ANTI-COLONIAL GLOBAL SCHOLARSHIP

Decolonization and Social Worlds

Series Editors: **Alana Lentin**, Western Sydney University,
Ali Meghji, University of Cambridge,
Syed Farid Alatas, National University of Singapore and
Jairo I. Fúnez-Flores, Texas Tech University

This series provides a radical new platform for high quality monographs which respond to the call for a decolonial revolution in sociology and the social sciences. Taking us beyond the boundaries of Eurocentrism, the series aims to expand the scope and imagination of the field.

Also available in the series:

Colonial Legacies and Global Inequalities in the Anglo-Caribbean
by **Meta Cramer**

Decolonizing Reproductive Rights in Latin America
by **Julieta Chaparro-Buitrago**

Decolonizing Feminist Economics
by **Gisela Carrasco-Miró**

Critical Racial and Decolonial Literacies
edited by **Debbie Bargallie** and **Nilmini Fernando**

White Supremacy and Racism in Progressive America
by **Miguel Montalva Barba**

Coloniality and Meritocracy in Unequal EU Migrations
by **Simone Varriale**

Find out more at:
bristoluniversitypress.co.uk/
decolonization-and-social-worlds

ANTI-COLONIAL GLOBAL SCHOLARSHIP

Contexts, Perspectives, and Debates

Edited by
Sujata Patel and Maureen A. Eger

First published in Great Britain in 2026 by

Bristol University Press
University of Bristol
1–9 Old Park Hill
Bristol
BS2 8BB
UK
t: +44 (0)117 374 6645
e: bup-info@bristol.ac.uk

Details of international sales and distribution partners are available at bristoluniversitypress.co.uk

© Editorial selection and matter © Patel, © Eger; individual chapters © their respective authors 2026

DOI: 10.51952/9781529245547

The digital PDF and ePub versions of this title are available open access and distributed under the terms of the Creative Commons Attribution-NonCommercial-NoDerivatives 4.0 International licence (https://creativecommons.org/licenses/by-nc-nd/4.0/) which permits reproduction and distribution for non-commercial use without further permission provided the original work is attributed.

British Library Cataloguing in Publication Data
A catalogue record for this book is available from the British Library

ISBN 978-1-5292-4552-3 paperback
ISBN 978-1-5292-4553-0 ePub
ISBN 978-1-5292-4554-7 OA PDF

The right of Sujata Patel and Maureen A. Eger to be identified as editors of this work has been asserted by them in accordance with the Copyright, Designs and Patents Act 1988.

All rights reserved: no part of this publication may be reproduced, stored in a retrieval system, or transmitted in any form or by any means, electronic, mechanical, photocopying, recording, or otherwise without the prior permission of Bristol University Press.

Every reasonable effort has been made to obtain permission to reproduce copyrighted material. If, however, anyone knows of an oversight, please contact the publisher.

The statements and opinions contained within this publication are solely those of the editors and contributors and not of the University of Bristol or Bristol University Press. The University of Bristol and Bristol University Press disclaim responsibility for any injury to persons or property resulting from any material published in this publication.

Bristol University Press works to counter discrimination on grounds of gender, race, disability, age and sexuality.

Cover design: blu inc
Front cover image: Shutterstock/Little River

Contents

Series Editors' Preface		vi
Notes on Contributors		viii
Preface and Acknowledgements		x
1	Anti-Colonial Global Scholarship: An Introduction *Sujata Patel and Maureen A. Eger*	1
2	Anti-Colonial Theory as a Peripheral Gaze *Sujata Patel*	20
3	The Meanings of Anti-Colonial Social Thought and Theory *Syed Farid Alatas*	58
4	The Promise of Anticolonial Social Theory *Julian Go*	83
5	Anticolonial Scholarship and the Politics of Location: Can Social Theory be Truly Democratic *and* Truly Global? *Satish Deshpande*	103
6	Decolonial Dialectics in an Inter-Imperial World *Laura Doyle*	123
7	Anti-Colonial Planetary Struggle: History, Humans, and Us *Neferti X.M. Tadiar*	153
8	Theorizing Hong Kong: From Colonial Collaboration to Inter-Imperial Zone *Hon-Fai Chen*	177
9	Humanizing Legacies of Caribbean Slavery and Colonialism in the Contemporary UK *Ann Phoenix*	197
10	The Horrors of Settler-Colonialism: Remote Sites of Refugee Detention in Australia's Carceral Archipelago *Claudia Tazreiter*	217
11	Sociology Besides Modernity? *Ontoformative Gestures* and Anti-Colonial Theories *Marcelo C. Rosa*	236
Index		252

Series Editors' Preface

*Syed Farid Alatas, Jairo Funez-Flores,
Alana Lentin, and Ali Meghji*

The *Decolonization and Social Worlds* series began at Bristol University Press as a response to the ongoing coloniality of knowledge. The series is co-edited by Syed Farid Alatas, Jairo Funez-Flores, Alana Lentin, and Ali Meghji, along with an international advisory board featuring some of the leading figures in the field.

A central aim of the series is to excavate how coloniality works – both historically, and in its contemporary expressions. It is undeniable that the social sciences emerged in the high era of colonial imperialism. Classical social scientists – from Durkheim to Weber, and Giddings to Geddes – were prominent exponents of the politics *and epistemologies* of European empires. From Weber's Orientalist reduction of the 'Hindu', 'Muslim', and 'Confucian' worlds, to Durkheim's assertion of indigenous people as being pre-modern, Geddes' colonial town-planning in India and Palestine, and Giddings' endorsement of 'democratic imperialism', social scientists have had significant relationships to colonial imperialism. We are now at a stage in social science where we know quite a lot about the histories of these relationships between social science and empire – both from the perspective of how social scientists worked in the service of empires (such as Britain's training cadets in sociology to better administer colonial populations), and from the perspective of how social scientists reproduced the epistemologies deployed by empires to legitimize colonialism (such as the idea of the colonized as being in need of development and progress). While the *Decolonization and Social Worlds* seeks to continue these discussions about social science and colonial imperialism, we also seek to further push the boundaries of social science knowledge by considering alternative histories, theories, movements, and social relations from the borders of the colonial world-system.

Within the series, we therefore seek to address multiple areas of social scientific inquiry. To name just some of these areas, we are interested in unearthing the work of forgotten (or denied) scholars, in decolonial and anti-colonial social movements and struggles, in new ways of thinking about the historical and contemporary relationships between the metropoles and colonies (or core, semi-peripheries, and peripheries of the world-system), in social scientific histories of colonial imperialism, in the evolution of empires, in indigeneity and indigenous critiques of coloniality, and in the historical and contemporary incarnations of the coloniality of being, knowledge, and power.

Now decades after the wave of decolonization of the mid-20th century, we still see clear colonial divisions in the contemporary world order: in terms of ongoing settler-colonial projects; in political economy, wealth, and poverty; in war and militarism; in international political order and organizations; and in knowledge production. There is always a vital need for conceptually and empirically informed decolonial scholarship to address all of these complexities, and we hope that the series goes some way towards contributing to this already rich, vibrant area of social scientific inquiry.

In its essence, this series looks for a world of many worlds.

Notes on Contributors

Syed Farid Alatas is Professor at the Department of Sociology and Anthropology at the National University of Singapore and Visiting Professor at the Department of Anthropology and Sociology at the University of Malaya. His areas of interest are the sociology of Islam, social theory, religion and reform, intra- and inter-religious dialogue, and the study of Eurocentrism.

Hon-Fai Chen is Head and Associate Professor of Sociology and Social Policy at Lingnan University, Hong Kong. His research interests include social theory, historical sociology, global modernity, colonialism and imperialism, and culture and knowledge. His current research aims to unravel the global/colonial formation of Chinese modernity and Chinese sociology.

Satish Deshpande retired from the Department of Sociology, University of Delhi in 2023, and is now an independent scholar living in Bengaluru. His interests include class and caste inequalities, social justice policy, higher education, and the history and politics of the social sciences, including questions of pedagogy and language.

Laura Doyle is Professor Emerita at University of Massachusetts Amherst and Co-director of the World Studies Interdisciplinary Project. Recent publications include *Decolonial Reconstellations*, a three-volume collection co-edited with Mwangi wa Gĩthĩnji and Simon Gikandi (Routledge, 2025) and *Inter-imperiality* (Duke University Press, 2020, Wallerstein Prize). Earlier publications include *Bordering on the Body* (Oxford University Press, 1994) and *Freedom's Empire* (Duke University Press, 2008).

Maureen A. Eger is currently Associate Professor in the Department of Sociology at Umeå University and a 2024–2025 Fellow at the Center for Advanced Study in the Behavioral Sciences at Stanford University. In 2026, she will join the Department of Sociology at the University of Southern California. Her interests lie broadly in political sociology, with an emphasis on immigration, nationalism, and the welfare state.

NOTES ON CONTRIBUTORS

Julian Go is Professor of Sociology at the University of Chicago where he is also Faculty Affiliate in the Center for the Study of Race, Politics & Culture and the Committee on International Relations, and a Fellow of the Chicago Center for Contemporary Theory.

Sujata Patel retired from the University of Hyderabad in India and is currently Visiting Fellow at the Freiburg Institute of Advanced Studies in Germany. Previously, she was the 2021 Kerstin Hesselgren Visiting Professor at Umeå University in Sweden. She works on the themes of global social theory, the history of Indian sociology, urbanization and city-formation in India.

Ann Phoenix, Professor of Psychosocial Studies, University College London, researches the intersectional interlinking of psychological experiences and social processes. Recent books include *Researching Family Narratives*, with Julia Brannen, Corinne Squire and the Novella project research team (SAGE, 2020) and *Nuancing Young Masculinities* (Helsinki University Press, 2022).

Marcelo C. Rosa is Professor of Sociology at Rio de Janeiro Federal Rural University, Researcher at the National Council for Scientific and Technological Development (CNPq) and Research Fellow at Huma/ University of Cape Town in the areas of social theory, land and collective action in the Global South.

Neferti X.M. Tadiar is the Moa Martinson Guest Professor (2024–2025) at Linköping University, Norrköping, Sweden, and Professor of Women's, Gender, and Sexuality Studies at Barnard College, Columbia University. Her most recent book *Remaindered Life* (Duke University Press, 2022) was awarded the John Hope Franklin Prize for Best Book in American Studies in 2023.

Claudia Tazreiter is Professor at the Institute for Research on Ethnicity, Migration and Society (REMESO) at Linköping University, Sweden. Claudia's research is grounded in sociology, cultural anthropology, and social theory and engaged in the fields of race, ethnicity, forced migration, and memory studies. She is currently serving as the elected Swedish representative on the European Advocacy Committee of Scholars at Risk (2023–).

Preface and Acknowledgements

This volume grew from the proceedings of an international workshop, 'Anti-Colonial Scholarship and Global Social Theory', held between 4 and 6 October 2023 at the Institute for Research on Migration, Ethnicity and Society (REMESO) at Linköping University, Norrköping campus in Sweden. This event brought together international and Swedish scholars with an interest in the legacy of colonialism in societies throughout the world as well as in the social scientific production of knowledge. Organized by Maureen A. Eger of Umeå University and Stefan Jonsson of REMESO as a pandemic-delayed capstone event of Sujata Patel's 2021 Kerstin Hesselgren Visiting Professorship in Sweden, the workshop featured scholars whose draft papers became the intellectual foundation for this volume: Syed Farid Alatas, Manuela Boatcă, Hon-Fai Chen, Keti Chukhrov, Satish Deshpande, Laura Doyle, Faisal Garba Muhammed, Julian Go, Nacira Guenif, Ann Phoenix, Marcelo Rosa, Neferti Tadiar, and Madina Tlostanova.

This collection is only possible because of the remarkable efforts of the authors of its chapters. Not only did these scholars enthusiastically engage on the theme of anti-colonial global scholarship, but they also extended their previous work, stretched their thinking, and refined (and in some cases reformulated) their ideas to ensure that they spoke to the key questions raised in this volume. We are extremely grateful to the authors for their intellectual contributions, trust, openness, and collaborative spirit. We regret that Manuela Boatcă, Keti Chukhrov, Faisal Garba Muhammed, and Madina Tlostanova could not participate in this volume and express our sincere gratitude for their participation and intellectual contributions at the Norrköping workshop.

We owe enormous thanks to Stefan Jonsson and the advisory committee at REMESO, Linköping University. We thank Peo Hansen, Anders Neergaard, Carl-Ulrik Schierup, and Claudia Tazreiter for their unwavering commitment in making the Norrköping workshop a success and Frida Log for handling each and every administrative detail with care and consideration. The workshop was generously funded by Linköping University Humanities, Sveriges Riksbankens Jubileumsfond (RJ Grant no F22–0128), and the Royal Swedish Academy of Letters, History and Antiquities.

We also thank the paper discussants, session chairs, and panelists whose insightful comments also informed the content of this book: Seema Arora-Jonsson, Anna Bredström, Ulrika Dahl, Maria Eriksson Baaz, Peo Hansen, Stefan Helgesson, Christina Kullberg, Patricia Lorenzoni, Edda Manga, Ali Meghji, Diana Mulinari, Anders Neergaard, Carl-Ulrik Schierup, Ted Svensson, Claudia Tazreiter, Håkan Thörn, and Aleksandra Ålund. We are extremely appreciative of the help and support provided by the REMESO student volunteers, who gave their time and energy and contributed to the workshop discussions: Anyhua Bobba, Laus Damgaard Jørgensen, Gvantsa Gatenadze, Laura Ricardo Marchese, Sarah Goosens, Ellen Rahm, Samuel Richter, and Max Waleij.

The two editors of this volume met for the first time online in early 2021, when the Department of Sociology at Umeå University made Maureen the host for Sujata's visiting professorship, financed by the Swedish Research Council (VR Grant no 2019–00711). In this role, Maureen organized Sujata's lectures across the various institutions that had supported her application: the Department of Sociology and Umeå Centre of Gender Studies at Umeå University, the Department of Sociology at Uppsala University, REMESO at Linköping University, and the Swedish South Asian Studies Network at Lund University. In addition to facilitating cross-national, interdisciplinary dialogue and exchange, these lectures helped lay the foundation for the introduction of Sujata's ideas on anti-colonial social theory, which coalesced at the workshop in Norrköping.

We thank the many individuals who contributed to the successful grant application and welcomed Sujata to Sweden. Specifically, we wish to record the help and support of Per Wisselgren, the original applicant, who with Hannah Bradby, Jenny-Ann Brodin-Danell, Andreas Johansson, Stefan Jonsson, Britt-Inger Keisu, Ilkka Henrik Mäkinen, Sandra Torres, and Ted Svensson, supported Sujata's application. Additionally, we thank Minoo Alinia, Maria Carbin, Samuel Merrill, Ted Svensson, and Ulrika Widding for organizing seminars at their institutions to discuss the promise of anti-colonial social theory, which inspired the subsequent scholarly discussions that helped formulate this volume. We are also grateful to Karin Nilsson and Sophia Wård at Umeå University for navigating the various bureaucracies, which only became more complicated during and immediately after the pandemic, to ensure Sujata could assume this role in person rather than on Zoom. We also thank Eva Renholm at Linköping University for helping coordinate Sujata's stay in Norrköping in 2022.

This book is being published in the series, *Decolonization and Social Worlds*, at Bristol University Press. We thank the series editors and, in particular, Ali Meghji who supported this project from the beginning. We are extremely appreciative of Bristol University Press and its staff and as well as the anonymous peer reviewers for their advice and support during the journey from proposal to publication.

Funding for Open Access publishing came from the research budgets of Marcelo C. Rosa (CNPq – Bolsa de Produtividade em Pesquisa, Grant no 408973/2021–8), Maureen A. Eger (Umeå University), and Sujata Patel (Humboldt Research Award, Alexander von Humboldt Foundation).

We recognize that this book is the result of many conversations – intentional dialogue across disciplinary, regional, and national boundaries – some of which is in this volume while some remains outside it. This journey has been rewarding for the two editors, who learned much not only from each other's perspective but also from the chapter authors through the multistage process of writing, reading, and revising. We believe that such conversations hold potential for greater understanding of the world – its past, present, and future. The chapters that follow collectively make a case for an approach to social science that is fundamentally anti-colonial. It is our sincere hope that this volume will help carry the conversations forward, inspiring scholarly dialogue and eventually a more complete understanding of our imperfect world.

Sujata Patel
Pune, India
Maureen A. Eger
Stanford, United States
30 April 2025

1

Anti-Colonial Global Scholarship: An Introduction

Sujata Patel and Maureen A. Eger

This volume explores the diverse manifestations of anti-colonial scholarship around the world. It critically examines the relationships among colonialism, society, and academic knowledge, while advancing perspectives that challenge the dominance of colonial frameworks in the social sciences. It also proposes alternative ways to understand the colonial and imperial world. The volume traces distinct genealogies of anti-colonial thought globally and considers how these can inform critical scholarship on both historical and contemporary forms of colonialism and imperialism. It asserts that colonialism and anti-colonial resistance are essential lenses for understanding the world, offering tools to analyze global conflicts and ongoing struggles for social justice and liberation. Anti-colonial scholarship calls for new conceptual frameworks rooted in a deeper understanding of humanity and ethical responsibility. It invites reflection on what it means to be human and urges a moral reckoning with our role as one – albeit dominant – species among many on this planet.

Like Chabal (2019: 436–7), we understand anti-colonialism to be a 'philosophy of action' and, because anti-colonialism exists *only* in opposition to colonialism, it is a word that requires hyphenation. However, some of the contributors to this volume prefer anticolonialism without hyphenation. As it will become clear, collectively, the chapter authors articulate a variety of perspectives on anti-colonial scholarship, not least its spelling. Allowing for both versions, we believe, is consistent with an approach to social science that values diverse knowledge and points of view.

According to the *Oxford English Dictionary*, the word *colonialism* does not appear (at least in English language dictionaries) until 1791 (OED, 2024), despite the fact that the political and economic project of colonialism, or control over territories and groups of peoples and acquisition of their wealth and resources, has a much longer history. This history is fundamentally about slavery, racism, forced migration, genocide, violence, and diaspora. It is also about the superimposition of cultures over many groups of displaced and exiled peoples with their own distinct identities and socio-philosophical worldviews. In this long project against peoples and groups living in Africa, Asia, the Americas, and Europe, only a relatively small group benefited while most did not. The beneficiaries of colonialism have for the most part been Europeans and the descendants of European colonists, but some are 'natives', who historically collaborated or, in contemporary times, collaborate with imperial projects.

After the Second World War, when post-colonial countries in Africa and Asia emerged as independent nation-states through anti-colonial movements and Latin American scholarship began confronting imperialistic control of its economies, a clearer understanding of colonialism's totalizing campaign of exploiting peoples and resource extraction emerged. Consequently, we now know that the first Spanish colony was established in the 15th century in today's Dominican Republic, while the first English settlement was in the early 1600s in today's United States. Osterhammel (2005) identifies three modular types of colonialism: colonies of exploitation (or non-settler colonialism) where the primary goal was to exploit raw materials, land, and 'native' labour (for example, British India); colonies of settlement (for example, Spanish, Portuguese, French and British America, the Antipodes, as well parts of Africa); and territories of strategic military and now financial significance (for example, Portuguese control in the Indian Ocean, American territories in the Caribbean, or China's administration of Hong Kong).

As mentioned earlier, the political and economic project of colonialism is also a cultural project and is associated with intellectual axioms of the capitalist system across the world. It has a long history and its economic and political ideas, practices and institutions of capitalist exploitation have changed over time. However, one element that persists is the notion that certain powerful cultures are superior and more civilized than other cultures in the world. This self-serving bias motivates continuous intervention in new and interesting ways to suggest that the barbarians, the backwards or any other group of peoples that can be termed 'less developed' can and should be moulded to be like themselves. This self-serving bias of colonizers justifies and legitimizes this politico-economic project. A characteristic of the first colonizers – the elite of Europe, from Iberia and later the British, French, German, Dutch, and Danish – it has since been adopted by other colonizers and contemporary imperial elites who are of different ethnicities and from distinct language groups, such as the Russians, Japanese, the Chinese, or the Indians. This sentiment is also expressed in distinct ways within academic scholarship and in academia.

Thus, as colonialism and imperialism, or neo-colonialism, have progressed and spread across various regions of the world in various guises and as different national European empires and other empires effected their domination globally, the modular forms as described by Osterhammel (2005) have got increasingly mixed in actual experience of power and control. At its peak, in the late 19th and early 20th centuries, major European countries together with the United States colonized most of Americas, Africa, Oceania, and Asia, with Great Britain controlling one-fifth of the landmass and one quarter of its population until the Second World War. From the late 19th century, the Japanese and the Russian empires also embarked on a similar process and the Japanese colonized Korea and Taiwan and later parts of China and most of the Far East. In different ways, contemporary semi-imperial regions continue to emulate this formula.

It is generally accepted that, after the Second World War, the era of colonialism ended. While it is true that empires slowly withdrew from the colonized regions of Asia and Africa and began recognizing former colonies as independent nation-states, it is also true that, to this day, colonialism persists not only in the form of dependent territories, protectorates, overseas departments, and other descriptions signifying colonial status, but also through the occupation of Palestine, the invasion of Ukraine, and the intention of the current president of the United States to control and incorporate Canada, Greenland, and the Panama Canal into US territory.

However, this volume is not focused as much on the political and economic project of colonial control over such regions as it is directed towards the ways in which colonialism has influenced how we think about, reflect on, and understand the world around us. Ideas about the impact that colonialism has had on knowledge first emerged when colonialism was at its peak in the late 19th and early 20th century. Early anti-colonial thought recognized that colonialism was an organized system of knowledge based on very specific principles that resonated with a mythology of progress and divisions between those who are civilized and those who are not. Importantly, it also recognized that these ways of thinking continued to frame ideas regarding our tools of thought with consequences for social scientific analysis and the production of knowledge. Since then, these ideas have been sedimented within policies and political strategies of the empires and within professional assumptions inspiring intellectual and academic scholarship. Consequently, colonial ideas are embedded in academia, continuing to influence, shape, and design concepts and theories about societies – and even norms for what constitutes a good human society. The chapters in this volume are efforts to bring attention to these processes and to illuminate the promise of anti-colonial scholarship for understanding human societies not only in the past but, importantly, in the present and future. In the next two sections, we provide a concise overview of the historical and contemporary context from which this volume emerges, the perspectives that constitute anti-colonial scholarship, and the questions and debates that the authors in this volume pursue in their respective chapters.

The context

The link between colonialism and anti-colonialism is decolonization. The idea of and for decolonization emerged in the late 18th century. However, a discussion on decolonization became part of extensive academic scholarship only around the mid-20th century when anti-colonial movements in parts of Asia and Africa demanded independence and sovereignty for their peoples. In this form, decolonization implies the unravelling and undoing of colonialism, its systems and practices, its ideas and relationships with the aim to disengage, and even cancel and thereby reverse, processes organizing colonialism's control and economic exploitation. Thus, there is a symbiotic link between decolonization and the growth of anti-colonial ideas and the development of anti-colonial social scholarship in academia.

However, unlike the 20th-century understanding of decolonization (mentioned earlier), the word anti-colonialism meant something else. As already mentioned, it was in the late 18th century when this word was introduced in the English language. Decolonization then was used in a very restricted sense and was associated with anti-colonial ideas of a settler group against the Iberian, British, and French royalists. It is in this context and, in these conflicts, that both the words colonial and anti-colonial emerged. No wonder the OED lists the origin of the words colonialism and anti-colonialism around the same time, with both these words signalling the growth of a set of ideas that queries and opposes the colonial and imperial powers and its interests. However, decolonization at this time implies the establishment of white settler nation-states in the Americas (Young, 2016). Anti-colonial thought in this phase was about distancing colonists whose ancestry was European from the European powers and of white settlers from white colonialists in England, France, Spain, and Portugal, and subsequent establishment of new sovereign nation-states in the Americas. After their success, these settler-colonists set up a new regime of internal colonialism, wherein they overpowered and almost decimated the original inhabitants, known today as indigenous groups or the First Nations in the Americas, Aborigines in Australia, and the Māori people in New Zealand. The independence of these colonies led to territorial expansion of the European empires across the world from mid to late 19th centuries the increasing militarization of these powers, and wars among them to control more territories.

Robert Young (2016) has suggested that this phase of decolonization was followed by two other phases. In the second phase of decolonization, from the late 18th and early 19th century up to the first quarter of the 20th century, if colonial countries competed for territories across the world, they also had to counter both humanitarian and libertarian ideas from within Europe and slave revolts in large plantations in the Caribbean. In the early to mid-19th century, the banning of slavery found support from the economic elite across Europe who promulgated the policy of free trade but neither disputed nor questioned the need for colonialism for the European empires. It is during this time that Europeans refashioned the notion of national identities within Europe, defining the 'others' against Europeans and, in the process, institutionalizing racism. By the late 19th century, with no space left for territorial expansion, the unsatiated empires turned inwards and attempted to devour each other. This led to the decline and decolonization of the Austro-Hungarian (a significant portion of this region was known after the Second World War as East Europe) and Ottoman empires (Turkey but also Southern Europe, West Asia and North Africa) and the creation of new nation-states. This also led to the displacement of groups who were 'othered' across territories within Europe, as geopolitical boundaries changed and regions and peoples were absorbed by other European powers. Germany's defeat in the First World War also deprived it of its overseas colonies, which led Aimé Césaire to suggest that the Second World War and fascism was a form of colonialism brought home to Europe (Young, 2016).

It is in this context that new critical perspectives emerged to comprehend the political economy of capitalism. The key contribution to this debate was made by Karl Marx, whose theorizing has continued to influence the understandings of colonialism and its relationship to capitalism. Marx's ideas on colonialism were shaped by contemporary humanitarian and libertarian ideas within Europe. In its initial stages Marx saw colonialism as separate from capitalism. As many commentators have contended, Marx's initial statements as expressed in his discussions on British India were at best ambiguous and contended that capitalism and thus colonialism could play a revolutionary role in freeing pre-capitalist productive forces stifling productivity in colonies such as India. However, in his later comments on this theme in connection to Ireland and Russia, Marx was able to take a critical stance and spell out the organic linkages between capitalism and colonialism and assess its negative implications (Lindner, 2022). Since then, Marxism has been the theoretical scaffolding that has lent itself to an understanding of colonialism. For example, Marxist thinkers such as Lenin, Trotsky, and Rosa Luxemburg dissected colonial capitalism's negative impact on the rest of the world as it has changed its avatar over time in and through its various imperialist strategies. Their framework helps us to understand current imperial strategies such as neo-liberalism and, recently, efforts to seize wealth and resources of sovereign nations and displace citizens and immigrants in the name of national interests and security.

Thus, it is of no surprise to note that, since the 1930s and 1940s as anti-colonial movements emerged in Asia and later Africa and continued to impact global politics, it has been Marxist ideas that have influenced the theory and practice of decolonization and led to the consolidation of anti-colonialism as a worldwide movement. In this third phase, these anti-colonial nationalist movements reinvented Marxist perspectives and reformulated Marxist propositions to present programmes and policies that can aid post-colonial nation-states to become economically autonomous and forge supportive political institutions. Unlike Marxist critiques that developed in Europe after the Second World War, Marxist perspectives that appeared in Africa and Asia through anti-colonial thought were in some ways new and remained flexible as these reacted and adapted to the specific socio-historical conditions in which these materialized. And as they articulated these concerns, each of these also enunciated the humanitarian values of equity and justice prevalent within Marxist and other radical European critical perspectives.

One example is that of Kwame Nkrumah (Langan, 2017), who formulated the concept of neo-colonialism. He contended that the system of economic exploitation of ex-colonies continues even though the political control remains in the hands of its 'native' elite. Recognizing a need for a new institutional arrangement to combat colonial influences, he suggested that an Africa-level political institution needed to be established to counter and confront this trend. This critique affirmed that there was historical continuity between imperialism as it developed in the 19th century and neo-colonialism as it has been imposed after independence of colonized territories; imperialism in the context of anti-colonial struggles continued to create a 'colonial situation' (Balandier, 1966 [1951]) when the newly independent nation-states remained caught in complex problems internal to its formation and thereby retained de facto colonial status. This complicated colonial situation allowed imperialism to become the ideology of the empires and intervene in global power politics using militarization and nationalism, be these be European nation-states, the United States, Russia, or China. Consequently, it was able to refashion a set of programmes to control the economies of the post-colonial nation-states.

However, as it is argued in some of the chapters in this volume, these critiques, despite some of their limitations, helped to challenge existing ways of thinking about the nature of self, of collectivities/nations, and social identities in colonized countries. They also led to philosophical queries that searched for theoretical foundations for understanding the contemporary social, be it the economic, political, or cultural and historical. These questions, together with the growing nationalism, impacted the development of formal scholarship from the late 19th century within Africa and Asia and later in Latin America. In addition, these found reflection within the African, Asian, and Latin American diaspora based in England, France, Portugal, and Spain, and within the discussions in the Communist International. Consequently, this led to an intermingling of various critiques fashioned both in Europe, within Marxism, and in the colonies. And as university education emerged, such ideas institutionalized themselves within formal academic scholarship and moulded themselves as practices of and for expanding knowledge of the colonized and now autonomous and conscious nations compared to the one created by colonial arrangements. The origin of anti-colonial scholarship lies in these nascent interventions made in these three continents to establish an academic scholarship that elaborated and used anti-colonial thought to theorize ways to see the world and provide a critique of the world as construed by the colonialists.

This growth of ideas and scholarship has led to the fourth phase of decolonization, wherein anti-colonial critiques now focus on academic scholarship and academia itself. This phase emerged from the late 1970s onwards and continues as we write and speak about it. In this phase, imperial capitalism reinvented itself as globalization and framed policies of neo-liberal interventions to ensure expanding markets across the world. If the introduction of new technologies of information and communication led to growing inequalities within post-colonial nation-states and between these countries and the rest of the world, a demand was made for understanding these global divisions its histories in colonialism and imperialism. These new technologies also impacted the global division of scholarship (UNESCO, 2010), leading to paradoxical results: an aspirational cultural political economy, the growth of migration from the ex-colonies to the empires, leading to – ironically – the circulation of some ideas regarding anti-colonial critiques of the empires through new perspectives such as postcolonialism and decoloniality. Consequently, we are today in a new phase of decolonization in the arena of ideas, within fields and disciplines and in all forms of knowledge. This phase has been termed intellectual decolonization (Hull, 2023).

The two new intellectual anti-colonial critiques that emerged in the late 1970s and early 1980s – that of Orientalism (Said, 1978) on one hand and of Eurocentrism (Amin, 1989) on the other – both recognized their origin within anti-colonial scholarship that had emerged within the continents of Africa, Asia, and Latin America but distinguished themselves from it. Orientalism found its footing in North America academia and has been called postcolonialism and was followed soon by another intellectual intervention: the decoloniality/modernity critique. The second, Eurocentrism, was developed among Marxist and radical intellectuals and activists located in Asia, Africa, and Latin America. This critique was associated with the world-system and dependency theories and was in reaction to: the failure of the post-colonial nation-state in Africa, Asia, and

Latin America; the back-tracking of Marxist anti-colonial critiques; the growth of culturist explanations to comprehend the colonized and, with it, the failure of the politico-ideological project of Thirdworldism (Nash, 2003); and the imposition of new forms of imperial domination by empires among other things. Called Eurocentrism by Samir Amin (1989), it was later reformulated in new ways within the scholarship of Anibal Quijano (2000) and Immanuel Wallerstein (1997). Both postcolonialism and Eurocentrism were critiques of dominant/hegemonic perspectives that had emerged in the late 18th century and were institutionalized through university education in Europe in the late 19th century. These explored in different ways how Eurocentric epistemologies embedded themselves in popular culture and within fields and disciplines.

For Samir Amin, Eurocentrism grew in tangent with the growth of capitalism and remains the critical and the most significant element of capitalist colonial culture and ideology; this being bred within Europe and which had embedded itself within dominant social theories by the period of the Renaissance. Amin, who extended Martin Bernal's argument on Eurocentrism elaborated in *Black Athena* (1987), defined it as a theory of world history that asserted Europe's uniqueness and superiority. It was a global political project which legitimates expansionism with such notions as 'manifest destiny' and 'the white man's burden'. Amin contends that Eurocentrism is implicated in official histories of the world. It has now interpellated itself as a myth such that when discussing Europe's 'real' history most commentators signal to Greece and later Rome while Europe's history lies in Ancient Egypt and with the Phoenicians. Likewise, social science theories borrowed from Europe have not been able to excavate local histories and challenge these ideological perceptions of social sciences. His solution is to use Marxist historical sociological analysis to critique the cultural and intellectual assumptions of European epistemologies.

The questions asked by postcolonialism and decoloniality were similar, but their answers were different and distinct. Unlike the historical sociological approaches of Amin, Quijano, and Wallerstein, both postcolonialism and decoloniality promoted discursive critiques. Postcolonialism brought back the voices of those who were silenced from the three continents of Africa, Asia, and Latin America through a critique of how the Orient was conceptualized by the literary icons of Europe and North America. It was a discursive critique that argued that language/literature of the Orient represents a field of power. Though it distanced itself from the European version of Marxism, its various manifestations combined perspectives from anti-colonial critiques of Marxist orientation with existentialism, poststructuralism, postmodernism, feminism, and anti-colonial thinking. On the other hand, the decoloniality critique distinguishes itself from postcolonialism by borrowing from Anibal Quijano's discussion on Eurocentrism and its organic linkages with colonialism since the 1600s. Thus, for decolonialists, modernity was fashioned in this period and thus need to be interrogated epistemically. A search for an alternative episteme needs to be framed from outside the modern.

Samir Amin (1989: x) has argued that it is difficult to unravel the nooks and corners within which Eurocentrism is embedded. It needs focused attention as it has spread across the world in different and distinct ways and re-articulated itself in many varieties. A critical global scholarship on this theme is fragmented, not only because of different schools of thought but also because of unequal development of social sciences across the world. In addition, many fields within post-colonial countries have developed as mere reflections rather than as scientifically oriented analysis. Critical social thought remains embedded within ideological positions drawn from reconstructed orientalist and Eurocentric perspectives or from imperial ideas refashioned by neo-liberalism.

It is in this context that scholars have carved out the theme of anti-colonial scholarship. Small conferences[1] and incisive intellectual interventions characterize these efforts. They have initiated a long journey of asking arduous questions which involves complex tasks not only of reformulating new tools but also of reconstruction of existing ways to think. Our endeavour in this volume is to contribute to these existing initiatives (Dei and Ashgarzadeh, 2001; Dei and Lordan, 2016; Dei and Demi, 2021; Elam, 2017; Lee, 2018; Chabal, 2019; Kamola, 2019; Nunn and Whetung, 2020; Gatechew and Mantena, 2021; Go, 2023a, 2023b; Patel, 2023, 2024, in press; Al-Hardan and Go, 2025, in press). This volume's chapters aim to initiate dialogue with readers about the promise of anti-colonial global scholarship for revealing new ways of making sense of the present while improving our understanding of the past.

Perspectives and debates

What is anti-colonial scholarship? Neither Orientalism nor Eurocentrism define it, nor do they examine it as a critical perspective in academic scholarship. And yet, there is a broad agreement among scholars that anti-colonial thought gives us a framework to understand challenges stemming from and resistance against colonial ideologies and its power structures (Dei and Lordan, 2016; Dei and Demi, 2021). However, it is rare to find a text that compares and contrasts anti-colonial ideas across the continents of Asia and Africa, or with those of the anti-imperialist ones from Latin America, despite a popular understanding that these ideas have resonance. We can, however, gain insights from Robert J.C. Young's book, *Postcolonialism: An Historical Introduction* (2016), and work by some historians such as Frederick Cooper (2005, 2023), or descriptions in dictionaries and handbooks on postcolonialism (for example, Schwartz and Ray, 2005; Albrecht, 2020;

Nunn and Whetung, 2020; OED, 2024). Through an assessment of such interventions, it is possible to begin to constitute a theoretical framework for anti-colonial global scholarship.

Anti-colonial thought is a cluster of ideas that confront dominant and authoritative ways of thinking about the colonized self and collectivities/groups within colonial/imperial geographies. Some scholars have examined the way the colonial/imperial state and its stakeholders have appropriated land, labour, natural and material resources of the colonized. Other scholars have examined the displacement and forced migration of peoples through peonage, bondage, and slavery. In addition to assessing economic exploitation and subjugation, anti-colonial thought has revealed ways in which cultures and ways of living have been eroded.

Anti-colonial thought is further understood as a narrative of a set of historical events and a methodological critique (Patel, 2023, 2024, 2025) which also provides a set of perspectives on political philosophy (Gatachew and Mantena, 2021), and articulates alternative economic philosophies and utopian visions of how to be human. Scholars argue that it should be understood as a resistance movement directed against colonial and imperialist powers containing parallel strategies for emancipation – from non-violent resistance to violent revolution (Elam, 2017). In addition, there have been discussions on anti-colonial ideas regarding equality and social justice and as well assessments of strategies for self-determination in the form for national independence and political sovereignty (Kamola, 2019). Anti-colonial thought has also interrogated the idea of whether sovereignty and territoriality are intrinsically linked, given that its contemporary manifestations are often cultural rather than territorial.

This volume debates what anti-colonial scholarship is – beyond what has been presented by postcolonialism, decoloniality/modernity, and the world-system perspectives – and in consideration of intellectual traditions, both old and new in countries within Africa, Asia, the Americas, and Europe. Its authors are geographically located in different parts of the world and, with two exceptions, are sociologists. In defining and describing what constitutes anti-colonial scholarship, these authors differ in many regards. For example, some trace themselves as coming from specific intellectual traditions; yet, they have committed to using this concept and framework because they agree that contemporary scholarship must comprehend how events and processes defining the contemporary world follow directly from colonialism and how this has consequences for knowledge about our world. If their concerns are about the immediate, these are also epistemic and methodological. With the use of tools sharpened by contemporary scholarship, the authors' collective aim is to assess the ways in which the past impacts the present and the future. Through their chapters, the authors reveal how anti-colonial scholarship offers an ontological-epistemological and a moral perspective to examine and evaluate the impact of colonialism/imperialism, while imagining more solidaristic and inclusive futures.

Next, we provide an overview of the aforementioned authors' respective chapters, highlighting their main arguments and where they stand on key debates in this field. Throughout this introduction, we have referred to anti-colonial scholarship, which we see as including anti-colonial social *thought*, anti-colonial social *theory*, and everything in between. Some authors make explicit distinctions between thought and theory, while others do not. This is one of the debates. Other debates include the legacy of the three perspectives – of postcolonialism, the decoloniality/modernity perspective, and anti-colonial critiques developed within Africa and Asian intellectual traditions.

The chapters combine different styles to debate and discuss anti-colonial scholarship. While some authors make a theoretical exegesis of anti-colonial social theory, others use an anti-colonial framework to understand a specific empirical case. The authors provide their respective definitions of anti-colonial social thought and social theory, identifying similarities and differences between their understanding and other intellectual traditions opposing colonialism and critiquing the colonialization of knowledge production in the social sciences. Collectively, they offer new theoretical concepts and ideal-typical typologies and discuss the promises and challenges of anti-colonial scholarship in the 21st century.

In Chapter 2, Sujata Patel defines anti-colonial social theory as a metatheory emerging from the peripheral gaze. Patel argues that as metatheory – a theory *about* theory – anti-colonial social theory is fundamentally a reflection on assumptions underlying and ways of approaching academic scholarship. She borrows the notion of the periphery from the world-systems approach and contends that anti-colonial social theory is a resistance, a critique, and a standpoint against the way the core regions of the world determine ways to think about the colonized. Patel identifies three important characteristics of anti-colonial social theory. She suggests, first, that anti-colonial social theory makes explicit the ontological claim that we live in a colonial world. Second, she contends that this framework provides a methodology to debunk colonial logics and hegemonic 'knowledge'. Third, she theorizes that anti-colonial social theory offers a framework to comprehend the 'social' as it has been constituted by colonial modernity. She argues that anti-colonial social theory implies imagining new perspectives of theoretical analysis and methods to centre the point of view of the colonized rather than the colonizers. In her chapter, Patel shows how these specific attributes have emerged in various social theoretic formulations over time and in different geographies since the 1940s. Patel further argues that a benefit of anti-colonial social theory is that it goes beyond the binaries of east and west. She asserts that not all nationalist thought is emancipatory and scholarship should not be discounted because of the geography from which it emerges, whether it comes from the so-called Global North or South. She argues that anti-colonial social theory's methodologies are multiple and diverse, which she sees as a benefit not a limitation.

According to Syed Farid Alatas, in Chapter 3, anti-colonial social scholarship first emerged in the 16th century. Alatas distinguishes between social thought and social theory in that the former is less formal. Specifically, anti-colonial social thought is less systematic in its articulation (that is, a lack of formal definitions or concepts) and may contain personal reflections, opinions, and valuations compared to anti-colonial social theory. Alatas also points out that social thought involves a greater plurality of methods of argumentation. However, he argues that social thought is not of lesser importance and may actually serve as the foundation of social theory. Like Go and Patel, Alatas critiques the notions of binaries and 'absolute opposition' between different parts of the globe, or rejection of Western knowledge on the basis of its geographical origins. However, he emphasizes that anti-colonial thinkers already tend to reject nativism. A major contribution of Alatas' chapter are his two typologies – the varieties of anti-colonial social thought and the dimensions of anti-colonial social thought. First, he identifies five ideal types of colonialism: trade, exploitation, settler, semi-, and internal colonialism. These can be distinguished from each other in terms of appropriation of economic surplus, the organization of labour, and the nature of the colonial state. Second, he identifies different dimensions of social thought opposing colonialism – content (normative or positive), author (colonizer or colonized), and temporality (colonial, post-colonial, and contemporary colonialism). In his chapter, Alatas also provides rich examples of scholarship from the colonial and post-colonial periods, bringing attention to scholars often ignored or simply unknown in the West and beyond.

Julian Go's chapter, 'The Promise of Anticolonial Social Theory', builds on his arguments presented earlier (Go, 2023a, 2023b). Specifically, Go makes a case for what he sees as the potential of anti-colonial social theory, as a global social theory, to rival an imperial and Eurocentric approach to understanding societies. According to Go, what distinguishes this framework from other extant approaches is an explicit anti-colonial standpoint, forged through struggles against specific instances of colonialism, combined with a rejection of what he calls geoepistemic essentialism, or the notion that the solution to the dominance of the Northern-Western standpoint is to replace it with a Southern/Non-Western standpoint. While he does not contend that geography is irrelevant, Go argues against the notion that geographic regions map onto knowledge or that 'geography equals *qualitatively different kinds of knowledge*'. Instead, he maintains that 'anticolonial thought is necessarily *general*'. Go argues that a strength of anti-colonial social theory, which recognizes the existence of a 'complex series of hegemonies and hierarchies that traverse the globe', is that it allows for generalizability. Indeed, it may reveal similarities across empirical cases despite differences in geographic location and time period. To illustrate how anti-colonial social theory can speak to general themes, he compares key aspects of the work of Frantz Fanon and W.E.B. Du Bois.

In Chapter 5, Satish Deshpande asks whether anti-colonial social theory can be truly *global*. He points out that the Global North still dominates the development of social theory, which potentially limits its scope. Moreover, even when a theory's origin stems from the Global South, when it gains global prominence, the theory and theorist tend to 'drift towards the North'. Deshpande argues that this sets up a situation where scholarship that offers a critique of colonial domination and extraction still depends on (former) colonial power to sustain it. He further argues that location should be *central* for anti-colonial theory because location may play a role in knowledge production; thus, location should not only be explicitly acknowledged but its implications for the intellectual project should also be considered theoretically. For example, Deshpande discusses how the 'industrial political economy of knowledge production' is inextricably linked to location, noting the inequalities that structure society (at large) also contribute to a system of stratification within academia (at large). What is more, these inequalities are persistent: not much has changed in the past few decades, when the internet and digital publications could have decreased the dominance of the Global North in the production of knowledge and thus our understanding societies worldwide. In this chapter, Deshpande also considers the implications and unintended consequences of anti-colonial social theory being defined as something opposed to rather than for something – and reflects on how to decide whether an argument is anti-colonial. He concludes with thoughts about the protests on Western university campuses during the 2023–2024 academic year, what has been called the 'Ivy Intifada'. He calls for a reimagining of 'we', a process that will determine whether a theory that aspires to be global can truly be so.

In her chapter, 'Decolonial Dialectics in an Inter-Imperial World', Laura Doyle makes the case for an anti-colonial and decolonial framework that is both critical of colonialism and takes a long historical view. Specifically, Doyle argues that societies have been shaped 'by a *field* of interacting empires, never just one'. Doyle explains that over the millennia, specific regions and communities have been subjected to repeated colonial projects, resulting in '"shatterzones" of inter-imperial jockeying'. Her analysis focuses on 'this dialectically shaped and accruing field of volatile interactions' whose afterlives shape subsequent empires and their coercive systems. Citing specific cases from across the globe and the centuries, Doyle shows how geographic location matters: certain communities have been more susceptible to (repeated) colonialization due to their strategic location at crossroads or sea lanes. Yet despite cases' particularities, her inter-imperial approach to understanding the long history of anti-colonial struggles helps reveal similarities across temporalities and geographies. For example, her analysis shows how institutions, infrastructures, media, and the arts are important sites for both colonial control and anti-colonial contestation. Doyle also uses the (recent) example of the resurgence of anti-woman laws and feminist counterprotests to highlight how intersectional thinking may contribute to decolonial and anti-colonial scholarship. She further discusses race, caste, and class identity politics in this context. Finally, using *One Thousand and One Nights*, she shows how art and, in particular, literature may both interrupt colonial temporalities while proposing alternative forms of relationality. She concludes by emphasizing the importance of cross-community, cross-disciplinary collaborations, such as this volume, for the development of an anti-colonial and decolonial intellectual project.

In Chapter 7, Neferti X.M. Tadiar invites the reader to consider the project of anti-colonialism as that of a planetary struggle. With evocative prose, she simultaneously captures the moment we are living in while also situating the 'current, a temporal movement, taking place, even inside the halls of the academy, but more so in the larger world outside of it, traversing it' in the long history of opposing colonialism. Her scope is planetary, but she zooms in on the 2022 Philippines presidential election and the notion of history repeating, asserting that '[c]olonial history is neither past event nor past structure'. With reference to her own life and that of her family, both living and dead, Tadiar reflects on time, conflicts over the telling of history, and the dominant story of the present that largely ignores subaltern lives and their descendants long subjugated to an imperial and racial capitalist order. To illustrate, Tadiar returns to the case of the Philippines, which has become the world's largest destination for US companies' business process outsourcing, such as call centres. She also draws attention to the experiences of migrant reproductive workers, and in particular overseas Filipina domestic and care workers, who act as 'vital infrastructures for the social reproduction of lives of value, wielded as human capital, as well as the means of reproduction of the global capital as a whole'. In a devastatingly accurate indictment of global servitude, Tadiar explains how Filipina migrants labour to save their employers' 'valuable life-times'. The past half millennium, which Tadiar refers to as the Capitolocene, is only a small part of the Anthropocene and even smaller period in much longer history of our planet, now under threat due to climate change. Yet Tadiar resists a narrative that makes humanity into 'a uniform biological being' and erases the dramatic differences in human experiences, due to the organizing force of colonialism, especially as societies impacted by colonialism also suffer the most devastating impacts of climate change. Using evidence from the Philippines, she maintains that 'a "natural disaster" in an already conquered land destroys life in the same patterns of destruction that decades and centuries of colonialism had laid down before'.

In 'Theorizing Hong Kong: From Colonial Collaboration to Inter-Imperial Zone', Hon-Fai Chen uses the theories of inter-imperiality, world-systems theory, and ocean studies to shed light on the characteristics of colonialism in Hong Kong. Chen points out that, despite having been a British colony, Hong Kong was not always understood as such. Scholars tended to view Chinese culture as playing a dominant role in Hong Kong society and politics, with British rule operating somewhat in the background. Additionally, with its economic prosperity and political stability, it has not been an obvious empirical case for colonial and postcolonial analyses. Yet Chen argues that examining seemingly 'anomalous' cases facilitates the development of anti-colonial social theory. His analysis rests on the premise that anti-colonial global scholarship must be informed by location in the world-system and global political economy. Eschewing the decolonial and postcolonial perspectives, Chen uses an inter-imperial framework to draw attention to the ways in which 'the Asian maritime world was conducive to collaborative colonialism at the interstices of empires'. In his analysis, Chen highlights the role of imperial power *in general* rather than examining the possible ways in which European and Asian powers impacted Hong Kong differently. In doing so, Chen contributes to a version of anti-colonial social theory that is generalizable while also combating a Eurocentric narrative that largely ignores the role of Asian economic and business elites in Hong Kong and the world's colonial and imperial projects.

In her chapter, 'Humanizing Legacies of Caribbean Slavery and Colonialism in the Contemporary UK', Ann Phoenix uses an anti-colonial framework to draw lines between the colonial era and the treatment of racial and ethnic minorities in contemporary British society. In addition to the more recent cases of Brexit and the collective violence against immigrants during the summer of 2024, Phoenix discusses the Windrush scandal of the 20th century, which involved thousands of British Caribbean nationals being denied their long-held British citizenship and then deported from the UK. Phoenix relies on a psychosocial methodology of narrative analysis that quite literally gives voice to the marginalized, dehumanized, and those rendered invisible by colonialism. According to Phoenix, implicit in this method is the notion that narratives stem from particular viewpoints 'in the present that build on the past but look to the future'. Moreover, people's stories and the ways in which they connect events sequentially reveals not only their understanding of events but also the meaning they want others to take away. This psychosocial method centres the experiences of the marginalized, facilitates agency, and actively opposes the erasure of their experiences from history. Importantly, her analysis allows us to see clearly how the Windrush scandal as well as the anti-immigrant and racist sentiment that inspired Brexit and recent attacks on immigrants are reverberations of colonialism. In doing so, Phoenix also makes visible current systems of stratification and inequality, whose origins are inextricably linked to colonialism.

Similarly, in 'The Horrors of Settler-Colonialism: Remote Sites of Refugee Detention in Australia's Carceral Archipelago', Claudia Tazreiter shows how Australia's contemporary approach to refugees is reminiscent of colonial treatment of indigenous populations. Tazreiter begins with a history of settler-colonialism in Australia, which meant the appropriation and theft of land and resources from the Aboriginal and Torres Strait Islander peoples, based on the colonial myth that indigenous peoples were inferior. Tazreiter argues that these ideas remain embedded in contemporary social attitudes in Australia, which have been amplified by security concerns since 9/11, and have, in effect, normalized contemporary migration policies of forced removal from Australia to remote, island detention centres. After providing a concise history of colonialism in and contemporary immigration to Australia, Tazreiter describes the impetus for Australia's externalization policies and development and use of refugee detention centres in the 21st century. In the second half of the chapter, Tazreiter centres the experiences of refugees held on a repurposed Australian naval base on Manus Island, Papua New Guinea. She argues that these immigrants' forms of resistance – activism, writing, and art – contribute to anti-colonial and decolonial thought in two main ways. First, through their embodied experiences, these refugees show how the Australian state's treatment of them resonates with the colonial experience. Second, through their activism and creative pursuits, they not only oppose contemporary colonial practices but also contribute to an empirical and epistemic understanding of their own experiences. In particular, Tazreiter discusses 'Manus Prison Theory (MPT)', which was developed by Behrouz Boochani based on his lived experience of Australia's carceral border. MPT and other scholarly and artistic expressions of resistance offer a unique and singular contemporary contribution to anti-colonial scholarship, providing powerful indictment of the 'totalizing system of domination and power in the Manus Prison' in the treatment of racialized migrants.

The last chapter in the volume is written by Marcelo C. Rosa, who befittingly in his contribution to anti-colonial social theory, argues for the consideration of 'other-than-modern' ontological components in theory development. Building on his previous work on ontoformative ethics, he proposes the idea of an 'ontoformative gesture', a theoretical-methodological alternative that goes beyond notions of modernity, emerging from colonialism. His goal is to 'to experiment with assembling anti-colonial thinking with other-than-modern components of contemporary existences ... to generate non-hegemonic theories from existences not accounted for in sociological analysis'. He argues that we must go beyond merely adding non-white, non-male, non-Western and indigenous scholarship to sociology because this step alone merely reinforces their existences as allegorical rather than the ontology on which to build theory. Rosa uses the scholarship of Gloria Anzaldúa, Silvia Rivera Cusicanqui, and Oyèrónkẹ́ Oyěwùmí not only to highlight contributions from Global South feminist scholars but to illustrate the promise of centring such work in the development of social theory that can make sense of and respond to the complexities of our lives.

Conclusion

This volume invites readers on a journey of discovery. We hope that this is true whether readers are new to scholarship that critically engages with the legacies of colonialism or established scholars in the field. In this introduction, we aimed to provide a road map for navigating the epistemological and ontological questions this volume raises and the debates and discoveries that ensue. While this volume endeavours to accomplish much, it should also be understood as a launching point for future theorizing and analysis. As one reads, it becomes clear there is neither perfect agreement about what exactly anti-colonial global scholarship entails nor a definitive answer to the question of whether any theory or framework, which fundamentally opposes the dominance of one perspective, can be ever be truly *global*. Within these pages are debates, tensions, and paradoxes. There are places of agreement but also instances of disagreement. We see this neither as a limitation of the volume, nor the enterprise of anti-colonial global scholarship more generally, but instead as emblematic of an approach to social science that strives to be interdisciplinary and anti-imperial while eschewing ethnocentrism.

Note

[1] For instance, 'Colonialism, Anti-colonialism, and Dissident Sociology Traditions', https://www.aub.edu.lb/aafp/Documents/AAFP_events-2020.pdf

References

Albrecht, M. (ed) (2020) *Postcolonialism Cross-Examined: Multidirectional Perspectives on Imperial and Colonial Pasts and the Neocolonial Present*, Routledge.

Al-Hardan, A. and Go, J. (eds) (2025) *Anticolonialism and Social Thought*, Cambridge University Press.

Amin, S. (1989) *Eurocentrism*, Monthly Review Press.

Balandier, G. (1966 [1951]) The colonial situation: A theoretical approach, in I. Wallerstein (ed) *Social Change. The Colonial Situation*, Wiley & Sons, pp 34–61.

Bernal, M. (1987) *Black Athena Vol 1: The Fabrication of Ancient Greece 1785–1985*, Rutgers University Press.

Chabal, E. (2019) Anti-colonialism, in M. Moriarty and J. Jennings (eds) *The Cambridge History of French Thought*, Cambridge University Press, pp 4360–445. DOI: https://doi.org/10.1017/9781316681572.049

Cooper, F. (2005) *Colonialism in Place: Theory Knowledge History*, University of California Press.

Cooper, F. (2023) Questioning colonialism, 2005–2023, *Ler Historia*, 83: 11–24. https://doi.org/10.4000/lerhistoria.11970

Dei, G.J.S. and Ashgarzadeh, A. (2001) The power of social theory: The anti-colonial discursive framework, *The Journal of Educational Thought/Revue de la Pensée Éducative*, 35(3): 297–323. https://doi.org/10.11575/jet.v35i3.52749

Dei, G.J.S. and Lordan, M. (eds) (2016) *Anti-Colonial Theory and Decolonial Praxis*, Peter Lang.

Dei, G.J.S. and Demi, S.M. (eds) (2021) *Theorizing the 'Anti-Colonial'*, DIO Press.

Elam, J.D. (2017) 'Anticolonialism', Global South Studies, Accessed April 5, 2025. https://www.globalsouthstudies.org/keyword-essay/anticolonialism/

Gatechew, A. and Mantena, K. (2021) Anticolonialism and the decolonization of political theory, *Critical Times: Interventions in Global Critical Theory*, 4(3): 359–88. https://doi.org/10.1215/26410478-9355193

Go, J. (2023a) Thinking against empire: Anticolonial thought as social theory, *British Journal of Sociology*, 74(3): 279–93. http://doi.org/10.1111/1468-4446.12993

Go, J. (2023b) Anticolonial thought, the sociological imagination, and social science: A reply to critics, *British Journal of Sociology*, 74(3): 349–59. http://doi.org/10.1111/1468-4446.13025

Hull, G. (2023) Varieties of intellectual decolonisation: An introduction, *Social Dynamics: A Journal of African Studies*, 49(2): 185–95. https://doi.org/10.1080/02533952.2023.2243077

Kamola, I. (2019) A time for anticolonial theory, *Contemporary Political Theory*, 18(2): 67–74. https://doi.org/10.1057/s41296-017-0161-8

Langan, M. (ed) (2017) *Neo-Colonialism and the Poverty of 'Development' in Africa*, Palgrave Macmillan.

Lee, C.E. (2018) Anti-colonialism: Origins, practices, and historical legacies, in M. Thomas and A.S. Thompson (eds) *The Oxford Handbook of the Ends of Empire*, Oxford University Press, pp 436–52. https://doi.org/10.1093/oxfordhb/9780198713197.013.24

Lindner, K. (2022) *Marx, Marxism and the Question of Eurocentrism*, Palgrave Macmillan.

Nash, A. (2003) Third worldism, *African Sociological Review/Revue Africaine de Sociologie*, 7(1): 94–116.

Nunn, N. and Whetung, M. (2020) Anti colonialism, in *International Encyclopedia of Human Geography*, 2nd edition, Volume 1, Elsevier, pp 1550–8. https://doi.org/10.1016/B978-0-08-102295-5.10800-5

OED (*Oxford English Dictionary*) (2024) Colonialism and anti-colonialism. https://www.oed.com/dictionary/anti-colonial_adj?tab=factsheet#1356643210

Osterhammel, J. (2005) *Colonialism: A Theoretical Overview*, 2nd edition, Markus Wiener Publishers.

Patel, S. (2023) Anti-colonial thought and global social theory, *Frontiers in Sociology*, 8. https://doi.org/10.3389/fsoc.2023.1143776

Patel, S. (2024) What is anti-colonial theory? *Sociological Compass*, 18(8). https://doi.org/10.1111/soc4.13259

Patel, S. (in press) Anti-colonial global social theory as meta theory: Its lineage, claims and deliberations, in J. Puri and V. Patil (eds) *Handbook on Anticolonial, Decolonial, Postcolonial Sociologies*, Edward Elgar.

Quijano, A. (2000) Coloniality of power, Eurocentrism, and Latin America, *Nepalta. Views from South*, 1(3): 533–80. doi.org/10.1177/0268580900015002005

Said, E. (1978) *Orientalism*, Pantheon Books.

Schwarz, H. and Ray, S. (eds) (2005) *A Companion to Postcolonial Studies*, Blackwell.

UNESCO (2010) *World Social Science Report: Knowledge Divides*, UNESCO and ISSC.

Wallerstein, I. (1997) Eurocentrism and its avatars: The dilemmas of social science, *Sociological Bulletin*, 46(1): 21–39. https://doi.org/10.1177/0038022919970102

Young, R.C. (2016) *Postcolonialism: An Historical Introduction*, John Wiley.

2

Anti-Colonial Theory as a Peripheral Gaze

Sujata Patel

Introduction

Is there an anti-colonial social theory?[1] I believe there is. In this chapter, I map and describe, explain and dissect anti-colonial social theory's *beginnings* (Said, 1975)[2] and locations in multiple colonized/imperialized geographies. I define anti-colonial social theory as a viewpoint that explores the way power, authority and domination imbricate themselves within knowledge while asserting a need to displace it for new alternative(s) that reflect the experiences of the colonized Other. I also suggest anti-colonial social theory is intimately linked with anti-colonial thought, which should be understood as a set of proto-philosophical/sociological ideas (Patel, 2023a, 2024). Additionally, I outline some of the theoretical challenges that anti-colonial social theory confronts as its diverse and manifold methodologies and perspectives are now recognized, organized and cohered into a body of thought (Go, 2023a; 2023b; Dei and Asgharzadeh, 2001; Patel, 2023a, 2024 and all chapters in this volume).[3]

Yet, to begin, I must emphasize that anti-colonial social theory is also metatheory, or a theory about theory. Metatheories query, interrogate and critically evaluate the assumptions governing categories and concepts, perspectives and theories that organize the past and the present of the social sciences. As metatheory, anti-colonial social theory integrates and combines three elements: its assumes that we live in a colonized/imperial worlds that needs a methodology to deconstruct its dominant/hegemonic knowledges that have emerged in these colonized processes historically; it frames a critical theoretical framework to comprehend the nature of colonially constituted modernities based on this methodology; and it introduces a method to study the new social and reflect on the anti-colonial ontological and epistemological standpoint. Together these attributes highlight the situated nature of anti-colonial social theory (Haraway, 1988), which I contend can be termed the peripheral gaze.

In Euro-American intellectual traditions, scholars have tended to distinguish between social theory and metatheory. It has been suggested that while social theory makes 'generalised statements about social realities or regularities of social life' (Joas and Knobl, 2009: ix),[4] metatheories question and provide alternatives to the philosophical, sociological and scientific assumptions needed to comprehend contemporary world(s) and discuss ways to engage with the empirical real through reflexive thinking (Rutzoe, 2018). Some scholars have argued that Pierre Bourdieu's approach of reflexivity or the viewpoint of critical realism or that of feminist standpoint theory, among many others, incorporate metatheoretical claims, for these draw attention to the philosophical and scientific assumptions of and for constituting social science theories and examine them through the lens of the relationship between the ontological and epistemological (Bourdieu and Wacquant, 1992; Archer et al, 2016; Rutzoe and Steinmetz, 2018).

By contrast, anti-colonial social theory presents us with a critical and a subversive interrogation of the epistemic foundations of fields and disciplines that were formalized within the Euro-American intellectual traditions from the late 18th to the late 19th centuries onwards. Consequently, anti-colonial social theory charts a distinctly different pathway to understand metatheory. Unlike the Euro-American intellectual traditions, it does not necessarily make a clear distinction between metatheory and social theory. Nor is it concerned with ways to delineate and comprehend an 'objective' real in the context of a post-positivist fashioning of social sciences. However, though it shares with the post-positivist traditions an exploration of some philosophical assumptions framing the social sciences and its fields, in the case of anti-colonial social theory, this exercise is attempted for a different goal. It wishes to interrogate the imbrication of power within colonial knowledge formations and search for the *political* moorings of received social theory in order to constitute alternative assumptions for framing new ways to think of colonized modernities.

In other words, all anti-colonial perspectives share the following characteristics: an ontological claim that we live in a colonial/imperial world; a search for a methodology to comprehend the way colonized power frames dominant/hegemonic and an elaboration of methods to debunk these; a quest to constitute new methods to conceive of the colonized social and thereby to reframe ways to think. Thus, anti-colonial social theory supports designing new perspectives of theoretical analysis and methods to frame knowledge from the point of view of the colonized rather than the colonizers. These perspectives may draw its intellectual resources from dissenting Euro-American positions and or combine these with pre-colonial thought in its search for a new analytical stance. Consequently, anti-colonial social theory's focus is on interrogating with critical insights the sociological assumptions – the nature of the dominant social[5] – embedded within late 19th-century theories and within current fields and disciplines and formulates alternate visions. Its goal is to present to us an assessment of the colonial/imperial and its mediations of our perceptions consequent to its formulations as a dominant/hegemonic position. It juxtaposes the categories and concepts fashioned within these fields and disciplines against the experiences of being colonized in particular geographies and counters these through information and data, and narratives and testimonials, of those in the periphery – the critical voice of individuals and collectivities/groups located within colonized/imperialized and sub-imperialist places. It thereby provides us with new meanings for the received categories and concepts of the social, as it reformulates and overturns these to capture the experiences of those in the periphery. Thus, if anti-colonial social theory offers to us critical methodologies to displace existing concepts and theories of modernity, it also suggests ways to design fresh ones based on the capitalist modern experience of being colonized. Subsequently, anti-colonial social theory is a standpoint that constantly reformulates itself.

Though I write about anti-colonial social theory in the singular, I also contend that it incorporates a set of distinct and separate methodologies based on these assumptions to dissect the power-knowledge unity within colonial/imperialist positions when it proposes alternative methods and new ways to think. These have emerged from engagement with and displacement of dominant/hegemonic theories and paradigms. The emergence of these discrete methodologies in particular settings and in distinct time periods should not imply that its applications are restricted to these contexts. Rather, I am suggesting that placing these together in one continuum allows us to open up ways to unravel and comprehend colonialism's imbrication in knowledge production and offers steps to frame comparatively the use of these as global social theory. These multiple perspectives, like an umbrella, harbour social theory at two levels. First, as mentioned earlier, anti-colonial social theory manifests itself as distinct methodologies which lay bare the embeddedness of colonial politics on knowledge construction. One of the goals of this chapter is to map these.

Second, these methodologies allow us to decouple the distinct space-time histories of critical perspectives against domination/hegemony of colonized knowledge within varied colonized geographies. Just as there are diverse and multiple methodologies of anti-colonial social theory, so are there numerous intellectual traditions and multiple theoretical perspectives with which these are assessed as specific histories of the colonized modern within localities, regions, nation-states and across the planet. These critiques have commenced in different times in distinct regions of the world in the context of distinct concerns that spilled out as protests, struggles and resistances against colonialism/imperialism. The first recorded *beginnings* of anti-colonial social theory are associated with discussions within certain parts of Asia and Africa in the 1940s and 1950s, and evidence suggests that it occurred in the context of the mobilizations of anti-colonial nationalism and later of Thirdworldism (Nash, 2003). We see a further development of this trend in the 1960s in Latin America with the growth of dependency and underdevelopment perspectives, which were deeply embedded with Marxist positions emerging out of social movements in and of the region. In the late 1970s and 1980s these questions are reformulated and asked within academic scholarship in North America and, since the late 1990s, in Europe. Simultaneously, further critiques of anti-colonial social theory (such as subalternity and extraversion) developed in the fledging academia within some Asian and African regions.

Consequently, distinct intellectual traditions regarding anti-colonial social theory have developed within these regions, and its multiple theories portray in varied ways colonized modernities. These distinct intellectual traditions provide us with a social scientific language that give us new meanings to older concepts and novel methods to constitute new concepts and hypotheses regarding transitions to the modern in an unequal global world. If, as mentioned earlier, there are a common set of attributes defining anti-colonial social theory's location within global geopolitics, there are also differences within it that need to be recognized and highlighted. I argue that the diversities that characterize anti-colonial social theory's understanding of colonized modernities are among its intellectual strengths (Patel, 2010).

Anti-colonial social theory's *beginnings* are in anti-colonial social and political thought which emerged in the mid to late 19th century.[6] In some of these colonized geographies, wherein oppositions and resistances emerged to dominant/hegemonic perspectives over the *longue durée*, anti-colonial social theory has engaged with changing concerns and turned its critical gaze on its own long history including on the colonial antecedents in understanding the concepts of nation, nationalism and the nation-state (Chatterjee, 1986; Chen, 2010; Patel, 2017). In addition, given that some anti-colonial movements have their *beginnings* in the mid to late 19th century and others emerged in the mid to late 20th century,[7] it is possible that these movements of resistance combine earlier trends or formulate new ways for understanding colonialism/imperialism. In this chapter, I distinguish between three phases of anti-colonial social theory.

What is the epistemic foundation of anti-colonial social theory? I suggest it is the peripheral gaze – a relational perspective of power that emerged within anti-colonial thought and later came to be embodied within anti-colonial social theory. The peripheral gaze is a standpoint to think from the margins of colonial/imperialist/sub-imperialist/nationalist-colonial situated structures; it posits itself in juxtaposition to colonial ways of seeing and perceiving the world,[8] and thereby alludes to its emergence in context to the core perspective. The latter draws its standpoint from an assessment of how global geopolitics intervene in the production, re-production and circulation of knowledge across the world within specific space-times. While acknowledging these relational moorings, its project is to critique and reconceptualize the colonially mediated modern and outline various interdisciplinary perspectives and methodologies that can make it possible. As such, anti-colonial social theory situates itself as a critical protagonist of colonial/imperial dominant/hegemonic knowledge(s) and maps ways through which knowledge fields need to be reconstituted to confront the contemporary colonial social. It positions itself as a language that queries old ways of comprehending the past and the present and constitutes new ways of perceiving the present and the future(s) of the planetary world. In this form, anti-colonial social theory perceives itself as a global political project and challenges scholarship to initiate changes in its philosophical, sociological, and political assumptions about the world. Further, it offers itself as a critical intellectual stance that can provide positionality for scholars and thereby locate their scholarship.

The present conjuncture is an apposite moment; this moment not only helps us to comprehend anti-colonial social theory's methodologies but gives us an opportunity to rethink critically its extensive repertoire, to trace its *beginnings* and comprehend the continuities of methodologies and built-in assumptions that have structured its intellectual traditions. The increasing flow of information and knowledge has opened up spaces for scholars to recognize different ways of doing social sciences, coinciding with a moment when critical stances are also being queried. In this context, the lessons that anti-colonial social theory provides us with are important. This chapter presents, describes and explains the various methodological positions associated with anti-colonial social theory and to relate these to the peripheral gaze as a continuing critique from the colonial/imperial peripheries. It contends that the *beginnings* of anti-colonial social theory stretch back to late 19th century and lies in the new language it generated in and within the growth of protests, struggles and resistance against colonialism/imperialism, sub-imperialist and increasingly dominant and authoritarian nationalisms across the world. After explaining its early *beginnings* in the 1940s and 1950s, the focus of this chapter shifts to a set of methodologies that developed within academic scholarship in the late 1970s and early 1980s onwards. Sometimes called 'high theory' (Mbebe, 2008), these are the perspectives are associated with subaltern scholarship, endogeneity and extraversion, coloniality of power, postcolonialism and modernity/decoloniality approaches. I argue that these perspectives build on a critique of the first phase and then outline their contributions to social theory. My perspective draws from the current debates within historical sociology of epistemology on this theme (Dayé, 2018).

On the basis of this description and assessments, the chapter first makes an evaluation of how anti-colonial social theory has contributed to an understanding of colonial modernities. I discuss how these methodologies have aided scholars to contribute to various fields of study. Second, on the basis of this description, I suggest that there needs to be a discussion on distinct models of colonized modernities in the world – those associated with settled, non-settled, semi-colonial and sub-imperial colonialisms – and go on to discuss some of their respective features. Lastly, in this chapter, I ask how contemporary geopolitics defines the current knowledge economy and reflect on the challenges it presents to anti-colonial scholarship.

The peripheral gaze

What is the peripheral gaze? I borrow the notion of the periphery from the world-systems perspective (Hopkins and Wallerstein, 1982). This analytical framework situated itself against the linear and evolutionary position embedded within modernization theories – that is, the idea that societies move from 'pre-modern' to 'modern' in a linear fashion over time. Critiquing this before-and-after understanding of history on the basis of the assumption that, because European nation-states transited to modernity earlier, others would also do so later, the world-systems approach maintains that nation-states cannot be the site for investigations. Rather, the world should be understood as one unit for investigation. Specifically, world-system theorists argue that this unit of analysis is determined by a continuous expanding capitalist economy wherein the core regions, that is, the Euro-American countries, have produced its wealth and profits by continuously exploiting the less advantageous – the periphery – through the control of the latter's economic, political, cultural and natural resources and wealth, as well as its people. The world-systems approach also argues that capitalist relations that flow across the world has integrated the world regions into a market economy based on monetary exchange over the course of its 500-year-long history through the processes of colonial and imperialist systems of power. Accordingly, this perspective promotes a view of history based on the evolving spatial power connections of domination and subordination structured in and through core–peripheral relations of economic and cultural inequalities. Methodologically, it proposes that each particular unit and sub-unit is a relationship of power, that is, when a unit is observed, it needs to be perceived in its power relation with the other, with each relational aspect in this unit occupying a distinctive spatial-temporal position within the evolving ensemble of power relations comprising the world economy (Hopkins, 1982).

In *Open Social Sciences* (1996), Wallerstein and his colleagues have expanded this perspective to bear upon the framing of universalistic social sciences. At one level, *Open Social Sciences* presents to us a history of the growth and expansion of fields and disciplines in five core countries of the world-system – England, France, Germany, Italy and the United States – and assesses its consolidation over the long 19th century (1776–1945). At another level, it is a narrative of the growth of a dominant episteme – Eurocentrism – in the context of colonial/imperial expansion of the world-system. Rather than discussing how the world was worlded (Spivak, 1985),[9] and thereby how Eurocentric philosophical and scientific assumptions were circulated and imposed across colonized/imperialized geographies, the arguments in the book focus on the production and reproduction of Eurocentric episteme in fields/disciplines within Europe. The book elaborates on: how the knowledge binary of nomothetic versus ideographic knowledges emerged; how the Eurocentric distinction between the I and the Other led to the separation of nomothetic social science fields of sociology, political science and economics from anthropology – with the former promoting itself as modern universalistic social sciences while the latter presenting itself as particularistic perspective that analyses non-modern societies; and how the legitimation of this disciplinary boundaries within separate departments in university structures helped to spread this dominant/hegemonic episteme as part of the continuously expanding world-system (Wallerstein et al, 1996).

Despite its focus on the Euro-American core regions[10] and the integration of the knowledge economy within it, *Open Social Sciences* provides us with key methodological assumptions to understand the relational nature of production and reproduction of fields and disciplines as global power relations alter and change continuously. In turn, it helps to comprehend ways to think about the received and reconstituted scholarship across the world. Contrary to the notion that all knowledge fields and disciplines can be understood exclusively in terms of their national concerns, *Open Social Sciences* argues that these need to be placed within a specific historically encompassing and unified world economy. It contends that Eurocentric episteme has been formulated in the core Euro-American regions and its manifestations in terms of ideas and thoughts, hypothesis and methods dominate the world culturally and intellectually. Thus, it is imperative to study the growth and nature of the world-system and observe the interconnections between its elements. Second, it suggests that, though Eurocentrism is an intellectual project, it is also a political project and needs to be studied contextually in terms of changing power relations between the core, semi-peripheries and peripheries. Lastly, it argues that its institutionalization was related with the establishment of university systems in core countries and later the semi-peripheries and peripheries; through these institutions global colonial connections were organized and reorganized, including the knowledge of the 'Other' as a way to comprehend the colonized self.

On the basis of this, I argue that the peripheral gaze is a standpoint that questions the Eurocentric epistemology;[11] assesses the processes of its consolidation within the peripheries through the relational prism; and examines its re-articulation in various projects of colonial conscription(s) imposed by colonial authorities (Asad, 1992) and its eventual confrontations with and against it. The peripheral gaze needs to be studied as situated knowledge that emerges over the *longue durée* in different space-times as it confronts a changing world knowledge economy. To this set of propositions, I add that the peripheral gaze has been actualized within anti-colonial thought and anti-colonial social theory and continues to do so currently in discrete ways. What is needed is that social sciences observe its historical and contemporary manifestations across the world in its distinct space-time settings as anti-colonial thought.

Anti-colonial thought includes many variants of philosophical-political ideas; these range from liberal and to left perspectives (Young, 2016). Each of these contain their own theories of power and elaborate the terms of their relationship with dominant/hegemonic positions through different perspectives. In turn these assessments have influenced the way theories of colonial modernity have been formulated. Given that the first theorizations on the relationship between capitalism and colonialism were presented by Karl Marx, and which were extended later by Lenin and other Marxists, research and analysis of colonialism and anti-colonial thought follows most often a Marxist intellectual legacy (Gandhi, 1998).[12] Consequently, anti-colonial social thought incorporates a political economy approach, a critique of colonial modernity and of the colonial state in understanding the constitution of the colonized social.

I have suggested earlier (Patel, 2023a, 2024) that anti-colonial thought should be understood as proto-philosophical/sociological thought. Thus, it alerts us to the impact of colonial domination to the economy, it delineates political strategies being used to impose it, it narrates the way rules and law together with violence and force are expended and leads us to comprehend the social of the colonized regions while signalling us to its project of continuously reframing old hierarchies though new dominant frameworks. Anti-colonial thought also frames the political strategies needed for confronting the military might and the violence perpetuated by the colonial authorities. Subsequently, anti-colonial thought takes the first step towards building an epistemic and methodological exercise that uses reason and rationality to search for a new logic to comprehend the relationship between power and knowledge under colonialism/imperialism. Together with the ideas of what constitutes a good society, and how to constitute human solidarities, anti-colonial thought offers an ontological-epistemological and a moral perspective to examine and evaluate colonial capitalism. Through this proto-sociological approach, it contributes to the formation of a situated standpoint and alerts us to the queries that need to be asked to comprehend fields and disciplines within contemporary colonial/imperial processes. It only becomes social theory when it frames and then articulates the assumptions needed to constitute an alternative way of thinking regarding the social. This happens when it becomes associated with academic scholarship and makes itself a methodological perspective. I describe these methodologies next.

Anti-colonial social theory: the first steps

How do we know what we need to know? And how can we displace what others think they know about us and present our ways to know? What does it mean when we say 'ours'? Which individuals and groups signify 'us'? Who and what are we and what are our histories? Why is this knowledge useful? How does this knowledge make us humans and allow us to live freely, autonomously and without violence?

These ambitious queries organized the debates from 1940s onwards of intellectuals within anti-colonial nationalism and subsequently the scholars of the newly independent Asian and African nation-states. These were not new questions; these were raised in different ways within the Asian and African colonialized regions of the world since the late 19th century. What was distinctive was their promotion as a new epistemological stance that could assist in reframing ways to look at 'us' as against the world outside 'us'. For most of the newly independent nation-states, decolonization was not only about the transfer of political sovereignty to the 'natives', but it was also about designing new intellectual pathways to free themselves from economic and cultural/intellectual dependencies generated by colonialism and, through these processes, to constitute sovereign knowledge. Readers used to the sophisticated elaboration of Michel Foucault's power/knowledge critique may not recognize the strategies used to dismember colonial knowledge. But these were extremely significant and in context to the post-Second World War geopolitics, because it created an important political-intellectual space to posit a theory of the 'third path to modernity' (Dirlik, 2007: 14).

At the Bandung conference in 1955, 29 Asian and African countries met to constitute themselves as a political bloc distinct from colonial/imperial powers. At this conference, these nation-states organized themselves as a non-aligned bloc of 'third world' countries and committed themselves to a model of social change outside the one presented by the American-led 'first world' promoting a capitalist democracy and the Russian-led 'second world' of a state-led planned economy bolstered through communist principles. In this context, public intellectuals from these newly independent countries came together to develop domestic economic policies that synced with the idea of Thirdworldism (Nash, 2003) that endorsed independent and autonomous economic programmes for growth and development of its peoples outside the ones designed by the first and the second worlds.[13]

As mentioned earlier, this was not a new idea. Since the late 19th century, in many countries, anti-colonial thought cohered around what contemporary historians have called economic nationalism, that is, a nationalist ideology where colonial rule was understood as economic exploitation (Chandra, 1979).[14] While each colonized region articulated distinct assessments of the same, in the case of India, these ideas were promoted in the late 19th century by a group of English-speaking literate professionals – lawyers, teachers and administrators who used English and regional language newspapers to create public opinion against the British rule. In various articles and subsequent discussions in these newspapers, they created a public that were convinced that the British were draining India of its wealth and its capital,[15] and using the revenues they were extracting from India to benefit the British people, British industries and British military exploits across the world in order to further usurp land and in turn to exploit various peoples and their territories. More specifically, these public intellectuals discussed how continuous famines were impacting land and its productivity and how the peasants were being forced to pay high rents, leading many to become destitute. They also argued that while there was little to no encouragement for modern industry, existing pre-colonial industries such as textiles[16] were being ruined, leading both to distress, migration and transportation of enslaved people to plantations across the world. The revenues so obtained were diverted to maintain the British administration in India rather than aid and help the people of India.

Given this legacy, intellectuals and political leaders presented a new economic programme of import substituting industrialization that could not only decrease substantively trade and market linkages with the colonizing countries but also allow postcolonial nation-states to depend on each other for trade and thereby sustain their project across the third world. Critical to the programme for economic nationalism was the need for political autonomy and for the establishment of intellectual infrastructure – educational institutions of teaching and research and financial sponsorship for new publications. It was hoped that this intellectual infrastructure would build frameworks for autonomous economic development.[17] The Bandung initiative thus provided a prelude to and a background for developing alternate social science models for economic growth and development and breaking the knowledge circuit controlled by Euro-American regions. Over the next two decades, a series of conferences made possible an exchange of ideas and models.[18] In 1973, at the first Asian Conference on Teaching and Research in Social Sciences, the discussions concretized to ask what are the methodological interventions needed to create sovereign and non-colonial ways of thinking and doing social sciences (Atal, 1981).

Termed the indigenization of social sciences, it included strategies that combined methodological interventions for doing sovereign social sciences with the aid of nation-states' institutional support. Scholars delineated four aspects of methodological significance. The first demanded that scholars search for local/native and regional language based primary sources which could in turn generate new frameworks for understanding local cultures. This query was significant for archaeologists, historians and anthropologists, given that colonial knowledge was sparse in these domains. The second query shifted the discussion to the scholar's positionality. It asked: does one's location outside the Euro-American intellectual traditions help to frame new and novel hypotheses and theories to comprehend post-colonial societies? Does being a 'native' help to re-do theoretical frameworks? These enquires signalled the methodological need of being an insider to identify particular cultural factors and subsequently develop theories relating to one's culture.[19] This question was linked to the discussions among anthropologists regarding emic versus etic perspectives. From these discussions emerged another question: given that the nation-state imagined a new nation and because it had been constituted through anti-colonial struggles should not the nation-state's agendas define the agendas of social scientists? This question was significant not only to economists who self-identified as policy social scientists and legitimized their role as planners but also to political scientists and sociologists who wished to study political and social changes after independence. Ultimately this query led to the setting up of a new specialization called development studies. Lastly, these debates led to another set of questions, these being discussed by philosophers, anthropologists and sociologists. Do scholars need new philosophical and sociological assumptions to conceive of sovereign theoretical and methodological paradigms? If so, which assumptions regarding one's culture and its philosophical notions can be extracted and how could these help to reorganize social sciences of post-colonial societies (Atal, 1981)?

This set of queries produced extensive scholarship in various fields and disciplines across the post-colonial nation-states. It is difficult to summarize the extensive contributions made to knowledge, but suffice to state that if it created new pathways to interrogate the universals embodied in Euro-American intellectual traditions, it also led to a discussion of how best social sciences can represent its nations/communities, its cultural histories and social lives. It promoted an idea that doing indigenous social sciences within each nation-state would lead to new culturally sensitive perspectives, theories and concepts regarding the social. Indigenous sociologies gave themselves an alternate epistemic voice to displace the power of

Euro-American intellectual traditions with its language of 'universal social sciences' and to substitute it with other ways of doing social sciences, in terms of 'one's own' traditions.

As mentioned earlier, for most social scientists the project of indigenization was juxtaposed against a perspective that universalized a nation's sociabalities through a colonially organized 'outsider' knowledge. Thus, doing indigenization meant the study to comprehend one's culture through an emic perspective. Consequently, anti-colonial social theory placed itself against colonial knowledge and positioned itself as creating new knowledge through the use of new primary sources and aligning its queries to culture-specific assumptions which it contended were located in the country's nation and its histories. It was suggested that anti-colonial social theory captures particular experiences and practices of groups/nations/communities within the country and should remain particularistic in character. Indigenization of social sciences should thus be based on understanding these particular values. In taking this pathway, it argued, it follows the road already traversed by Euro-American social theory, which constituted its perspectives from its particular cultures and values. In this case, the mission was to reflect similar insider practices and experiences and to develop new methodological and epistemological precepts to examine these. Within parts of Africa and Asia, wherein these intellectual projects developed, the philosophical and cultural roots of national knowledge traditions were extracted and identified to constitute the national social.

To illustrate, I briefly summarize the scholarship of two sociologists who elaborated an emic viewpoint of social theory: D.P. Mukerji (1894–1961) from India and Akinsola Akiwowo (1922–2014) from Nigeria. For Mukerji, the questions were: how does one understand India's current economic and social problems, the nature of change in India and why has British/Western social science language proved inadequate in comprehending this change and India's social problems? Mukerji contended that the discipline of sociology needs social theories that can capture practices and experiences of the groups living in a region given that actions and agency are defined within received cultural practices. Such practices are in turn related to specific ideals/values of these groups. In his scholarship, he deliberated how change has been conceptualized within pre-colonial intellectual traditions in India and concluded that an Indian sociology needs to create a vocabulary that assesses contemporary changes in terms of its past theories. On this basis, he identified four attributes of social change in India; acceptance, adaptability, accommodation and assimilation. He posited that Indian modernity cannot be assessed in a social scientific language of conflict, as suggested by Karl Marx. Rather it should be formulated as a theory based on cultural symbiosis, which he argued is the outstanding feature of India's long civilizational history (Madan, 2007).

As against Mukerji, Akiwowo (1986, 1999) suggested that sociology and social theory can be constituted from tales, myths and proverbs of the people together with 'the laws of true African wisdom'. These sources reflect, according to Akiwowo, the values of the region. At the Department of Sociology of the University of Nigeria, he and his colleagues attempted to put together a social theory extracted from the poetry of the Yoruba tribe of Nigeria. Akiwowo and his colleagues argued that the key philosophical principle of the Yoruba tribe is represented in the concept of *asuwada*. It is through an examination and analysis of this concept that social theorists can organize a theory of sociation and thereby constitute a general theory of the social. They argued that the concept of *asuwada* asserts that though the unit of all social life is the individual, an individual as a 'corporeal self needs fellowship of other individuals' (Makinde, 1988: 62–3). As a consequence, community life based on a common good is *sui generis* to the existence of the individual within the Yoruba tribe.

How did contemporary scholarship receive these reflections? Did it agree that emic perspectives provide us with epistemic voices to reframe social theory? As emic perspectives percolated across the post-colonial regions, critical Marxist positions interrogated these perspectives. By the 1970s and 1980s a new generation of social scientists queried these emic positions and searched for new epistemic voice(s) to revisualize once again anti-colonial social theory. Next, I discuss five such interventions: subaltern studies; endogeneity and extraversion; coloniality of power; postcolonialism; and modernity/decoloniality.

Anti-colonial social theory: its reformulations in Africa, Asia and Latin America

In the 1980s, anti-colonial social theory reframed itself in context of two geopolitical changes. First, from the mid and late 1970s postcolonial nation-states faced economic crisis together with balance of trade deficits and were forced to shift their political alliances and adopt the economic models of the first or second world blocs. This led to the slow demise of the project of autonomous economic development. Consequently, the political projects of non-alignment and Thirdworldism also lost their political legitimacy. The decades of the 1970s and 1980s were also a period of global upheavals and impacted the weight and power of the Soviet bloc. The global balance of power was impacted by: the fall of the Berlin Wall in the late 1980s; the demise of communism in the Eastern and Central European countries and Russia; and later China's decreasing ideological and economic influence on the left-oriented anti-colonial nationalist nation-states and anti-colonial movements. This period also saw the expanding capitalist market and subsequent financialization of the economy. In this context, the Euro-American core countries, with their control of new technologies (ICT), asserted their place in the world and promoted a unipolar world. They reinforced this goal through the formation of the G8 in the early 1990s. There were some attempts to regroup the non-aligned movement and make it into a Global South political grouping. Though this venture has not been as successful as the political project of Thirdworldism, it did create a small intellectual space for the growth of southern studies (Connell, 2007; De Souza Santos, 2014; Fiddian-Qasmiyeh and Daley, 2018). However, today the world reflects the late 19th century unequal divisions of West–East, though it is now called North–South; if the earlier bipolar world perspective was about two political-economic systems, today it is about inequalities between the periphery – the post-colonial nation-states – and the core regions, that of the Euro-American world (World Inequality Report, 2022).

Second, at the moment when the Euro-American countries reasserted their domination in the world, paradoxically their knowledge fields and disciplines were caught in an internal crisis – that of their own self-identity. While the entry of postmodernist positions challenged knowledge universals promoted by Euro-American fields and disciplines, a subsequent critique of the 19th-century positivist perspective affirmed a need to overhaul and radically reorganize received social science models that promoted value neutrality, regularities of social life, certainties of knowledge and law-like analysis of the same based on regression models. This crisis of self-identity led some scholars to use new methodologies, such as hermeneutics and interpretative analysis or constructivist analysis, poststructuralism and deconstruction, while others suggested a need to historicize the discipline in order to comprehend whether late 19th-century positions had contemporary relevance. Simultaneously, the growth of feminist and ecological/environmental perspectives raised queries and concerns regarding the dystopias of modernities. It is in this space that anti-colonial social theory reinvented itself in new ways. It initiated its project by criticizing the emic approaches within the indigenization perspective and contended that it merely reproduces colonial assumptions as nationalist perspectives. It queried these perspectives at three levels: for standardizing and homogenizing pre-colonial intellectual traditions of one group and universalizing these to all nation(s)/community(ies) within the nation-state; for using ethnophilosophical/Orientalist ideas and perspectives uncritically as primary sources; and lastly for not following critical scientific procedures in order to constitute analytical perspectives. These critiques searched for new perspectives and outlined distinct ways to study the anti-colonial social. Next, I elaborate how the new positions of subalternity, endogeneity/extraversion and coloniality of power challenged these received understandings. It is important to mention that these perspectives drew their frames of reference from contemporary critical Marxist positions.

Subalternity

It is difficult to summarize the range, breadth and depth of subaltern scholarship. Beginning with 1982 and running through until 2005, the 12 edited volumes of *Subaltern Studies*, together with various monographs written by scholars of this collective, have overturned many of the received assumptions of mid-20th-century anti-colonial historiography and by extension of social theory.

Ranajit Guha (1913–2023) initiated the debate and discussion on indigenous nationalist historiography and social sciences by stating the following: 'The historiography of Indian nationalism has for a long time been dominated by elitism-colonialist elitism and bourgeois-nationalist elitism' (Guha, 1982: 1). He contended that the nationalist historiography, whether liberal or Marxist, was about the elites and its interests. The elite in India were British-educated middle-class groups who were in collusion with the colonial state and wanted to share political power. He argued that these elite groups, while projecting their nationalism as anti-colonial, reproduced in their politics the language of colonialism. Given that colonial and nationalist historiographies, whether liberal or Marxist, drew their understanding of politics and power from these elite and their languages, these historiographies reflected elite conceptualizations.

According to Guha, there was another set of politics and another notion of power within anti-colonial nationalist movements. This was articulated in the politics of the 'people' – the subalterns. They were the masses of labouring poor and the intermediate strata in the country and in the towns; these were peasants, women, the lower castes, the tribals, the informalized workers, and those who are the underprivileged and considered inferior. The subalterns understood politics and power differently from the elite. He argued that the recovery of their voices against colonialism will lead to a new understanding of two 'indigenous protagonists' (Guha, 1997: xvi) against colonialism – the elite and the subalterns.

But how do scholars understand subaltern politics and their notions of power? How does one 'hear' and 'read' the voices of the illiterate subalterns who also did not build class solidarities? How does one understand them as 'new sovereign subjects of history' (Chatterjee, 2012)? Subaltern scholarship used oral records and testimonies and analysed these to comprehend fragmented expressions articulated by the subalterns. These could be in and through religious idioms, in songs and ballads. In addition, they argued for a need to assess how community identities of kin/subcaste/caste or tribal groups helped the subalterns to forge new identities and to articulate a new language of power.

The subaltern scholars made a critique of the colonial archive, a collection of written records of colonial authorities that oftentimes also included documents and testimonials of the elite. In this context, subaltern scholarship used poststructuralist methodologies to deconstruct the voices of the 'rejects' of colonial/nationalist scholarship and framed new histories of these 'peoples'. This scholarship presents to us a new methodology of interrogating archival documents and has mined popular beliefs, folklore and rumours to explain the political logic of religious-political assertions during colonial and postcolonial/nationalist times. Subaltern historiography reformulates our understanding of the 'social' as it critiques dominant nationalist knowledge and suggests ways to capture the voices of the subjugated groups.

Subaltern scholarship shifted the discussion from the received binary of colonially dominant knowledge versus anti-colonial nationalist knowledge to an interrogation of dominant elite nationalist knowledge against autonomous/emancipatory subaltern knowledge. It suggested that scholars needed to align with subaltern emancipatory knowledge and search for new epistemic voices which are not aligned to colonial assumptions. It presents to us methodologies to reframe anti-colonial social theory from outside nationalist perspectives.

Despite the potentialities of doing alternate scholarship that the subaltern scholarship posited, it has faced widespread theoretical criticisms from historians and social scientists.[20] First, scholars have asked how subaltern historians comprehend the relationship of the subalterns with the dominant nationalist groups. Was this a dialectical relationship or were the subalterns completely autonomous from the elite? According to the historian Sumit Sarkar (1997), in early volumes, the subaltern historians presented the complex dynamics between dominant and subaltern groups in context to colonialism which was in tune with the Gramscian notions. Authors highlighted the subalterns' moorings within economic structures and their conflictual relationship with dominant group as the latter continuously tried to control their aspirations. Yet, in the later volumes, Sarkar argues, this scholarship lost its original agenda to reformulate orthodox and economistic oriented Marxist historiography in dialectical terms. Instead, a significant number of articles in the later volumes followed Partha Chatterjee's proposition that the subaltern is autonomous, fragmented and outside modernity and thus indigenous.[21] Sarkar contends that this position makes subaltern historiography essentialist. Not only does it propose that the various subalterns – the unorganized, informalized workers, women, tribes, inferior caste groups and peasantry – were almost a 'class' group, but it also indicates a lack of sociological sensitivity to the way these groups defined their distinctive subjectivities and thereby distinguished themselves from each other. In addition, do we not see the same blindness reflected in the definition of the elite? For example, landlords, capitalist peasantry, moneylenders, traders, business persons and small capitalists with factories are lumped together when there is historical evidence that each of these groups have played distinctly different political roles with or against the subalterns in context to colonialism. Beyond the discussion on categories, the key issue that most Indian social scientists have queried relates to the conceptualization of anti-colonial nationalism. Is it 'derivative', as suggested by Partha Chatterjee (1986), and has it been compromised by colonial assumptions?[22]

In a previous work, I argued that there is a need to move beyond binaries (Patel, 2017). Although I agree that subaltern thought cannot be posited as being autonomous from dominant perspectives and considered as pre-modern, this should not imply that all nationalist thought was necessarily emancipatory. While some trends within nationalist thought engaged with Marxist perspectives and presented in (limited) ways critical stances, this was not so for trends that popularized emic nationalist perspectives. In this context, I examined the indigenous perspective promoted within Indian sociology from the 1940s onwards. In its search for an alternate ontological language, indigenous nationalist sociology excavated the Hindu past through Orientalist literature to delineate the Indian principles of the social. Consequently, Oriental and later Indological studies and those regarded as precursors of 'modern' sociology (such as D.P. Mukerji, mentioned earlier) legitimized the idea that India's social can be derived from its Hindu religious texts. These texts, I argued, carried not only a colonized gaze but also an upper-caste male gaze as these texts represented the Brahmin voices and members of this group were instrumental in translating these texts for the Orientalists (Dalmia, 1996). I contend that the use of these sources to define the Indian social denied contemporary India's colonial capitalist social. Consequently, Indian sociological traditions were coproduced in the post-independence period by the episteme of colonial modernity and of methodological nationalism that legitimized India as a traditional society rather than one which was colonially constituted (Patel, 2017).

Endogeneity and extraversion

Some of the arguments presented earlier are also reflected in the discussions initiated by the Beninese philosopher Paulin Hountondji (1942–2024). Hountondji has been highly critical of the anthropological search for the indigenous in Africa (1995, 1997, 2009). He has queried the scientific relevance of using folk material to comprehend the African social. Hountondji's (2009) critique of the indigenous is at two levels, the discursive and the analytical. First, he argues that the term 'indigenous' was immersed in colonial connotations and was conceptualized within European African studies programmes and assumes European methods of studying the 'Other'. This programme became associated with disciplinary practices linked to colonial intellectual histories that valorized an ethnophilosophical approach for Africa. He questions the African nationalists that promoted this perspective and contends that they were promoting a kind of populism. The indigenous perspective, according to Hountondji, was ideological because it objectified and promoted a partial understanding of the 'Other'; in addition, it was also racist. Hountondji contends that scholars should first assess the processes that reorganized and erased the many memories of cognitive thought in Africa, for example, that of forced migration and slavery, before identifying local sources for investigation. Local sources and oral traditions may have been overlaid by the objectifications made by colonial authorities in different space-times and in diverse regions, and when received today need to be studied as colonial and ideological. In these circumstances, a search for pre-colonial local knowledge and cognitive traditions can only be possible if scholars unravel the colonial cognitive traditions and assess the local that is not tainted by colonial knowledge. Scholarship in Africa, Hountondji contended, needs a new perspective, which he calls the endogenous perspective; an emancipatory and liberated production of knowledge

Second, Hountondji suggests that this should not imply that local and/or native-insider knowledge cannot be used to constitute new theoretical perspectives but these perspectives can only be conceptualized consequent to their filtration through scientific protocols. For him, locating philosophical queries within science is important, rather than locating science in philosophical positions. He contends that local resources and local languages or native/insider research can yield good practices only if such work incorporates scientific validity. For this to happen, African studies need to develop critical scientific rationalities to interrogate African knowledge traditions; without these, it would be difficult to separate the ideological from the scientific. Such critical stances can be borrowed from perspectives from across the world and Hountondji argues that these scientific rationalities would help to interrogate the local – a dismantling of which is a necessity in the context of the late 1990s. Unfortunately, there has been little to no debate on this perspective. Recently Táíwò (2021) has reasserted the need to use Yoruba literature to comprehend contemporary sociation practices in Africa.[23]

Hountondji is also concerned with another question: how can African scholarship develop endogenous critical stances? His answer: this can only happen if there is in place an intellectual infrastructure. He suggests that African scholarship is full of weaknesses because it has been locked into extraversion: knowledge that is externally produced. Obviously, there has been uneven investments in intellectual infrastructure in various parts of Africa and Asia and this has had an implication in developing anti-colonial perspectives.

According to Hountondji, Africa has for long been in a relationship of unequal exchange not only in terms of trade and agricultural goods but also in terms of knowledge production. For Hountondji, the lack of autonomous control of the academic community over scientific practices is related to its lack of intellectual infrastructure which in turn can enable it to reproduce new knowledge goods. If there is an 'uncritical and imitative mind dominated by an external source' (Alatas, 1972: 692), this is because of economic dependencies within knowledge infrastructure. For Hountondji, these dependencies are related to the knowledge market and include financial, physical and human resources, critical education and teaching and learning programmes, a publishing industry that can print books and journals and circulate these in domestic and global markets together with physical and managerial infrastructure to house documents, books and journals in libraries and archives. Hountondji contends extraversion, that is, externally produced knowledge, has reproduced uncritically topics and questions from the Euro-American intellectual traditions and that this has impacted research and the framing of various specializations within fields and disciplines. Such dependent scientific cultures, Houtondji argues, are fuelling brain-drain and promoting academic tourist circuits with diasporic scholars circulating between the core and the periphery gathering information for analysis in the North by the Northern academics.[24]

Coloniality of power

Anibal Quijano's (1928–2018) concept and theory of coloniality/coloniality of power (Quijano, 1989, 1993, 2000, 2007) are like Paulin Hountondji's understanding of extraversion, embedded in the Latin American dependency theories. But unlike Hountondji, Quijano, being a historical sociologist, shifts the discussion of academic dependencies to an interrogation of colonial assumptions organizing social sciences. He contends that these assumptions were consolidated and universalized in the Euro-American social sciences as these developed step by step in consort with colonial capitalism from the 16th century onwards. Quijano's focus is on Eurocentrism, which Samir Amin (1989) had earlier defined as the cultural and intellectual ideology of capitalism.[25] To comprehend the genealogy of Eurocentrism across 500 years of its history, Quijano combines dependency theory with other perspectives: world-systems approach, poststructuralism and the history of critical thought in Latin America. In the process, Quijano's theory of coloniality of power overturns orthodox Marxist analysis of structure-superstructure with a new perspective that argues that the ontological-epistemological is always coproduced with material and sociological processes.

Sensitive to local, regional and global scales, Quijano analyses the growth of colonialism through trade circuits that connected Iberian capitalism with the Americas, and which in the 16th century integrated with Africa through the slave trade. Quijano argues that this model of colonial capitalism institutionalized in the Americas – that of land appropriation, resource extraction and in-migration, became over time a global model not only because it organically interconnected with colonial ideology but it also coproduced dominant knowledge regarding modernity. Over time, this perspective became not only dominant/hegemonic knowledge but expressed itself as embedded scientific assumptions. Coloniality is thus not only about Eurocentrism, 'a peculiar dualist/evolutionist historical perspective' (Quijano, 2000: 556), but also about the organic interconnections between racism and division of labour (based on peonage and slavery). It is about how these attributes reconstitute existing hierarchies and thereby influence values and norms of everyday life, including the family system, marriage alliances, sexualities, the learning processes and its various pedagogies.

Quijano also cautions us against implementing new methodologies uncritically. He contends that although there is a necessity to develop novel methodologies to unravel the consequences of what has occurred, it is also necessary to continuously deconstruct these methodologies' relationship with established and institutionalized knowledge and power. This, he asserts, needs to be done because methodologies have a history of becoming embedded in ideological positions and can even serve dominant interests. Consequently, both theories and methodologies need constant scientific interrogation, even if these have had emancipatory origins.

Like the subaltern school, Quijano's theory of coloniality as a holistic understanding of social change has faced a gamut of criticisms by Latin American social scientists (Domingues, 2019; Salvatore, 2010; Bortoluci and Jansen, 2013). These scholars have raised two sets of queries. First, they ask whether coloniality can persist over 500 years without changes? And further, does it even have an ontological relevance given the sweep of contemporary capitalist modernity (Domingues, 2019) and the genocide against the indigenous groups? Second, they ask whether coloniality has had differential spatial impacts in the Latin American continent and have asked if it can be generalized as a category across the region?

Scholars agree that Anibal Quijano has highlighted a key attribute of settler-colonialism: the usurpation of land from the indigenous groups and the establishment of a settler society. The ideology to rebuild a new society after this displacement has encouraged various legal interventions for the continuation of land appropriation and new forms of its incorporation, such as miscegenation. Historians have contended that empirical studies have affirmed that conquest/genocide of the 'indigenous' groups and their displacement together with modernity has led to neo-colonial domination and backwardness; these two have walked hand in hand in Latin America, creating sometimes mixed and uneven spatial processes (Salvatore, 2010: 339). In addition, scholars who have accepted the idea that the 15th- and 16th-century encounters of the Spanish and the Portuguese were colonial have argued that there is a very specific Latin American historical process consequent to the Iberian invasion into the region. While agreeing that Latin America is an important site for examining the representational and discursive practices that were developed for and through the operation of early European colonialism, they argue for a need to make an assessment of the implications of Catholicism, the contrasting effects of a centralizing state juxtaposed by local bureaucracies and an analysis of its peculiar racial ideologies across the region before accepting the coloniality thesis (Bortoluci and Jansen, 2013). Particularly, social scientists in Latin America have raised fundamental questions regarding the coloniality thesis. One of the major problems seems to be the lack of engagement with the various ways race and racialization have been organized across the Americas (Benzi, 2021).[26] This begs the question whether all forms of difference emerging from Iberian colonial experience since the 16th century can be categorized as racial and theorized as being part of coloniality. These critiques have led to the growth of further research on Quijano's propositions.

Anti-colonial social theory: the shift to North America

An appraisal of an intellectual legacy-exceptionalism and a legislation that opened up immigration to non-European migrants provide strangely the context for the growth of the postcolonial perspective and later of the modernity/decoloniality positions in the United States.

Post-Second World War geopolitics benefited the United States, which took over the leadership of the democratic capitalist world from England and Europe. In the context of an expanding economy and global ambitions, changes were inaugurated in US domestic policies, one of which was its immigration policy. The 1965 immigration policy abolished an earlier quota system in favour of the British and the Europeans and created conditions for immigrants from Asia, Africa and Latin America to find a place and, with it, an intellectual and professional space in the United States. These changes occurred at a time when there were domestic convulsions impacting the WASP hegemony – the growth of the Civil Rights movement of the mid-1950s, the anti-draft movement and the growth of youth countercultures. This ambience provided the conditions for providing a critique of the nationalist American ideology of exceptionalism by a group of new immigrants recruited in academia in the 1970s and 1980s and who were experiencing racism (Schwarz, 2005).[27]

Mainstream American academia promoted the doctrine of exceptionalism. Some efforts to create small changes, such as the establishment of the Afro American, American Indian and Asian American studies departments, were made. These helped to create new ways of thinking but their influence on mainstream disciplines was limited (Schwarz, 2005). This was also true for the area studies departments such as the Middle Eastern, South Asian,

African and Latin American, where different regions were discussed without understanding its connections with each other and to US imperial ambitions. These were also often funded by American military and state departments and had courses and research projects that catered to US global foreign policy concerns.[28] The introduction of the policy of multiculturalism in the 1980s also did not change the situation radically (Sharpe, 2000). Rather it naturalized these divides which came to be graded and were permeated by knowledge politics. The only mainstream department in the United States which discussed the rest of the world was, curiously, the English literature department, which in the wake of growing interest in Commonwealth literature floated courses in comparative English literature. These departments soon started recruiting scholars from various post-colonial countries who brought with them the memories of the anti-colonial movements which was overlaid by contemporary experience of racist discrimination in the United States; these experiences permeated their teaching, research and writing (Schwarz, 2005). Soon a new intellectual movement was inaugurated called postcolonialism, drawing from and extending Edward Said's *Orientalism* (1978), which argued that colonial ways of thinking had infused literature and language studies even though colonialism as a political system of control had formally ended.

Postcolonialism

Said's study, and that of others who established the postcolonial standpoint, was focused on the Western consumption of an imaginary Orient. Said's description of Oriental studies/Middle East studies considered it as a Western style of thought and an institution of power for exercising control over the Arabs and Islam. This idea, that Oriental thought controls the consciousness of the 'natives', pre-dates Said's work and is associated with anti-imperialist approaches popular in the Arab world subsequent to the war of independence in Algeria (Halliday, 1993). However, while borrowing from this idea, Said made a clean break from its Marxist genealogy, integrating Michel Foucault's structuralist/poststructuralist critique of disciplinary knowledge to an assessment of Orientalism. Using Foucault's concepts of power/knowledge and discourse, Said and his colleagues made connections between images and institutions in the production of knowledge and the securing of power.

This method flowed through the book *Orientalism* (1978) and defined what it was. He argued that Orientalism was not only a set of institutions, disciplines and activities of Western universities concerned with the study of Oriental societies and cultures,[29] nor was it only a corporate institution primarily concerned with the Orient. Rather he contended Orientalism was a mode of thought based on a particular epistemology and ontology which established a division between the Orient and the Occident. Said used Foucault's concept of discourse to argue that it combined power with knowledge and thereby produced its objects for a discourse of power which is resistant to change and transformation because of its linguistic constitution. In Said's conceptual framework, there was no phenomena outside that of language, for language is self-referential. Language/literature defines the character of Orientalism; it not only produces the Orient as an object of knowledge but also establishes its outcome in terms of relations of power. Postcolonial studies, in this sense, is a radical methodology that interrogates both the past history and ongoing legacies of European colonialism in order to undo them and integrates in its interrogation its epistemic authority with institutional power.[30]

In the late 1980s, with the migration of some subaltern scholars to the United States, postcolonial positions were integrated with subalternity. Indeed, today the two are rarely distinguished within US academia. This reinvention of postcolonialism helped to cement the place of subaltern scholarship within North American area studies departments and mainstream academia. If Said used literary texts to analyse the West's project of domination of the Orient, the newly inducted subaltern scholars argued that the recovery of the subaltern subject was possible only by deconstructing the historical documents in the archive. In following this path, they made a break from their earlier concerns of the subaltern studies project[31] and shifted their discussions from a search of the subaltern and a critique of elite nationalist historiography in colonial, nationalist and Marxist historiography to the discourses and texts that represent 'the fabric of dominant structures and manifest ... itself as power' (Prakash, 1994: 1482). Though they assert that the search for the subaltern has not been abandoned they also contend that the subaltern and subalternity are organically connected and both can be located in the historical archive.

Their position now fits in intimately with the postcolonialists, who have argued that doing postcoloniality is doing politics against colonialism/ imperialism. The Oriental archive, they contend, lays bare the West's framing of the 'Other' and its politics. This perspective has led Said and his colleagues and the subalterns to confront their own fields of knowledge; in Said's case it is Oriental studies/Middle Eastern studies and, in the case of the subalterns, the discipline of history whose procedures they argue are enmeshed in the authority of the West. Thus, postcolonialism becomes not only a theory of knowledge but a 'theoretical practice', a methodology that can transform knowledge from static disciplinary competence to activist intervention. It gives this privilege to scholars and scholarship who can use it to expose unequal power, make it visible and involve them in ending it. As can be seen, this anti-colonial social theory is very far removed from those developed not only within the indigenization perspective but also elaborated in subaltern studies. The latter searched for a new language to comprehend the power of colonial modernity while postcolonialism is about surface dismembering; that is of deconstruction of literature/languages and documents in the archives. There is little to no engagement within postcolonialism with the relationship of processes and structures which produces literature/documents or with the way these are embedded within events, processes and systems of power and of hierarchies.

Modernity/decoloniality

Decoloniality emerged within the Latin American studies programme in the United States in engagement with postcolonialism. It draws on Quijano's concept of coloniality of power but breaks away from Quijano's methodology that assessed the epistemic linkages with that of the historical empirical processes and presents to us a global perspective that argues that all modern knowledge(s) is embedded within the discursive circle of colonial/capitalist modernity. It divides modern knowledge in terms of the binaries of 'I' and the 'Other' and contends that its formation was initiated in the 16th century. This knowledge spread itself across the world and over time came to be institutionalized soon after the expulsion of Jews and Muslims from Spain and the elevation of Western Christianity to religious dominance. These developments promoted an early racial classification (Mignolo, 2005, 2011). Following Quijano, decoloniality theorists argue that the American continent became the first contact zone and battleground for deploying Eurocentric ideas of civilization, evangelization, empire, racial difference and subalternation of the knowledge of the colonized. It presents a repertoire of epistemic concepts such as Occidentalism (the formation of specific forms of racialized and gendered Western selves) as the effect of Orientalist representations of the non-Western Other (Coronil, 1996); colonial difference (the epistemic division of modernity from coloniality and its use to create further divisions and differences in knowledge); and imperial difference (the downgrading and hierarchization of European Others, for example, the Ottomans, the Chinese or the Russians) to assess and examine the constitution of the 'Other' in European and North American fields of knowledge making in social sciences, art, literature and aesthetics. It argues for a need to excavate alternate epistemologies, thus the use of the term decoloniality as a perspective which is not tainted by Enlightenment thought. In this formulation, its key theorist, Walter Mignolo (2007, 2017), suggests decolonial scholars can articulate their novel perspectives by using the methods of border epistemology, de-linking and pluriversality to create alternate knowledge(s).

Without the introduction of these approaches, mainstream American and European academia embedded in various degrees of dominant perspectives associated with varieties of Occidentalism (Coronil, 1996) would not have engaged with colonialism and reflected on how it has affected both American and European history and the history of its social science disciplines. Indeed, the study of Occidentalist assumptions in literature, literary criticism, historiography and now sociology, political sciences (Gatechew and Mantena, 2021) and more generally social science theories has led to the recovery of the work of scholars such as the sociologist W.E.B. Du Bois (1868–1963) (Morris, 2017) and an assessment of the way racism, ethnicity and discrimination against the First Nations can revitalize the disciplines in North America.

As has been the case for these perspectives of anti-colonial social theory, both postcolonialism and decoloniality have been facing stringent questionings of their methodological and theoretical assumptions. This is more so for postcolonialism given its longer history within contemporary Euro-American intellectual traditions. In the following, I highlight some significant criticisms made of these two perspectives, which I suggest share similar theoretical and methodological orientations though I am aware that scholars would like to see them as distinct from each other (Asher and Ramamurthy, 2020), First, both these perspectives seem not to be interested in understanding specific historical events, processes and structures in different parts of the world in their engagement with colonialism and its knowledges. This is also related to an indifference towards using specific empirical information and an aversion to use the political economy approach. Consequently, there is an absence of self-reflection about the strengths and weakness of its own formulations (Parry, 1987; Dirlik, 1994; Cusicanqui, 2012; Naicker, 2023).

Second, following from this, there is an implicit or explicit belief that intellectual traditions within disciplines and fields are merely discourses located within the binaries of 'I' and the 'Other'. This assumption promotes a scholarly attitude that rejects methodologically 'true' descriptions of the 'real world', including how the real world impacts fields and disciplines making these perspectives anti-foundational (Turner, 1989). Third in continuation of this, there is a lack of self-awareness of their own location within the core regions of the world which reproduce dominant/hegemonic fields and disciplines. In the absence of perspectives regarding the way dominant knowledges control the global knowledge economy, the strategy used by scholars is to merely displace Eurocentric assumptions and not to comprehend how global modernities are distinctly constituted in various parts of the world and relate these to the global knowledge economy. Consequently, these perspectives inadvertently promote methodological nationalism by default. A lack of the understanding of one's location in the core region of Euro-American intellectual traditions can paradoxically lead to overturning its own manifest goals, as has happened recently with the appropriation of Walter E. Mignolo's concept of decoloniality by some Indian rightist intellectuals (Sen, 2023).

The discussion here raises a problem which needs further deliberation. The core regions of the world dominate the globe's intellectual infrastructure – universities, research institutes, institutes of excellence and the publishing industry. The neoliberal corporatization of these intellectual infrastructure and its use of new digital economies (Streckeisen, 2018) has increased the English language production and circulation of the region's published articles, book chapters and books across the world (UNESCO, 2010). Thus, the introduction of new communication technologies has belied the hope of democratizing the knowledge economy; instead, it has increased and facilitated access of knowledge products from Euro-American intellectual traditions to global consumers (who have access to the internet). Consequently, in terms of content, there continues to be little to no circulation of knowledge products from the rest of the world except those produced by the diasporic community within the core regions (Knöchelmann, 2021; Patel, 2023b). This control has also implied that Euro-American understandings of how to write and argue, what to write about and what are the protocols for reviewing papers – this being the symbolic capital of the current Euro-American-dominated knowledge economy – flourishes more intensely than before.[32] Both postcolonialism and decoloniality and various new critical studies that have emerged recently, such as critical race and migration studies, contend that they wish to decolonize dominant perspectives. In this context, a significant challenge is constituting a peripheral perspective, from within core regions, that has global relevance.

Conclusion

How does one assess the contributions of the last eight decades?

In the last few decades anti-colonial social theories have constituted new intellectual cultures across distinct intellectual traditions around the following questions regarding modernities. Is modernity universal? Has it always been produced in similar ways in all parts of the world? Does one need to distinguish between its many differences as these are articulated globally? What are these? How are these related to colonial/imperial capitalism and its contemporary manifestations? How do these modernities differ in terms of a region's or a territory's changing placement in the global world-system? What structures of inequalities and violence do we deal with when discussing modernity in colonized, colonizing and postcolonial regions? How does colonial/imperial capitalism intersect with patrimonialism, patriarchy, racism, ethnicities, caste-ism, religiosities and linguistic identities? How does this influence subsequent hierarchies and redefine them differentially across the world? How do these hierarchies interface with power and politics as well as with nation/community, nation-states, democracy/authoritarianism and knowledge production? How does one develop critical stances towards these knowledges and what intellectual genealogies do we extract to do so?

Intellectual cultures focused on these questions are both general and specific. Generally, these initiate discussions and debates by engaging with dominant/hegemonic social sciences to dismember the inherent ethnocentrism of social sciences that projects a superiority of European experience of modernity. Subsequently, they critique the European historical and cultural patterns of modernity that promote the idea of emulation. In doing so, they assert that Euro-American traditions efface partially or fully non-European history in order to reproduce it through binaries, using divisions of social sciences to promote an Orientalist way to perceive the non-European world and an Occidentalist way to present the Euro-American world.

However, these general questions use specific methodological strategies to interrogate Eurocentric embeddedness and distil its assumptions to comprehend colonized patterns of modernities. These methodological strategies are not necessarily new. What is specific is the way strategies are combined to derail power dimensions within knowledge. Thus, we find some scholars combining structuralism, poststructuralism, deconstruction analysis with dependency theory and world-system analysis to critique Eurocentrism while others use critical Marxist historical sociology to analyse contemporary processes organizing modernities is specific time-spaces. Consequently, scholars have created new concepts to examine the politics of power: for example, Hountondji and Guha use endogeneity and subalternity respectively to explore ways to refashion new practices of doing social sciences. They, with Quijano, have queried Marxist orthodoxies through concepts such as extraversion and coloniality of power, thereby displacing the structure-superstructure argument. In the earlier phase of the subaltern school, and in Quijano's oeuvre, an historical sociological approach helped to provide a new vocabulary. This can be seen in the way Guha built his critique of dominant historiography by distinguishing between the nationalist elite and the subalterns, and Quijano elaborated the way class and race are intermingled in the colonially capitalist exploitative process. This use of old and new methods has provided an entry point to review the past and present assessments in the constitution of hierarchies within colonized territories and to present an alternate standpoint.

These perspectives imply a shift away from a linear theory of time/history and its associate perspectives of evolutionism. Thus, for anti-colonial social theory, its *beginnings* lie in the colonial/imperial encounter and history needs to start from this point. Consequently, most anti-colonial theories of modernity shift their gaze towards assessing the colonial/imperial spatial connections that organize the flows of commodities, ideas and ideologies as well as imaginaries and fields and disciplines between metropole(s), semi-peripheries and peripheries of the world in the context of specific time-spaces.

Subsequently, knowledge fields and disciplines present themselves as distinct intellectual traditions within the overall global system defining core, semi-peripheries and peripheries. As these intellectual traditions have multiplied, they engage with each other within the changing global system to define its knowledge projects and elaborate new ways to define the peripheral gaze. Indeed, as I have argued previously, anti-colonial social theory is diverse and presents itself as multiple methodologies to displace dominant/hegemonic positions and to constitute new ones (Patel, 2010).

We can see the impact of these innovations on various interventions made by this new scholarship. While it is difficult to summarize these trends, it is important to flag the following interventions. In the context of the decolonization process in Africa and Asia, there have been debates on the limited nature of democracy and assessment of what constitutes citizenship in these new post-colonial countries: on the character and quality of the post-colonial state and the attributes of its civil society; on the different kinds of practices related to racism, ethnicity and religiosities and its relationship with colonially imposed nativism; on the nature of its rightist nationalism and its relationship to civilisationalism (Chatterjee, 1986; Mamdani, 1996, 2021; Kaviraj, 2005; Chen, 2010; Domingues, 2019; Gatechew and Mantena, 2021). Others have contended that these ambiguities have impacted the constitution of the self and the formation of subjectivities and identities of the colonized (Nandy, 2009). Similar interventions have been made regarding concepts and theories of class, caste/race and gender; inequalities and exclusions; work, labour and informality; secularism and the constitution of majorities and minorities; on internal migration, urbanization and modernities.

While this scholarship has mapped key themes that structure colonial modernity, recent scholarship has suggested a need to highlight the differences between different forms of colonialism and assess its impacts on knowledge production and the peripheral gaze. Of particular significance are the discussions on settler-colonialism, which is now distinguished from mainstream colonialism or non-settler-colonialism. Veracini (2011) suggests that given the nature of settler-colonialism, where a community of exogenous settlers permanently relocate and eliminate or displace indigenous populations and their control of land, in this case, knowledge structuring is significantly different from other forms of colonial knowledge. Settler-colonialism has built continental projects, such as the United States or Australia. Here it eliminated the original inhabitants to appropriate their land and resources and imposed domination. In the case of non-settler colonialism, the efforts have been to continuously produce, shape and design inequalities between colonizers and the colonized through the reconstruction of pre-modern notions of hierarchy, such as caste or ethnicity or religious affiliations in order to continuously extract surplus from 'native' labour. Thus, in settler-colonization there were rarely projects of decolonization, unlike non-settler colonialism – nor did they have anti-colonial national movements from which scholars have extracted critical stances. In settler-colonization, race, class and geopolitics combined to impose violent annihilation of original inhabitants. Consequently, notions of nation and the nature of nation-state have different and distinct meanings within settler-colonialism. And so have concepts such as indigenous and indigeneity. Scholars have contended that there are also differences within various regions of settler-colonialism and that the Central and Latin American experience should not be equated with the North American one. In addition, these regions need to be distinguished from the experiences of colonialism in the Antipodes (Veracini, 2011) and with contemporary forms of colonialism and genocide in Rwanda, Armenia, Cambodia and Palestine (Wolfe, 2006).

This leads us to another query. How does one evaluate dominant knowledge in regions of the rest of the world which has not experienced colonialism in the forms of settler and non-settler colonialism? Recent literature on eastern regions of Europe and Russia as well as the 'Far East' have argued that the assumptions defining coloniality have also impacted social sciences in these regions. Earlier, Coronil (1996) had argued that forms of Occidentalism had impacted the reproduction of knowledge in various parts of Europe. Scholars have explored methods needed to assess and reconstruct social sciences in territories which were not earlier part of capitalist colonial/imperial system, such as Russia and eastern parts of Europe, but had their own set of (socialist) imperialist premises (Tlostanova, 2012). These scholars tend to use the approach of decoloniality to comprehend the post-socialist worlds and query the relevance of anti-colonial approaches. (This is a surprise given the way discussions on Ukraine have proceeded [Couch, 2023].) Such discussions have also assessed the social sciences in Japan, which was colonized at one point but had in turn also colonialized parts of East Asia. Recently, the historian of the 'Far East', Tani Barlow (2012), has argued that we need a new perspective, one which does not use static categories such as nation, modernity, tradition, culture, stages of development and civilization but rather those that assess multiple and overlapping projects of contemporary colonialism and imperialisms. She suggests that today these overlapping projects of colonialism and imperialism are reshaping intellectual discourses, thereby legitimizing domination-subordination structures defining the metropole(s) with the peripheries actualized first during colonialism. Such overlapping structures have led to new ways to think of the anti-colonial social theory as the complexity of present geopolitics reflects on the blurry spatial-temporality of histories, borders, boundaries and modes of becoming.

Taken together, this body of scholarship assesses how contemporary imperialist geopolitics continues to dictate multi-scaler global geographies of knowledge flows reproducing dominant/hegemonic knowledge. Importantly, there is a recognition that the world has changed significantly since the colonial and postcolonial interventions of the mid to late 20th century. Rather than the West–East axis or the North–South axis, there exists currently, sub-imperial regions which have their own semi-peripheries and peripheries (for example, Singapore, Korea, Taiwan and Japan). These have reorganized flows of commodities, ideas and ideologies and fields of knowledge (Chen, 2010; Lee and Cho, 2012). These flows define all spaces of everyday life, even those which have not experienced colonialism. This position has found support among scholars who work in China, Japan, Korea, Thailand, Cambodia and Hong Kong (Mackie, 2018).

I am suggesting that anti-colonial social theory has resources to confront the current challenges. Its growth in the last eight decades has led it to formulate itself as a standpoint – a point of view and a stance that thinks from the periphery and relates the periphery to changing geopolitics. I also contend that this is situated knowledge because it demands a contextualization of this knowledge in terms of colonially constituted time-spaces. I have shown how anti-colonial social theory is metatheory with an ontological-epistemological perspective. As mentioned earlier, it combines three elements: its assumes that we live in a colonized/imperial world which needs a methodology to deconstruct its dominant/hegemonic knowledges that have emerged in these colonized processes historically; it frames a critical theoretical framework to comprehend the nature of colonially constituted modernities based on this methodology; and it introduces a method to study the new social enabled though a reflection on the anti-colonial ontological and epistemological standpoint. Understood as a collective whole, it provides a positionality to scholars and their scholarship to reframe critical stances.

One of anti-colonial social theory's major contributions is assessing pathways structuring cognitive geographical circuits organizing the metropoles, its semi-peripheries and, in turn, the continuously expanding peripheries of the semi-peripheries and its cores. It argues that these global divisions have created knowledge territories and borders of debate and deliberations which have been sustained by divided academic language communities. These multiple and overlapping knowledge projects connect the global, regional, national and local academic communities and simultaneously reflect on the ways in which these circuits reproduce themselves across various scales in unequal and uneven discourses of modernities. The many circuits that one can identify and the many terms it has used to self-define itself suggests a need to comprehend the diversities that organize anti-colonial social theory. While acknowledging that geopolitics continues to organize flows of knowledges, anti-colonial social theory, I argue, is best equipped to intervene in these geopolitics of knowledge production and circulation given its analysis of the same.

Notes

1. This chapter synthesizes and expands earlier texts (Patel, 2015, 2021a, 2021b, 2023a, 2024).
2. For Said, the concept of beginning (as against origins) traces a genealogy; a line of inquiry. It is a first step in comprehending the meaning of an intellectual tradition as distinct from other traditions of thought. It authorizes that which comes after and enables and limits what is acceptable in this discussion (Said, 1975).
3. See the reference list in the Introduction.
4. Most often than not, such definitions of social theory confuse the particular with the general.
5. For example, a critique of individualism/individuation or a need to re-think the relationship between nature and culture or understanding meanings given to the concepts of nation and nationalism; or that of democracy and secularism in colonized regions.
6. There is a possibility that we may find written records pre-dating 19th century anti-colonial thought which would imply changing this statement.
7. For example, critical anti-colonial thought on the First Nations in Canada and the United States.
8. This juxtaposition leads it to conceive itself as a binary, such as East versus West or South versus North. I would suggest that these binaries should be perceived as political positions rather than conceptual assumptions of anti-colonial social theory.
9. To be correct, Spivak (1985: 253) calls it 'worlding the world'.
10. I agree with Mignolo (2014: 586) that this document 're-westernises social sciences'. Yet, given its moorings within the world-system approach, it helps us to reconstruct the peripheral gaze by alerting us to the changing spatio-temporal specificities of the periphery as against the core.
11. Since the time Samir Amin wrote *Eurocentrism* (1989), this concept has acquired many meanings. Here I am using it as an episteme that is produced through exchange of ideas about the world and later – since the 18th century – has been produced, reproduced and circulated within the world-system in context to shifts of power relationships between the core, semi-periphery and peripheries.
12. Some trends within anti-colonial thought, in particular within postcolonial and decolonial scholarship, set themselves apart from Marxist perspectives and contend that Marx and Marxist perceptions are part of Orientalist positions. Lindner (2022) contends that Marx's writings on Russia and Ireland included recently in the comprehensive edition of his work suggests a more critical orientation to colonialism.
13. For the Indian experience of this programme, see Chakravarty (1987).
14. After the establishment of CEPAL (UN Economic Commission for Latin America and the Caribbean), similar arguments were made by the Latin American intellectuals of the dependency school through a more systematic study of underdevelopment. They suggested that the control of raw materials, technology, capital and markets by the Euro-American regions led to an increase in poverty.
15. In 1901, Dadabhai Naoroji (1825–1917) published a volume titled *Poverty and Un-British Rule in India*, a book that elaborated his ideas on British rule. Earlier, he had started a campaign against British control of India's economy in the 1860s and had mobilised the Indian public on this theme. Later he associated himself with the Indian National Congress established in 1885. He became the Indian National Congress' president for 1886 and also represented it at the Amsterdam Congress of the Second International in 1904 (Chandra, 2010).
16. From 1600 to 1800 Indian textiles dominated the global trade of cloth.
17. For example, as part of the project to indigenise social sciences, the Indian government invested in establishing universities and promoted research institutes. In addition, the state set up a social science research funding body, a regulatory body for universities and

18. encouraged the growth of professional associations in the social sciences. These bodies sponsored journals while various international publishers set up branches in India to publish new monographs.
19. Post-Bandung, the first conference to exchange economic models of development was held in 1957 in Cairo and it brought together 19 Arab and African countries to discuss alternate third world models of development.
20. Subsequently some postcolonial nation-states implemented a policy for hiring only citizens in universities and social science institutes.
21. Ludden (2002) brings together a number of critical assessments on the subaltern studies project which raises methodological issues that confront this scholarship.
22. Recently, quoting Dipesh Chakrabarty, Partha Chatterjee suggests that in point of fact the subaltern studies scholars wanted to study the 'archaic in the modern' and not archaic against the modern (Chatterjee, 2012: 46).
23. Chatterjee (2012) has argued that the subaltern moment has passed, given the deepening and widening of the apparatuses of governmentality in India. No longer is there rebelliousness of the kind that has emerged against the colonial authorities.
24. Recently there has been a revival of Akiwowo's arguments. A series of articles published in 2021 in the *Journal of Contemporary Studies* (Vol. 39, No. 3) debate the legacy of Akiwowo.
25. See, in this context, the experience of Nigeria as illustrated by Onwuzuruigbo (2018) and, for South Asia, see Chatterjee (2002).
26. One early intervention of using Eurocentrism as a critique and a method to constitute new knowledge is Martin Bernal's *Black Athena* (1987).
27. See Bortoluci and Jansen (2013: 217) on how the biracial model cannot be generalized to Latin America.
28. Exceptionalism was a nationalist ideology. It claimed that because the American nation did not carry its antecedents in feudalism, nor had a class of aristocracy or left-wing socialist and communist intellectual traditions like Europe, it was an original nation. It came to be the bearer of values such as freedom and liberty, individual responsibility, republicanism, representative democracy, laissez-faire economics where all its citizens were equal before the law. In this ideology, political conflicts remained within the tight boundaries of a liberal consensus, that celebrated private property, individual rights, representative government and a religiosity based on Puritanism (Shafer, 1999).
29. On the investment by the US military and the State Department in South Asian studies programmes, see Dirks (2013).
30. The first Chair in Arabic at Cambridge was established in 1643. By the mid-19th century, Oriental studies was a well-established academic discipline in most European countries.
31. Though Homi Bhabha and Gayatri Chakravorty Spivak with Edward Said are considered the trinity of postcolonialism, Bhabha's and Spivak's positions are different from that of Said. For the latter, Orientalism is a closed and coherent system of domination and is a discourse which is not real and that reproduces itself across the world. For Bhabha, on the other hand, the discursive is enmeshed in colonial material practices and, for Spivak, it is about the discourse's reproduction in texts defining various fields such as history and literature.
32. Dipesh Chakrabarty (2000: 15) has argued that 'subaltern historiography necessarily entails (a) relative separation of the history of power from any universalist histories of capital, (b) a critique of the nation form, and (c) and interrogation of the relationship between power and knowledge (hence of the archive itself and of history as a form of knowledge)'. When it adopted the postcolonial perspective, the subalternist project shifted to the second and third aspects of its project. This led historians associated with Marxist persuasions to walk out of the group.

[32] This concentration of power has also increased the migration of students and scholars to the core regions of the world, allowing possibly for the increase of academic tourism, as suggested by Paulin Hountondji.

References

Akiwowo, A.A. (1986) Contributions to the sociology of knowledge from an African oral poetry, *International Sociology*, 1: 343–58.

Akiwowo, A.A. (1999) Indigenous sociologies: Extending the scope of the argument, *International Sociology*, 14: 115–38.

Alatas, S.H. (1972) The captive mind in development studies, *International Social Science Journal*, 24(1): 9–25.

Amin, S. (1989) *Eurocentrism*, translated by R. Moore, Monthly Review Press.

Archer, M., Decoteau, C., Gorski, P., Little, D., Porpora, D., Rutzou, T., et al (2016) What is critical realism? *Perspectives: A Newsletter from ASA Theory Section*, 39(2): 4–9. https://www.asanet.org/wp-content/uploads/2023/11/Perspectives-2016-vol38-issue2.pdf

Asad, T. (1992) Conscripts of western civilization, in C.W. Gailey (ed) *Dialectical Anthropology: Essays in Honour of Stanley Diamond*, University of Florida Press, pp 334–51.

Asher, K. and Ramamurthy, P. (2020) Rethinking decolonial and postcolonial knowledges beyond regions to imagine transnational solidarity, *Hypatia*, 35: 542–7. doi.org/10.1017/hyp.2020.16

Atal, Y. (1981) The call for indenisation, *International Social Science Journal*, 33(1): 189–97.

Barlow, T. (2012) Debates over colonial modernity in East Asia and another alternative, *Cultural Studies*, 26(5): 617–44. doi.org:10.1080/09502386.2012.711006

Benzi, D. (2021) Coloniality of power, Eurocentrism and Latin America from the perspective of macro-historical sociology, in J.G. Gandrilla, M. García-Bravo and D. Benzi, *Two Decades of Aníbal Quijano's Coloniality of Power, Eurocentrism and Latin America*, Contexto Internacional, 43(1): 212–18.

Bernal, M. (1987) *Black Athena Vol 1: The Fabrication of Ancient Greece 1785–1985*, Rutgers University Press.

Bortoluci, J.H. and Jansen, R.S. (2013) Toward a postcolonial sociology: The view from Latin America, *Political Power and Social Theory*, 24: 199–229.

Bourdieu, P. and Wacquant, L.D. (1992) *An Invitation to Reflexive Sociology*, Chicago University Press.

Chakrabarty, D. (2000) Subaltern studies and postcolonial historiography, *Nepalta. Views from the South*, 1(1): 9–32.

Chakravarty, S. (1987) *Development Planning: The Indian Experience*, Oxford University Press.

Chandra, B. (1979) *Nationalism and Colonialism in Modern India*, Orient Longman.

Chandra, B. (2010) The rise and growth of economic nationalism in India. *Economic Policies of Indian National Leadership, 1880–1905* (Revised Edition), Har-Anand.

Chatterjee, P. (1986) *Nationalist Thought and the Colonial World: A Derivative Discourse?*, Oxford University Press.

Chatterjee, P. (2002) Institutional context of social science research in South Asia, *Economic and Political Weekly*, 37(35): 3603–12.

Chatterjee, P. (2012) After subaltern studies, *Economic and Political Weekly*, 47(35): 44–9.

Chen, K.H. (2010) *Asia as Method: Towards Deimperialisation*, Duke University Press.

Connell, R. (2007) *Southern Theory: The Global Dynamics of Knowledge in Social Science*, Polity.

Coronil, F. (1996) Beyond Occidentalism: Toward nonimperial geohistorical categories, *Cultural Anthropology*, 11(1): 51–87. http:// doi.org/10.1525/can.1996.11.1.02a00030

Couch, E. (2023) Is the Ukraine war an anti-colonial struggle? *Foreign Policy*. https://foreignpolicy.com/2023/03/07/russia-colonialism-imperialism-solidarity-ukraine/

Cusicanqui, S.R. (2012) Ch'ixinakax utxiwa: A reflection on the practices and discourses of decolonization, *The South Atlantic Quarterly*, 111(1). DOI 10.1215/00382876-1472612

Dalmia, V. (1996) Sanskrit scholars and pandits of the old school: The Benares Sanskrit college and the constitution of authority in the late nineteenth century, *Journal of Indian Philosophy*, 24(4): 321–37.

Dei, G.J.S. and Asgharzadeh, A. (2001) The power of social theory: The anti-colonial discursive framework, *The Journal of Educational Thought/Revue de la Pensée Éducative*, 35(3): 297–323. https://doi.org/10.11575/jet.v35i3.52749

Dayé, C. (2018) A systematic view on the use of history for current debates in sociology, and on the potential and problems of a historical epistemology of sociology, *The American Sociologist*, 49(4): 520–47. https://doi.org/10.1007/s12108-018-9385-1

De Souza Santos, B. (2014) *Epistemologies of the South: Justice Against Epistemicide*, Paradigm Publishers.

Dirks, N. (2013) *South Asian Studies: Pasts and Futures*, South Asia Institute, Harvard University (video). https://mittalsouthasiainstitute.harvard.edu/event/south-asian-studies-pasts-and-futures/

Dirlik, A. (1994) The postcolonial aura: Third world criticism in the age of global capitalism, *Critical Inquiry*, 20(2): 328–35. doi.org/10.1086/448714

Dirlik, A. (2007) The global south: Predicament and promise, *The Global South*, 1(1&2): 12–23. https://doi.org/10.2979/gso.2007.1.1.12

Domingues, J.M. (2019) *Critical Theory and Political Modernity*, Palgrave Macmillan.

Fiddian-Qasmiyeh, E. and Daley, P. (2018) *The Routledge Handbook of South-South Relations*, Routledge.

Gandhi, L. (1998) *Postcolonial Theory: A Critical Introduction*, Allen & Unwin.

Gatechew, A. and Mantena, K. (2021) Anticolonialism and the decolonization of political theory, *Critical Times: Interventions in Global Critical Theory*, 4(3): 359–88. https://doi.org/10.1215/26410478-9355193

Go, J. (2023a) Thinking against empire: Anticolonial thought as social theory, *British Journal of Sociology*, 74(3): 279–93. http://doi.org/10.1111/1468-4446.12993

Go, J. (2023b) Anticolonial thought, the sociological imagination, and social science: A reply to critics, *British Journal of Sociology*, 74(3): 349–59. http://doi.org/10.1111/1468-4446.13025

Guha, R. (1982) On some aspects of historiography of colonial India, in R. Guha (ed) *Subaltern Studies, Vol. 1*, Oxford University Press, pp 1–9.

Guha, R. (1997) Introduction, in R. Guha (ed) *A Subaltern Studies Reader: 1986–1995*, Oxford University Press, pp 1–8.

Halliday, F. (1993) 'Orientalism' and its critics, *British Journal of Middle Eastern Studies*, 20(2): 145–63.

Haraway, D. (1988) Situated knowledges: The science question in feminism and the privilege of partial perspective, *Feminist Studies*, 14(3): 575–99.

Hopkins, T. (1982) The study of the capitalist world economy: Some introductory considerations, in T. Hopkins and I. Wallerstein, *World Systems Analysis: Theory and Methodology*, SAGE, pp 9–38.

Hopkins, T. and Wallerstein, I. (1982) *World Systems Analysis: Theory and Methodology*, SAGE.

Hountondji, P. (1995) Producing knowledge in Africa today: The second Bashorun M. K. O. Abiola distinguished lecture, *African Studies Review*, 38(3): 1–10.

Hountondji, P. (ed) (1997) Introduction, in *Endogenous Knowledge: Research Trails*, CODESRIA, pp 1–42.

Hountondji, P. (2009) Knowledge on Africa. Knowledge by Africans. Two perspectives on African studies, *RCCS Annual Review*, 1: 121–31.

Joas, H. and Knobl, W. (2009) *Social Theory. Twenty Introductory Lectures*, Cambridge University Press.

Kaviraj, S. (2005) An outline of a revisionist theory of modernity, *European Journal of Sociology*, 46(3): 497–526, DOI: 10.1017/S0003975605000196

Knöchelmann, M. (2021) The democratisation myth: Open access and the solidification of epistemic injustices, *Science & Technology Studies*, 34(2). DOI: https://doi.org/10.23987/sts.94964

Lee, H. and Cho, Y. (2012) Introduction: Colonial modernity and beyond in East Asian contexts, *Cultural Studies*, 26(5): 601–16.

Lindner, K. (2022) *Marx, Marxism and the Question of Eurocentrism*, Palgrave Macmillan.

Ludden, D. (ed) (2002) *Reading Subaltern Studies: Critical History, Contested Meaning and the Globalization of South Asia*, Anthem.

Mackie, V. (2018) Whispering, writing and working across borders: Practising transnational history in East Asia, in K. Okano and Y. Sugimoto (eds) *Rethinking Japanese Studies: Eurocentrism and the Asia-Pacific Region*, Routledge.

Madan, T.N. (2007) Search for synthesis: The sociology of D.P. Mukerji, in P. Uberoi, N. Sundar and S. Deshpande (eds) *Anthropology in the East: Founders of Indian Sociology and Anthropology*, Permanent Black, pp 256–89.

Makinde, M. (1988) *African Philosophy, Culture, and Traditional Medicine*, Ohio University Center for International Studies.

Mamdani, M. (1996) *Citizen and Subject: Contemporary Africa and the Legacy of Late Colonialism*, Princeton University Press.

Mamdani, M. (2021) *Neither Settler nor Native: The Making and Unmaking of Permanent Minorities*, Harvard University Press.

Mbebe, A. (2008) What is postcolonial thinking? An interview with Achille Mbebe, *Eurozine*. https://www.eurozine.com/what-is-postcolonial-thinking/

Mignolo, W.D. (2005) On subalterns and other agencies, *Postcolonial Studies*, 8(4): 381–407.

Mignolo, W.D. (2007) Delinking: The rhetoric of modernity, the logic of coloniality and the grammar of de-coloniality, *Cultural Studies*, 21(2–3): 449–514. doi.org/10.1080/09502380601162647

Mignolo, W.D. (2011) *The Darker Side of Western Modernity: Global Futures, Decolonial Options*, Duke University Press.

Mignolo, W.D. (2014) Spirit out of bounds returns to the East: The closing of the social sciences and the opening of independent thoughts, *Current Sociology*, 62(4): 584–602. https://doi.org/10.1177/0011392114524513

Mignolo, W.D. (2017) Interview, Walter D Mignolo/Part 2 key concepts, *E-International Relations*, 21 January. https://www.e-ir.info/2017/01/21/interview-walter-mignolopart-2-key-concepts/

Morris, A. (2017) *The Scholar Denied: W. E. B. Du Bois and the Birth of Modern Sociology*, University of California Press.

Naicker, V. (2023) The problem of epistemological critique in contemporary decolonial theory, *Social Dynamics: Journal of African Studies*. doi.org/10.1080/02533952.2023.2226497

Nandy, A. (2009) *The Intimate Enemy*, 2nd edition, Oxford University Press.

Nash, A. (2003) Third worldism, *African Sociological Review / Revue Africaine de Sociologie*, 7(1): 94–116.

Onwuzuruigbo, I. (2018) Indigenising Eurocentric sociology: The 'captive mind' and five decades of sociology in Nigeria, *Current Sociology Review*, 66(6): 831–48.

Patel, S. (ed) (2010) *The ISA Handbook of Diverse Sociological Traditions*, SAGE.

Patel, S. (2015) The Problematique of Indigenous and Indigeneity: South Asian and African experiences, in H. Sabea and F. Biegal (eds) *Academic Dependency: the Challenge of Building Autonomous Social Sciences in the South*, EDIUNC-SEPHIS, pp 55–64.

Patel, S. (2017) Colonial modernity and methodological nationalism: The structuring of sociological traditions of India, *Sociological Bulletin*, 66(2): 125–44. http://doi.org/10.1177/0038022917708383

Patel, S. (2021a) Sociology's encounter with the decolonial: The problematique of indigenous vs that of coloniality, extraversion and colonial modernity, *Current Sociology*, 69(3): 372–88. doi.org/10.1177/0011392120931143

Patel, S. (2021b) Colonialism and its knowledges, in D. McCallum (ed) *The Palgrave Handbook of the History of Human Sciences*, Palgrave Macmillan. https://link.springer.com/referenceworkentry/10.1007/978-981-154 106-3_68-2

Patel, S. (2023a) Anti-colonial thought and global social theory, *Frontiers in Sociology*, 8. https://doi.org/10.3389/fsoc.2023.1143776

Patel, S. (2023b) Open, access, predatory journals or subscription-based journals, *Global Dialogue*, 13(2): 34–5.

Patel, S. (2024) What is anti-colonial theory?, *Sociological Compass*, 18(8). https://doi.org/10.1111/soc4.13259

Parry, B. (1987) Problems in current theories of colonial discourse, *Oxford Literary Review*, 9(1–2): 7–58.

Prakash, G. (1994) AHR forum: Subaltern studies as postcolonial criticism, *The American Historical Review*, 99(5): 1475–90.

Quijano, A. (1989) Paradoxes of modernity in Latin America, *International Journal of Politics, Culture and Society*, 3(2): 147–77.

Quijano, A. (1993) Modernity, identity, and utopia in Latin America, *boundary 2*, 20(3): 140–55.

Quijano, A. (2000) Coloniality of power, Eurocentrism, and Latin America, *Nepalta. Views from South*, 1(3): 533–80.

Quijano, A. (2007) Coloniality and modernity/rationality, *Cultural Studies*, 21(2–3): 168–78. http://dx.doi.org/10.1080/09502380601164353

Rutzou, T. (2018) Crisis!? What crisis!? On social theory and reflexivity, *Political Power and Social Theory*, 34: 1–22.

Said, E. (1975) *Beginnings: Intention and Method*, Columbia University Press.

Said, E. (1978) *Orientalism*, Pantheon Books.

Salvatore, R.D. (2010) The postcolonial in Latin America and the concept of coloniality: A historian's point of view, *A Contracorrinte*, 8(1): 332–48.

Sarkar, S. (1997) The decline of the subaltern in *subaltern studies*, in S. Sarkar, *Writing Social History*, Oxford University Press, pp 82–108.

Schwarz, H. (2005) Mission impossible: Introducing postcolonial studies in the US academy, in H. Schwarz and S. Ray (eds) *A Companion to Postcolonial Studies*, Blackwell, pp 1–20.

Shafer, B.E. (1999) American exceptionalism, *Annual Review, Political Science*, 2: 445–63. https://doi.org/10.1146/annurev.polisci.2.1.445

Sharpe, J. (2000) Postcolonial studies in the house of US multiculturalism, in H. Schwarz and S. Ray (eds) *A Companion to Postcolonial Studies*, Blackwell, pp 112–25.

Spivak, G.C. (1985) The Rani of Sirmur: An essay in reading the archives, *History and Theory*, 24(3): 247–72.

Streckeisen, P. (2018) Neolibrealism in European higher education policy. Economic Nexus and changing patterns of power and inequality, in C. Sin et al, *European Higher Education and the Internal Market, Tensions between European Policy and National Sovreignty*, Springer Nature.

Táíwò, O. (2021) Doing sociology in Africa: Notes towards advancing the Akìwọwọ project, *Journal of Contemporary African Studies*, 39(3): 364–83. DOI: 10.1080/02589001.2020.1858227

Tlostanova, M. (2012) Postsocialist ≠ postcolonial? On post-Soviet imaginary and global coloniality, *Journal of Postcolonial Writing*, 48(2): 130–42. https://doi.org/10.1080/17449855.2012.658244

Turner, B.S. (1989) From Orientalism to global sociology, *Sociology*, 23(4): 629–38.

UNESCO (2010) *World Social Science Report: Knowledge Divides*, UNESCO and ISSC.

Veracini, L. (2011) Introducing settler colonial studies, *Settler Colonial Studies*, 1(1): 1–12.

Wallerstein, I., Juma, C., Keller, E.E., Kocka, J., Lecourt, D. and Mudkimbe, V.Y., et al (1996) Open the Social Sciences. Report of the Gulbenkian Commission on the Restructuring of the Social Sciences, Standford University Press.

Wolfe, P. (2006) Settler colonialism and the elimination of the native, *Journal of Genocide Research*, 8(4): 387–409.

World Inequality Report (2022) *Executive Summary*. https://wir2022.wid.world/insights/

Young, R.C. (2016) *Postcolonialism: An Historical Introduction*, Wiley Blackwell.

3

The Meanings of Anti-Colonial Social Thought and Theory

Syed Farid Alatas

Introduction

What has come to be known as postcolonialism, decolonial thought and other varieties of anti-Eurocentric and anti-Orientalist thought, constitute, among other things, anti-colonial thought.[1] Anti-colonial thought, however, refers to a vast and diverse body of writings across a variety of disciplines and genres. It means many things that ought not to be conflated with each other. Indeed, it is useful to differentiate the meanings of anti-colonial thought, its histories and current status. This chapter analytically distinguishes among the varieties of anti-colonial thought that correspond to five types of colonialism, as well as different dimensions of anti-colonial thought. These dimensions may exist within each type of colonialism. To illustrate these varieties and dimensions, I draw on examples from 16th-century Spanish America, 17th-century India, 19th-century Indonesia and the Philippines, and contemporary Malaysia and Singapore, from among both the colonized and the colonizers.

Anti-colonial discourse against European colonialism began in the 16th century.[2] Various types and dimensions of this discourse had emerged. As the social sciences in Europe took shape, they were often appropriated by the colonized and turned into anti-colonial thought, expressing themselves through sociology, anthropology, literature and other disciplines. Despite this rich history of anti-colonial thought, it is only recently that we are beginning to chart its development and take stock of its varieties and dimensions.

From the 1950s, scholars from the postcolonial world called for indigenous social science, endogenous intellectual creativity, autonomous knowledge, postcolonial theory, decolonial thought, globalization of knowledge, deimperialization of knowledge and the decolonization of knowledge. While the labels are different, in practice these calls often overlap in terms of objectives, theoretical approaches and methods, despite their distinct features and premises.

Three interesting points can be noted about this literature. One is that the category 'anti-colonial' did not emerge in this literature. 'Anti-colonial' can, nevertheless, be viewed as an umbrella term that encompasses the variety of perspectives that critique Eurocentrism and Orientalism (Patel, 2023a: 4). Second, it was generally assumed that such critical discourses only began to emerge in the 19th century and continued into the 20th. Third, and most importantly, there was little metatheoretical reflection on the types of anti-colonial thought that had emerged thus far.[3]

Much of the existing literature is informed by these three limitations. This chapter is an attempt to overcome these limitations by taking a longer-term historical perspective, tracing anti-colonial thought to the 16th century (Patel, 2023a: 2), and offering a typology of anti-colonial that had developed during the last 400 years.

The chapter begins with a definition of anti-colonial thought. This should be seen within the context of the decolonization of knowledge, which can be understood to consist of the following three moves, that is, the critique of colonialism/coloniality, the discursive reconstruction of history, society and ideas in a non-colonial mode, and the original construction of ideas and applications from hitherto unknown, lesser known and under-utilized non-Western intellectual traditions and experiences. The critique of colonialism/coloniality make up the anti-colonial move in the decolonization of knowledge. I then turn to a discussion of the different types and dimensions of anti-colonial thought. These are discussed in terms of the following categories.

With regards to the types of anti-colonial thought, they can be grouped according to the types of colonialism they are directed against. Here I refer to the five principal types of colonialism, that is, exploitation, trade, settler, semi-, and internal colonialism. The typology of anti-colonial thought can be further complicated by bringing in the different dimensions of anti-colonial thought. Whatever the types of anti-colonial thought, they can be seen to exist along several dimensions, some being mutually exclusive and some not. These dimensions are as follows: anti-colonial thought that ranges from being normative to positive, anti-colonial thought emerging from the colonizer during the colonial period; anti-colonial thought emerging from the colonized contemporaneous with the colonial period; anti-colonial thought that developed during the postcolonial period, that is, after political independence; anti-colonial thought directed against colonial ideologies, that is, the subjective dimension; anti-colonial thought that is critical of objective dimensions of colonial society, that is, political economic and legal structures, for example; anti-colonial thought directed against existing colonialism today in a largely postcolonial world; and anti-coloniality thought in both its subjective and objective dimensions.

This chapter will proceed as follows. The first section attempts a definition of anti-colonial thought. The section following after this discusses the varieties of anti-colonial thought that correspond to the five types of colonialism mentioned earlier. The third section discusses the dimensions of anti-colonial thought and is followed by a conclusion.

A definition of anti-colonial social thought

As suggested earlier, the decolonization of knowledge can be understood to consist of the following three moves, that is, the critique of colonialism and colonial knowledge of the social, the discursive reconstruction of colonial history, society and ideas in a non-colonial mode, and the original construction of ideas from hitherto unknown, lesser known and under-utilized non-Western intellectual traditions and historical experiences. The critique of colonialism, reconstruction and original construction together constitute the decolonization of knowledge. Anti-colonial social thought comes under the first move, critique, while reconstruction and original construction represent the constructive rather than deconstructive dimension of the decolonization of knowledge. To give an example, Syed Hussein Alatas (1977) provides a critique of colonial capitalism as well as of colonial ideology by showing that the discourse of laziness was erroneous or carried out without considering the proper context. This work also provides a reconstruction of colonial history by providing an alternative account of the role of colonial ideology on laziness in promoting colonial capitalists' interests (Alatas, 1977). Alatas also makes an argument against colonial capitalism by an original sociological construction, partly influenced by Rizal's essay, 'The indolence of the Filipino' (Rizal, 1963).

Here, it is necessary to make a distinction between social thought and social theory. As noted by Parker, social thought encompasses a much broader category of thinking than sociological theory, and is found in the history of non-Western traditions (Parker, 1997: 137). In the effort to broaden the canon to include thinkers from outside of the Western tradition, it is important to make that distinction. Social thought differs from social theory in terms of its lesser formality. It is also expressed in less systematic terms and contains more reflection on experiences, opinions, assessments and valuations, in comparison with sociological theory. Social thought is often not couched in terms of formal definitions, concepts and theories. Patel correctly notes that anti-colonial thought is interdisciplinary (Patel, 2023a: 9). I would add that anti-colonial social thought, as opposed to sociological theory, is also characterized by a plurality of methods of argumentation. Sociological theory generally resorts to the scientific method of argumentation and employs deductive and inductive reasoning. But, the Ancient Greek, medieval Christian and Islamic traditions recognized that demonstration was not the only method of reasoning that led to valid truth claims. Other forms of argumentation include dialectics, rhetoric and poetics (Ibn Khaldun, 1967: 140–1, 2005: 93–4).

As an example, Rizal's works constitute a critique of various aspects of colonial life as experienced by the colonized. He principally engaged in this critique via a poetic mode of argumentation, specifically through his novels, *Noli Me Tangere (Touch Me Not)* and *El Filibusterismo (The Revolution)* (Rizal, 1990 [1887], 1992 [1891]). These novels diagnosed the problems of Filipino society and were socially descriptive texts in which the various characters represent the social malaise and wrongs of his time (Majul, 1999: 3). Rizal's essays and journalistic writings, however, were based more on demonstration. In the case of Ibn Khaldun, all four methods of argumentation, that is, demonstration, dialectics, poetics and rhetoric, were employed (Alatas, 2013: 71–5).

Apart from Rizal, mention must be made of the novel of the Malayan writer, Harun Aminurrashid (1907–1986), *Panglima Awang*, which attempts to give an identity and role to Enrique of Malacca, the probably Malay slave that Magellan bought in Malacca and who aided Magellan in his attempt to circumnavigate the globe in 1519 (Harun, 1957). More importantly, we must not forget the renowned Indonesian novelist, Pramoedya Ananta Toer (1925–2006), who wrote critical, anti-colonial works and is the best known novelist to have come out of the Malay world after José Rizal. Among his novels, the *Buru Quartet* (Indo. *Tetralogi Buru*), consisting of *This Earth of Mankind*, *Child of All Nations*, *Footsteps* and *House of Glass*,[4] were written while Pramoedya was under detention on Buru Island in Maluku.

All these differences by no means render social thought less important than the more formal sociological theory and may in fact be the basis of the systematic constructions of what we call sociological theory (Alatas and Sinha, 2017: 13). But, the distinction is important in the consideration of candidates for the expanded canon. Thinkers like Ibn Khaldun, Karl Marx, Max Weber, Ziya Gökalp, Benoy Kumar Sarkar and Fei Hsiao-tung were clearly theorists. The same may not be said for Pandita Ramabai Saraswati, Florence Nightingale, Rizal and Pramoedya Ananta Toer. While they did write about broad-ranging social issues, they were far less systematic in their approach than the theorists, and tended not to engage in formal concept formation and theory building. Furthermore, they usually employed non-demonstrative methods in their works. Nevertheless, they are indispensable for the task of our understanding modern society, having provided original contributions in this respect.

It is also relevant to point out that anti-colonial social thought and theory are both metatheoretical (Patel, 2023a: 9), to the extent that they reflect on the state of the social sciences in the context of colonialism and coloniality, as well as theoretical to the extent that they theorize about colonial society itself.

Much of anti-colonial thought is cosmopolitan. However, as Go suggests, projects to overcome Eurocentrism by offering alternatives theories (Alatas, 2006; Connell, 2007; Mignolo, 2011; Bhambra, 2014a; de Sousa Santos, 2014) can be misappropriated and domesticated by what he calls geoepistemic essentialism, that is, the assumption that 'the world can be divided into distinct essentialized geographical spaces – such as North and South or "West" and "non-West" – and that those spaces map directly onto cultures and knowledge formations' (Go, 2023a: 290). According to Go, geoepistemic essentialism is founded on the assumption that (i) if a thinker is from the non-West, then their knowledge is necessarily in opposition to Western knowledge, and (ii) that any thinker from the West is to be rejected (Go, 2023a: 290). Go does not claim that the approaches of Bhambra, Connell, Mignolo, de Sousa Santos and myself are essentialist, but he does state that our approaches can be easily deployed in an essentialist manner as they are not clear regarding their positionality with regard to the proposed alternative theories (Go, 2023a: 290). But Bhambra, Connell, Mignolo, de Sousa Santos and myself have all distanced ourselves from what he calls geoepistemic essentialism, a problem that has been written about for decades under the heading of nativism. I myself, in proposing alternative discourses, had written 30 years ago about the need to avoid nativism, including calls for the rejection of Western knowledge on the grounds of its geographical origins. I had critiqued nativist social science for celebrating the absolute opposition between Western and Eastern culture, which often resulted in a wholesale rejection of Western thought (Alatas, 1993: 312). Mignolo, in a thoughtful piece written about ten years ago, is also clearly against nativism when he lauds border thinkers for being able, for example, to think with both Ibn Khaldun and Max Weber, as opposed to captive minds who can only think *with* Weber and *about* Ibn Khaldun (Mignolo, 2014: 593).

Patel has consistently warned against adopting essentialist positions in her writings against binaries. She notes that the call for a sociology of and for the South draws attention to binaries, such as that of the South against the North. Furthermore, as postcolonialism tells us, this binary is

> part of a matrix of other binaries, such as the other against the I, the East against the West, the Orient vs the Occident, the colonized against the imperialist, the traditional against the modern, the particular against the universal, and are part of an episteme that represents the project of modernity. (Patel, 2006: 382)

Elsewhere, Patel notes that binaries have plagued Eurocentric knowledge to the extent that it is informed by multiple divisions or oppositions. These divisions are by no means harmless. Binaries like reason and body, subject and object, culture and nature, and masculine and feminine are also hierarchies that 'scale, from superior to inferior, the different peoples of the world in terms of principles of race and gender' (Patel, 2020: 9).

Patel discusses the Beninese philosopher, Paulin Houtondji's (1942–2024) critique of the indigenous–endogenous distinction in knowledge creation. While Houtondji accepts endogenous knowledge creation as a valid, scientific activity, he regards indigenization as ideological. This is so because the idea of the indigenous arises from the West–East binary and is therefore a part of colonial knowledge (Patel, 2021).

Anti-colonial social thought is the deconstructive move of the decolonization of knowledge, the others being reconstruction and original construction. For the most part, anti-colonial thinkers reject nativism. Anti-colonial thought has a number of varieties that correspond somewhat to the types of colonialism, to which we now turn.

The varieties of anti-colonial social thought

Colonialism in general refers to the practice of one polity taking political control of another with the aim of benefiting from the exploitation of its land and resources. It is the subjugation of one people by another (Kohn and Reddy, 2023). There are several types of colonialism. The types of anti-colonial thought can be grouped according to the types of colonialism they are directed against. The five principal types of colonialism are trade, exploitation, settler, semi- and internal colonialism. What is discussed in the following are ideal types. Each type is distinguished from another in terms of the mode of the appropriation of the economic surplus, the organization of labour, as well as the nature of colonial state. For example, trade colonialism often did not require extensive rule of a European power over the colonized territory and did not involve much control of labour. On the other hand, exploitation colonialism required intervention to the extent that made it possible to control both labour and capital. This required the setting up of a more elaborate colonial state structure. In reality two or more types of colonialism may co-exist. For example, in the case of settler-colonialism, other forms of colonialism such as exploitation colonialism can be found.

Trade colonialism

Trade colonialism refers to the control of territory by a foreign power for the purpose of supporting trade opportunities for merchants. This was an early form of colonialism that began in the 16th century but remained prominent through to the 19th century. Trade colonialism should be understood in the context of the need of mercantile capitalism to have control over trade relationships. The function of trade colonialism was to feed the metropole with raw materials which would be turned into finished products such as textiles, weapons and other goods which would be sold to the colonies. The need for control over the colonies arose from the necessity of imposing tariffs and policing smuggling such that capital accumulation in the metropole was ensured (Shoemaker, 2015).

A prominent critic of trade colonialism was the Indian political leader, scholar and merchant, Dadabhai Naoroji (1825–1917). He was a strong proponent of the drain theory of wealth, according to which there was the continuous transfer of wealth from India to Britain during the colonial period without sufficient economic benefits accruing to India. The channelling of wealth to Britain from India, instead of its use to improve the well-being of Indians, was made possible because of the tools of coercion available to the British under colonial rule. India's poverty was attributed to the drain of its wealth to Britain (Naoroji, 1901; see also Naik, 2001).

Exploitation colonialism

The use of the term exploitation here should not be taken to mean that other types of colonialism are not exploitative. Exploitation as used in exploitation colonialism refers to a narrower meaning of term. Exploitation colonialism is a colonial system in which the objective is the exploitation of natural and human resources of the colony, whether through extraction of minerals and fossil fuels or through the establishment of plantation economies. In plantation colonialism, the colonizers establish bases in the colony to plant cash crops destined for export globally. Exploitation and plantation colonialism often existed together. For example, both forms were to be found in British Malaya and the Netherlands East Indies.

An example of the critique of exploitation colonialism is Stephen Bunker's work on modes of extraction. Bunker examines the demographic, ecological and infrastructural effects of extraction on underdevelopment, with a focus on extractive export economies in the Amazon Basin from the early days of the colonial period up to 1980 (Bunker, 1984). This work is in the area of the sociology of development, but other examples of anti-colonial sociology that fall within the area of social thought can be cited. Rizal's work is an important and obvious candidate for an alternative sociology of colonial society. He wrote on topics and theorized problems that should be of interest to those studying the broad-ranging macro processes that have become the hallmark of classical sociological thought and theory. Rizal theorized about the nature of society in ways not done by Western sociologists. He provides us with a different perspective on the colonial dimension of the emerging modernity of the 19th century (Alatas, 2009).

An example of anti-colonial writing against plantation colonialism is that of Selvaratnam (2021). This work discusses the impact of imperialism, colonial capitalism and racism on the South Indian coolies whom the British recruited through a 'new system of slavery' to work for the development of the British Malayan colonial economy.

Another example is Jan Breman's *Coolies, Planters and Colonial Politics* (1992). This work is a critical study of large Western agricultural enterprises on Sumatra's east coast at the end of the 19th century that were characterized by the large-scale deployment of Chinese and Javanese contract coolies, but who were in fact attached to their plantations as forced labourers.

Settler-colonialism

The obvious example where settler-colonialism is violently contested is Palestine/Israel. This was also the case in South Africa. However, settler-colonialism is also on the agenda of critical thought regarding the histories of the United States, Canada, Australia and New Zealand. In settler-colonialism, there is *en masse* migration from the colonizing country or countries to the colonized territory. The objective of colonization is to establish a new life in the colonies. This requires either the extermination of the indigenous peoples of the colony, forced expulsion or their subjugation.

An early example of anti-settler-colonial thought in the form of the conceptualization of settler-colonialism is from Arab thinkers in the 1960s and 1970s, beginning with the work of the Palestinian Fayez Sayegh, followed by several other Arabs (Sayegh, 1965; Rodinson, 1973; Said, 1980; Said, 1999; Sabbagh-Khoury, 2021).

Anti-settler-colonial thought in the context of Palestine/Israel is indeed contentious. Those who believe that the concept of settler-colonialism applies to the Palestine/Israel situation face criticism from Zionist ideologues, who contend that certain features of European Jewish migration to Palestine render the concept inapplicable. It is said that there was no mother country unlike the other cases of settler-colonialism. Europeans had migrated to Palestine from various countries in Europe. Rodinson, however, supported the applicability of 'settler-colonialism' to the case of Israel, stating that the creation of Israel in 1948 on Palestinian soil perfectly fits into the European-American expansion in the 19th and 20th centuries 'whose aim was to settle new inhabitants among other peoples or to dominate them economically or politically' (Rodinson, 1973: 91). Granted, there was no mother country from which the settlers hailed. Rather, the mother country, Great Britain, facilitated the creation of a new state via a series of backdoor deals, subterfuge and deception, making it possible for Jews from Europe to emigrate to Palestine over a period of decades, a process that culminated in the establishment of Israel in 1948.

Semi-colonialism

Semi-colonialism refers to a form of colonialism that took shape in geographies that were not formally colonized but nonetheless experienced the ravages of imperialism in other ways. The concept originated in the writings of Lenin and Mao Tse-tung. A semi-colony is a country that is formally a sovereign and independent one, but is nevertheless dominated by an imperial power in economic, ideological, military or political terms. Such states maintain their juridicial independence but suffer from the penetration of foreign, imperial capital and unwanted political influence. This has been vividly described by Mao, who had noted how Western imperialism had used its military, political, economic and cultural power such that China gradually became a semi-colony.

While China maintained its juridical independence, it was dominated in various ways by imperialist powers. These include the following:

- wars of aggression against China, for example, the Opium War launched by Britain in 1840, the war launched by the Anglo-French allied forces in 1857, the Sino-French War of 1884, the Sino-Japanese War of 1894, and the war launched by the allied forces in 1900. After these wars, the powers had seized or 'leased' parts of China's territory;
- the imperialist powers forced China to sign many unequal treaties which gave them rights to station land and sea forces and exercise consular jurisdiction in China, control of the vital trading ports of China, and control of China's customs, foreign trade and air, sea and land communications. The result was that they had been able to dump their goods in China;
- the imperialist powers monopolized China's banking and finance by establishing banks in China and by extending loans to the Chinese government. Thus, they had not only overwhelmed China's national capitalism in commodity competition, they had also secured a stranglehold on her banking and finance;
- the imperialist powers exerted control via the supply of munitions and military advisors to the government. This facilitated continued fighting among the warlords;
- the cultural dimension of semi-colonialism is the creation of pro-imperialist people among the semi-colonized through the establishing of hospitals and schools, publishing newspapers and encouraging Chinese students to study abroad (Mao, 1939).

Internal colonialism

The theory of internal colonialism was developed by Robert Blauner in the late 1960s in order to account for exploitative relationships between groups that were geographically proximate (Blauner, 1972). Barrera notes that as the civil rights movement in the United States in the 1960s switched to organize along racial lines, it consequently adopted third world national liberation movements as models and, therefore, saw US racial minorities as colonized peoples (Barrera, 1979: 188). The concept of internal colonialism had been developed from that of the more traditional colonialism with the difference that it introduced the idea of the 'domination and exploitation of natives by natives' rather than the 'direct domination of foreigners over natives', as is the case with traditional colonialism (Gonzales-Casanova, 1969).[5] The natives referred to here are not a homogeneous group, however. Crucial is the element of cultural heterogeneity. In internal colonialism, therefore, there is a 'structure of social relations based on domination and exploitation among culturally homogeneous, distinct groups' (Gonzales-Casanova, 1969).[6] Along the same lines is the work of Cotler, who looks at the domination by urban groups of the mestizos, who in turn dominate the indigenous people of Peru. Furthermore, Cotler's contribution had been to develop the social psychological dimension of internal colonialism (Cotler, 1970).[7]

Stavenhagen, on the other hand, looks at regional differences, at how the less developed regions of Latin America have been internal colonies of the more developed urban centres or the more productive agricultural sectors (Stavenhagen, 1965). Also important in this regard is Frank's contribution to the internal colonialism concept. This is seen in the context of the theory of economic dependency in which there are exploitative relationships between the metropolis and satellite in a nation-state or within a region (Frank, 1967).[8]

The concept of internal colonialism was also used to analyse the exploitation of ethnic minorities in the United States and Britain. These were said to be domestic or internal colonies of white American society and Britain (Bailey and Flores, 1973; Hechter, 1975). The internal colonialism concept has also been used to discuss colonial situations in several other states such as Israel, Pakistan, South Africa, Sudan and Thailand (Hind, 1984: 543).

An important critique of internal colonialism, used to develop a theory of racial inequality, can be found in the work of Barrera, cited earlier. Barrera's work is not only important because of the empirical research that documents racial inequality but also for the rich theoretical discussions on internal colonialism and racial inequality (Barrera, 1979: 174–220).

The dimensions of anti-colonial thought

Apart from the varieties of anti-colonial thought which are to be understood in terms of the context of the types of colonialism, we can also distinguish between different dimensions of anti-colonial thought. These dimensions may be found to exist within each of the types of anti-colonial thought discussed previously.

Anti-colonial thought: from the normative to the positive

It should be known that in the earlier days of European colonialism to the 18th century, anti-colonial thought tended to be normative and prescriptive rather than positive and analytical. Many examples of these can be furnished. Some are lesser known than others.

Here I discuss the example of Shaykh Zayn al-Din al-Maqdum (1530–1583) who wrote the *Tuhfat al-Mujahidin fi ba 'd akhbar al-Burtughaliyin* (*Gift to the Holy Warriours Concerning the Deeds of the Portuguese*).[9] The Shaykh, a Muslim scholar of Arab origin and born in Chombal, northern Malabar, dedicated this work to Sultan Alī Adil Shah of Bijapur (r. 1557–1580). The work was intended to not only expose the 'shameful deeds' of the Portuguese in the war that they waged against the Muslim inhabitants of Malabar throughout the 16th century, but also to encourage the Muslims to take up arms and wage jihad against them. Indeed, the *Tuhfat* can be said to be an early example of an anti-colonial tract. The book deals with, among other things, the history of the Portuguese in Malabar, from their arrival in the late 15th century to the period after the loss of the fortress of Chalé in 1571. The main thrust of the book is to encourage Muslims to take up arms against the invading Portuguese.

In this work, al-Maqdum praises the Indian rulers of Malabar, the Zamorin, for the support they lent to the Muslims against the Portuguese. He noted that the war consumed much of the Zamorin's money. In order to get assistance, the Zamorin sent letters to Muslim Sultans. None of them stepped up to assist him (Makhdum, 2006: 52).

> The Zamorin, who paid due regard to the peace, endured their evil doings with patience, because he was apprehensive of their wickedness. Nevertheless, he secretly sent letters to the Muslim Sultans urging them to make preparations for war with the Portuguese, hut it was no avail. It was what Allah willed. (Makhdum, 2006: 60)

The *Tuhfat al-Mujahidin* is one of the earliest examples of anti-colonial writings against European colonialism in the normative mode.[10] It is also said to be the oldest historical work on Kerala. The first section, entitled 'A treatise on the necessity of jihad and instructions thereof', is a plea for Muslims to engage in war against unbelievers who invade Muslim territories, the situation that the Malabari Muslims were facing then. Al-Maqdum praises the Muslim-friendly Zamorin but has harsh words for the Muslim sultans and emirs who did not take any interest in the plight of the Muslims of Malabar and did not take up jihad against the Portuguese as a holy duty (Makhdum, 2006: 15). Al-Maqdum makes a case for the legitimacy of jihad against the Portuguese to its readers on religious grounds.

Anti-colonial thought among the colonizers

Albert Memmi (1920–2020), the French-Tunisian novelist, is well-known for several works, including the more sociological *Portrait du colonisé–Portrait du colonisateur*, translated as *The Coloniser and the Colonised* (1957, 2002). In this work, Memmi makes a distinction between the colonialist and the colonizer. The former is firmly committed to the colonization project while the latter, although from the home country, sometimes becomes sympathetic to the sufferings of the colonized. It is from among the colonizers that we may see the emergence of thought that is critical of colonialism. While, strictly speaking, these cannot be termed as anti-colonial works, because they in principle support the colonial project, yet, at the same time they undertake serious criticisms of colonial policies and practices and become intellectual resources for the more decisively anti-colonial thinkers and activists.

The libertarian tradition in 16th-century Spain produced scholars who became strong critics of colonialism. These include Father Antonio Montesinos (1475–1540), Francisco de Vitoria (1483–1546), Domingo de Soto (1494–1560) and Bartolomé de Las Casas (1484–1566) (Watner, 1987). All were critical of the inhumane treatment by the Spaniards of the natives of Spanish America but never went so far as to proclaim colonialism itself as an illegitimate project. Rather, they agitated for reform to be implemented within colonialism.

Another interesting figure was the Italian novelist, Emilio Salgari (1862–1911), author of *Le Tigri di Mompracem* (*The Tigers of Mompracem*), his first adventure novel in the Sandokan series. Set in the northern part of Borneo, in what is today part of Malaysia, it tells the story of Sandokan, a native nobleman orphaned and dethroned by the murder of his family by the British. He leads a legion of natives against the British imperialists to avenge his family and retake lost territory. In doing so, he gains the support of the weak and oppressed (Alatas, 2009: 31). Among European novelists, Salgari was the first to invent a Malay literary hero, Sandokan, who fought against James Brooke, the British imperialist (Alatas, 2022).[11]

Salgari's *The Tigers of Mompracem* was certainly anti-British but not necessarily anti-colonial. This is suggested by, among other things, Sandokan being a European caricature of a Muslim hero (Alatas, 2009: 39).[12]

Perhaps the most well-known critical colonizer was the Dutch colonial officer and writer, Eduard Douwes Dekker (1820–1887), known by his pen name, Multatuli. He is celebrated for his novel, *Max Havelaar; of, De koffi-veilingen der Nederlandsche Handel-Maatschappy* (*Max Havelaar; or, The Coffee Auctions of the Dutch Trading Company*), an 1860 novel in which the protagonist, Max Havelaar, wages a battle against a corrupt Dutch colonial government on Java in the Netherlands East Indies. The colonial economy from the mid-19th century was based on the *cultuurstelsel* or cultivation system. This system required Indonesian farmers to replace staple foods such as rice with commercial crops such as coffee and sugar. The colonial government also put in place a tax collection system in which the collecting agents were incentivized by commission. The resulting abuse of power, particularly by the native elite through whom the Dutch ruled, created starvation and poverty. Max Havelaar, the fictitious colonial officer, encounters similar problems in the novel as those encountered by Eduard Douwes Dekker, the colonial officer in real life. *Max Havelaar*, therefore, was written by Multatuli as a protest against colonial policies and their abuses, although he also attempted to use the threat to publish the novel as leverage to be reinstated to the job that he had resigned from. Whatever his motivations, *Max Havelaar* succeeded in raising the awareness of the Dutch in the Netherlands of the impact of colonial exploitation and was influential in at least modifying colonial policy.

In the field of Indonesian history, the problem of its Eurocentric nature was first raised by Dutch and not Indonesian scholars. One of the firast among the Dutch in particular, and Europeans in general, to challenge Eurocentrism in the social sciences was Jacob Cornelis van Leur, a scholar who died at a young age in the Battle of the Java Sea against the Japanese (Van Leur, 1940a, 1940b).[13] Van Leur was critical of Eurocentric tendencies in Dutch scholarship on the Netherlands Indies. He is well-known for having written against a perspective arrived at from 'the deck of the ship, the ramparts of the fortress, the high gallery of the trading house' (Van Leur, 1955: 261). For example, he questioned the appropriateness of the 18th century as a category in the history of the Netherlands Indies, as it was a category borrowed from Western history (Van Leur, 1940a). Another important contribution to the discussion on the need for Indocentric history from the Dutch was that of the sociologist and historian, B.J.O. Schrieke.[14]

These Dutch scholars did not take an anti-colonial position in the sense of calling for an end to colonialism. However, their critical views towards aspects of colonialism and on the need for reforms often resulted in their ideas being appropriated by anti-colonial scholars.[15]

Anti-colonial thought among the colonized during the colonial period

The classical examples of anti-colonial thought that emerged from among the colonized during the colonial period are those of Aimé Césaire, Frantz Fanon and Albert Memmi. What is often missed out are the earlier examples of anti-colonial thought. I have in mind those of the Haitian anthropologist, Anténor Firmin, and the Filipino thinker, José Rizal.

Joseph Auguste Anténor Firmin (1850–1911) was a Haitian anthropologist and among the first to systematically critique racists ideas about the hierarchy of human beings that was widely circulating in Europe during his time. In his *De l'égalité des races humaines* (*On the Equality of Human Races*) (1885) he critiqued Arthur de Gobineau's *Essai sur l'inégalité des races* (*Essay on the Inequality of the Races*) which developed the idea of the superiority of the Aryan race and the inferiority of Black people. Firmin, on the other hand, wrote that 'all men are endowed with the same qualities and the same faults, without distinction of color or anatomical form. The races are equal'.

Firmin was able to assert this because he recognized the difference between anthropological data and its theoretical analysis. The anthropologist enters after the ethnographer and ethnologist have done their work.

> Anthropology is comparative, separating Man from the other animals addressing the questions: 'What is the true nature of Man? To what extent and under what conditions does he develop his potential? Are all of the human races capable of rising to the same intellectual and moral level?' Anthropology requires the effort of the best minds – 'It goes without saying that if they are to come up with valid results, anthropologists must do more than establishing some arbitrary ranking of the human races and their respective aptitudes'. (Firmin, 2000: 12–13)[16]

Needless to say, his views were not well-received among the social scientists of his time (Lobban, 2000, 2005, 2018; Bernasconi, 2008). But, Firmin had the foresight to see that racist anthropology had no future.

> Their science will face certain discredit when, in the twentieth century, it is subjected to the critique of Black and White, Yellow and Brown scientists who can write as well and handle as expertly the instruments manufactured by the Mathieu Company [producers of anthropometric instruments], instruments that bring such eloquent results, even in the hands of scientists who doubt their effectiveness. (Firmin, 2000: 102).[17]

Rizal had also dealt with a form of colonial racism. He was the first to theorize the phenomenon of laziness when it was an unfounded accusation made by Spanish colonialists against the Filipinos. He undertook a critique of the discourse on the lazy Filipino native that was perpetuated by the Spaniards. The theme of indolence in colonial scholarship is an important one that formed a vital part of the ideology of colonial capitalism. Rizal was probably the first to deal with it systematically. This concern was later taken up by Syed Hussein Alatas in his *The Myth of the Lazy Native*, which contains a chapter entitled 'The indolence of the Filipinos', in honour of Rizal's essay of the same title (Rizal, 1963).

The basis of Rizal's sociology is his critique of the myth of the indolent Filipino. It is this critique and the rejection of the idea that the backwardness of Filipino society was due to the Filipinos themselves but rather to the nature of colonial rule, that provides the proper background for understanding Rizal's criticisms against the clerical establishment and colonial administration. In Rizal's treatment of the myth of Filipino indolence in his famous essay, 'The indolence of the Filipinos', he defines indolence as 'little love for work, lack of activity' (Rizal, 1963: 111).

Rizal's important sociological contribution is his raising of the problem of indolence to begin with as well as his treatment of the subject matter, particularly his view that indolence was not a cause of the backwardness of Filipino society. Rather it was the backwardness and disorder of Filipino colonial society that caused indolence.

Anti-colonial thought during the postcolonial period

There are many examples of anti-colonial thought that were products of the period after formal independence. I mention one example in the following as it recalls Rizal's and Alatas' concerns discussed earlier.

According to Zawiah Yahya '[r]esistance is necessary because the pen is mightier than the sword for those who can read' (Yahya, 1994: 9). It is possible for a discourse to be alluring if we read it without question, fall for its charm and unconsciously adopt the ideology it conceals. Discourse has the ideological capacity to persuade the reader that claims are true, especially when those claims are supported by institutions or disciplines.

One such discourse is that of colonialism. Yahya analyses literary texts that are representative of British colonialist constructions of Malaya from the 1890s to the 1950s. She shows how much of what is read in these texts are colonialist assertions about colonizer and natives that are uncritically accepted as universal truths but are also implicated in justifying colonial rule.

On the theme of 'native laziness' Yahya, refering to Alatas (1977), discusses how British colonialist literature reproduced the image of 'Malay indolence' and functioned in tandem with colonial ideology to justify the import of labour on the grounds that Malay labour was not productive in the colonial capitalist sense (Yahya, 1990: 120).

Anti-colonial thought is resistance discourse and is necessary. This requires understanding that there are possibilities for 'native' rather than colonialist readings of colonialist literature that provide alternative experiences of colonial rule, therefore relativizing the universal meaning attributed traditionally to such literature by Eurocentric literary criticism (Yahya, 1994: 11).

For Zawiah Yahya, anti-colonial thought comes from the realization that literary discourse is a great seducer. If we are to be thinking readers, we must wilfully resist this seduction and, therefore, engage in real criticism. Not to do so is 'to decide to give up our rights as a reader and to abandon intellectual responsibility' (Yahya, 1994: 9).

Anti-colonial thought against subjective colonial realities

In order to understand the meanings of anti-colonial thought, it is necessary to make a basic distinction between the objective and subjective dimensions of the subject matter under study. The objective refers to material conditions 'out there', while the subjective refers to thought, values and emotions, that is, the subjective internal states. Anti-colonial thought directs its attention to both the objective and subjective.

The subjective may refer to ideology, ideas, emotions, feelings, attitudes and, indeed, all other subjective states. The critical study of colonial ideology is an example of the study of subjective states. In my part of the world, examples of such work are Syed Hussein Alatas' studies on colonial ideology, that is, on the political philosophy of the colonial founder of Singapore, Raffles (Alatas, 1971), and on the critique of the ideological function of the colonial view of native indolence in colonial Southeast Asia (Alatas, 1977).

Anti-colonial thought against the objective dimensions of colonial society

Anti-colonial thought also deals with the objective dimensions of colonial realities. A good example of that is an insightful but under-appreciated work of S.B.D. de Silva on political economy, published decades ago (de Silva, 1982). Central to de Silva's argument is distinction between settler and non-settler colonies. De Silva argues that in the latter type of colony, colonial policies functioned to stunt development by preventing or restricting capital accumulation.

Other examples are works on colonialism and capitalism. Sergio Bagú refers to the system that is based on coerced cash-crop labour as colonial capitalism (Bagú, 1969). The same term is used in Alatas' study on the colonial construction of native indolence (Alatas, 1977). Alavi et al (1982) explore the relationship between colonialism and capitalism as well as how capitalism had changed the communities it has dominated, using numerous Asian countries as material to address the problems. By re-evaluating the issues at hand, identifying pre-colonial modes of production, and closely examining the specifics of the changes brought about by colonial dominance, they contend that capitalism and feudalism do not co-exist in these nations, but rather that colonialism gave rise to unique forms of capitalism that are characterized by their reliance on pre-colonial modes of production. Also important is Banaji's theorization of the colonial economy in terms of 'colonial modes of production' (Banaji, 1972).

Anti-colonial thought directed against contemporary colonialism

An obvious example would be anti-colonial writings on settler-colonialism in Palestine/Israel that I discussed earlier. Another example is the case of Puerto Rico.

Puerto Rico, among the world's oldest colonies, has been under occupation or 'protectorate' status since 1508. The 'discoverer' of America, Christopher Columbus, made a second voyage to the region in November, 1493, during which time he arrived in Puerto Rico. At that time, the island was inhabited by the Taíno people that dominated the island, numbering some 30,000 people (Rouse, 1992).

This is an important dimension of anti-colonial thought because it functions as a reminder that colonialism is still very much a contemporary reality and not just a phenomenon of the past.

Anti-coloniality

The last dimension of anti-colonial thought I refer to is thought against the continuing coloniality of knowledge creation as well as of the world itself, outside of a formally colonial context. The coloniality is not only an attribute of knowledge but also of the material world. It is not only knowledge that is colonial or Eurocentric in nature but the political economic structures and cultures of the world that are in a state of coloniality. Strictly speaking, this may be referred to as anti-neocolonial thought. Both postcolonialism and decolonial thought address themselves against such coloniality.

Postcolonial theory or postcolonialism refers to an intellectual tradition that studies the cultural legacy of colonialism while at the same time opposing the persistent continuity of coloniality in knowledge creation, in both bourgeois as well as leftist discourses (Prakash, 1992). Influenced significantly by the ideas of Edward Said, Homi K. Bhabha and Gayatri C. Spivak, most of the work in postcolonialism is confined to the cultural disciplines such as literature. Geographically, postcolonialism has its origins in the work of diasporic scholars from West and South Asia. In terms of time frame, postcolonialism refers to the 19th and 20th centuries (Bhambra, 2014b: 115).

Decolonial thought, on the other hand, while dealing with much of what postcolonial theory contends with, has a different intellectual and geographical genealogy and some differing concerns. Associated with scholars such as Anibal Quijano, Mario Lugones and Walter Mignolo, decolonial thought is more closely linked to political economy and sociology, in particular to world-systems theory (Bhambra, 2014b: 115). Unlike postcolonialism, decolonial thought emerged from the work of scholars from Latin America. In terms of time frame, decolonial thought roots the problems of coloniality in an earlier history that begins with the 'discovery' of the Americas in the 15th century (Bhambra, 2014b: 115).

Both postcolonial and decolonial thought are critical of the coloniality of not only knowledge production but also of the material world. I have mentioned postcolonialism and decolonial thought here, but this is not to say that these are the only approaches that deal with the persistence of coloniality in an otherwise postcolonial world.

Conclusion

Regardless of the type of colonialism and anti-colonial thought, some points can be made regarding what unites them. Each anti-colonial thinker or theory can be located in a specific way vis-à-vis colonialism in terms of the type of colonialism; the political economic nature of colonialism, such as, for example, colonial mercantilism, economic extraction, or genocide; the dominant ideology of colonialism to be found in a particular colonial society; and the central arguments and objectives that inform the thought of the anti-colonial thinker. The last is the most important as it gives form and content to anti-colonial thought.

Anti-colonial thought can be seen to be informed by a specific structure which can be identified as consisting of subject-matter, problematic, method of argumentation and objective. A body of work or discipline can be assessed in terms of its choice of subject-matter, formulation of research problems, theorizing, the methods of argumentation it deploys, and the objectives it wishes to achieve.

Let us take colonial society as an example of the subject-matter of anti-colonial social thought. With regard to the problematic formulated for this subject-matter, an example is the identification of a central pathology of colonial society. Examples would be Rizal's characterization of the brutalization of Filipinos or W.E.B. Du Bois' theorizing of American society as racially fractured (Go, 2023a: 286). Concerning the methods of argumentation, I have already discussed the idea that social thought has a wider repertoire of such methods, not confining itself to the scientific procedures but availing itself of dialectics, poetics and rhetoric, in addition to demonstration, the staple of the modern social sciences. This makes for a more methodologically pluralist anti-colonial social thought.

Concerning the objective of anti-colonial thought, this depends on the type of anti-colonial thought under consideration. Anti-colonial thought that emerged in the colonial period often had as its objective the understanding of the nature of colonial society and its practical contribution to national liberation. Anti-colonial thought directed against contemporary settler-colonialism also has as its objective national liberation, partly by way of creating international sympathy for its cause. Palestine/Israel provides the most vivid example for today. On the other hand, the anti-colonial thought of the past colonial period that we undertake today has as its objective the identification of non-European, non-Eurocentric traditions of thought, exemplars of thought that are to be found outside of the colonial centres of knowledge creation. Beyond that, some scholars and activists undertake anti-colonial research on exploitation and plantation colonialism in order to push the agenda of reparations for the formerly colonized.

At least four conclusions emerge from this chapter. One is that the origins of anti-colonial thought should be correctly identified as being prior to the 19th century. Second, anti-colonial thought has been pursued by both the colonized and the colonizers. Third, it should be recognized that anti-colonial thought is to be found not only in theoretical-empirical writing based on the modern scientific logic of induction and deduction, but also in literary works and the visual arts based on a poetic logic. Fourth, it should be known that the vast accumulation of anti-colonial thought over the centuries has had little impact on the discipline of sociology and other social sciences in terms of the formal curriculum.

After centuries of colonization we now have an accumulation of ideas and systematic thought that emerged in the postcolonial era. These ideas, nevertheless, remain marginal to the discipline of sociology, in particular social theory. In social theory texts and courses there is a failure to account for, first, broader contexts of the development of social theory, that is, not just developments in modern Europe, but also colonial capitalism, racism and slavery; and, second, the context of the rise of non-Western social thought.

While social forces such as the Industrial Revolution and the rise of capitalism are the proper contexts in which to understand the emergence of social theory (Ritzer, 1992: 5–10), the fact that colonialism, slavery, racism and misogyny were all complicit in the rise of capitalism is generally not taken into account.[18] Holton refers to classical social theory as having 'emerged in the nineteenth and early twentieth centuries as a critical commentary on the major socio-economic and political processes shaping the modern world' (Holton, 1996: 25). Here, colonialism, slavery, racism and misogyny do not feature as major social and political processes that shaped the modern world. Giddens notes that the 19th and early 20th-century ideas that continue to make a strong imprint on contemporary social science must be 'radically overhauled today' (Giddens, 1979: 1). This overhaul, however, does not seem to include references to the major sufferings of humanity that took place under colonialism, an inherent and major dimension of the emergence of capitalism since the 15th century, and the proper context within which to understand the rise of modern slavery and racism.

The problem in ignoring social and political processes outside the West that shaped the modern world – such as colonialism – is that it removes any attention that may be given to the emergence of thinkers in the non-Western world in that context (colonialism). As we have seen, there were many such thinkers throughout the colonial period that many in the West and the Third World remain ignorant of.

Notes

1. I would like to thank Maureen A. Eger and Sujata Patel for their very helpful comments on an earlier draft of this chapter. I am also grateful to Syed Imad Alatas and Syed Ubaydillah Alatas for their help with the formtting of this chapter.
2. My concern in this chapter is with European colonialism. This is not to suggest that non-European colonialism did or does not exist.
3. As noted by Patel (2023a: 1), such discussions on anti-colonial social theory are mostly recent and include Sefa Dei and Asgharzadeh (2001); Go and Watson (2019); Go (2022). To these we can add Go (2023a); Go (2023b); Cramer (2023); Patel (2023a); Patel (2023b).
4. For a useful introduction to Pramoedya's works, see Lane (2017, 2023).
5. Cited by Chaloult and Chaloult (1979: 85).
6. Cited by Chaloult and Chaloult (1979: 85).
7. Cited by Chaloult and Chaloult (1979: 86).
8. See the section 'Internal colonialist development and capitalist underdevelopment', pp 190–201.
9. Al-Maqdum (nd); Makhdum (2006).
10. For an historical background to anti-colonial struggle in Malabar, see Randathani (2007).
11. I am grateful to Masturah Alatas for translating the relevant passage in her introduction from the Italian.
12. For a more extended discussion on Salgari and colonialism, see Annunziato (2019).
13. For the English translations of his works, see Van Leur (1955).
14. For a comprehensive discussion on both van Leur and Schrieke, see Vogel (1992).
15. See, for example, Pané (1951) and Soedjatmoko (1957).
16. Cited by Lobban (2018).
17. Cited by Lobban (2018).
18. For discussion on the complicity of misogyny, slavery, racism and colonialism in the making of the modern world, see Grosfoguel (2013) and Federici (2014).

References

Alatas, M. (2009) Sandokan's daughter: Emilio Salgari meets his first Malaysian reader, *Heteroglossia*, 10: 29–54.

Alatas, M. (2022) Introduzione, in E. Salgari, *I pirati della Malesia* [*The Pirates of Malaysia*], Giunti-Barbera, pp 7–20.

Alatas, S.F. (1993) On the indigenization of academic discourse, *Alternatives*, 18: 307–38.

Alatas, S.F. (2006) *Alternative Discourses in Asian Social Science: Responses to Eurocentrism*, SAGE.

Alatas, S.F. (2009) Religion and reform: Two exemplars for autonomous sociology in the non-western context, in S. Patel (ed) *The ISA Handbook of Diverse Sociological Traditions*, SAGE, pp 29–39.

Alatas, S.F. (2013) *Ibn Khaldun*, Oxford University Press.

Alatas, S.F. and Sinha, V. (2017) *Sociological Theory Beyond the Canon*, Palgrave Macmillan.

Alatas, S.H. (1971) *Thomas Stamford Raffles 1781–1826: Schemer or Reformer*, Angus and Robertson.

Alatas, S.H. (1977) *The Myth of the Lazy Native: A Study of the Image of the Malays, Filipinos, and Javanese from the Sixteenth to the Twentieth Century and its Functions in the Ideology of Colonial Capitalism*, Frank Cass.

Alavi, H., Burns, P.L., Knight, G.R., Mayer, P.B. and McEachern, D. (1982) *Capitalism and Colonial Production*, Croom Helm.

Annunziato, S. (2019) Lions and tigers and piracy! Colonialism in two versions of Emilio Salgari's Sandokan, *MLN*, 134: S-286–S-302.

Bagú, S. (1969) La Economía de la sociedad colonial ('The Economy of Colonial Society'), *Pensamiento Critico*, 27: 30–65.

Bailey, R. and Flores, G.V. (1973) Internal colonialism and racial minorities in the U.S.: An overview, in F. Bonilla and R. Girling (eds) *Structures of Dependency*, Stanford University Press, pp 149–60.

Banaji, J. (1972) For a theory of colonial modes of production, *Economic and Political Weekly*, 7(52): 2498–502.

Barrera, M. (1979) *Race and Class in the Southwest: A Theory of Racial Inequality*, University of Notre Dame Press.

Bernasconi, R. (2008) A Haitian in Paris: Anténor Firmin as a philosopher against racism, *Patterns of Prejudice*, 42(4–5): 365–83. doi:10.1080/003132208023377321

Bhambra, G. (2014a) *Connected Sociologies*, Bloomsbury.

Bhambra, G. (2014b) Postcolonial and decolonial dialogues, *Postcolonial Studies*, 17(2): 115–21.

Blauner, R. (1972) *Racial Oppression in America*, Harper & Row.

Breman, J. (1992) *Koelies, planters en koloniale politiek: het arbeidsregime op de grootlandbouwondernemingen aan Sumatra's Oostkust in het begin van de twintigste eeuw* (Coolies, planters and colonial policy: the labour regime in the large-scale agricultural enterprises on Sumatra's east coast in the early twentieth century), KITLV.

Bunker, S.G. (1984) Modes of extraction, unequal exchange, and the progressive underdevelopment of an extreme periphery: The Brazilian Amazon, 1600–1980, *American Journal of Sociology*, 89(5): 1017–64. https://doi.org/10.1086/227983

Chaloult, N.B. and Chaloult, Y. (1979) The internal colonialism concept: Methodological considerations, *Social and Economic Studies*, 28(4): 85–79.

Connell, R. (2007) *Southern Theory*, Polity Press.

Cotler, J. (1970) The mechanisms of internal domination and social change in Peru, in I.L. Horowitz (ed) *Masses in Latin America*, Oxford University Press, pp 407–44.

Cramer, M. (2023) Colonial scholars and anti-colonial agents: Politics of academic knowledge production between the West Indies and London in the mid-20th century, *Social Lens*, 1–15. DOI: 10.1111/johs.12417

de Silva, S.B.D. (1982) *The Political Economy of Underdevelopment*, Routledge.

De Sousa Santos, B. (2014) *Epistemologies of the South*, Paradigm Publishers.

Federici, S. (2014) *Caliban and the Witch: Women, Body and Primitive Accumulation*, Autonomedia.

Firmin, A. (1885) *A De l'égalité des races humaines:Anthropologie positive* (*On the equality of human races: Positive anthropology*), Cotillon.

Firmin, A. (2000) *The Equality of the Human Races*, translated by A. Charles and introduced by C. Fluehr-Lobban, Garland Press.

Frank, A.G. (1967) *Capitalism and Underdevelopment in Latin America: Historical Studies of Chile and Brazil*, Monthly Review Press.

Giddens, A. (1979) *Central Problems in Social Theory*, University of California Press.

Go, J. (2022) Thinking against the empire: Anticolonial thought as social theory, *LSE Online Event*. https://www.youtube.com/watch?v=gb7ACmyW-4A

Go, J. (2023a) Thinking against empire: Anticolonial thought as social theory, *British Journal of Sociology*, 74(3): 279–93. DOI: 10.1111/1468-4446.12993

Go, J. (2023b) Anticolonial thought, the sociological imagination, and social science: A reply to critics, *British Journal of Sociology*, 1–15. DOI: 10.1111/1468_4446.13025

Go, J. and Watson, J. (2019) Anticolonial nationalism: From imagined communities to colonial conflict, *European Journal of Sociology*, 60: 31–68. doi: 10.1017/S000397561900002X

Gonzales-Casanova, P. (1969) Internal colonialism and national development, in I.L. Horowitz, J. de Castro and J. Gerassi (eds) *Latin American Radicalism*, Vintage Press, pp 118–39.

Grosfoguel, R. (2013) The structure of knowledge in Westernized universities: Epistemic racism/sexism and the four genocides/epistemicides of the long 16th century, *Human Architecture: Journal of the Sociology of Self-Knowledge*, 11(1): 73–90. http://www.okcir.com/Articles%20XI%201/Grosfoguel.pdf

Harun, A. (1957) *Panglima Awang*, Pustaka Melayu.

Hechter, M. (1975) *Internal Colonialism: The Celtic Fringe in British National Development, 1536–1966*, University of California Press.

Hind, R.J. (1984) The internal colonial concept, *Comparative Studies in Society and History*, 26(3): 543–68.

Holton, R.J. (1996) Classical social theory, in B. Turner (ed) *The Blackwell Companion to Social Theory*, Blackwell, pp 25–52.

Ibn Khaldûn, A.A. (1967) *Ibn Khaldun: The Muqadimmah – An Introduction of History*, 3 volumes, translated from the Arabic by F. Rosenthal, Routledge & Kegan Paul.

Ibn Khaldun, A.A. (2005) *Al-Muqaddimah (Prolegomenon)*, 5 volumes, 'Abd al-Salam al-Shaddadi, Bayt al-Funun wa al-'Ulum wa al-Adab.

Kohn, M. and Reddy, K. (2023) Colonialism, in E.N. Zalta and U. Nodelma (eds) *The Stanford Encyclopedia of Philosophy, Spring 2023 Edition*. https://plato.stanford.edu/archives/spring2023/entries/colonialism

Lane, M. (2017) *Indonesia Tidak Hadir di Bumi Manusia: Pramoedya, Sejarah dan Politik* (Indonesia is Not Present on This Earth of Mankind: Pramoedya, History and Politics), Djaman Baru.

Lane, M. (2023) *Indonesia Out of Exile: How Pramoedya's Buru Quartet Killed a Dictatorship*, Penguin Random House SEA.

Lobban, C.F. (2000) Antenor Firmin: Haitian pioneer of anthropology, *American Anthropologist*, 102(3): 449–66. doi: 10.1525/aa.2000.102.3.449

Lobban, C.F. (2005) Anténor Firmin and Haiti's contribution to anthropology, *Gradhiva – Musée du Quai Branly*, 1: 95–108. doi:10.4000/gradhiva.302.

Lobban, C.F. (2018) A 19th century Haitian pioneering anthropologist: An intellectual biography of Anténor Firmin, in *Bérose – Encyclopédie internationale des histoires de l'anthropologie*, Paris.

Majul, C.A. (1999) Rizal in the 21st century: The relevance of his ideas and texts, *Public Policy*, 3: 1–21.

Makhdum, S.Z. (2006) *Tuhfat al-Mujahidin: A Historical Epic of the Sixteenth Century*, translated by S. Muhammad Husayn Nainar, Islamic Book Trust.

Mao, T. (1939) The Chinese revolution and the Chinese communist party, in *Selected Works of Mao Tse-tung* [online]. https://www.marxists.org/reference/archive/mao/selected-works/volume-2/mswv2_23.htm

Al-Maqdum, S.Z.A. (nd) *Tuhfat al-Mujahidin fi ba 'd akhbar al-Burtughaliyin* (*A Gift to the Warriors Concerning Some Accounts of the Portuguese*), Maktabat Tirurangadi.

Memmi, A. (1957) *The Colonizer and the Colonized*, Beacon Press.

Memmi, A. (2002) *Portrait du colonisé – Portrait du colonisateur* (*Portrait of the Colonised – Portrtait of the Colonider*), Gallimard.

Mignolo, W.D. (2011) *The Darker Side of Western Modernity*, Duke University Press.

Mignolo, W.D. (2014) Spirit out of bounds returns to the East: The closing of the social sciences and the opening of independent thoughts, *Current Sociology*, 62(4): 584–602. https://doi.org/10.1177/0011392114524513

Naik, J.V. (2001) Forerunners of Dadabhai Naoroji's drain theory, *Economic and Political Weekly*, 36(46/47): 4428–32.

Naoroji, D. (1901) *Poverty and Un-British Rule in India*, Swan Sonnenschein & Co.

Pané, A. (1951) Indonesia di Asia Selatan: Sedjarah Indonesia sampai ± 1600 [Indonesia in Southern Asia: Indonesian history till ± 1600], *Indonesia*, 2: 1–36.

Parker, D. (1997) Why bother with Durkheim, *Sociological Review*, 45(1): 122–46.

Patel, S. (2006) Beyond binaries: A case for self-reflexive sociologies, *Current Sociology*, 54(3): 381–95.

Patel, S. (2020) Social theory today: Eurocentrism and decolonial theory, *MIDS Working Paper* No. 240, Madras Institute of Development Studies.

Patel, S. (2021) Webinar 5, decolonial research methods: Resisting coloniality in academic knowledge production webinar series, National Centre for Research Methods, University of Southampton, 30 November. https://www.youtube.com/watch?v=MrHXUlWmeTU

Patel, S. (2023a) Anti-colonial thought and global social theory, *Frontiers in Sociology*, 8: 1–13. doi: 10.3389/fsoc.2023.1143776

Patel, S. (2023b) Doing anti-colonial social theory, *Global Dialogue*, 13(2).

Prakash, G. (1992) Postcolonial criticism and Indian historiography, *Social Text*, 31/32: 8–19.

Randathani, H. (2007) *Mappila Muslims: A Study on Society and Anti Colonial Struggles*, Other Books.

Ritzer, G. (1992) *Sociological Theory*, 3rd edn, McGraw-Hill, Inc.

Rizal, J. (1963) The indolence of the Filipino, in *Political and Historical Writings*, The National Historical Institute, pp 111–39.

Rizal, J. (1990 [1887]) *Noli Me Tangere (Touch e not)*, translated from the Spanish and introduction by J. Ventura Castro, Nalandangan Press.

Rizal, J. (1992 [1890]) *The Revolution*, translated from the Spanish and introduction by J. Ventura Castro, Nalandangan Press.

Rodinson, M. (1973) *Israel: A Colonial-Settler State?*, Monad Press.

Rouse, I. (1992) *The Tainos: Rise and Decline of the People who Greeted Columbus*, Yale University Press.

Sabbagh-Khoury, A. (2021) Tracing settler colonialism: A geneaology of a paradigm in the sociology of knowledge production in Israel, *Politics and Society*. DOI: 10.1177/0032329221999906

Said, E. (1980) *The Question of Palestine*, Vintage Books.

Said, E. (1999) Zionism from the standpoint of its victims, *Social Text*, 1: 7–58.

Sayegh, F. (1965) *Zionist Colonialism in Palestine*, Research Center, Palestine Liberation Organization.

Sefa Dei, G.J. and Asgharzadeh, A. (2001) The power of social theory: The anti-colonial discursive framework, *The Journal of Educational Thought*, 35(3): 297–323.

Selvaratnam, V. (2021) Malaysia's South Indian 'coolies': Legacies of imperialism, colonial capitalism and racism, in R. Rasiah, A. Hashim and J.S. Sidhu (eds) *Contesting Malaysia's Integration into the World Economy*, Springer, pp 169–99.

Shoemaker, N. (2015) A typology of colonialism, *Perspectives on History*, 1 October. https://www.historians.org/research-and-publications/perspectives-on-history/october-2015/a-typology-of-colonialism

Soedjatmoko (1957) *An Approach to Indonesian History: Towards an Open Future* (An address before the Seminar on Indonesian History, Gadjah Mada University, Jogjakarta, December 14), Ithaca, New York: Translation Series, Modern Indonesia Project, Southeast Asia Program, Department of Far Eastern Studies, Cornell University, 1960.

Stavenhagen, R. (1965) Classes, colonialism, and acculturation. Essay on a system of inter-ethnic relations in Mesoamerica, *Studies in Comparative International Development*, 1(6): 53–77.

Van Leur, J.C. (1940a) Eenige aanteekeningen betreffende de mogelijkheid der 18ᵉ eeuw als categorie in de Indische geschiedschrijving [Some notes on the possibility of the 18th century as a category in the writing of the history of the Indies], *Tijdschrift voor Indische Taal-, Land- en Volkenkunde uitgegeven door het (Koninklijk) Bataviaasch Genootschap van Kunsten en Wetenschappen*, 80: 544–67.

Van Leur, J.C. (1940b) De Wereld van Zuidoost-Azië [The world of Southeast Asia], in J.C. de Haan and P.J. van Winter (eds) *Nederlanders over de Zeeën: 350 jaar Nederlandsche koloniale geschiedenis* [*Dutchmen Over the Seas: 350 Years of Dutch Colonial History*], De Haan, pp 101–44.

Van Leur, J.C. (1955) *Indonesian Trade and Society: Essays in Asian Social and Economic History*, W. van Hoeve.

Vogel, J. (1992) *De opkomst van het Indocentrische geschiedbeeld: Leven and werken van B. J. O. Schrieke en J. C. van Leur* [*The Rise of the Indocentric Image of History: Lives and Works of B. J. O. Schrieke en J. C. van Leur*], Verloren.

Watner, C. (1987) 'All mankind is one': The libertarian tradition in sixteenth century Spain, *The Journal of Libertarian Studies*, 8(2): 293–309.

Yahya, Z. (1990) Resisting colonialist discourse, *Akademika*, 37: 107–33.

Yahya, Z. (1994) *Resisting Colonialist Discourse*, Penerbit Universiti Kebangsaan Malaysia.

4

The Promise of Anticolonial Social Theory

Julian Go

Introduction

Social scientists and social thinkers seek to understand, know and represent society through concepts, categories and frameworks drawn from existing social theories.[1] These theories offer conceptual frameworks that dictate *what* about the world is to be perceived and understood. By now, however, it is painfully clear that the dominant social theoretical frameworks in use by social scientists – particularly in the Global North but not exclusively there – are inadequate. Critics have pointed out that conventional social theories are plagued with blinders and biases. In sociology, the canonical theories of thinkers like Karl Marx, Max Weber, Emile Durkheim, Talcott Parsons, Irving Goffman among many others have theorized modernity but their theories are often Eurocentric, ignorant of social dynamics in the Global South and ex-colonial world, and blind to colonial and imperial histories in the making of modernity. We might extend to this to political theory and social thought more broadly, whether it be social contract theorists like Kant and Locke, historicists like Hegel, or even critical theorist like Michel Foucault and Judith Butler. The blinders of these conventional, canonical and dominant social theories – which for short-hand we might call 'Northern-metropolitan' because they originate and are prominent in the Anglo-European fields of the Global North – have compelled scholars to seek alternative social theories by which to overthrow or at least transform and supplement the existing Northern-metropolitan canon. The goal is to find new conceptual frameworks and theories that are more inclusive and capacious; that overcome the limits of Northern-metropolitan thought and offer a new sociological imagination that is adequate to our global social worlds.

But what *are* these conceptual frameworks and theories that offer an alternative to Northern-metropolitan social thought? Which traditions or bodies of social thought should we enlist or create to generate a more capacious sociological imagination? Who are the thinkers to whom we should turn and by what criteria do they qualify? On what basis or by which warrants do we decide and choose different frameworks and theories to change the Northern-metropolitan canon? If we look at the vast literature that ponders the problems of Northern-metropolitan theory, we can find a number of apparent solutions, as Boatcâ et al (2010), Connell (2007) and Patel (2010), among others, trace. They include the 'decolonial' solution articulated by the likes of Mignolo (2011) and Quijano (2000), and movements in sociology since the 1990s such as 'indigenous' sociology, 'connected sociologies', 'non-Western' sociology, 'alternative discourses', 'Southern theory' or 'global social theory' (Alatas, 2006; Connell, 2007; Mignolo, 2011; Bhambra, 2014; Sousa Santos, 2014). In this chapter, I argue that anticolonial thought offers another solution. In prior work, I have already proposed that anticolonial thought can and should be the basis for a reconstruction of sociology and social theory. I have argued that anticolonial thought feeds into and sets the precedent for what I call 'postcolonial' social theory. I argue that anticolonial thought, along with its inheritor, postcolonial thought, can help us overcome the limitations of conventional Northern-metropolitan theory. It can offer the basis for an alternative 'canon' or, if we hesitate about canonization, it can significantly expand our sociological imagination (Go, 2016, 2020, 2023a, 2023b).[2] The present chapter builds upon this prior project to centre anticolonial thought as an alternative to Northern-metropolitan thought by addressing some crucial issues attendant with the project. Foremost: how does the turn to anticolonial thought as an epistemic project for reconstructing social theory relate to, or differ from, the many other alternatives that have been offered?

In a recent essay, Patel (2023) suggests that 'anti-colonial' theory encompasses a range of different perspectives:

> Anti-colonial ... is an umbrella term to describe a range of different methodological positions that have emerged in the wake of colonialism: indigenous sociology, indigeneity, and indigenous methodology (Atal, 1981; Akiwowo, 1986, 1999; Smith, 1999; Odora, 2002); endogeneity and endogenous thought; extraversion (Hountondji, 1995, 1997, 2009); autonomous and independent sociologies (Alatas, 2006); subaltern theory, derivative nationalism, and colonial difference (Guha, 1982; Chatterjee, 1986); colonial modernity

> (Barlow, 2012; Patel, 2017); internal colonialism (Martin, 2018); coloniality of power (Quijano, 2000); border thinking and de-linking (Mignolo, 2007); connected sociologies (Bhambra, 2014a); and postcolonial sociology (Go, 2016), south theories (Fiddian-Qasmiyeh and Daley, 2018). Undoubtedly these different positions highlight unique attributes, but they also flag an imperative for a common denominator that binds these perspectives. I suggest that this common denominator is the affiliation of these approaches to an anti-colonial social theory as an ontological–epistemological perspective. (Patel, 2023: 4)

Patel thus intimates that anticolonial social theory has important *commonalities* with these other movements for a more global sociology. In the present chapter, I ponder the *differences* between my approach to anticolonial social thought and these other projects. I want to ponder the *distinct value* that anticolonial social thought might offer. In other words, while Patel does the important work of highlighting commonalities, I want to highlight some of the 'unique attributes', in Patel's words, of anticolonial social theory while also dealing with some of the challenges the project might face – and how they might be overcome. What are the distinct affordances of the anticolonial standpoint compared to other critical projects that try to critique and expand the canon?

In this chapter I suggest that, first of all, the project of recovering anticolonial social theory is best thought of in terms of a postcolonial sociology of knowledge that recognizes that anticolonial thought represents a distinct standpoint: the anticolonial (or 'anti-imperial') standpoint.[3] Mounted upon this claim, I then suggest that one of distinct affordances of anticolonial theory is that it facilitates a critique of Northern-metropolitan theory's *imperiality* or, as I have put it elsewhere, its 'imperial standpoint' (Go, 2016, 2023a). This makes it distinct from other projects because it allows us to overcome what I call *geoepistemic essentialism*. As I will suggest in this chapter, many existing alternatives to Northern-metropolitan theory operate from the premises of geoepistemic essentialism and thus only critique the *Eurocentrism* of Northern-metropolitan social theory rather than its imperiality. Anticolonial thought does not fall into this problem.

Further and relatedly, this chapter suggests that the project of mobilizing anticolonial thought to revitalize social theory offers another distinct affordance: generalizability. One of the limitations of approaches that operate from geoepistemic essentialism is that they remain specific to the geocultural location they purport to represent. While this specificity to social theory is useful in some respects, like all social theories it has limitations, one of which is generalizability. A standpoint approach to anticolonial social theory enables us to resolve this problem. To make this argument, I will compare some key aspects of the thought of W.E.B. Du Bois and Frantz Fanon.

The discussion cannot be exhaustive of their thinking, only suggestive of how anticolonial social thought can speak to general themes.

The imperial standpoint and social theory

Criticisms of Northern-metropolitan social theory need to specify what it is about such theory that requires remedy. What exactly is wrong or limiting with Northern-metropolitan social theory that warrants the search for an alternative canon, different theoretical frameworks or theorists? Too often, this question is not addressed. I therefore wish to be clear: I suggest that Northern-metropolitan theory suffers from its *imperiality* or more precisely, its *imperial standpoint*. Understanding this requires clarifying what I mean by 'standpoint.'

By the term 'standpoint,' I draw upon standpoint theory offered by Marxists like Lukács (1971), feminists and Black feminists (Collins, 1997; Smith, 1997) and post-positivist philosophers (Harding, 2004, among others). Elsewhere I connect standpoint theory with 'perspectivalism' in the philosophy of science (Giere, 2006) to formulate a postcolonial sociology of knowledge (Go, 2016: 162–6; 2023b). For the purposes of this chapter, the fundamental usable point from standpoint theory is that social location shapes consciousness and knowledge, including scientific knowledge. Differential social locations allocate different experiences, concerns and interests to people and this in turn guides how people see the world and what they see in it. Social location does not determine knowledge but it conditions and shapes it. As Wylie (2003: 28) summarizes, 'social location systematically shapes and limits what we know, including tacit experiential knowledge as well as explicit understanding, what we take knowledge to be as well as specific epistemic content'. Patricia Hill Collins adds that there is a

> commonality of experiences and perspectives that emerge for groups differentially arrayed within hierarchical power relations ... [G]roups who share common placement in hierarchical power relations also share common experiences in such power relations. Such shared angles of vision lead those in similar social locations to be predisposed to interpret these experiences in comparable fashion. (Collins, 1997: 377)

Even early sociologists of knowledge like Mannheim (1936) recognize this point. Mannheim claims that 'modes of thought' are not free floating but have 'social origins'. They are produced by people in definite social contexts as 'responses' to 'situations characterizing their common position' (Mannheim, 1936: 2–3).

A 'postcolonial sociology of knowledge' extends these insights by specifying a social ontology of empire upon which epistemic production is based

(Go, 2023b). Lukács (1971) claims that the class is the primary social determinant of knowledge. Feminist standpoint theory, or its variant of Black feminist theory, adds that gender and race are also crucial (Collins, 1997). By contrast, a postcolonial sociology of knowledge extends the social map to the global level. It recognizes that the history of colonialism and imperialism has created global socioeconomic, political and social hierarchies that also shape knowledge production just as intra-societal hierarchies of race, class or gender do. For example, the sociologists who founded disciplinary sociology in the United States and Europe in the late 19th and early 20th century resided at the top of a global hierarchy. They were men of the white middle classes in the United States and Europe who, as university professors, provided knowledge for the imperial state, its managers and capitalists. They operated within a culture of empire that dictated the parameters of their concerns and categories and so the sociology they produced embedded an *imperial standpoint*. The problems that these metropolitan sociologists identified, the categories and concerns that oriented their theories, and the interests guiding their knowledge projects reflected their position as elites within imperial metropoles.

Some history needs to be recounted. As I have shown in previous work (Go, 2013, 2020), drawing upon the seminal scholarship of Connell (1997), disciplinary sociology was created at a particular historical moment in global history. Over the course of the 19th century and into the early 20th century, Anglo-European imperialism was reaching its pinnacle. This was the moment of the 'new imperialism' or 'high imperialism' (as it would later be called) – the unleashing of violent power as nations like England, France, Germany, the United States, Belgium, Italy and others mounted new territorial assaults upon Africa and Asia. By 1900, the new empires were ruling 90 per cent of Africa, 56 per cent of Asia and 99 per cent of the Pacific. By the First World War, imperial powers occupied 90 per cent of the entire surface area of the globe (Young, 2001: 2). As all of this was occurring, the first ideas about 'society' emerged and resonated among elites in metropolitan centres, contributing to the formation of the social sciences as we know them today. Ideas about society thus emerged in imperial metropoles within this culture and context of empire. The very notion of the 'social' – as a space between nature and the spiritual realm – that emerged in European thought was generated in the 19th century and resonated among European male elites who were trying to make sense of and manage social upheaval, resistance and revolt from workers, women and colonized natives (Borch, 2012; Owens, 2015).

Later, in the early 20th century, the categories and concerns of the early sociologists reflected the interests of elites and imperial power. Assimilation theory in the early 20th century expressed the concern of white elites fretting about the incoming non-white hordes. Inscribed in the early theorizations of 'social order' were imperial anxieties about resistance from subaltern peoples, embedding the horrors of elites desperately attempting to maintain the racial status quo (read: 'social order'). Anxieties about social disorder; sociology's attachment to Social Darwinism; its focus upon the so-called 'Negro problem' in the United States; Weber and Durkheim's Orientalist and essentialist lenses for discussing other cultures – in all of these respects and more, sociology reflected the questions of interest to imperial centres and embedded the worldview of those metropoles (Connell, 1997; Go, 2009, 2013, 2020; Boatcâ, 2013; Jung, 2009).

Even after the period of formal colonialism beginning in the mid-20th century, sociology continued to embed an imperial standpoint, reflecting dreams of the new US empire. The rise of 'systems theory' and 'structural functionalism' offered by Talcott Parsons (1951) drew from cybernetics, reflecting a managerial view from on top of a social order whose smooth functioning and maintenance of hierarchy served the interests of state managers and capitalists. As Steinmetz (2005) argues, these and other theories of order resonated across metropolitan societies like the United States because the seemingly stable regime of global accumulation fostered coherence. Parsons' work in particular fomented modernization theory that the US neo-imperial state employed as it sought to change postcolonial societies in directions that matched its interests (Gilman, 2003). Many aspects of sociology today still carry the imprint of its imperial history. As I have discussed elsewhere (Go, 2016: 75–101), sociology's current imperial standpoint is seen in sociology's persistent essentialism, its analytic bifurcations and its metrocentrism. It is seen in the *objects* of sociology's theorizing, which still include issues like 'assimilation' and 'social order'. It is reflected in our epistemology and methods which often universalize from European experiences or distinct 'model cases' taken from Europe (Krause, 2021). It is reflected in not just the occlusion of colonialism and imperialism from our accounts of modernity, but also the related denial of the *agency* of colonized and ex-colonized peoples in the making of modernity. The imperial standpoint remains with us.

The anticolonial standpoint

Anticolonial thought emerges from a different history. While the history of imperial-metropolitan sociology lies in imperial conquest, the history of anticolonial thought lies in resistance, protest and struggle against it (Al-Hardan and Go, in press). Empire was always contested. Resistance included nationalist movements seeking reform, eventual independence or full integration into the metropole as equal territories (Go and Watson, 2019). It also included transnational organizing, expressed in the various pan-African conferences and the Bandung meeting of 1955, among other forums.

These movements were vital for spelling the collapse of formal colonial empires in the latter part of the 20th century. They also produced an array of critical thinking, giving rise to anticolonial thought.

I propose that anticolonial thought reflects not just a different history but also a different standpoint than the imperial standpoint. While conventional disciplinary sociology embedded the categories, concerns and interests of imperial elites in the metropolitan centres, anticolonial thought represents the categories, concerns and interests of colonized peoples who stood up against empire. It reflects the ideas of colonized peoples who were conquered, dispossessed and exploited but who resisted domination. Just as disciplinary sociologists in Europe and the United States embed the experiences and concerns of metropolitan elites, so did anticolonial writers, thinkers, activists and leaders embed the experiences and concerns of colonized peoples who fought against colonial control and imperial conquest.[4]

Who were anticolonial thinkers? They are far too numerous to name; they constitute a diverse and eclectic group offering a variety of different ideas. But despite the diversity, they shared some basic characteristics. First, most were born in or lived in the colonies and drew upon their experiences there. This would include Apolinario Mabini and Jose Rizal in the Philippines, Eugenio Maria de Hostos in Puerto Rico, or Frantz Fanon and Aimé Césaire in Martinique. It would also include Kwame Nkrumah, Amilcar Cabral, the Vietnamese anticolonial activist Nguyen An Ninh, and the Martinican surrealist Suzanne Césaire (to offer only a handful of examples). Second, many were educated in imperial capitals like Paris, London or Barcelona where anticolonialists often met, mobilized and theorized (Goebel, 2015; Matera, 2015). Ho Chi Minh and Fanon were among the many who studied in France, Jose Martí and Jose Rizal studied and travelled through Spain, Nkrumah and C.L.R. James joined many other anticolonial leaders in London. A different group of anticolonial thinkers lived and operated within the *internal colonies* of metropolitan centres. W.E.B. Du Bois, operating mainly within the United States, is an obvious example. But there are others. For example, Laura Cornelius Kellogg was an indigenous activist born on the Oneida Indian reservation in Wisconsin. She and other indigenous thinkers represent an anticolonial thinking that operated within the confines of settler-colonialism, struggling within the internal colonized spaces of empire.

Anticolonial thought emerged from a variety of social positions along a continuum of professionalization. Some anticolonial thinkers were actual academics teaching in lower schools or universities. This list would include W.E.B. Du Bois, but it would also include the Indian sociologist Radhakamal Mukerjee, the Algerian sociologist Abdelmalek Sayad (who was one of Pierre Bourdieu's collaborators) and the Lebanese theorist Mahdi Amel. Many others, and likely most others, were journalists, writers or artists. Some were activists and political leaders. Journalists and political activists included Mabel Dove in the Gold Coast. Political leaders included Nkrumah or Pedro Albizu Campos in Puerto Rico. The list is almost infinite. The point is that anticolonial social thought did not typically come in the form of academic writing. It was articulated in journalistic writings, political pamphlets, speeches, art, or through the chants of activists in the streets.

Hence the larger claim. Despite the fact that they were not card-carrying social scientists, they nonetheless offered up important ideas and knowledges about the world that imperial sociology either ignored or completely overlooked. It is already known, for example, that anticolonial thinkers wrote about and thought about anticolonial revolution and struggle. This is perhaps why Fanon is typically thought of as a key anticolonial thinker. His ideas of anticolonial revolution and the role of violence have become prominent in some circles (Macey, 2010). But I claim that anticolonial thinkers also offered a variety of other ideas about society, the social and social relations that we might learn from. They even offered, although not always intentionally, a kind of sociology, one that contained potentially generalizable concepts and theories. Anticolonial social thought does not just offer particularistic ideas pertaining only to anticolonial revolt, or the dilemmas of colonized or racialized peoples. As I have shown elsewhere, it offers insights into society more broadly (Al-Hardan and Go, in press; Go, 2023a).

Beyond geoepistemic essentialism

How is this project of recovering anticolonial social thought different from other attempts to critique and reach beyond the blinders of Northern-metropolitan social theory? First, the project of recovering anticolonial thought offers a proper alternative to social theory's imperiality where other projects do not. For instance, one of main critiques over the past decades of Northern-metropolitan theory has been its 'Eurocentrism', where Eurocentrism is understood in terms of the geographic origin and focus of the theories (cf Getachew and Mantena, 2021). In other words, according to these critiques, the problem with Northern-metropolitan social theory that needs to be remedied is that it focuses upon Europe alone, and/or uses European social theorists only. In other words, the problem that requires remedy is that Northern-metropolitan social theory is *from the Global North* (that is, from the United States or Europe), by *Northern theorists*, and *only focuses on the Global North*, consistently and repeatedly only drawing upon Karl Marx, Max Weber, Emile Durkheim, Georg Simmel, Talcott Parsons, Irving Goffman, Bruno Latour, Michel Foucault, Judith Butler, Pierre Bourdieu among many others, including scholars today located in the Global North.

The solution, or rather the alternative to Northern-metropolitan theory, follows directly from this critique. We should locate theorists *from the Global*

South who write theories that focus on the Global South. In other words, the way in which social theorists should fix the Eurocentric canon is by replacing it a more 'indigenous' or 'local' one rooted in 'non-Western' or geographically 'Southern' cultures (and hence regions or countries), thus ostensibly replacing the Northern-Western standpoint with a Southern/ Non-Western standpoint. Rather than read Karl Marx or Max Weber, we read Ibn Khaldun or thinkers from Latin America. Rather than use the theories of Talcott Parsons, Emile Durkheim or Michel Foucault, we should turn to the ideas of 'indigenous' scholars, poets from Yoruba, 'Asian' discourses, or other presumably 'non-Western' or 'non-European' traditions of social thought.

These 'indigenous' or 'non-Western' solutions are worthwhile and important, but they do not address the imperiality of social theory. Rather than critiquing and offering an alternative to the imperial standpoint of social theory, they only critique and offer an alternative to its geographic location. The project therefore runs the risk of falling into the trap of 'geoepistemic essentialism', by which I mean the ontological assumption that the world can be divided into distinct essentialized geographical spaces – such as North and South or 'West' and 'non-West' – and that those spaces map directly onto cultures and knowledge formations. By this assumption, if a thinker is 'in' or 'from' the Global South or a 'non-Western' country their knowledge is necessarily oppositional to dominant 'Western' sociology and therefore should count as alternative knowledge. Simultaneously, according to this geoepistemic essentialism, any thinker in or from the 'Global North' or 'the West' or 'Europe' is to be rejected.[5] Therefore, by this criterion, someone like W.E.B. Du Bois would not count for this alternative sociological canon, nor would the indigenous activist Laura Kellogg in Wisconsin whose ideas I have explored elsewhere, because they spent most of their lives in the United States. Note too that by this criteria, Ibn Khaldun has been heralded as a critical voice offering an alternative to Eurocentric sociology on the grounds that he represents the 'Middle Eastern' view, even though Khaldun's standpoint was not a critical one. In fact, Khaldun was a court scholar; his theories of *assabiyah* and of cyclical state-formation represent the standpoint of dynastic power intent upon preserving and prolonging dynastic rule (Khaldun, 2015). His is the standpoint of power and empire, even if it is the standpoint of a 'non-Western' power. Therefore, while Khaldun takes us far and is valuable if we want to cultivate a so-called 'non-Western' or 'non-Eurocentric' social theory, it does not pose a true alternative to the imperiality of social theory. If anything, turning to thinkers based upon their geography on the grounds of geoepistemic essentialism *reproduces* the imperial standpoint, for it was the imperial standpoint that divides the world into geographic categories and presumes that culture and knowledge map correspond directly with those categories. Geoepistemic essentialism is a corollary to regional or cultural Orientalism, as Edward Said might suggest (Said, 1979, 1995).

Note, finally, that if we rest our alternative social theories on geography, what do we do with thinkers from or in China? If we operate from the assumption of geoepistemic essentialism, we will be forced to conclude that social thinkers in or from China offer the best frameworks for crafting an alternative to the imperial standpoint, even though China itself can be seen, and should be seen, as an imperial power. Surely, some overlooked Chinese thinkers adopted a standpoint that was close to that of their anticolonial counterparts. Some parts of Mao Tse-tung's thought, for example, could be said to embed an anticolonial perspective. But what about other Chinese thinkers, including contemporary ones? If the heads of the Chinese Communist Party wrote a sociological treatise, are we supposed to take that as a body of thought that we should enlist as an alternative to imperial sociology from Europe, just because it comes from China?

By making the case for anticolonial social theory, I am arguing something different. I do not think the *only* problem with Anglo-European sociology is its Eurocentrism. In my view, the problem with Northern sociology is much deeper than this. The problem is sociology's *imperial standpoint*. That is, conventional social theory (that we might lazily label as 'Northern' or 'Western') views the world from the standpoint of power at the top. It embeds the interests, concerns and categories of only those at the height of imperial systems. It is not a view from the dominated, repressed, excluded or marginalized of global hierarchies. The imperial and anticolonial standpoints do not map onto opposed geographical or spatial locations. They refer to *social* locations within a global hierarchy of power and domination. Surely there is some amount of correlation between geography and social location, but the geoepistemic assumption that they are the same would lead one to overlook how the imperial standpoint even permeates the 'Global South'.

Indeed, through the global academic division of labour and hierarchies that Alatas (2003) and others highlight, and through the spread of sociology through colonialism to all parts of the world, even to the so-called non-West, the imperial standpoint has not stayed put; it has spread around the world. In many parts of the colonized world, colonizers created new universities and schools creating academic departments modelled upon academic disciplines in the imperial metropole. With some exceptions – including anticolonial thought to be discussed in what follows – social science in the colonies thus reproduced the imperial episteme (Connell, 2019). And the legacies remain, for today, imperial sociologies remain in the ex-colonial world too. The extent to which it does so, the exact reasons for why, the precise institutional configurations that embeds it, and the forms of opposition and resistance to it probably varies greatly across contexts.

But available evidence does suggest the imperial standpoint persists across sociology departments in the so-called 'non-Western' Global South that rely upon conventional Northern-metropolitan sociologies, even if this standpoint is nestled alongside more critical social theories that represent an anticolonial perspective (Banzon Bautista, 2000: 181; Patel, 2021).[6] There are thus colonized epistemes residing in the so-called Global North just as the imperial episteme circulates in the so-called Global South. There are colonized standpoints and knowledges in the United States or England or China and there are imperial-colonial standpoints them too. The same goes for other countries, including those in 'non-West' or Global South.

The alternative to imperial social thought, therefore, is not switching geographies, but rather switching epistemic frames and standpoints which may or may not align with geography.

Herein lies the promise of anticolonial social thought. By looking at anticolonial social thought as a true alternative to the imperial episteme, we are not relying upon the ontology and epistemology of geoepistemic essentialism. The project does not depend upon an ontology or vision of the world that divides up the world into distinct geographic regions that map onto knowledge. The ontology underlying the epistemic project of turning to anticolonial social thought is rather one that sees in the world a complex series of hegemonies and hierarchies that traverse the globe but which were first forged through imperialism and colonialism that generated a series of colonial epistemic formations traversing geographies. As opposed to geoepistemic essentialism, the anticolonial standpoint is grounded in an ontology of global hierarchy forged by histories of colonialism and empire. The anticolonial standpoint does not mark out an essential position of geography or culture (or race, for that matter) but rather a *relational* position of experience, of subordination, erasure and struggle that may or may not map onto geographical, national or cultural differences.[7]

My claim is not that geography is irrelevant or that we cannot speak about the 'Global North', the 'Anglo-American world' or 'Europe' as geographic locations from which knowledge springs. To the contrary, we can use these categories. The problem is not geography but the assumption of geographic essentialism: the assumption that geography equals *qualitatively different kinds of knowledge*. Nor is my claim that we should reject social theories from the Global South or from different geographic locations than the Global North. I do not reject attempts to locate theories that offer 'Asian' discourses on society, 'non-Western' theories, 'indigenous' theories or 'theories from the South' (Alatas, 2006; Connell, 2007). I *do* reject mistaking these theories for *anticolonial* theories. Southern, 'indigenous', 'Asian' discourses, 'non-Western' theories or 'theories from the South' are not necessarily anticolonial. They might be non-Western or even non-Eurocentric, but to assume that non-Western or non-Eurocentric *equals* anticolonial would be a problematic insinuation of geoepistemic essentialism – which to my mind is intellectually and sociologically untenable.[8]

From the particular to the general

There is another affordance of anticolonial social thought: it permits a certain kind of generalizability that is necessary for social theory. One of the common critiques of some attempts to globalize social theory and unmoor it from its Northern-metropolitan standpoint has long been this *lack* of generalizability. Critics have long pointed out that alternatives to global sociology that seek to 'indigenize' it or rely upon 'Southern' knowledge suffer from parochiality. In the late 1980s and early 1990s, the African scholar Akiwowo (1986, 1999) argued that one way to globalize sociology was to replace Western-based, Northern or metropolitan social thought with African-based parochial oral traditions. Critics wondered whether social theories rooted in the distinct traditions of the Yoruba, for instance, could at all offer any social knowledge beyond that particular locality. If not, a 'global social theory' or 'global sociology' would be only an array of local knowledges that have no commonalities or shared basis: a 'plethora of pluralisms', as Burawoy (2014: xvi) puts it. Similarly, some readings of 'Southern' theory claim that the pursuit of theories developed in the Global South, and about the Global South, have little to say about other parts of the world, including other countries in the Global South itself besides the country in which the social theorist resides (Connell, 2007). At issue, therefore, is not universality but some base form of generality that would make social thought approximate social *theory*. Even Akiwowo (1986: 95) strives for a 'general body of explanatory principles for sociology across the world'. Connell (2007: 196) similarly declares that generalization is 'vital' and 'theory' provides it. But as yet, existing approaches operating from an ontology of geoepistemic essentialism do not offer a solution. How can we have generalization if our challenge to Northern social theory is to go 'native'?

Here again anticolonial theory can be enlisted. Anticolonial thought emerged in response to and as a critique of imperialism and colonialism that historically has extended to almost the entire world. Up until the last few decades, the world had long been organized into empires and their colonies. For centuries, societies were not bounded as nation-states but rather parts of empires. By the early 20th century, nine-tenths of the globe had been occupied by imperial powers and their colonies. Imperialism – and its distinct form as colonialism – has therefore generated similar hierarchies, typically racialized but at the very least ethnoracial, across societies and around the globe. Concomitant with capitalism, colonialism has generated structures of extraction and modes of oppression that transcend particular localities and are often similar across them. Anticolonialism challenged these structures that have been always been translocal and similar across distinct localities.

Anticolonial thought, therefore, is not parochial but rather targets more global structures and shared hierarchies. Unlike local social theories or theories bounded by geography and presumed cultures, anticolonial thought is necessarily *general*. Of course, not all societies and social systems are exactly the same; hence not all colonialisms are the same. But as I've argued elsewhere, colonialism has generated shared *problematics of domination* that gives anticolonial social thought translocal relevance – that is, a certain generality – around which local particularities are organized (Go, 2024). To see this, let us briefly look at some examples of anticolonial thinkers and their social concepts. Consider two obvious examples of anticolonial thinkers: W.E.B. Du Bois and Frantz Fanon. Each wrote their anticolonial tracts in very different colonial contexts. Fanon wrote as a colonial subject in the context of French colonialism in Algeria, with all of its particularities and logics of domination, amidst a violent anticolonial nationalist struggle. Differently, Du Bois wrote much earlier and was a colonial subject of the United States, residing in the centre of an imperial metropole. He wrote in a situation of 'internal colonialism' with a dominant white majority on the one hand and on the other, ex-slave populations and migrant peoples racialized as non-white and hence inferior.

Despite these different contexts, however, Fanon and Du Bois shared a basic problematic of domination that the French and US empires had generated. As such, they produced emergent sociological concepts that were similar, hence revealing that their 'local' insights were in fact more general than we might initially believe. And their social thought together provided an alternative to the dominant sociological imagination of their respective times.

Let us start with Du Bois. Du Bois wrote when American sociology was just beginning to try to theorize what 'society' is. Du Bois offered his own notion, theorizing society as fundamentally fractured. He conceptualized American society as bifurcated along racial lines, separated by a 'veil'. He introduced this concept at the beginning of *The Souls of Black Folk* (2007 [1903]) where he discusses his first experience of being rejected by white children on the basis of his race: 'it dawned upon me with a certain suddenness that I was different from the others; or like, mayhap, in heart and life and longing, but shut out from their world by a vast veil'. To this, Du Bois would later add the concept of the 'color line': a racial division that cuts through modern society and extending globally. And throughout his work, he theorized the logics and dynamics of this type of fractured society. He discusses the two sides of the colour line marked by the veil – the white and Black world in America – and elaborates upon the latter's internal structure and dynamics. He examines the impact of this fractured society upon Black Americans and white Americans, delving into the social, economic, cultural and even psychological effects of informal and formal segregation. Hence Du Bois' famous concept: 'double-consciousness' (Du Bois, 2007 [1903]).

This was a nascent theory of internal colonialism, and the picture it paints of modern society is a far cry from that painted by Northern social theory in the United States at the time (dominated by neo-Spencerians like Albion Small or social contract theorists influenced by Thomas Hobbes) (Breslau, 2007). Rather than a society arranged by an underlying social contract, or a society of men pursuing their self-interest in freely associating with each other, nor similarly an organic whole evolving through time, Du Bois paints a picture of society as racialized and bifurcated; a society of exploitation and domination. And his related concepts also offered an alternative. His concept of 'double-consciousness' differed significantly from conventional social theory at the time which, as in George Herbert Mead's theory of the self, emphasized how individuals' identities were solidified through 'recognition'. For Du Bois, racialized exclusion impeded such recognition. Rather than a cohesive singular self, racialized society generated a split self.

Fast forward to French Algeria and Fanon. On the one hand, Fanon's experience was different from Du Bois and he wrote in a different context. Fanon traversed the African-Francophone world. The colonial context in which he wrote was not a context of racialized minorities in a metropole but rather of racialized peoples colonized by a foreign power – a situation of external colonialism rather than internal colonialism (or, put differently, of invasion and rule rather than displacement and internal domination). Because of this different situation of invasion, colonial conquest and then administrative colonialism, Fanon's social thought encompassed different matters than those articulated by Du Bois. It encompassed questions of anticolonial revolution in Africa and the role of peasantry. It dealt with the dilemmas of a foreign occupying power, questions of religious difference in colonial contexts and resource extraction from Africa. Du Bois would later write about colonialism in the African continent (and elsewhere) but mostly from a distance.

On the other hand, Fanon's social thought was strikingly similar to key components of Du Bois' thought. For example, Fanon offered a conceptualization of society that emphasized social fissures and fractures rather than order and integration. This was similar to Du Bois while also offering an alternative to dominant French social theory at the time. In Fanon's work, neither metropolitan French society nor colonial Algeria figure as organic cohesive wholes but rather as bifurcated. Society is divided into two distinct worlds, Fanon notes, those of the colonizer and those of the colonized, the settler and 'the native'. These are two distinct spaces, 'a Manichean world, a world divided up into compartments' (Fanon, 1968 [1961]: 43). 'The colonized world is a world divided in two', Fanon declares (1968 [1961]: 3). The only difference with Du Bois perhaps is that, for Du

Bois, the Black and white worlds are separated by a veil, for Fanon, the two worlds of colonial society are marked by a 'dividing line, the border' which is 'represented by the barracks and the police stations' – a line whose coercive and violent basis is much more transparent than in Du Bois' veil. But otherwise, the conceptualization of society is similar.

Fanon also theorized the subjectivity associated with this sort of social system in similar ways to Du Bois. As Du Bois argued that one of the effects of America's 'veil' upon the sense of self of African Americans was 'double-consciousness', Fanon wrote of the colonized's 'third person consciousness' emerging from colonial compartmentalization – a compartmentalization that reflected the hierarchical structure of empire itself. In this structure, subjects of the French empire, like Fanon, were inculcated with supposedly universal French ideals of *liberté*, *égalité* and *fraternité* but were not allowed to experience them on the basis of their race. The universal was denied to those rendered particular by racialization. The 'black man aims for the universal but on-screen his black essence, his black "nature" is kept intact' (Fanon, 1967 [1952]: 163). This produces a 'third person consciousness' that is unique to racialized subjects – a form of racial alienation whereby the racialized subject, by consistently being particularized on racial grounds, is forced to see themselves not as an 'I' but as a 'him' or 'her'. As Fanon says: 'I wanted to be a man, nothing but a man.' But alas, he was forced into his inferior position and consistently reminded of it. 'In the white world, the man of color encounters difficulties in the development of his bodily schema. Consciousness of the body is solely a negating activity. It is a third person consciousness' (1967 [1952]: 110).

Unlike Du Bois, Fanon was here contending primarily with Hegelian themes about self-consciousness, not with Mead's theory of the self. And his notion of third-person consciousness is not exactly the same as Du Bois' 'double-consciousness'. But the two concepts are nonetheless similar. Both speak to senses of the self that are fractured and incomplete due to the experience of compartmentalized, bifurcated societies wherein racialized subjects are not recognized as full citizens. Both refer to the subjectivity of racialized and subjugated peoples in modern society. And both are theorized first and foremost based upon direct experience. As Du Bois writes that he first noticed the veil as a child, when he was rejected by his white peers, Fanon similarly relates his initial experiences with racism. On the train to Paris, a white child exclaimed: 'Look, a Negro! Mama, see the Negro! I'm frightened!' The novel social concepts of both Du Bois and Fanon began with the experiences, concerns and problems of racialized subjects of empire.

The lesson? Du Bois' and Fanon's social thought mark both particularity *and* generality at once. They are particular in that they represent the specific dilemmas faced by different subjugated peoples. But they are general in that they share similarities based upon the shared social situations of those subjugated peoples. While Du Bois wrote about the dilemmas faced by African American minorities within the rising American empire, and while Fanon wrote in the context of French overseas colonialism, both of their theories embed the problematic of racialized exclusion in the context of the modern colonial empires. African Americans in the United States or Africans in the French Caribbean and Algeria: they were each exploited for their labour and denied the full rights and privileges of citizenship. Empire created shared experiential problems and similar socio-theoretical innovations across different contexts of colonial domination – from 'internal colonialism' impacting African Americans in the United States to the treatment of French colonial subjects within France's empire.

Given this shared situation, both Du Bois and Fanon confronted similar (though not identical) issues of racialized hierarchy, domination and subjectivity. The knowledge they generated was situated within this shared situation. Their concepts and ideas were birthed as they confronted and critiqued colonialism and the problematic of exclusion marking it. It is true that all knowledge is situated and local, hence particular in that limited sense. However, because the contexts in which Du Bois and Fanon wrote themselves shared certain sociostructural features of exclusion and hierarchy based upon social difference, so too did the concepts and their theorizations. This was made for anticolonial thought that was not parochial, particularistic or limited but also generalizable and potentially global.[9]

Conclusion

Anticolonial theory is useful for changing the landscape of social theory today, but not because it comes from a certain geographic location. Note that neither Du Bois nor Fanon's theories are just 'non-Western' or 'Southern' or 'indigenous'. They are not defined by their geography. They are rather defined by social position, social experience (a 'subaltern' experience of being subjected to colonialism) and their critiques of colonial, imperial and hence global structures (Go, 2016). What makes them useful and important for rethinking the sociological canon is not that they are from certain geographical locations but rather because they offer sustained critiques of colonialism and empire. They challenge the *imperiality* or the *imperial standpoint* of social theory, not the *geographic origins* of social theory. One can offer a 'non-Western' theory that is perfectly amenable to or justify Chinese or Arab imperialism. But one would be hard pressed to argue that the theories of Du Bois or Fanon would be easily supportive of imperialism anywhere.

This critique of empire is what anticolonial social theory is about. And this is one of the many reasons for why anticolonial social theory is necessary as well as potentially generalizable: it offers a critique not of 'the West' or the 'North' because of empire. Most of the world has been imperial in some form or colonized in some form. And both colonialism and imperialism continue in various guises. Russia, the Ottoman Empire, China, Japan have all been colonial empires based upon exclusions and hierarchies. And Russia, China or Japan might continue to do so today or in the future. All colonialisms generate exclusion; they are predicated upon it. Colonialisms everywhere depended and continue to depend upon a 'rule of colonial difference' that in turn forms the basis for social hierarchy, exploitation and exclusion from the presumed universals that colonizers purported to offer and yet monopolize. The basis of difference varies. In the US and European empires, the differences were largely about race, rooted in scientific racism. But in other contexts, including perhaps the Russian, Chinese and Japanese empires, the basis of difference might have been different. Ethnoracial or ethnic differences, cultural differences, or even religious differences have served as the 'rule' of the rule of colonial difference, exclusion and hierarchy in various contexts. Therefore, anticolonial thought, which by definition challenges these exclusions and hierarchies, will always have shared problematics that in turn lead to the development of a shared theoretical repertoire. Anticolonial thought can thus not only offer a true alternative to the imperial standpoint, it can also form the basis for general social theories – quite unlike those social theories whose worth is only measured by their geographical or geocultural origins.

Notes

[1] For helpful feedback, I thank the editors of this edited collection, the participants of the workshop 'Anti-Colonial Scholarship and Global Social Theory' at Linkoping University, Sweden (4–6 October 2023) and anonymous reviewers of the book volume.

[2] I further explore these ideas through a conference on 'anticolonial thought as social theory' with Anaheed Al-Hardan at the University of Chicago-Paris Center in 2022, that is forthcoming as an edited volume (Al-Hardan and Go, 2025).

[3] For the purposes of this chapter, I think of 'anticolonial' and 'anti-imperial' as functionally the same.

[4] This is not to flatten the social variety of the colonized. Colonized populations represented a variety of economic class positions, genders, sexual orientations, religious orientations, ethnicities and cultures. But standpoints emerge from relational positions not essential ones. And given their shared location in social, economic, political and ethnoracial global hierarchies created by empire, anticolonial thinkers shared certain similarities when compared to imperial elites living in the metropoles of England, the United States, Germany, France or other imperial states.

[5] I do not claim that these approaches are intrinsically essentialist – and indeed for Connell (2007), for instance, 'Southern' is not just geographical – but I do claim that they are too easily deployed as such when they do not clarify the standpoint and positionality of their proposed alternative canons.

[6] Indian sociology for the most part has long struggled with the hegemony of S.N. Srivinas who was hardly representative of an anticolonial standpoint. As Patel's work on Srivinas hints (Patel, 2005), he was more of an indigenous and nationalist sociologist whose thinking relied upon the classic exemplar of the imperial episteme: British anthropology. Is this the same thing as 'anticolonial' sociology? Patel even goes so far as to say that Srivinas and

much of Indian sociology is itself an effect of colonial modernity that reproduces rather than challenges 'the language of colonialism' (Patel, 2021: 37).

7   I am not assuming that sociostructural position within a global hierarchy automatically confers an anticolonial standpoint. Drawing from post-positivist feminist scholars, I conceive of the anticolonial standpoint as an accomplishment that *conveys* or *expresses* the experience of subaltern colonial domination and exploitation in a certain conceptual language (wherein subalternity is the relational sociostructural position). This means that any individual knowledge producer articulating an anticolonial standpoint need not be themselves subaltern, nor do all subaltern positions automatically conference an anticolonial standpoint.

8   As I stated, Ibn Khaldun's theory is 'non-Western' but that does not, in itself, make it anticolonial or anti-imperial.

9   The other ways in which anticolonial thought – exactly because its key object of critique is colonialism and all of its correlates – is more generalizable than the particular site of colonialism itself. First, colonialism's effects linger. Even though formal colonialism has dissipated, despite some persistent pockets, a vast body of research shows that the legacies of empire remain throughout social systems. Modern colonialism is a social force that is not historically parochial, even if it is historically specific. Second, colonialism did not only impact the colonized. As both Du Bois and Fanon noted, and as other anticolonial thinkers like Aimé Césaire pointed out, colonialism impacted the colonizer and the colonized, the metropole and the colony.

References

Akiwowo, A. (1986) Contributions to the sociology of knowledge from an African oral poetry, *International Sociology*, 1(4): 343–58.

Akiwowo, A. (1999) Indigenous sociologies: Extending the scope of the argument, *International Sociology*, 14(2): 115–38.

Alatas, S.F. (2003) Academic dependency and the global division of labor in the social sciences, *Current Sociology*, 51(6): 599–613.

Alatas, S.F. (2006) *Alternative Discourses in Asian Social Science: Responses to Eurocentrism*, SAGE.

Al-Hardan, A. and Go, J. (2025) *Anticolonialism and Social Thought*, Duke University Press.

Banzon Bautista, M.C.R. (2000) The social sciences in the Philippines: Reflections on trends and developments, *Philippine Studies*, 48(2): 175–208.

Bhambra, G. (2014) *Connected Sociologies*, Bloomsbury.

Boatcâ, M. (2013) From the standpoint of Germanism: A postcolonial critique of Weber's theory of race and ethnicity, *Political Power and Social Theory*, 24: 55–80.

Boatcâ, M., Costa, S. and Rodríguez, E.G. (2010) Decolonizing European sociology: Different paths towards a pending project, in E.G. Rodríguez, M. Boatcâ and S. Costa (eds) *Decolonizing European Sociology: Transdisciplinary Approaches*, Ashgate, pp 1–10.

Borch, C. (2012) *The Politics of Crowds: An Alternative History of Sociology*, Cambridge University Press.

Breslau, D. (2007) The American Spencerians: Theorizing a new science, in C. Calhoun (ed) *Sociology in America: A History*, University of Chicago Press, pp 39–62.

Burawoy, M. (2014) Preface, in W. Keim, E. Çelik, C. Ersche and V. Wöhrer (eds) *Global Knowledge Production in the Social Sciences*, Ashgate, pp xiii–xvii.

Collins, P.H. (1997) Comment on Hekman's Truth and method: Feminist standpoint theory revisited: Where's the power?, *Signs* 22: 375–81.

Connell, R. (1997) Why is classical theory classical?, *American Journal of Sociology*, 102(6): 1511–57.

Connell, R. (2007) *Southern Theory*, Polity.

Connell, R. (2019) *The Good University*, Books.

Du Bois, W.E.B. (2007 [1903]) *The Souls of Black Folk*, Oxford University Press.

Fanon, F. (1967 [1952]) *Black Skin, White Masks*, Grove Press.

Fanon, F. (1968 [1961]) *The Wretched of the Earth*, Grove Press.

Getachew, A. and Mantena, K. (2021) Anticolonialism and the decolonization of political theory, *Critical Times*, 4(3): 359–88.

Giere, R. (2006) *Scientific Perspectivism*, University of Chicago Press.

Gilman, N. (2003) *Mandarins of the Future: Modernization Theory in Cold War America*, The Johns Hopkins University Press.

Go, J. (2009) The 'new' sociology of empire and colonialism, *Sociology Compass*, 3(5): 775–88.

Go, J. (2013) Sociology's imperial unconscious: The emergence of American sociology in the context of empire, in G. Steinmetz (ed) *Sociology and Empire*, Duke University Press, pp 83–105.

Go, J. (2016) *Postcolonial Thought and Social Theory*, Oxford University Press.

Go, J. (2020) Race, empire and epistemic exclusion: Or the structures of sociological thought, *Sociological Theory*, 38(2): 79–100.

Go, J. (2023a) Anticolonial thought, the sociological imagination, and social science: A reply to critics, *British Journal of Sociology*, 74(3): 345–59.

Go, J. (2023b) Thinking against empire: Anticolonial thought as social theory, *British Journal of Sociology*, 74(3): 279–93.

Go, J. (2024) Towards an alternative canon? Particularity and generality across 'black' and 'red' social theory, in E. Macé (ed) *Toward a Non-Hegemonic World Sociology*, Rowman & Littlefield, pp 141–66.

Go, J. and Watson, J. (2019) Anticolonial nationalism: From imagined communities to colonial conflict, *European Journal of Sociology*, 60(1): 31–68.

Goebel, M. (2015) *Anti-Imperial Metropolis*, Cambridge University Press.

Harding, S. (ed) (2004) *The Feminist Standpoint Theory Reader*, Routledge.

Jung, M.-K. (2009) The racial unconcious of assimilation theory, *Du Bois Review*, 2: 375–95.

Khaldun, I. (2015) *The Muqaddimah*, Princeton University Press.

Krause, M. (2021) *Model Cases: On Canonical Research Objects and Sites*, University of Chicago Press.

Lukács, G. (1971) *History and Class Consciousness*, MIT Press.

Macey, D. (2010) 'I am my own foundation': Frantz Fanon as a source of continued political embarrassment, *Theory, Culture & Society*, 27(7–8): 33–51.

Mannheim, K. (1936) *Ideology and Utopia*, K. Paul, Trench, Truber & Co.

Matera, M. (2015) *Black London: The Imperial Metropolis and Decolonization in the Twentieth Century*, University of California Press.

Mignolo, W. (2011) *The Darker Side of Western Modernity*, Duke University Press.

Owens, P. (2015) *Economy of Force: Counterinsurgency and the Historical Rise of the Social*, Cambridge University Press.

Parsons, T. (1951) *The Social System*, The Free Press.

Patel, S. (2005) On Srinivas's 'Sociology', *Sociological Bulletin* 54, no. 1 (2005): 101–11.

Patel, S. (2010) *The ISA Handbook of Diverse Sociological Traditions*, SAGE.

Patel, S. (2021) Nationalist ideas and the colonial episteme: The antinomies structuring sociological traditions of India, *Journal of Historical Sociology*, 34: 28–40.

Patel, S. (2023) Anti-colonial thought and global social theory, *Frontiers in Sociology*, 8: 1143776. doi: 10.3389/fsoc.2023.1143776

Quijano, A. (2000) Coloniality of power, Eurocentrism and Latin America, *Nepantla: Views from South*, 1: 533–80.

Said, E. (1979) *Orientalism*, Vintage Books.

Said, E. (1995) Orientalism: An afterword, *Raritan*, 95(4): 32–59.

Smith, D.E. (1997) From the margins: women's standpoint as a method of inquiry in the social sciences, *Gender, Technology and Development*, 1(1): 113–35.

Sousa Santos, B. (2014) *Epistemologies of the South*, Paradigm Publishers.

Steinmetz, G. (2005) Scientific authority and the transition to post-Fordism: The plausibility of positivism in U.S. sciology since 1945, in G. Steinmetz (ed) *The Politics of Method in the Human Sciences*, Duke University Press, pp 275–325.

Wylie, A. (2003) Why standpoint matters, in R. Figueroa and S. Harding (eds) *Science and Other Cultures*, Routledge, pp 26–48.

Young, R. (2001) *Postcolonialism: An Historical Introduction*, Blackwell Publishing.

5

Anticolonial Scholarship and the Politics of Location: Can Social Theory be Truly Democratic *and* Truly Global?

Satish Deshpande

Introduction

At its most general level, 'anticolonial scholarship' is any kind of scholarship that challenges unjust intellectual domination, particularly the kind that is exercised by the Global North over the rest of the world. At the same time, like any scholarship, anticolonial scholarship too must ground itself in some kind of *theory*. However, in the real world of scholarship – the academic world – the Global North tends to dominate and monopolize the production of any theory that can claim to be global, including anticolonial theory. Even when such theories are born in the Global South, as soon as they acquire a global reputation they (and their producers) tend to drift towards the North, and are eventually housed in some enclave of the Western/Northern academy. This produces a peculiar predicament where anticolonial theory, which defines itself as a critique of the contemporary avatars of colonial domination, depends for its sustenance on the very regime(s) that it seeks to critique.

This is the problem that I want to describe. A description is all that can be attempted today, since effective solutions are yet to be imagined.

But even a description poses difficult challenges. To begin with, many would question whether the predicament described, admittedly in too terse and too abstract a fashion, constitutes a 'problem' at all. How does it matter *where* a theory is produced, they would ask; what matters is what it does and how well it does it. Some would cast doubt on the empirical claims made;

it is not true that *all* the centres of theory production (or its producers) are located in the North, they would say – look at theory X or theorist Y that are indeed located in the Global South. Others would see this as an *old* problem, or as a special case of a more general predicament that is at least as old as modern/Western social science: isn't this, they would ask, the fate of a so-called 'liberal academy' anywhere – dependence on the very power that it wishes to 'speak truth' to? Finally, there are those who would go on the offensive: any attempt to consecrate the 'where' (and the 'who') of social theory, they would insist, undermines the very idea of social science and surrenders to the dangerous essentialism of 'identity politics'.

I will try to address these and related objections on the way to my destination, which is an enabling description of why 'location' matters, and *should* matter, for anticolonial theory, despite – or perhaps even because of – the well-known dangers of essentialist perspectives. What I am referring to as 'location' here is a collection of relationships that together situate a theory or theorist in a self-reflexive manner and allow her/him/they/it to be connected in a concrete, transparent and accountable manner to an intellectual project. This assemblage of relationships is perhaps best described by the phrase 'the politics of location', which is introduced in the first section. The second section provides reasons why a politics of location is particularly relevant for, indeed even central to, the broad enterprise of anticolonial theory in its evolving avatars and contemporary variants. The focus here is on the concentration of intellectual resources and power in the Global North and the use of terms like 'decolonizing' or 'colonial mindset' in unanticipated and dangerous ways for ends that are antithetical to the liberal and progressive goals of anticolonial theory. The third section summarizes some implications of the preceding argument. Finally, the conclusion points to the mismatch between the material conditions for the production of theory and the requirements for a legitimate and defensible idea of 'global theory' that is compatible with the implicit/explicit objectives of anticolonial theory taken as a whole, a mismatch highlighted in the academic consequences of the continuing genocide by the Israeli state in Palestine.

A brief history of the politics of location

The phrase 'politics of location' first gained traction in the 1980s in feminist and postcolonial theory.[1] As used in these contexts, the word 'location' is an umbrella term that includes at least three distinct elements: a geographical place (such as a country or a region); an identity (such as race, gender, religious affiliation, and so on); and a standpoint, which is a perspective or worldview shaped by, but not fixed or determined by, the other two aspects. An awareness of 'location' in this sense emerges from the 'interrogation of "the West" as an institutional site of enunciation' (John, 1996: 26). This is a site where the postcolonial (or more generally, the non-Western) intellectual subject seems to disappear in her/his specificity, mimicking at least in part the place-less universality of the white male Western intellectual. The politics of location is thus born of a 'struggle for accountability' (Rich, 1986: 211), the renewed effort to name one's positionality among multiple intersecting axes of power and inequality. One's location is thus sought to be defined not only in terms of the particular position from where one speaks and acts, but also with reference to a 'place of accountability' – the communities or interests to whom an intellectual chooses to be answerable (John, 1996: 110).

As feminism evolved from a primarily political movement into a broader epistemological perspective that laid claim to being a legitimate source of knowledge, it introduced a radically new conception of method into the academy. The ethics of feminist politics, when transplanted onto the scholarly world, gave rise to the demand that the framework of research include the socio-cultural location of the researcher herself. This was in sharp contrast to the conventional (male-dominated) traditions of science, where the (usually male) researcher routinely performed, in a phrase made famous by Donna Haraway (1988: 581), the 'god trick of seeing everything from nowhere'. In refusing the 'god trick', feminist scholars insisted that the vantage point of the researcher had a bearing on what she was able to see and how she interpreted what she saw. This was, after all, the epiphanic origin of feminism – the realization that the world, when seen through female eyes, looked very different than it did from the supposedly universal viewpoint of 'Man'. Having already figured out that ideals like 'perfect objectivity' or 'pure scientific neutrality' were not only impossible to attain, but also potential masks for various forms of power, feminist scholars advocated the opposite move of explicitly including the researcher's location as a mandatory component of a truly *scientific* research methodology (Harding, 1986).

Questions of location had a special resonance in postcolonial studies where both scholars and subject matter were inevitably enmeshed in shifting networks of unequal global relationships. In a collection of essays written in the 1980s which retrospectively became one of its manifesto texts, Homi Bhabha pointed out that the 'post' prefix used to designate the late 20th-century present (postmodern, postcolonial) pointed to a beyond that 'is neither a new horizon, nor a leaving behind of the past' (Bhabha, 1994: 2). Rather, it inaugurated a historically unprecedented kind of experience:

> The move away from the singularities of 'class' or 'gender' as primary conceptual and organizational categories, has resulted in *an awareness of the subject positions – of race, gender, generation, institutional location, geopolitical locale, sexual orientation – that inhabit any claim to identity in the modern world*. What is theoretically innovative, and politically crucial, is

> the need to think beyond narratives of originary and initial subjectivities and to focus on those moments or processes that are produced in the articulation of cultural differences. (Bhabha, 1994: 2, emphasis added)

Apart from the fact that it emerged from an evolutionary process that began in the newly postcolonial, Cold War world that was pushed in new directions by second wave feminism and postcolonial theory (itself shaped by poststructuralism and neo-Marxism), what precisely was *theoretically* new about the politics of location? The short answer is that the politics of location combined and extended prior theoretical perspectives to the point where something recognizably different emerged – or at least it can retrospectively be seen as having done that.

The two most proximate theoretical initiatives that are extended by the politics of location are those of Pierre Bourdieu on the imperative for sociology/social anthropology to be reflexive, and Talal Asad's influential interventions explicitly highlighting the symbiotic relationship between British functional social anthropology and colonialism. For instance, in his seminal edited volume, *Anthropology and the Colonial Encounter*, Asad voices a complaint:

> It is not a matter of dispute that social anthropology emerged as a distinctive discipline at the beginning of the colonial era, that it became a flourishing academic· profession towards its close, or that throughout this period its efforts were devoted to a description and analysis – carried out by Europeans, for a European audience – of non-European societies dominated by European power. And yet there is a strange reluctance on the part of most professional anthropologists to consider seriously the power structure within which their discipline has taken shape. (Asad, 1973: 14–15)

This complaint and the subsequent efforts that Asad and others undertook to confront the existential fact that anthropology is rooted not only in 'the ideas and ideals of the Enlightenment' but also 'in an unequal power encounter between the West and the Third World which goes back to the emergence of bourgeois Europe, an encounter in which colonialism is merely one historical moment' (Asad, 1973: 16), could be seen (in retrospect) as the birth of a politics of location in the discipline of social anthropology.

Talal Asad's complaint can itself be seen – arguably – as a historically and politically specific case of a more general complaint that Pierre Bourdieu was raising at around the same time[2] about the epistemological foundations of the disciplines of sociology and social anthropology. In his classic work, *Outline of a Theory of Practice*, Bourdieu points to 'the practical privilege in which all scientific activity arises' and complains that, when this privilege is 'unrecognised as privilege, it leads to an implicit theory of practice' that neglects 'the social conditions in which science is possible' (Bourdieu, 1977: 1). This leads him to an important insight on the epistemological frame of anthropology:

> Knowledge does not merely depend ... on the particular standpoint an observer 'situated in space and time' takes up on the object. The 'knowing subject' ... inflicts on practice a much more fundamental and pernicious alteration. ... [I]n taking up a point of view on the action, withdrawing from it in order to observe it from above and from a distance, he constitutes practical activity as an *object of observation and analysis*, a *representation*. (Bourdieu, 1977: 2, emphasis original)

At the risk of oversimplification, using Bourdieu and Asad as exemplars of broader trends, we could see the reflexive turn (Bourdieu) as the most abstract origin of an evolutionary process that eventually arrives, via a newly awakened sensitivity to colonialism and its impact on knowledge production (Asad), at the politics of location. Bourdieu's 'observer' or 'knowing subject' is noticeably unmarked – though a male pronoun is used, this is a subject without any concrete identifiers, in the classic European Enlightenment tradition of Western 'Man' who claims to subsume all of humanity within himself. Interestingly, Bourdieu's complaint is a strictly epistemological one which, despite his being embedded in the field of 'culture', neither offers, nor does it seem to feel the need for, any socio-cultural identifiers. A theoretically similar reflexive gaze is deployed by Asad to ask questions about the *location* of anthropology as a discipline, questions that seek to interrogate its epistemological claims by making explicit its socio-political conditions of possibility. We can see that when reflexivity chooses (and is able) to 'see' colonialism, it has become more grounded and less abstract – the European Enlightenment figure of 'Man' can no longer be the taken-for-granted reference point. However, this sensitivity to location (in the sense of taking seriously the constitutive impact of colonialism on anthropology) still remains at the level of a discipline – it is yet to consider (with the partial exception of race) the further levels of concreteness that are listed by Bhabha, namely 'gender, generation, institutional location, geopolitical locale, sexual orientation'. Bhabha's list is, of course, indicative and not intended to be a definitive one, but it is sufficient for my purpose here, which is to interpret the politics of location as an extension and deepening of prior tendencies in social theory.[3]

There are two further points to note about the politics of location before I go on to discuss its relationship to anticolonial theory. The first has to do with its 'built-in' intersectionality. Originating at a time when the grand identities of the early 20th century – gender, race and class – were proving to be inadequate to address contemporary concerns and the so-called new social movements that emerged in the post-1960s context, the politics of location could not but be intersectional. Its two main sources – feminism and postcolonial theory – had also emerged as a response to the demands for recognition of distinct groups and identities within the older categories – gay, lesbian, queer and, later, transgender, for example, or the newly salient intersections of race and class, race and nationality and so on. In the late 20th century, it was amply clear that no identity could remain singular or one-dimensional, regardless of the intentions of the bearers of identity. Given that identity is also irreducibly relational – it is partly in the eyes of the beholder – intersectionality is now a taken-for-granted aspect of the politics of location.

The second, even more consequential though less obvious, aspect of the politics of location is that it is accompanied by the recognition that no identity – even an intersectional one – can automatically produce an authentic politics. In other words, the political stance taken by individuals or groups cannot be derived in a deterministic fashion from the mere fact of the identities they bear. This is well captured in Stuart Hall's felicitous phrase 'without guarantees' – the politics of location recognizes that location cannot guarantee a particular political-ethical stance (Hall, 1986). All those who live in the Global South, for example, cannot – by virtue of that fact alone – be said to hold particular political views. Women may not necessarily endorse feminist beliefs, working-class people may have deeply right-wing views and so on, just as bourgeois individuals may espouse communist beliefs. In short, location cannot become an epistemology, guaranteed to produce one and only one kind of knowledge or beliefs. This is important to point out because the politics of location carries with it, as a sort of 'occupational hazard', the risk of essentializing specific aspects of identities or positioning.

Let me now end this section with two examples that I hope will begin to clarify the ways in which the politics of location is crucial for any variety of anticolonial theory. These are deliberately chosen from timepoints that are more than three decades, or a generation, apart.

The first example is that of an early and particularly productive instance of engagement with the politics of location in the larger context of postcolonial cultural studies. This was a conference on 'Predicaments of Theory' organized by the Centre for Cultural Studies at the University of California, Santa Cruz in 1989, which resulted in a special issue of the journal *Inscriptions* (1989) titled *Traveling Theories, Traveling Theorists*.[4] The Preface to this volume lists the questions that the conference hoped to address:

> How can we conceive of the complex predicaments of theories and theorists both in terms of location (in travel and intercultural translation) and in terms of the accountability and self-positioning of the theorist?

What conditions govern the export and import of theories in changing post- and neo-colonial situations? What are the crucial inequalities of power and experience? How do theorists ('cosmopolitan,' 'postcolonial,' 'postmodern,' 'engaged,' etc.) negotiate the asymmetries, discrepancies in their travel among different audiences, languages, histories? What counts as 'theory' in specific traditions? What are its 'proper' idioms? Who counts as a 'theorist?' (Clifford and Dhareshwar, 1989: v)

Three papers presented at the conference (and included in the volume cited) are especially important to mention here as insightful and precocious attempts to get at the problem of location in relation to theoretical perspectives that seek to challenge colonial and/or neo-colonial worldviews. Together, these essays amply justify the observation made in the preface that the '[p]redicaments of theory have often presented themselves as issues of location' (Clifford and Dhareshwar, 1989: vi).[5] Mary E. John (1989) describes the discrepant dislocations of the postcolonial feminist scholar in the West, who may be privileged in her home society, but is placed in a relatively subaltern position in the host society, and must act as both a native informant and an anthropologist. As a Western-trained Jamaican who did fieldwork in Sri Lanka, David Scott (1989) reflects on the peculiar predicaments of the postcolonial anthropologist who chooses to study an ex-colonial society other than his own. And Vivek Dhareshwar 'attempts a negotiation between metropolitan theories and postcolonial narratives' (Dhareshwar, 1989: 136) that might produce useful descriptions of postcolonial intellectual journeys to the West and eventual return to non-Western locations.

Each of these papers is attempting to grapple with specific problems or predicaments highlighted by location. John, for example, is trying to figure out the politically and ethically appropriate response that a non-white, third world woman scholar should make when she is unthinkingly equated and compared to women scholars of colour who are citizens of the United States but lack the cultural capital that she herself has acquired, ironically because of being educated as a privileged upper caste woman in an ex-colony. Scott is wondering whether and in what ways the 'concept' of anthropology – identified as a 'white' discipline – changes when the practitioner, the anthropologist, is Black and is studying a non-white people who see him as, so to speak, a 'strange' stranger, a person who is neither a native nor a white man. Dhareshwar is grappling with the existential predicament of the ex-colonial scholar who, once interpellated by metropolitan theory but now able to take a critical view of it, must nevertheless map the possibility of a return to the ex-colony without giving up the difference that separates him from the metropolis but also without erasing the experience of the journey.

If their distance in time – after all, this was before most of the theoretical tendencies that are extant now, like the decolonial perspective or anticolonial theory had emerged – makes these examples hard to relate to, my second example is taken from a 2023 essay. Gustavo Lins Ribeiro, the (partly) US-trained Brazilian anthropologist now working in Mexico, has long been concerned with questions of global theory in and from the South. In an essay titled 'From decolonizing knowledge to postimperialism: A Latin American perspective' published in the *American Ethnologist* (Ribeiro, 2023), he is trying to envision 'postimperialism as a framework that aims to deimperialize the world, overcoming the hierarchical positions between hegemonic and nonhegemonic anthropologies'.

What interests me here is his use of the term 'positionality'. Ribeiro is claiming that his 'Latin American positionality is especially productive to think about postimperialism', and he provides explicit reasons why this is so (Ribeiro, 2023: 2): Latin America is the earliest and the largest settler-colony of the world; the majority of its citizens are Christians, speak European languages and see themselves as part of the West; metropolitan dominance ended long ago and there is only a thin memory of it today; US imperial might has been exercised on this region since the 19th century; and contemporary Latin America is the area where the United States' 'invisible postwar imperialism' holds sway. The reader may or may not agree with Ribeiro that Latin America is a specially well-suited site for theorizing postimperialism, but my point is that what Ribeiro terms 'positionality' is basically location, and what he is trying to do is to foreground it and to connect it to the content of his work. Even if positionality is here restricted to the geopolitical dimensions of location, it is the manner of its placement in the argument that I wish to highlight.

This is what I believe a politics of location should be doing – it should explicitly acknowledge one's location, and try to work out its implications for the intellectual content of the work being done. Conversely, when this is *not* done, something important is being left out of the account, something that may very well be shaping content. After all, this was precisely what the nationalists of the early 20th century – the first explicit practitioners of anticolonial theory – were accusing colonial theory of. Their claim was that the colonists' location coloured the knowledge-claims they made, so that what was asserted to be universal and 'place-less' was in fact firmly located in the geopolitical contexts of the colonists and their (intellectual and material) interests. Colonial knowledge systems were predicated on a metropolitan location, and could assert their supposed universality only by eliding this location. It is worth reiterating that the need to declare location remains an imperative regardless of the fact that location offers no guarantees – the claims made (from any location) will always need to be evaluated for their truth value. I am not arguing for or against some particular location (like the South or the North, or a public or private academic institution, for example); rather, I am arguing that explicitly marking one's location and relating it to one's project (as best as one can) should be an imperative for social scientists in the 21st century.

The uses of a politics of location (without guarantees) for anticolonial theory

There are two main sites, or grounds, where the salience of the politics of location becomes visible: one is the layered field of *material and social inequalities* and the other is the contentious arena of *divergent political projects*. This is a contradictory commonality because what is shared – the salience of the politics of location – becomes the basis for the emergence of differences and incompatibilities. Let me explain.

The politics of location unmasks material and social inequalities

We still suffer, to some extent, from the hangover of the intoxicating 20th-century quarter-truth that knowledge, especially 'pure' or disinterested knowledge, is somehow outside and above the world of material wealth and resources. Even if we are aware today that knowledge production is as much of an industry as the production of automobiles or IT services, the implications of this awareness are not worked through. The dependence on material resources – equipment, personnel, long-term investments in the raw materials of knowledge production – is readily visible in the science, technology, engineering and mathematics fields, but is equally important today in the social sciences and humanities and, arguably, even in the arts.

The industrial political economy of knowledge production is a major feature of 'location'. When, along with engaging with the content of knowledge, we begin to ask questions about its producers – Who is speaking? What sort of institutional context are they speaking from? What kind of resources do they command? and so on – rifts and ruptures become visible within the intellectual field. It is hardly surprising that the inequalities that structure society at large should structure academia as well. What is unexpected, however, is that these inequalities have not changed significantly in the era of the internet and digital publication, often hailed as enabling the democratization of knowledge.

For example, a comparison of the distribution of social science journals by world regions in the years 2000 and 2018 shows that not much has changed in terms of the overwhelming dominance of the Global North, specifically Western Europe and North America. The share of these two regions of all journals listed in the Scimago Journal and Country Ranks[6] went from 94 per cent (in 2000) to 85 per cent (in 2018). This may seem to show a decline in dominance, but the real story is in the Q1 journals list, that is, journals in the top quarter of the journal rankings. In this elite group, Western Europe and North America have together maintained a near monopoly, their combined share going from 99 per cent to 98 per cent between 2000 and 2018. The stark way of stating this inequality is to say that, as late as the year 2018, the *combined share* of Asia, Africa, Latin America, Eastern Europe, the Middle East and Oceania of journals in the top quarter of the Scimago list amounted to *less than 2 per cent!* The only silver lining in this very dark cloud is the increase in the Global South's share of all journals more than doubled (though starting from a very low number) from about 6 per cent in 2000 to about 15 per cent in 2018 (Demeter, 2020: 91).[7]

The author of these estimates, the Hungarian communications scholar Márton Demeter, concludes that '[a]lthough the number of journals has increased dramatically and the share of the periphery as a whole has increased, in the elite field – among Q1-ranked journals, in the top quartile – the center's exclusive share has remained the same over the last 20 years'. Moreover, in the social sciences, the pattern of 'elitist exclusion is perhaps even more dramatic, as no peripheral region has been able to raise its share of Q1-ranked Scopus-indexed journals over 1% in the past two decades' (Demeter, 2020: 91). While more refined analysis is needed, the overall point is well taken – the massive explosion in academic publishing over the past two decades has done little to reduce inter-regional inequalities in academic publishing.[8]

Language is another axis of deep inequalities. Consider the suggestive 'visualisation of global scholarly publishing' offered by researchers Kirsten Bell and David Mills in the *LSE Impact* blog (Bell and Mills, 2020).[9] Using a cartographic analogy, they argue that 'much like the early-modern cartographic representations of the globe, with their civilized European centre and dangerous uncharted peripheries, the inequalities embedded in scholarly publishing have been similarly naturalised'. Their comparative chart (not reproduced here for technical reasons) of global academic publications (essentially, the number of journals including both print and digital versions) in English and 'Other Languages', shows the overwhelming dominance of English in global knowledge production. English dwarfs all other languages combined in indexed journals. The dominant and well-known 'mainstream' of academic publishing is overwhelmingly in the English language, with other languages being mostly *terra incognita* – unknown territory. Bell and Mills say that they wanted to 'highlight how little we know about non-English scholarly production, and how our views of the global landscape are skewed by the dominant databases ... especially Web of Science and Scopus'. Their subsequent finding is worth quoting at length:

> When we attempted to go beyond the English-language journals, our simultaneous reliance on indexes and ignorance of those outside of

English-language contexts (except where hosted by Web of Science) became abundantly clear. Thus, the map quickly became highly speculative, hindered by our attempts to find non-English journal databases via English-language Google searches, which mostly directed us to English-language journals focusing on non-English regions and languages (given the growing centrality of Google to academic research, the problem is clearly one of databases the whole way down). Consequently, the dotted circles signal whole 'unknown' publishing continents: non-indexed publications, non-English journals, and non-mainstream journals. (Bell and Mills, 2020)[10]

Comparable illustrative evidence could be presented on academic appointments, on the funding of academic institutions in different regions of the world, and so on, but the point should be clear enough by now.[11] And we haven't even begun talking about the intangibles – the immense social and cultural capital that Western/Northern institutions and scholars have accumulated over the past two centuries as a direct dividend flowing from the colonial-imperial power and wealth of the society and economy they are embedded in.[12]

The institutionalized apparatus of contemporary knowledge production is a product of these deep inequalities, and it in turn reproduces them. This *matters* – even the production of anticolonial knowledge is shaped by inequalities. Material inequities are epistemologically consequential, even if they are not exhaustive or always-and-fully-determining causes. Economic, social and cultural capital exerts an inexorable gravitational pull on the sites and agents of intellectual production. A list of the biggest names in anticolonial theory would show that the majority – and in recent times, the vast majority – are located in Western institutions, and that those who were not tend to belong to the generation born before 1950. In itself this is not exceptional – the same is likely to be true for most fields of knowledge. But a field founded as a challenge to inequalities cannot be blind to them in its own house.[13]

The politics of location exposes conflicting goals

One of the 'founding problems' (that is, problems built into the very foundations) of anticolonial theory is that it defines itself negatively. Perhaps this is a problem common to all perspectives that claim (or acquire) the prefix 'anti', but in the specific case of anticolonial theory it serves as a special source of vulnerability. Because it does not insist on an explicit prior statement of what it is *for*, anticolonial perspectives leave the door open for their recruitment to widely divergent – even diametrically opposed – political projects and social agendas.

A case in point is the trending term 'decolonization'. This term is proliferating in public discourse as it is deployed as an alibi for the pursuit of a wide range of sectarian agendas.[14] In contemporary India, for example, decolonization is the preferred term used by the current regime to justify a variety of government-backed or legislated 'reforms' ranging from changing names of streets and towns to changing curricula in schools, colleges and universities. The term can be used for measures designed to reverse egalitarian and secular laws and conventions in keeping with a right-wing Hindu-centric ideology. The key moves here involve a selective invocation of history, with a heavy reliance on social media to disseminate and amplify popular prejudices. In fact, in an ex-colonial context where the postcolonial state had thus far been reasonably liberal and progressive (at least formally and publicly), 'decolonization' is being used as licence to dismantle neutral and non-discriminatory structures in favour of majoritarian measures designed to stoke Hindu pride and legitimize prejudice against minorities and lower castes.

The invocation of broadly anticolonial ideas and insights as the intellectual-ethical grounds for profoundly illiberal projects is such a pervasive phenomenon today that it requires its own full treatment. Here I will only briefly mention some points on this broad spectrum that have gained prominence in contemporary India, the context that I am writing from and am most familiar with. The three points, or sites, I have in mind can be provisionally labelled as theory (for want of a better word), pedagogy, and policy.

Theory

The Hindu right-wing has had a strong on-the-ground presence but no significant theorist or scholar who could carry credibility as a modern academic or public intellectual, at least not in the English-based segment which has dominated social science since independence.[15] There have been (and still are) many serious scholars attracted to indigenous thought and ideas, but their stance has proved too mild and lukewarm for the aggressive agendas of contemporary Hindutva. Serious efforts are on to remedy this lack in the Modi era, with vigorous state support and the backing of a formidable social media apparatus. One name that has emerged in this context is that of J. Sai Deepak, a lawyer who has attained celebrity status through his role in cases important to the Hindu right wing. Deepak has authored a book, announced as the first volume of a trilogy, titled *India that is Bharat: Coloniality, Civilisation, Constitution* (Deepak, 2021) that explicitly invokes anticolonial theory, especially the decoloniality perspective.[16] He quotes extensively from Walter Mignolo (who also wrote a laudatory blurb for the book, but later retracted it after protests) and other scholars like

Anibal Quijano, Enrique Dussel, Ramon Grosfoguel, Sylvia Winter, Nelson Maldonado-Torres and others. The ultimate aim (of the proposed trilogy) seems to be a radical overhaul of the Indian constitution to undo the damage caused by 'colonializing reforms'. The conclusion to this first volume of the forthcoming trilogy expresses the

> fervent hope ... that readers would, at the very least, become aware of their own preconceived notions about Bharat brought about by unconscious and conscious coloniality before holding forth on the need for 'reform' or the virtues of 'secularism'. ... Hopefully, some day transformative constitutionalism will acquire a decolonial hue in Bharat, thereby strengthening indigeneity instead of shaming and silencing it through the unending and secularised Protestant project of 'reform'. (Deepak, 2021: 374)[17]

Pedagogy

There have been recurring and increasingly systematic efforts to change prescribed curricula at all levels of education to reflect the present regime's Hindu-majoritarian version of indigenous Indian thought. High level panels were formed in 2023 for the express purpose of integrating 'Indian Knowledge Systems' into the school curriculum by revising textbooks.[18] This sounds harmless and even desirable at first glance, but the specific changes brought about have revealed the actual agenda. Passages to do with caste discrimination or communal riots, the assassination of Mahatma Gandhi by a person associated with Hindu right-wing organizations, and discussions of authoritarianism (including of Indira Gandhi's imposition of Emergency in 1975) have been purged. At the college level, texts considered 'controversial' from a Hindu right-wing perspective have been removed, and there is an overall attempt to promote an uncritical, exclusively celebratory and triumphalist view of ancient Indian culture and civilization, subjects which have been taught for a long time. 'Decolonization' is offered as a general justification for these moves, though indigenization is also emphasized.

Policy

This is the extreme end of the spectrum, and may not involve the explicit invocation of decolonization, but is animated by the same spirit, this time expressed as national pride. Ever since the Modi regime came to power at the national level, it has attempted to discourage, forbid and even suppress social statistics that highlight problems of the Indian economy or society, such as poverty, unemployment, lack of growth, malnutrition and so on. The methodology used to calculate gross domestic product was arbitrarily changed because the old methods showed a drop in the growth rate; unemployment statistics, showing that it had reached unprecedented levels, were suppressed and then the data collection machinery was centralized and regulated; the demographic data collected through the National Family Health Survey was sought to be questioned and withdrawn; and attempts have been made to 'revise' or 'reinterpret' data on anaemia among women and stunting and wasting among children. Apart from these attempts to control the state's own statistical infrastructure, the government and government-allied experts have tried to question and reject the findings of international agencies that show India in a poor light. These include the World Health Organization, and recently, the International Labour Organization. A campaign is on to reject 'Western' standards (of stunting in children, for example) and to replace them with 'indigenous' ones which will present a more favourable view of India.[19] Independent researchers, activists and experts worry that lowered standards will be used to further reduce state expenditure on social services in health and education, which would have a disastrous impact on the poor and vulnerable sections of the population.

Argument and implications

My purpose in mentioning these instances of the conscription of anticolonial theory to further ends that are antithetical to its own emancipatory intent (in the third section) is not to suggest that the theory or theorists are somehow at fault. Ultimately, no theory can predict or control the uses to which it might be put, even if appropriation can be made more or less difficult. My point is that theories – and theorists – need to be *located* with reference to things outside the theory itself, and then this location has to be *politicized*, that is to say connected to an *ethics* that is transparent and open to contestation.

Challenges to a theory – any theory, including anticolonial theory – may be based on four kinds of argument.[20] First is an argument about the correctness of the theory. This may take the form of a claim that the theory does not correctly (truthfully, accurately) explain or describe the phenomenon it studies. The location of the theory (or theorists associated with it) may or may not be relevant for this argument.

Cases where location (or some aspect following from location) is a necessary component of the challenge to the theory lead to the second type of argument. This type of argument does not (necessarily) contest the correctness of the theory, but claims that some aspect of its location gives rise to an external reason (that is, outside the content of the theory) for a fault (deficit, shortcoming) in the theory such that an alternative theory without that fault is always preferable.

An example of this kind of argument is found in the section titled 'The politics of location unmasks material and social inequalities': The political economy of theory-production today has created an unwarranted (that is, ethically indefensible) geographical monopoly based in the West; anticolonial theory, too, is produced within this monopolistic framework that allows the colonizer locations (that is, the West) overwhelming dominance; this creates the potential for the perpetuation of colonial relations in the field of knowledge production, including in the production of anticolonial theory; therefore, variants of anticolonial theory that avoid or resist or overcome this geo-cultural monopoly are always to be strictly preferred over variants that are embedded in the monopoly and show no evidence of any effort to dis-embed themselves.

A third kind of argument is of a generic kind and (like the second kind) is agnostic about the correctness of theory. It is made possible by the insights of feminist standpoint theory as it segues into the politics of location (see the discussion above in the section 'A brief history of the politics of location') and involves the following stages: Universal standpoints – at least those we have known thus far – have proved to be partial (that is, both biased or partisan as well as partial or non-exhaustive) and exclusionary in some significant way; the remedy for this cannot be the search for an all-inclusive standpoint since such an all-seeing 'god's-eye view' is not available (at least within the social sciences); therefore the only option we have is to mitigate and counterbalance the partiality of particular views by insisting on always considering many different viewpoints simultaneously. There is no one-to-one correspondence between locations and theories – a single location in a geographical sense may be a home to many standpoints or perspectives, just as persons who share a single identity in the sense of class or race may have divergent standpoints.

Finally, there is a fourth kind of argument. This kind asserts that the presence of a fatal flaw in the location of the theory/theorists (its/their current site, past behaviour, and probable future trajectory) renders the theory's claim to being a certain kind of theory – here anticolonial theory – morally and conceptually incoherent to the point where it must be rejected outright. An example of this kind of argument is found in 'The politics of location exposes conflicting goals', where a case is not actually made, but merely outlined. Had the case been developed in detail, it would have tried to establish that: A standpoint broadly labelled as 'Hindu-right-wing' is a coherent empirical reality in India; this standpoint is defined by a combination of essential (that is, essence-based) glorification (of a particular version of Hindu culture-religion) and hatred (towards 'non-Indic' minority religions and 'Westernized' intellectuals); based on its stated core beliefs and its past history, it can be reasonably expected that it will continue to practice a majoritarian and authoritarian politics; in other words, it has practised and will continue to practise a form of colonialism-like oppression on groups it identifies as enemies; anticolonial or decolonial theory/concepts used in the service of neo-colonial domination and oppression present an irreconcilable contradiction; therefore, anticolonial theory or concepts deployed from a Hindu right-wing standpoint cannot be considered anticolonial.

Conclusion: Global theory after the 'Ivy Intifada'

In this chapter, I have not been concerned with the internals of anticolonial theory, its different strands, their relative merits or the mutual relationships between them. Instead, I have been concerned with establishing not just the relevance but the *centrality* of the politics of location for any kind of anticolonial theory. Given this centrality, the politics of location needs to be integrated as a core component of all kinds of anticolonial theories, in the insistent plural. We should not have to bring to bear the politics of location from the outside, so to speak, but a commitment to the ethics of location must be inseparable from anticolonial theory itself. It is worth emphasizing that this commitment needs to be constantly renewed, because anticolonial theory must by definition deal with subtle and increasingly complex forms of intellectual domination. Forms of domination keep mutating and reinventing themselves in response to changing contexts and conjunctures – they do not stop obediently at the shores of continents, the borders of nations, the boundaries of disciplines or any other markers of difference or identity. Because the politics of location comes without guarantees, it demands constant collective vigilance.

Fifteen years ago, in an attempt to summarize the argument (based on a pragmatic economies-of-scale-in-knowledge-production logic) made for accepting and even celebrating the concentration of knowledge production in the West, I had written the following words:

> It is unreasonable to fetishise geography, race or ethnicity in the production of social scientific knowledge when the producers of this knowledge are more mixed and multicultural today than ever before in human history. The composition of the global intellectual elite has never been as diverse in terms of ethnic, racial or national-regional identities as it is today. The western university may indeed be located in the west, but it is the closest thing to the proverbial global village in today's world, and a relatively egalitarian one too. The whole world is represented there, and so are 'we'. (Deshpande, 2009: 43)[21]

These words and the hopeful expectations they carried seem hopelessly naïve today, after what has been referred to as the 'Ivy Intifada', namely the widespread and resilient student protests against the state of Israel's ongoing genocide in Palestine. The ferocious attacks on these protests by the state establishment and university administrations have not only decisively ended the century-long ideological reign of the idea of 'Western liberalism', they have also destroyed the location from where the elite Western university could be imagined as special sort of community, a really-existing utopia.

Where do 'we' go from here? Whatever the answer, it will have to begin by renewing and reimagining the 'we' that is the subject of this question. The shape of the new 'we's that emerge will determine the ways in which something called 'global theory' (whatever its definition) can be genuinely global.

Notes

1. The originary texts that brought this phrase into play are Adrienne Rich's famous talk given at Utrecht, Netherlands in 1984 (collected in Rich, 1986) and the Black feminist group, the Combahee River Collective's statement of 1977 (collected in Smith, 2006 [1983]). A parallel originary strand emerged from Michel Foucault's writings on intellectuals, particularly his distinction between the 'universal' and the 'specific' intellectual (Foucault, 1977) and his more general reflections on intellectuals and power (such as the essays/interviews in Rabinow [1984], especially 'Politics and ethics: An interview') and the critical responses to this work. Contemporary articulations of similar concerns often use the term 'positionality', as, for example in the work of Gustavo Lins Ribeiro (Ribeiro, 2023, discussed further later in this chapter).
2. The original French edition of *Outline of a Theory of Practice* was published in 1972, though the English translation appeared in 1977. Talal Asad's edited collection *Anthropology and the Colonial Encounter* consists of papers first presented at a seminar in September 1972 and published as a book in 1973.
3. I am well aware of the dangers of presentism here – of appearing as though I want to create a retrospective, teleologically fixed origin myth for the politics of location – but the risk seems worth taking for reasons of concise and clear exposition.
4. Full disclosure: I was part of the committee that helped organize the conference.
5. These themes are the concerns of the time and are also echoed in the work of well-known theorists such as Chandra Talpade Mohanty (1984), Walter Mignolo (1995), or Gayatri Spivak (1988).
6. According to its website, the SJR, or Scimago Journal and Country Rank, 'is a publicly available portal that includes the journals and country scientific indicators developed from the information contained in the Scopus database (Elsevier B V)'. The portal is run by a research group from the University of Granada, 'dedicated to information analysis, representation and retrieval by means of visualisation techniques'. Available at: https://www.scimagojr.com/aboutus.php
7. All the statistics quoted here have been computed from the Scimago Journal and Country Rank data by Márton Demeter in his book *Academic Knowledge Production and the Global South* (Demeter, 2020).
8. This is merely indicative evidence; a more disaggregated analysis is needed to bring out the relevant trends. For example, according to Demeter, the 'Developing Asia' region shows a significant increase in the proportion of authors (rather than journals) published in indexed journals; but there is no break up of authors in Q1 journals, and the region clubs together an academic powerhouse like China with India, Malaysia and other less-developed countries.
9. Available here: https://i2.wp.com/blogsmedia.lse.ac.uk/blogs.dir/9/files/2020/10/mapping.png?ssl=1
10. On the 'centrality of Google to academic research', the reference is to Gusenbauer (2019).

[11] For recent examples, see Martin Rojo (2021) or Pennycook and Makoni (2020: ch 2). In his International Sociology Association's Presidential Address of 2014 'Facing an unequal world', Burawoy (2015) has detailed the global inequalities that mark the profession.

[12] In their recent monograph, Gurminder Bhambra and John Holmwood argue that 'modern social theory begins by being saturated with the presence of colonialism and the interpretive issues it posed' (2021).

[13] Sujata Patel has captured well the importance of tackling material inequalities in the context of anticolonial theories when she argues that 'sociology/social sciences are constituted in and within the politics of "difference"' that is 'being reproduced in everyday knowledge practices and is being structured through the political economy of knowledge'; it can be destabilized and democratized 'only when there is a fulsome interrogation of this political economy, and its everyday practices of knowledge production within universities and research institutes' (Patel, 2020: 1).

[14] For a report on how decolonization is being used in Eastern Europe, see Koziura et al (2024).

[15] There is of course Vinayak Damodar Savarkar, the figure who weaponized the concept of Hindutva, but for reasons I do not fully understand, he seems to be out of favour with the dominant sections of the Hindu right today.

[16] A different, and differently positioned, example seems to be the academic philosopher Ambika Dutt Sharma, who writes mainly in Hindi. Sharma appears to be headed in the same general direction as Deepak, but grounds himself in Indian social thought (though he also mentions Western thinkers). His essay (in Hindi) is titled *Decolonising the Indian Mind*, and its subtitle may be translated as *A Project for Recommuning with the Authentic Cultural Self*.

[17] The printed version of this book (published by Bloomsbury, New Delhi) does not have page numbers listed in the contents page. It continues to carry Walter Mignolo's laudatory note as the lead item in the blurbs published at the head of the book. See Sen (2023) for a critical review.

[18] https://www.hindustantimes.com/india-news/panel-set-up-for-indian-knowledge-system-s-integration-in-books-101699469738912.html

[19] https://thewire.in/health/govt-moves-to-set-indian-standards-for-stunting-in-children-report

[20] The order of these arguments is not significant – that is, this is an ordering for convenience, not a hierarchy or logically necessary sequence.

[21] Just to clarify, this is not what I myself believed, even in 2009, but an attempt to fairly summarize some dominant views on the matter.

References

Asad, T. (ed) (1973) *Anthropology and the Colonial Encounter*, Ithaca Press.

Bell, K. and Mills, D. (2020) What we know about the academic journal landscape reflects global inequalities, *LSE Impact Blog*, 12 October. https://blogs.lse.ac.uk/impactofsocialsciences/2020/10/12/what-we-know-about-the-academic-journal-landscape-reflects-global-inequalities/

Bhabha, H. (1994) *The Location of Culture*, Routledge.

Bhambra, G.K. and Holmwood, J. (2021) *Colonialism and Modern Social Theory*, Polity Press.

Bourdieu, P. (1977) *Outline of a Theory of Practice*, Cambridge University Press.

Burawoy, M. (2015) Facing an unequal world, *Current Sociology*, 63(1): 5–34.

Clifford, J. and Dhareshwar, V. (1989) Preface, *Inscriptions*, 5: v–vii.

Deepak, J.S. (2021) *India that is Bharat: Coloniality, Civilisation, Constitution*, Bloomsbury.

Demeter, M. (2020) *Academic Knowledge Production and the Global South: Questioning Inequality and Under-Representation*, Palgrave Macmillan.

Deshpande, S. (2009) The practice of social theory and the politics of location, *Economic and Political Weekly*, 44(10): 40–6.

Dhareshwar, V. (1989) Toward a narrative epistemology of the postcolonial predicament, *Inscriptions*, 5: 135–57.

Foucault, M. (1977) The political function of the intellectual, *Radical Philosophy*, 17: 12–14.

Gusenbauer, M. (2019) Google Scholar to overshadow them all? Comparing the sizes of 12 academic search engines and bibliographic databases, *Scientometrics*, 118: 177–214. DOI: 10.1007/s11192-018-2958-5

Hall, S. (1986) The problem of ideology: Marxism without guarantees, *Journal of Communication Inquiry*, 10(2): 28–44.

Haraway, D. (1988) Situated knowledges: The science question in feminism and the privilege of partial perspectives, *Feminist Studies*, 14(3): 575–99.

Harding, S. (1986) *The Science Question in Feminism*, Cornell University Press.

John, M.E. (1989) Postcolonial feminists in the Western intellectual field: Anthropologists *and* native informants?, *Inscriptions*, 5: 49–74.

John, M.E. (1996) *Discrepant Dislocations: Feminism, Theory and Postcolonial Histories*, University of California Press.

Koziura, K., Palm, D. and Matus, A. (2024) Decolonisation as a progressive force? In eastern Europe, think again, *Times Higher Education*, 27 August. https://www.timeshighereducation.com/blog/decolonisation-progressive-force-eastern-europe-think-again

Martin Rojo, L. (2021) Hegemonies and inequalities in academia, *International Journal of Socio-Linguistics*, 267–8: 169–192. DOI: 10.1515/ijsl-2020-0077

Mignolo, W. (1995) *The Darker Side of the Renaissance: Literacy, Territoriality and Colonization*, University of Michigan Press.

Mohanty, C.T. (1984) Under Western eyes: Feminist scholarship and colonial discourses, *boundary 2*, 12–13(3&1). DOI: 10.2307/302821

Patel, S. (2020) Sociology's encounter with the decolonial: The problematique of indigenous vs that of coloniality, extraversion and colonial modernity, *Current Sociology*, 69(3): 372–88. DOI: 10.1177/0011392120931143

Pennycook, A. and Makoni, S. (2020) *Innovations and Challenges in Applied Linguistics from the Global South*, Routledge.

Rabinow, P. (ed) (1984) *The Foucault Reader*, Pantheon Books.

Ribeiro, G.L. (2023) From decolonizing knowledge to posimperialism: A Latin American perspective, *American Ethnologist*. DOI: 10.1111/amet.13186

Rich, A. (1986) *Blood, Bread and Poetry: Selected Prose 1979–1985*, W.W. Norton.

Scott, D. (1989) Locating the anthropological subject: Postcolonial anthropologists in other places, *Inscriptions*, 5: 75–84.

Sen, A. (2023) J Sai Deepak's India that is Bharat: Coloniality, civilisation, constitution, *Social Dynamics*, 49(2): 376–385. DOI: 10.1080/02533952.2023.2236899

Smith, B. (ed) (2006 [1983]) *Home Girls: A Black Feminist Anthology*, Rutgers University Press.

Spivak, G.C. (1988) Can the subaltern speak?, in C. Nelson and L. Grossberg (eds) *Marxism and the Interpretation of Cultures*, Macmillan, pp 66–111.

6

Decolonial Dialectics in an Inter-Imperial World

Laura Doyle

Introduction

Important transformations are underway in decolonial, postcolonial, and anti-colonial studies, in both practice and theory. Over recent decades activists and scholars around the world have collaborated and debated across disciplines, generated fresh concepts, and cultivated more community-based projects – despite appropriations, suppressions and depleted budgets. In turn they have generated new, interconnected articulations, as reflected in this edited collection.

I hope to contribute to these conversations by offering a methodology for what I will refer to as dialectical decolonial thought. This approach combines three methods: a long-historical analysis of accruing colonial and anti-colonial dynamics; an intersectional understanding of anti-colonial struggle, over labour as well as land; and the cultivation of collaborative interdisciplinarity to deepen both our understanding of the dialectics of history and our alliance-based engagement with the present. This combination of methods can, I propose, at once dismantle colonialist epistemologies and generate liberatory decolonial thought.

After a discussion of terms in this introduction, the chapter proceeds in five sections. The first three sections elaborate on the historical and intersectional methods already mentioned, making visible the key sites of dialectical contestation between colonial systems and decolonial thought and practice. The fourth and fifth sections analyse how labour becomes both an existential matrix of struggle and a resource for collective sustenance as negotiated through epistemological, material, and aesthetic formations. Across all the sections, I point to the importance of interdisciplinary collaboration for this kind of multi-dimensional analysis.

Some stipulation of key terms is important at the outset in light of recent debates about decolonial, postcolonial, and anti-colonial vocabularies. Some scholars have distinguished decolonial studies from postcolonial studies, arguing that postcolonial studies has mainly critiqued the modern/colonial Anglo-European world order, while decolonial studies has highlighted visions originating outside of that order, especially among Indigenous peoples. I concur with theorists who argue, however, that these projects are connected at the root and are best developed as complementary rather than separate or fundamentally divergent (Ramamurthy and Tambe, 2017).[1] Although it remains important to take stock of how different locations call for distinctive theoretical formulations, the postcolonial versus decolonial binaries too often overlook the interconnected legacies across hemispheres, a trend that can re-trigger old colonialist divisions among peoples and regions.[2]

The term 'anti-colonial' helpfully avoids the postcolonial versus decolonial territorializing of critical thought. For some, it also counters recent appropriations of 'decolonial', for instance in India where it is used to justify anti-Muslim, anti-Dalit and other violence. There is a limit to this choice however, since the term 'anti-colonial' could be coopted next. Most valuably, in my view, 'anti-colonial' emphasizes a stance of 'refusal', as formulated by thinkers such as Audra Simpson (2014) and Max Liboiron (2021: 6–9). As I explain next, I prefer the term decolonial, but I do sometimes use anti-colonial to emphasize energies of refusal or as a term that avoids the postcolonial–decolonial binary.

'Decolonial' has a multitude of meanings and genealogies that are important to keep in mind. In 'Decolonization is not a metaphor', Eve Tuck and K. Wayne Yang (2012: 31) argue that 'decolonization is not [equivalent] to other anti-colonial struggles' and they stress that, in the context of the Americas and many other invaded lands, decolonization is always a call for the repatriation of land to Indigenous communities. Certainly the reclamation of land and other forms of reparation stand at the centre of many decolonizing struggles, and it's crucial not to overuse the term or conflate different histories, places or forms of decolonization, or to think solely in terms of discursive and ideological decolonization. Yet it is likewise important not to think about the materiality of colonization solely in terms of land or to underestimate the interlocking formations of land and ideology. Furthermore, in the Americas, histories of slavery complicate a singular focus on land.[3]

For many, including myself, the term decolonial is the most salient because it conveys an anti-colonial stance and simultaneously acknowledges other dimensions of existence and community. That is, decolonial analyses often encompass critique, but they also register realities and epistemologies generated from outside colonialism, even if these are also entangled with colonialism. This kind of work was introduced decades ago by thinkers such as Ngũgĩ wa Thiong'o (1986), and it has been further developed by diverse scholars across the world, ranging from Caribbean thinker Sylvia Wynter (2003) to Maori scholar Smith, Linda Tuhiwai Smith (2013), Zimbabwean scholar Sabelo Gatsheni-Ndlovu (2013, 2020), Pacific Islander scholar Tiara Na'puti (2017, 2025), and South American scholars Catherine Walsh (2008), Catherine Walsh and Walter Mignolo (2018), Arturo Escobar (2007, 2018, 2020), and Walter Mignolo (2005, 2018). Attention to these diverse legacies affords fresh possibilities both for 'de-linking' from dominant systems (Amin, 1990) and for 'relinkings' with epistemologies and communities beyond or alongside the colonial order of things (Suárez-Krabbe, 2025). Moreover, as shown in this chapter, notions of interdependent relationality in non-dominant epistemologies dovetail fittingly with dialectical approaches to the history of struggle.

In what follows, I begin by establishing how colonizing formations have been shaped by *a field* of interacting empires, never just one – both over the *longue durée* and in any one period.[4] Attention to this *inter*-imperial, accruing field of competitive, colonialist manoeuvres makes more visible both the shrewd character of anti-colonial maneuvers and the sustaining power of decolonial epistemologies, clarifying the roles of both in long-historical dialectics.

In this light, the second section more specifically traces the inter-imperially shaped processes through which institutions, infrastructures, and media become sites of control and contestation. These sites include not only engineered infrastructures (ports, roads, buildings) and state institutions (temples, schools, government buildings) but they also encompass record-keeping systems and knowledge traditions (including science, philosophy, law, history, and art forms). This section demonstrates how these systems and sites have all been instrumentalized both for and against empire: they operate as matrices of colonial, anti-colonial, and 'mediating' negotiations. Although we often understand texts and performances as less 'material' than buildings and bridges, it takes only a moment to see that they are not. They require hands, pens, paper, performing bodies, and built spaces for their production. Critical social theory concerned with the history of struggle would be enriched by fuller incorporation of these dimensions of the dynamics of history. For this, we need collaboration across disciplines.

The third section outlines how intersectional thinking further sharpens dialectical decolonial thought. Here I take up the materialist dialectics of labour but recast them within an intersectional and inter-imperial framework that also centres the existential condition of interdependence. The existential fact of our dependence on others for survival explains why carework constitutes perhaps the most fundamental site of dialectical contestation – as displayed today in both the resurgence of repressive anti-woman laws and the protests against these laws. Especially given the sometimes decisive (if ignored) influence of gendered conflicts in world politics, a feminist analyses of intersectionally coercive systems belongs front and centre in critical theory. The fourth section extends the implications of this intersectional analysis in relation to non-Western and Indigenous epistemologies of time, place, and polity.[5] Tapping Johannes Fabian's critique (1983) of the European-colonialist 'denial of coevality' among peoples, I emphasize the gender and labour stakes in colonialism's *disavowal of interdependence*. I argue that non-dominant relational epistemologies based on interdependent coevality are not 'soft' knowledges but instead are re-structuring tools with under-appreciated potency.

The short final section of the chapter turns to literature. It aims to convey just a few ways that art forms are simultaneously sites of contestation and channels for decolonial imaginaries. Touching on texts from *One Thousand and One Nights* to contemporary fiction, I indicate how they model alternative forms of relationality while also interrupting colonialist, successionist, and 'modernist' temporalities. The chapter closes by reflecting on the larger claims of a dialectical decolonial framework and commenting on the importance of cross-community, interdisciplinary collaboration for cultivation of it.

One last remark is in order. This study of *longue-durée* histories uncovers pasts that are as complex as the present. Amid today's colonial politics, in which earlier imperial histories are romanticized or instrumentalized for recolonizing ends, such historical work can be fraught. Yet we cannot afford to cede this important historical ground to apologists for empire, such as Niall Ferguson (2003), or to civilizationalist discourses (as critiqued by Sucheta Mazumdar, 2003). Otherwise we lose the opportunity to fully de-centre European hegemony, to re-narrate these pasts in counter-hegemonic terms, and to recover the resources that can guide us in the present. A long-historical or 'deep time' decolonial framework that is also intersectional, dialectical, and interdisciplinary can make visible the deeper multi-dimensionality of decolonizing struggles, as recently laid out in the three-volume collection, *Decolonial Reconstellations* (Doyle et al, 2025). In turn, the study and teaching of these complex legacies offers our students richer resources for critical theory.

The inter-imperial political economy and the historical dialectics of struggle

As noted, this chapter's analysis of colonialism focuses on a key matrix of historical dynamics: the millennia-spanning, geopolitical field of vying empires that has formed together with manifold forms of anti-imperial dissent and alliance. As I have developed at length in *Inter-imperiality* (2020), empires have co-created infrastructures, institutions, ideologies, and forms of war, through both collusion and competition.[6] Over millennia, these have become sedimented into stratifying, determining, yet contested conditions. My use of the term inter-imperial foregrounds this dialectically shaped and accruing field of volatile interactions, which I understand as a matrix of the human political-existential condition. By giving simultaneous attention to multi-vectored, violent relations among empires *and* to the lived conditions of those who suffer, die, endure, and manoeuvre among empires, I aim to reveal the degree to which we all occupy a deeply sedimented condition of *inter-imperial positionality* – yet in distinctly unequal ways. I draw on the long tradition of dialectical philosophy from ancient to modern, and encompassing Mediterranean, Asian, and European dialectical thinkers. While diverse, most of these thinkers begin with the observation that the world's physical and social phenomena unfold inter-dependently and contingently, always 'co-arising' in relation to other phenomena.[7]

The focus on different empires in dialectical relation to each other does not equate them or imply that they have engaged in precisely the same projects. When we speak of 'international relations' we do not imply that all nations are the same; nor when we speak of interpersonal relations do we imply that all persons are the same. Accordingly, inter-imperial theory simply begins from the fact that different empires, of different sizes, locations, languages, and value-systems, form in dialectical relation: their differences and divergent histories as well as their linkages and alliances shape their interrelations and their degree of power. Here I understand an empire as an expansionist state that achieves sustained control over the labour, finances, administration, linguistic, artistic, and material resources of a foreign territory through political, financial, and violent coercion. The inter-imperial framework particularly highlights the fact that each empire's powers of control arise and develop in relation to other empires as well as to smaller polities and to resisting communities. These relations prepare the future contours of historical struggle.

The long-historical scope of this framework first of all brings into view the fact that certain regions and communities have particularly suffered in the dialectical force fields and 'shatterzones' of inter-imperial jockeying. Places such as the Middle East, Indonesia, Eastern Europe, Afghanistan, the Andes, the Caribbean, and the Maghreb have endured both successive and converging colonizations over centuries.[8] Situated at strategic crossroads and along sea lanes, parts of the Middle East and North Africa have, for instance, been repeatedly invaded by empires, reaching from Persianate and Macedonian empires, through Roman and Byzantine empires, to Ottoman and European empires. Likewise with parts of Kashmir: it has been repeatedly claimed by vying states – from the Chinese and the Mughals to the British – which in turn has influenced the vying claims on the region today by India and Pakistan. Much the same is true of Eastern Europe, as Manuela Boatcă and Anca Parvulescu (2022) address in their work on Eastern Europe.

These regions are therefore best understood and honoured not strictly as peripheral territories but as strategic inter-imperial zones, again and again vied over for their resources (including labourers) and their geopolitical location – including before, during, and since the rise of European hegemony. Although Immanuel Wallerstein's world-system framework broke important ground for anti-colonial and Marxist thought, as did Abu-Lughod's application of the world-system concept to Asian formations of the 13th and 14th centuries, the need for additional models becomes clear when we focus on the presence of *multiple* interacting empires in any one period, which together encompass multiple cores and peripheries. At minimum, we see afresh that the designation of a region as a periphery may shift depending which empire's perspective we take. Furthermore, attention to the fact of multiple, competing, manoeuvring empires forces us to notice the extreme volatility of relations between 'core' and 'peripheries', which includes, for instance, an empire's efforts to gain control of a rival's peripheries.

Perhaps most importantly, the long-historical perspective makes visible how the long succession of empires has complicated all relations. For, in regions that have been dominated by successive empires, each invading empire has left its sediments – in infrastructural, linguistic, epistemological, institutional, and political forms – which then persist to shape future conflicts. These zones have formed not only as palimpsests of inter-imperial systems and infrastructures, but also as vessels of layered collective memory and cross-hatched identifications that create both bonds and divisions, making trust fragile and straightforward alliances difficult. That is, the inter-imperially layered accretions over centuries have created frictions among identities, claims, languages, and other attachments. Long-standing cultures and communities thus hold rich cultural resources and seasoned forms of wisdom or wry humour; yet they are often also replete with memories of betrayal, violence, and sexual-racial trauma and with frustrated forms of imperialist, often masculinist desire. All of these may be re-triggered by events in the contemporary field of inter-imperial pressures. In contemporary Eurocentric discourses of international politics, these complexities often get reduced to 'tribal animosities'. But we might rather think of them as the long-accruing, empire-saturated relations that hamstring contemporary efforts to create healthy lives, communities, and alliances.

When we keep in mind this geopolitical history with its layered, conflicting interpellations, we see more clearly how the past has shaped later strategies of both domination and revolt, on a macro-political scale. Among other effects, the layered hierarchical stratifications installed by successive empires over centuries allow an empire to pit one population within it against another. Witness, for instance, the US political machinations that leverage differences of position among African-Americans, Native peoples, and diverse immigrant populations. This differential leveraging is not new.

Earlier Eurasian empires sometimes gave older conquered populations privileges or allowed them to marry into the elite but denied these rights to others or to newly conquered populations (Burbank, 2007; Lavan et al, 2016; Doyle, 2020: 45–6). Although such tactics have created unrest, they have also served colonizers' efforts to 'divide and conquer' minoritized communities.

Meanwhile these internal divisions have also been instrumentalized by empires in their competition with other states, enabling an empire to destabilize rival states by fomenting minority rebellion in them. As is well-known, many an empire has armed the colonized communities of rival states and held out promises of liberation to them, but ultimately for their own ends of gaining power over that state and its resources, including its colonized labourers. This inter-imperial practice of destabilization is widespread, yet it has been insufficiently understood as part of the dialectics of history. For instance, in their 18th- and 19th-century Atlantic-world contests, the British, French, Portuguese, and Spanish empires each fostered insurgency among Indigenous peoples and enslaved communities to destabilize the other empires, while the 'pawn' communities suffered the fall-out. Later, US imperial policy in many parts of the world, notoriously for instance in Cuba and in the Philippines, similarly supported independence fighters' efforts to oust the reigning empire and then afterward promptly jailed revolutionaries, dominated finance and trade, and reinforced the subordinate, racialized status of many labourers and women. Such was also the case in Russia's sponsorship of client communities in the Polish and Swedish empires in the 18th century (LeDonne, 1997: 23–37). As is apparent in today's geopolitical field, this cunning and classically imperialist strategy is widespread and long lived.

At the same time, however, colonized, disenfranchised, and other dominated communities have themselves shrewdly manipulated these inter-imperial rivalries, navigating precariously yet consciously within a multi-polar field of power relations. They have, for instance, regularly garnered support and weapons from one empire for resistance against 'their own' empire. Consider Toussaint L'Ouverture negotiating with agents of the British empire who offered arms and personnel to strengthen their battles against the French empire in their efforts to oust the British empire, while in the same period the Irish successfully solicited troops and arms from the French, capitalizing on the British–French rivalry. In the 19th century, the Serbian community played the Russians against the French and Austrian-Hapsburgs in order to win military support for their struggles against in the Ottoman empire. In the 20th century, Roger Casement negotiated with agents of the German empire to win Irish independence from the British empire. Sherif Hussein ibn Ali, emir of Mecca and the leader of the Arab Uprising against the Ottoman empire during the First World War, was encouraged, funded, and abetted by the British empire, although eventually betrayed by the British in the Balfour Declaration. The dialectical effects of this latter history find their criminal contemporary expression in the inter-imperially supported colonization of Palestine beginning in the first half of the 20th century.

Although the empires often 'win', resistance movements do sometimes make gains, or they have after-lives that inspire future movements (often sustained in the background by women's labours of care and relation-building).[9] At the end of the 18th century, uprisings and revolutions broke out around the world amid the machinations, wars, and rising taxes of empires (for their war chests), as discussed in *The Age of Revolution in Global Context* (Armitage and Subrahmanyam, 2009). Rebellions surged both East and West, both North and South. These included the White Lotus Rebellion in Qing China, Pugachev's Rebellion in Russia, the Serbian Revolution, and the invention of local *guerilla* warfare in the Spanish village uprisings against Napoleon; and they also included Irish and Caribbean rebellions as well as the interlocking Haitian, French, and North and South American revolutions.

All of these revolutionary movements laid down precedents and tactics for future movements; and they seeded what I have elsewhere analysed as an incipient post/colonial consciousness, insofar as communities began to imagine a time after colonialism (Doyle, 2020: 131–3). For instance, in his 1803 speech from the execution dock, Irish rebel Robert Emmet told his British executioners that 'by a revolution of power, we might change places', even insinuating 'with the confidence of intimate knowledge' that plans were already underway for Ireland's 'emancipation from the superhuman oppression' of the British (Emmet, nd). As scholars have shown, by the late 19th century, an internationalist consciousness emerged and was disseminated through literatures and journals (Chatterjee, 1993; Ledoux, 2013; Nwankwo, 2014; Martin, 2017; Doyle, 2020). Aware of these precedents, later leaders sometimes successfully manoeuvred among empires to win independence. India's decolonizing transformation, for instance, took shape partly through risky and ethically fraught affiliations between Indian nationalist leaders and Japanese imperial politicians, an alliance that worried Britain and eventually moved it towards conciliatory stances. Each wave of resistance and shrewd alliance has helped to keep alive an anti-colonial imaginary.

In other words, resistance and alliance have long unfolded together with domination in a dialectically volatile geopolitical surround. Accordingly, anti-colonial struggle is much more than a battle of us-against-them. It demands alertness to the 360-degree surround of jockeying actors and states. Independence thinkers of the 'third world' who promoted neutrality during the Cold War were raising awareness of exactly this predicament. They also understood that their 'third-world' positioning required multiple decolonizing strategies – including restructurings of epistemology and perception generated partly by literary and artistic movements, as emphasized by Ngũgĩ wa Thiong'o in *Decolonizing the Mind* (1986). More recently

Samir Amin's concept of 'delinking' from the Eurocentric colonial order (1990) and Julia Suárez-Krabbe's complementary concept of 're-linking' to relational epistemologies (2023, 2025) reflect ongoing efforts to challenge and reimagine geopolitics.

Sites of struggle: infrastructural, institutional, dialectical

A closer look at inter-imperially built techno-infrastructures, tools, and institutions can sharpen our understanding of these historical dialectics. We might start by recalling that, in the long history of agrarian uprisings, the pitchforks and digging tools provided by masters to peasants, slaves, or serfs have sometimes been retooled by these laborers as weapons of resistance. On a larger scale in later periods, as engineered infrastructures spread into rural as well as urban areas, 'uncredentialed' political actors have seized hold of or destroyed them. Thus have bridges, buildings, ports, trains, and telegraph lines sometimes become targets of vandalism or sabotage, as in the early 20th-century dismantling of telegraph lines by Arab-speaking and other provincial communities in the Ottoman empire (Ballantyne and Burton, 2014). The 'sit-ins' and takeovers of academic spaces in recent decades provide another kind of illustration. While many of us are aware of these histories, very few critical thinkers have taken sufficient stock of them in their analyses of the present.

In *Inter-imperiality*, I consider these infrastructural and institutional dynamics as they have accrued through competitive empire-building since roughly the first millennium CE (Doyle, 2020: 35–67). This history also further dismantles Eurocentric modernity myths, establishing that the first 'modern' states with 'advanced' governance and science long pre-dated the 'rise of Europe'. A summary of the historical patterns clarifies the accruing dialectics and conjunctures that complicate anti-colonial struggle. First of all, empires have not just *singly* engineered and conscripted labour to build massive infrastructure projects such as ports, roads, water management systems, and libraries (not just 'decadent' palaces). They have also imitated, borrowed, stolen, and extended each other's inventions, systems, and labourers. Sometimes they have conquered a territory exactly so as to seize control of the infrastructures built by others. The Incan state did so in the 15th century with the roads, mining sites, and terrace and drainage systems of the Chimor empire, just as the Spanish later did with Incan infrastructures. The Japanese engaged in the 1904–1905 Russo-Japanese War partly so as to gain control of the new railways built in Manchuria by Russians (Doyle, 2020: 52).

These takeovers of material infrastructure constitute dialectical co-formations not in any neutral or stable way but rather as driving forces of dialectical history, including as they involve relocation of labourers who themselves bring diverse languages, allegiances, and new cultural practices (Doyle, 2016, 2020: 55). As empires have expanded, they and their willing or coerced agents have installed infrastructures across ever larger distances, enabling empires to manage relations with faster, cheaper, more 'efficient' modes of production, transport, war, and communication. Simultaneously empires' relocations, dislocations, and stratifications of communities have exacerbated the conjunctures of identity – further igniting both anti-colonial dissent and reactionary conflicts.

Furthermore, as Michael Mann (1986) pointed out, as these competitive infrastructure-generating practices have intensified over centuries, they have performed 'track-laying' work that shapes future hierarchies and struggles. That is, past patterns of infrastructural 'development' determine the unequal spatial distribution of life-sustaining resources across many generations, inhibiting access to sustenance for some communities, while enabling it for others. For instance, the placement of good plumbing infrastructures in one area brings clean water to some communities while poisonous dumping brings polluted water to others. Hegemonic discourses of modernity implicitly encourage us to think of the privileged communities as living in 'modern' conditions while impoverished communities live in 'premodern' conditions. Yet these periodizing vocabularies elide the true operations underway and they simultaneously perpetuate racist images of exploited communities.

The full inscape of this dialectically generated field of contests over and through infrastructures comes into sharpest focus when we track developments that are at once cultural, material, and institutional. This attention also lays ground for a better understanding of literature's place in the dialectic – which again indicates the need for interdisciplinary methods. The material-cultural elements include, for instance, paper-making and printing technologies, first developed in China between the 1st and 7th centuries CE. While many peoples, from the Egyptian to the Aztec, had systems of writing and record-keeping, the relatively easy reproducibility of paper eventually made it a favoured medium. Its development not only led to the first paper money – and to treatises about it – but it also allowed the growth of China's literacy-centred state-building and its imperial expansion, helping to effect its self-representation and projection over increasingly vast territories, as Mark Edward Lewis (1999) analyses in *Writing and Authority in Early China*. At the same time, paper supported the launching of a large-scale civil service corps with state-controlled examinations, all of which enabled the wide interpellation of populations and the powerfully 'imagined community' of this expanding empire.

Given its state-building power, the capacity to manufacture paper provoked the interest of other expanding states and became a sought-after technology.

The first rival to emulate it was the Abbasid state, which, as it expanded eastward in the 8th century, collided with the westward-expanding Chinese Tang dynasty. Thereafter, Arabic-language states also developed a culture of 'the book', helped in this ambition by their incorporation of the intellectual and bureaucratic institutions of conquered Persian states. These dialectical co-formations allowed these states to extend their knowledge, institutions, and technologies further east and south across Afro-Eurasia.

Thus, by the time Europeans engaged at length with imperial Arabic-language courts in Spain and Africa (as when Crusading princes were hosted or forcibly held at royal courts in between pitched battles), these states had developed scholarly institutions as powerful organs of state (Doyle, 2020: 61–7). This knowledge and the institutions supporting it drew Northern European scholars and scientists south, to libraries in Spain and Africa, catalysing the turn towards so-called 'modern science' and 'European' scholasticism. It's worth recalling that in the 10th, 11th, and 12th centuries, when the largest libraries in Christendom held a couple of thousand volumes, libraries in Baghdad and African cities contained tens or hundreds of thousands, such as that of the vizier of the African Fatimid caliphate of al-Amin, which numbered half a million (Bloom, 2001: 118–22). Many of these books were scientific, which of course informed the states' technical, engineering projects. It should be no surprise, therefore, if in these centuries Europeans suffered from and were motivated by 'imperial envy', as Gerald MacLean argues (2007).

Like the engineering infrastructures, these intellectual and cultural infrastructures were co-constituted by vying states, that is, formed through inter-imperial competition and conquering. As Jonathan Bloom (2001) establishes, empires deliberately borrowed or stole from their neighbours' and rivals' library collections, seeking for strategic reasons to understand their science, religion, and arts. To allied empires they sent delegations of scholars who brought and hoped for manuscripts as gifts, and to enemy empires they sent officers with orders to capture manuscript collections as valuable booty, as in wars between Byzantine and Abbasid empires (Bloom, 2001: 117–19). Scholars too were booty – kidnapped or forced to serve new masters, creolizing knowledge while probably also manoeuvering in ways that have likely shaped scholarly codes and legacies.

Necessarily, translation projects stood at the centre of these empire-building activities and of competition over knowledge, both for infrastructure-building and for influence in contested territories. As Bloom points out, the 'translation of Persian, Greek, and Indian works into Arabic became a regular state activity' in the 8th-century Abbasid empire (Bloom, 2001: 117) – just as the ambitious state-supported translation of Indian-Buddhist manuscripts taken from India had helped some Chinese dynasties to consolidate power in central Asia. Likewise, in 7th-century Japan, translation of Chinese and Buddhist manuscripts served to build an island-wide hegemony for Japanese rulers, according to Joan Piggott (1997). In all cases, the translators participated, voluntarily or involuntarily, in the dialectical, globalizing processes of co-adaptation, co-production, and homogenization. We might think here of al-Hasan al-Wazzan, the 16th-century scholar who Europeans have called Leo Africanus and who was 'held' at the court of the Pope Leo X, where he was 'asked' to translate Arabic texts for the 'knowledge' of the Catholic Church (Davis, 2006).

A focus on translation reveals not only how central language has been to colonization and inter-imperial jockeying, as Mary Louise Pratt discusses (2015). It also clarifies how these dynamics have driven the accretion and growth of capitalist-imperial systems. The cultivation of mathematical knowledge most clearly illustrates this point. As we know, the decimal system for mathematical computation arrived with the publication of al-Khwarizmi's 9th-century book, *Calculation of the Hindu Numerals* (circa 825 CE), which elaborated on the Hindu-Arabic numerical system to describe computational methods using the zero and the notion of place value. His work depended on the inter-imperially generated availability of paper and it reflected the inter-imperial history of state-formation, for al-Khwarizmi was an Abbasid scholar of Persian descent. In turn, when his book was translated into Hebrew and Latin, this new computational practice became a transhemispheric accounting system. As Edmund Burke III points out, this translated knowledge helped to create 'a single market from Spain [and Africa] to India and China, with a single language of administration (Arabic) and a single monetary system (the trimetallic system of gold dinar, silver dirham, and copper fils)', thus facilitating the integration of European markets and eventually American markets into an increasingly global world-system (Burke, 2009: 183–4). In this accruing, dialectical way, 'translated' technologies at once homogenize, disseminate, and intensify inter-imperial systems.

In the last century, the increasing circulation of systems or translated knowledges via media and education have dramatically affected the dialectics of hegemony and dissent, as evident in student- and scholar-led movements and activism among writers in the international public sphere. Multi-lingual members of early 20th-century independence movements shrewdly undertook a transperipheral circulation of newspapers and journals, to expose colonial crimes, challenge propaganda, share strategy, and extend solidarities (Kelley, 1999; Boehmer, 2002). Combined with the falling and rising, shifting positions of warring empires complicated conjunctures and re-alignments emerged. As Ben Tran (2017) unpacks, sometimes when one colonial regime replaces another, new possibilities emerge – as when France invaded Vietnam and disrupted Chinese-Mandarin educational hegemony there, partly by allowing women to go to school. At once suppressing knowledge and creating new social formations, the French disruption of gender norms also came back to bite them by generating new readerships, subversive literatures, and unexpected, non-heteronormative alliances among Vietnamese men and women. This is just one example of the many ways that schools and their institutionalized languages have been sites of struggle.

When we thus track how anti-colonial actors grapple with multiple empires' unequal institutional and infrastructural legacies, how they transform them despite uneven distribution of resources, we give a proper place to the micro-manoeuvres of dissenting communities of all kinds within the macrophysics of state formation and historical change.

Reproducing empires: intersectional sites of struggle

This multi-sided theorization of inter-imperial projects and anti-colonial dialectics requires that we address at least one more dimension – intersectional labour formations – to capture the fuller nature of political struggle. Close attention to this structural dimension unveils the colonial instrumentalization of our existential interdependency, and it illuminates the often masculinist desire to denigrate and disavow this relationality. These insights allow a fuller analysis of intersectional stratification *as a structural and existential dimension of labour extraction*.

If we begin with the simple fact that both humans and polities emerge within a volatile existential condition of entangled co-formation, we can powerfully re-ground the terms of macro-political theory. Very basically, we might recall that a state's claim to sovereignty must be recognized by other states to have standing or force. Then too, most empires, nations, kingdoms, and villages depend materially on trade, a relational activity. Likewise are all persons are co-constituted and co-formed, despite all disavowals to the contrary.

This point becomes clear when we recall, as so few philosophies do, that a person's physical survival depends from birth on another person who brings sustenance from the material world. Our survival arises within a situation of fraught co-origination, with the labours of care-taking as the pivotal practice. In contrast to Giorgio Agamben's emphasis (1998), we might understand this fraught *co*-origination as the founding condition of 'bare life'. This fact of radical interdependence feels inadmissible for those who have been encouraged to dream of absolute autonomy or dominance, and for those interpellated into the gendered, racialized notion that bodily labours belong to others, not themselves. Under these conditions, there does indeed arise a core struggle over labour, but the fuller story of struggle differs from Hegel's as well as Agamben's and Marx's versions.

In in his famous 'lord and bondsman' analysis in his early work, *Phenomenology of Spirit*, G.W.F. Hegel captures some of the complexities of labour formations as shaped by interdependency. (Notably, Hegel was likely influenced not only by Ancient Greek thought but also indirectly by the dialectical Chinese and Buddhist notions of 'co-arising' phenomena, *via* Leibniz [Bernasconi, 2003]). Hegel first describes a primal encounter in which two men meet, feel threatened by each other, and battle to near death for domination. In this account, when one man gains enough control to threaten his rival with murder and the other concedes defeat, the winning man becomes 'master' of the other with, as Hegel glosses it, the right to demand his unrewarded labour. As Susan Buck-Morss (2005) has noted, this narrative of coerced labour provided an implicit justification for the Atlantic slave trade. Hegel's reduction of this coeval intersubjectivity to a competitive, violent, zero-sum battle also implicitly foreshadows his later, explicitly racist work in *Philosophy of History*. His founding 'lord and bondsman' scene may thus also be understood as a founding 'necropolitical scene', as defined by Achille Mbembe (2019).

Yet, as Karl Marx importantly apprehended, Hegel also pointed towards the dynamics of consciousness and disavowal in this encounter. Hegel traces how both the master's dependence on the labourer's production *and the labourer's awareness* of this fact destabilize the power of the 'lord' (Hegel, 1977 [1807]: 111–19). He lays bare how the *fear of interdependence* prompts the master to disavow and denigrate the bondsman's labour – exactly because the master *depends* on it. In effect, Hegel's philosophy unconsciously explains his own threatened consciousness and the disavowals embedded in that philosophy. It's worth recalling that 18th- and 19th-century African-descended persons who had escaped slavery in the Atlantic world were simultaneously writing counter-narratives in Anglo-European languages, which became widely read and drew adherents to anti-slavery movements. This written exposure of the disavowal of Euro-American dependency on enslaved labour was itself an engagement with and shaping of the dialectics of history (Bromell, 1993; Doyle, 2010). Thus are literary and other arts are historical engagements.

Marx of course also cultivated the critical seed germinating in Hegel's dialectical exploration of the self-consciousness of the bondsman, which Hegel had traced to the labourer's active engagement in materiality, and which Marx then analysed as the labourer's alienated self-consciousness under capitalism. Yet a core element remains untheorized here, by Marx and many others. For when Hegel positions a male lord and male bondsman's physical contest for control as *the* original intersubjective moment, much gets erased in one stroke. That is, his life-or-death story of struggle over labour has no women in it. Yet without women's labours as well as men's, there is neither lord nor bondsman in the first place. Unfortunately most non-feminist theorists of historical dialectics have repeated this erasure.

When we take stock of these gendered elisions and open out to the macro-political field, we see more clearly that women's labours for the physical, emotional health of households and communities also occupy a pivotal place in states, including but not limited to colonizing ones. As intersectional and social reproduction scholars have noted, ruling classes regulate sexuality through customs or laws that restrict their marriages within ranked and race-d identities in order to secure their group's power within kin lines and to ensure the reproduction of labouring classes especially in slavery, serfdom, caste, or wage regimes.[10] That is, female-gendered people are conscripted into giving life and providing care *within a sorting system*: they must reproduce not just humans but specifically positioned humans, sorted by lineage, religion, gender, and skin colour, whose position in the ranks determine their access to education, leisure, political power, and life-sustaining resources. While the larger systems also install a hierarchy for male labourers, the gendered regimes ensure that half of the human race – the half we call women – will provide free labour in the household and community. In short, these identity structures determine material conditions.

In the world of vying states, this gendered economy creates further pressures for women. While perpetuating gender hierarchies in their own states, colonizers may hold out promises of better lives for women in the communities they invade, in effect pitting these women against *their* communities. If these women show any interest in this promise, they often face defamation and punishment from their communities. Because some *have* resisted or manoeuvred within these conditions, women have been cast as a dangerously uncertain element in the field of relations – an Achille's heel in men's control of communities and states. Indeed, some of the most well-known stories of the world blame women for the downfall of the state, or for the colonization of it. Cleopatra, Helen of Troy, and the 'whore' of Babylon were blamed for the ruin of empires, while women of colonized communities have sometimes been blamed for 'letting in' the conquerors, as with the figure of Malinche in Mexican tradition or, in Irish tradition, 'the adultress' who brought 'the Saxon robbers here' (as parodied by James Joyce in *Ulysses*).[11] Thus is men's control of stratified labour intertwined with their control of literary and other arts, each reinforcing the other. Together they hinder the potential for alliances among men and women of colonized labouring groups and among women of different stations. No surprise, then, that Aristotelian political theory deemed the control of 'women and slaves' in the household the basis for control of the larger polis – a notion that has taken hold across states in the East as well as the West (Arjomand, 1999). Meanwhile, as I will touch on later, over the centuries women have told the other side of the tale, although often anonymously.

For now, the familiarity of the androcentric narratives of macropolitics reminds us that these legacies occupy the habitus over long-historical time, not only spatially in the built environment but also psychically and bodily – in art, memory, and feeling. These legacies affect men as well as women.

For men, the lesson centres on the trials and triumphs of male competition over control of states. In fact, succession narratives of vying and betraying brothers who compete and kill over rulership are canonical, in literary traditions as far flung as the Incan, the Islamicate, and European. Taken together, these macropolitical dramas make clear that gender, race, and caste constitute much more than mere 'identity politics' and that the arts are much more than mere superstructures. To appreciate the existential depth and often labour-centred matrix of art's *re*structuring project, it's necessary first to consider its affinity with the structuring projects of epistemology.

Time, labour, and coevality

Among the many things that empires aim to destroy is a community's *place-specific* ways of being-in-time together. Through what indigenous scholars such as Audra Simpson (2014) analyse as epistemic violence and what feminist philosopher Miranda Fricker (2007) has called epistemic injustice, masculinist colonialism seeks to control, destroy, or exploit a community's shared ways of naming, trusting, thriving, and knowing in the world.[12] Because colonialism seeks to prohibit a community's way of cultivating knowledge and longevity within a distinctive place, epistemologies of time and place also lie at the heart of anti-colonial struggle and historical dialectics.

As Johannes Fabian famously observed in *Time and the Other* (1983), the colonialist denigration of local epistemologies and of coevality (that is, simultaneous genesis) among peoples makes it evident that 'geopolitics has its ideological foundations in chronopolitics' (1983: 144). Fabian critiqued the 'denial of coevalness' embedded in European thought and particularly anthropology, tracing how it measures the 'progress' of 'races' on a modernity time line that marks so-called 'primitive' peoples as 'backward'. As Doreen Massey (1999) further pointed out, this denial of temporal coevality also generated a racialized spatial mapping of the world, building implicitly on Hegel's claims in *The Philosophy of History*. For it rendered all places outside North America and Western Europe as needing 'development' – and therefore also needing to borrow, in every sense, from the 'modern' states.

Fabian's discerning choice of the word *coeval* also enfolds connotations that link it more directly to decolonial thought. Etymologically, *coeval* connotes not just a shared temporality but also a shared project of *wellbeing*, or a *shared vitality* over a coterminous life span. The syllable '*eva*' in *coeval* derives from the proto-Indo-European Sanskrit root '*aiw*' or '*ayu*', meaning '*vital force, life; long life, longevity, eternity*' (which in Latin had become 'aevum' or 'age' and in Arabic 'eve'). '*Aiw*' is also the root of the word 'hygiene', traditionally understood to denote 'healthy' and literally meaning '*living well*' (all attributes personified in the Greek goddess Hygieia).[13] Given the Latin meanings of 'co' (that is, 'together' or 'in common'), the notion of coevality recognizes a collective project of well-being over the *longue durée*.

Many communities and polities have organized themselves around this recognition of interdependent, long-historical coevality, rather than around disavowals of it. A few examples may illustrate the point. Fabian's term coeval resonates, for instance, with the principle of *buen vivir*, or as named in the Quechua language of Andean peoples, *sumak kawsay*. As Eduardo Gudynas emphasizes (quoted in Balch, 2013), *sumak kawsay* is not solely about individual well-being but individual well-being in and through community, and as such it has recently inspired social movements and informed government policy in states such as Ecuador and Bolivia.[14] Other epistemologies particularly emphasize the need to cultivate shared knowledge across time and for a sustainable future. We might think here, for instance of the 'Seventh Generation' principle developed by the Native American Haudenosaunee people, which calls the community to gear its practices towards what will benefit the next seven generations (Starblanket and Stark, 2018). The principle of *Sankofa* embedded in the Akan Twi and Fante languages of Ghana expresses another aspect of temporal wisdom, in this case calling on the community to honour the importance of the past for the present. Translated literally as 'go back and get', or retrieve from the source (especially 'that which you may have forgotten'), the Sankofa principle is fittingly figured in the image of a bird carrying a precious egg in its mouth with its head turned backwards and its feet facing forward.[15] Likewise, as Tiara Na'puti and Judy Rohrer (2025) have discussed, the philosophies of Native Pacific peoples often feature temporal concepts that honour the past, and which inherently disrupt non-coeval or 'developmental' forms of linearity. These include, for instance, the Kanaka Maoli proverb, 'I ka wā ma mua, ka wā ma hope' (literally, in the time in front, the time in back), understood to translate as, 'The future is found in the past' (Trask, 1991: 164).

At the same time, the multiple ways that human communities render time – perennial, diurnal, and cosmological – make startlingly clear that there is not simply one '*longue durée*'. Rather there are as many 'deep-time' temporalities and 'deep-place' epistemologies as there are languages, places, and symbologies (see Doyle et al, 2025). At the same time, many of these knowledge legacies share a core element: they articulate principles of existential and planetary relationality. Thus have scholars used the term 'pluriversality' to emphasize that human and planetary communities encompass many worlds, many cosmologies and many ways of being and knowing.[16] Both the pluriversal philosophies of interdependence – which define time, place, and creaturely life – and the colonialist efforts to suppress these epistemologies deserve more attention as forces in world history and politics.

We might begin by noticing how colonizing and extractive states have often forcibly installed their own temporal orders and thus displaced temporal epistemologies organized around non-hierarchical interdependence. Most concretely, ruling states have created calendars which regulate labours of cultivation, extraction, and reproduction solely for the benefit of the rulers.[17] Furthermore, as queer theorists have emphasized, imperialist, successionist, and heteronormative ideologies of time not only control the narrative of the past, they also lay claim to the future, as they harness men and especially women into the role of reproducing the hierarchical stratifications (Freeman, 2007, 2010). Additionally, identity-structured hegemonies that control the temporalities of labour, especially of care, may be understood as central to what Achille Mbembe (2019) calls necropolitics and what Rob Nixon (2013) calls slow violence. As these thinkers emphasize, colonial violence entails more than genocides, massacres, and wars. It also unfolds over 'slow' time through gendered, racialized practices of environmental racism, resource extraction, territorial displacement, and barriers to physical, social, and cultural resources. In thinking about necropolitics and slow violence, we might also include the culture of rape and everyday acts of disrespect, as well as the ceaseless labours of care. Colonialist, racist, and masculinist disavowals of these debilitating conditions inflict yet deeper damage insofar as they deny the primal condition of relationality itself.

I propose that the time-place discourse of 'modernity' is currently the most stubborn and subtle colonialist narrative of this kind, despite its apparently neutral, rational vocabularies. Its periodization of pre-modern and modern stealthily undercuts the principles of coevality and interdependent 'co-arising'. Even when there is no condescending reference to 'pre-modern' periods, it is often implied in uses of the word modern. Furthermore, as indicated earlier, the everyday vocabularies of progress, of catching up, falling behind, and backwardness train us to segregate peoples and places and to distance 'us' from 'them'. Additionally, since the 19th century, modernity discourses have incorporated sexual, racial, and gender hierarchies, for instance through the 'modern sciences' of eugenics and phrenology (Doyle, 1994), which still circulate implicitly insofar as 'primitive' sexuality is attributed to darker-skinned and southern peoples, as well as sometimes to 'wayward' white women (those who have sex outside the caste/race/class rules of marriage).

Despite the widespread debunking of these stereotypes, and despite the rich, critical historiographic work I have been discussing, the pre-modern/modern political imaginary remains embedded. It is inscribed in the ahistorical presentism of much work in the social sciences, and it even implicitly frames a good portion of postcolonial, decolonial, and Marxist scholarship. It certainly permeates public discourses, with the effect that 'modernity' operates covertly as one of the most powerful afterlives of Western European colonialism. Its unconscious hegemony quietly undercuts some of the best efforts to dismantle Eurocentric epistemologies and craft new political imaginaries. We might ask what would emerge if we simply discontinued our use of the word modern. What if, instead, we simply spoke of early states and later states, or named the century being discussed? It's easier to do than we might think. And what if we took the existential condition of radical interdependence, and the caring labours that support it, as the starting points for our thinking? Might we dislodge, just a little, the assumption that zero-sum competition drives *all* human action? The history of care – not to mention of decolonial reimagination – stands right next to the history of violence. Why not theorize them together?

As I suggest in the next and final section, this 'theorizing' has long been a central project of the artists of the world. They have shaped the world we inhabit by dramatizing our entangled engagement with the dialectics of history.

The re-worlding arts

Authors, painters, film-makers, and performers have engaged with history not only as witnesses to the politics of their times but as historical actors shaping them. From diverse positionalities, artists have constituted aesthetics as a world*making* realm – not a world apart, as is commonly assumed. This latter myth fosters colonialist-capitalist practices that extractively appropriate art's power for 'messaging', while ensuring the impoverishment of artists (and humanities and arts programmes). Yet meanwhile artists structure and restructure our ways of being in the world, materially, psychically, emotionally, collectively. Witness the imprisonment, exile, and surveillance of writers and artists. If states pay them mind, why don't political and social analyses? As a literary scholar, in this last section I particularly focus on how and why fiction deserves full integration into anti-colonial social theory.

At the macro-political level, literature has been both instrumentalized by colonizers and turned against them, operating as a volatile site of contestation in the dialectics of struggle. Many artists have of course participated through patronage or pay in the creation of colonizing, hierarchizing hegemonies, even if not always by their own wishes. Yet they have also intentionally, if sometimes covertly, intervened critically in the dialectics of their time, encoding their own fraught inter-imperial conditions of production. Via this encoding, they have embarked, as Theodor Adorno (2014 [1966]) would say, on 'negative dialectical' projects, despite the risks of censorship, imprisonment, exile, or execution. These interventions can be found in literatures across hemispheres, reaching from early storytelling traditions to 19th-century Gothic novels, and to the 'non-linear' experimental fiction of the last century.[18] In the limited space I have, I highlight only a few examples to clarify literature's exposure and re-worlding of the political field.

As mentioned, literary productions entangle us as participants and witnesses, often literally by design – that is, their structural design. Literary genres structured around situations of address, such as soliloquies addressed to theatre audiences, do so most clearly. They implicitly cast us as witnesses, drawing a relational link between present-day historical 'reality' and the events on stage. In narrative forms, it is the very old genre of the 'framed tale' that most artfully involves the audience in these stagings of pressured relationality. For it ensconces a storyteller and listener in the text itself, mirroring the position of the text's audience. And among framed tales, *One Thousand and One Nights* is by far the most famous and the most widely translated, across states, centuries, and languages. Its long, travelling life itself reflects the dialectical retooling of arts and their technologies across historical time. That is, its frame-within-frame tales self-reflexively embody the history of literary interventions. As I've discussed elsewhere the *Nights* may thus be understood as an ur-text: a progenitor, example, and catalyst of decolonial maneuvering through aesthetic forms (Doyle, 2020: ch 2). Given the limits of space here, I will only say that, from her position *between* empires, both the storyteller Shahrazade and her anonymous creators quietly embody a political situation that many communities, generations, and historical actors – including artists – have shared with her: the situation of living dangerously among multiple empires and amid fraught layers of imperial formations. It meanwhile models ways to use art to expose the intersectionally structured violence and to practice alternative forms of witnessing, collectivity, and solidarity.

This artful project of interrupting violence is alive and well today in fiction and other aesthetic forms around the world. The compact discussion of recent fiction that follows showcases how authors continued to thematize the troubles of inter-imperial positionality and to *make felt* the already-existing, honest practices of being-together-in-time that have sustained communities over centuries. In effect, these artists not only offer mirrors to magistrates and paupers. They emplace and involve their audiences in the labours of care.

Many recent authors have called attention to their character's precarious inter-imperial positionalities. As Salman Rushdie puts it in his tale of two vying brothers in *Midnight's Children* (1981), in these texts, 'the ghosts of ancient empires [are] in the air' (although unfortunately the masculinist elements of this haunted condition lurk, disavowed, in Rushdie's own writing). The Irish writer-in-exile James Joyce had earlier named this problem and conjured its persisting afterlives in his 1922 novel *Ulysses*, which is laced with references to the *Odyssey*'s tale of post-war wandering as well as to *One Thousand and One Nights*. In the first pages, Joyce's Irish Catholic protagonist, Stephen Dedalus, laments his position as the 'servant of *two* masters ... the imperial British state ... and the Holy Roman Catholic Church' (1986: 17, emphasis added). Standing in the perennial, inter-imperial position between a rock and a hard place, Stephen also broods on the competitive 'brother motive' (1986: 173) that pervades literary texts from the Greek to the English, and meanwhile plague his relations with the men in his community.

Comparably, Mulk Raj Anand's 1935 novel *Untouchable* focuses on a laboring Dalit protagonist who perceives 'a common quality in the look of hate in the round white face of the Colonel's Wife and in the ... visage of the touched [Hindu] man' who had beaten and humiliated him that morning. By midday he is overcome by a 'spirit of resignation', which the narrator tells us derives from 'the serfdom of thousands of years' and which Bakha feels 'flowing like a wave through his body'. Writing amid yet another set of intersecting pressures in *Two Thousand Seasons* (1973), the Ghanian writer Ayi Kwei Armah traces the dialectics of a millennium of successive colonizations and successive resistance movements in the history of West Africa. Writing in the voice of a choral narrator, the story emphasizes that 'we are not Europeans, we are not Christians ... we are not Arabs, we are not Muslims' (1973: 24); and it records the struggle to maintain the long-standing values of the region's communities.

These and other authors simultaneously expose gendered structures as a key political matrix – not only of colonialism but also in failed efforts to resist colonialism. Bakha's brooding on his caste condition becomes most rageful when he learns that a Hindu priest has molested his sister during her round of house-cleaning labours for him. In Armah's *Two Thousand Seasons,* it is often the women who lead the struggles, through both tactical decisions and their everyday labours of care. The choral narrator implicitly praises their practices of 'reciprocity' and laments the resisting men's failure to engage in this practice through their refusal to ease the load of community caretaking and protection. In Indian author Arundhati Roy's *God of Small Things* (1997), when her female protagonist's Dalit lover is brutally beaten and eventually murdered, the narrator remarks that this caste-based, gendered violence 'actually began thousands of years ago' with 'Love Laws', put in place '[b]efore the British took Malabar, before the Dutch Ascendancy, before Vasco de Gama arrived, before the Zamorind's conquest of Calicut' (1998: 33).

It is no coincidence that many of these texts also restructure linear and 'realistic' temporality. They show us ways to live in time differently and see history from within deep-time perspectives. Both Joyce and Anand wrote full-length novels that however cover only a single day in the lives of their characters. By rendering the ways that each moment, each body, and each action in a day is steeped in centuries of successive regimes, they make us feel history 'flowing like a wave' through our material and social worlds. In his 800-page novel *Ulysses*, filled with allusions to the warring, wandering characters of *The Odyssey*, Joyce writes a profoundly anti-war novel, fathoming the two millennia of inter-imperial battles that flood our present.

Other texts render the dialectics of historical determinism and difficult choice-making by way of their reconfigurations of temporality. For instance, they create retrospective or looping temporal structures that, on the one hand, convey the overdetermined forces of history, and on the other hand, when looping back in time give readers a reprieve – an opening in which to imagine ways that these violent crises might not (have) happen(ed). And to ask ourselves what might have been done differently, what *we* might do differently.

Just one brief example may give some sense of this restructuring work. In Jamaican writer Michelle Cliff's *No Telephone to Heaven* (1987) we continually approach a moment of revolutionary action. Set during the upheaval of the 1970s in Jamaica, the novel exposes history as a violent struggle intertwined with efforts at care despite the complications of friendship and community. The scene that opens the novel and to which it returns at the start of many chapters is that of an old truck lumbering steeply uphill on a muddy, broken road, hauling guns and people in khakis to the site where (although we don't know it yet) they will organize their insurrectionary attack, which however will be fatally sabotaged. The novel unfolds in a looping temporal structure, repeatedly returning to this uphill journey before the insurrection and then circling back in time to approach it again from another perspective, each time carrying a new layer of backstory revealing ever more complex sexual and racial relations. In this way, readers experience both the inevitability of violence and the paradoxical necessity, nonetheless, to take responsibility for decolonial choice-making and care-taking within those violent conditions.

Not merely retrospective, texts such as *Telephone to Heaven* and many others undertake the re-worlding work that keeps alive a changing consciousness in the present and for the future. Whether written, painted, performed, or filmed, these artistic transformations of temporality re-cast history's 'progress' or 'development' as history's *questions*, including about how to act and who to befriend in a pressured, precarious field of relations. Re-creating how it feels to live inside the determinations of history while embracing suppressed possibilities for more sustaining relations, they immerse readers in decisions about 'when and where one enters' the dialectic, to paraphrase Paula Giddings.

Especially when understood as events in history, such texts model forms of open-ended listening and imagining that can inform our work as scholars, teachers, and community members in the present. Attention to their work can also loosen our attachments to Eurocentric paradigms and disciplinary key words (for example, 'development'). The dialectical engagements that they dramatize and catalyse beckon us to see that interdisciplinary collaboration is fundamental for decolonial studies.

Conclusion

This chapter has offered a decolonial and long-historical analysis of interacting empires in order to capture the long dialectics of resistance and to better understand the presence of pluriversal resources for collective sustenance. It has kept decolonial relational epistemologies and practices in view, including as expressed in the arts, so as to draw attention to their leveraging power in the dialectics of historical change. In this light, the chapter has argued that intersectional, historical, and interdisciplinary methods are essential to a dialectical, decolonial analysis.

As scholars, we have it within our reach to foster the conversations that can bring this decolonial understanding of historical struggle to fuller fruition. After all, many of us bring diverse resources and knowledges from our life histories and communities as well as from our academic learning, all of which can feed these reformulations. In fact to some degree, in some places, the academy and its standard curricula have already been changed by our presence and institutional activism. But, under neoliberal work conditions and with limited funding, few of us have found time or material resources for the sustained collaborations needed to share and connect these knowledges. Then too, since we all remain entangled in the colonial histories we seek to critique, and we inhabit unequal positionalities and incommensurable epistemologies, this work is difficult. It requires learning from and listening to each other beyond our comfort zones, and thereby cultivating the trust that coercion and division have discouraged. Yet if, as scholar-teachers, we commit ourselves to slow-time habits of collective care in whatever degree we can manage, perhaps we may begin to counteract slow-time violence. One path is to organize interdisciplinary decolonial forums like the one that has generated this book.

Ultimately, this building of alliances across differences, within and beyond academia, can itself become part of the decolonial dialectics of history.

Notes

[1] For other linkings of postcolonial and decolonial feminisms, see Lugones (2010) and Lugones et al (2022).

[2] Our approach here shares a spirit with, for instance, Catherine Walsh and Walter Mignolo's emphasis on pluriversality in *On Decoloniality*, but it demurs from their region-centred mapping of theory. They rightly gloss colonial divisions as 'the habits that modernity/coloniality implanted in all of us'. But their implication (2018: 4) that Africa and Asia have generated only pragmatic thought for state-building while Latin America have led the way in decolonial theory risks repeating some familiar, racialized binaries.

[3] Tuck and Yang's singular emphasis on land leads them to group the white-European settlers together with the captive Africans and their descendants who were exploited, tortured captives by white settlers (2012: 7). This grouping elides radical differences and risks repeating colonialist violence.

4   This discussion draws on the wealth of recent critical historiographies, cited in this chapter. Many took inspiration from Abu-Lughod's *Before European Hegemony* (1989) and some of these also correct her sidelining of Africa.
5   Indigenous and environmental thinkers join these scholars in emphasizing that labours of care are often inspired by forms of planetary and relational consciousness (see Barker, 2017).
6   The theoretical introduction and early chapters of *Inter-imperiality* discuss pre-1500 dialectical formations; later chapters move from the 16th through 20th centuries, analysing inter-imperial, anti-colonial, and literary formations in conjunction.
7   On interconnected legacies, see Doyle, *Inter-imperiality*, pp 8–15.
8   'Shatter-zones' appears in the title of Bartov and Weitz (2013).
9   At least since the anthology *This Bridge Called My Back* (Moraga and Anzaldúa, 1981), womanist and feminist thinkers of colour have noted that the energy for political struggles has depended on daily caretaking and labours typically undertaken by women. This critique also informs Caribbean theorists such as Donette Francis, Belinda Edmondson, and Michelle Stephens. More recently, scholars such as Neferti Xina M. Tadiar (2009, 2022) have foregrounded the relational practices and important influence of women domestic labourers who have organized labour movements.
10 For the early groundbreaking theorization of intersectionality, see Patricia Hill Collins' *Black Feminist Thought* (1990) and also her more recent publications on the concept. For a wide sample of recent work on social reproduction, see Bhattacharya (2017). For an interdisciplinary analysis of intersectional formations, see Doyle (1994).

    For useful overviews and assessments of the concept, see Brittney Cooper (2015) and de Lima Costa (2016). Other early intersectional work includes Lerner (1987), Rubin (1997), Rowbotham (2015 [1973]), and Sedgwick (1985).

    For relevant queer theory, see, for example, Freeman (2007, 2010) and Amar and El Shakry (2013).
11 Joyce, *Ulysses* (1986: 12.1156–58).
12 Some readers may also want to see Boaventura de Sousa Santos, *Epistemologies of the South: Justice against Epistemicide*, despite the evidence of the author's practices of harassment.
13 See https://www.etymonline.com/word/coeval and https://www.etymonline.com/search?q=hygiene
14 For a helpful analysis of this principle see https://www.theguardian.com/sustainable-business/blog/buen-vivir-philosophy-south-america-eduardo-gudynas
15 This understanding is expressed in the proverb, 'Se wo were fi na wosankofa a yenkyi' or 'Sankofa w'onkyir', which translates as 'It is not wrong to go back for that which you have forgotten'. It commonly refers to ancient traditions and customs that have been left behind, including due to colonialism.
16 Apparently first used by US philosopher William James in *A Pluralistic Universe* (1909, 1977), this term has since been developed by several scholars. See T.C. Mercier (2019) for a helpful overview. Most recently in decolonial studies, it has been developed by Suárez-Krabbe (2012); Walsh and Mignolo (2018), and Escobar (2018, 2020), as well as others. For edited collections, see Reiter (ed) (2018); Woons and Weier (eds) (2016); de Sousa Santos and Sena Martins (2012); Salleh et al (eds) (2019).
17 For the politics of calendars in diverse polities, including Chinese, Aztec, Islamicate, and Saharan, see: Olaniyi (2014); Steele (2007); Aveni (2016); Oxby (1998); and Drucker-Brown (1999); Stowasser (2014); and Holbrook et al (2008).
18 For discussion of early internationalist movements, see Doyle (2020: chs 2, 4, 5 and 6). Also see Boehmer (2002) and Kelley (1999).

References

Abu-Lughod, J. (1989) *Before European Hegemony: The World System 1250–1350, A.D*, Oxford University Press.

Adorno, T.W. (2014 [1966]) *Negative Dialectics*, translated by E.B. Ashton, Bloomsbury Academic.

Agamben, G. (1998) *Homo Sacer: Sovereign Power and Bare Life*, Stanford University Press.

Armah, A.K. (1973) *Two Thousand Seasons*, Per Ankh.

Amar, P. and El Shakry, O. (eds) (2013) Introduction: Curiosities of iddle East studies in Queer Times, *International Journal of Middle East Studies*, 45(2): 331–335.

Amin, S. (1990) *Delinking: Towards a Polycentric World*, Bloomsbury Publishing.

Arjomand, A. (1999) Law, agency and policy in medieval Islamic society: Development of the institutions of learning from the tenth to the fifteenth century, *Comparative Studies in Society and History*, 41(2): 263–93.

Armitage, D. and Subrahmanyam, S. (2009) *The Age of Revolutions in Global Context, c. 1760–1840*, Palgrave.

Aveni, A.F. (2016) 'The Measure, Meaning, and Transformation of Aztec Time and Calendars' in D.L. Nichols and E. Rodríguez-Alegria (eds) *The Oxford Handbook of the Aztecs*, Oxford, pp 107–16.

Balch, O. (2013) *Buen vivir*: The social philosophy inspiring movements in South America, *The Guardian*, 4 February. https://www.theguardian.com/sustainable-business/blog/buen-vivir-philosophy-south-america-eduardo-gudynas

Ballantyne, T. and Burton, A.M. (2014) *Empires and the Reach of the Global, 1870–1945*, Harvard University Press.

Barker, J. (ed) (2017) *Critically Sovereign: Indigenous Gender, Sexuality, and Feminist Studies*, Duke University Press.

Bartov, O. and Weitz, E.D. (2013) *Shatterzone of Empires: Coexistence and Violence in the German, Habsburg, Russian, and Ottoman Borderlands*, Indiana University Press.

Bernasconi, R. (2003) With what must the history of philosophy begin? Hegel's role in the debate on the place of India within the history of philosophy, in D.A. Duquette (ed) *Hegel's History of Philosophy: New Interpretations*, State University of New York Press, pp 35–50.

Bhattacharya, T. (ed) (2017) *Social Reproduction Theory: Remapping Class, Recentering Oppression*, Pluto Press.

Bloom, J.M. (2001) *Paper Before Print: The History and Impact of Paper in the Islamic World*, Yale University Press.

Boatca, M. and Parvulescu, A. (2022) *Creolising the Modern: Transylvania Across Empires*, Cornell University Press.

Boehmer, E. (2002) *Empire, the National, and the Postcolonial, 1890–1920: Resistance in Interaction*, Oxford University Press.

Bromell, N. (1993) *By the Sweat of the Brow: Literature and Labor in Antebellum America*, University of Chicago Press.

Buck-Morss, S. (2005) *Hegel, Haiti, and Universal History*, University of Pittsburgh.

Burbank, J. (2007) The rights of difference: Law and citizenship in the Russian empire, in A.L. Stoler, C. McGranahan and P.C. Perdue (eds) *Imperial Formations*, School for Advanced Research Press, pp 77–112.

Burke III, E. (2009) Islam at the center: Technological complexes and the roots of modernity, *Journal of World History*, 20(2): 166–8.

Chatterjee, P. (1993) *The Nation and its Fragments: Colonial and Postcolonial Histories*, Princeton University Press.

Cliff, M. (1987) *No Telephone to Heaven*, Plume Press.

Collins, P.H. (1990) *Black Feminist Thought: Knowledge Consciousness, and the Politics of Empowerment*, Hyman Press.

Cooper, B. (2015) Intersectionality, in L. Disch and M. Hawkesworth (eds) *The Oxford Handbook of Feminist Theory*, Oxford University Press, pp 385–406.

Davis, N.Z. (2006) *Trickster Travels: A Sixteenth-Century Muslim Between Worlds*, Hill & Wang.

de Lima Costa, C. (2016) Gender and equivocation: Notes on decolonial feminist translations, in W. Harcourt (ed) *The Palgrave Book of Gender and Development*, Palgrave Macmilllan, pp 48–61.

de Sousa Santos, B. and Sena Martins, B. (eds) (2012) *The Pluriverse of Human Rights: The Diversity of Struggles for Dignity*, Routledge.

Doyle, L. (1994) *Bordering on the Body: The Racial Matrix of Modern Fiction and Culture*, Oxford University Press.

Doyle, L. (2010) *Freedom's Empire: Race and the Rise of the Novel in Atlantic Modernity, 1640–1940*, Duke University Press.

Doyle, L. (2020) *Inter-imperiality: Vying Empires, Gendered Labors, and the Literary Arts of Alliance*, Duke University Press.

Doyle, L. (ed) (2016) Labor travels, art forms, *Literature Compass*, 13(5): 261–5.

Doyle, L. (2025) Embedded interventions: undoing disavowal, witnessing coeval time, in L. Doyle, M. wa Gĩthĩnji and S. Gikandi (eds) *Dynamics of Deep Place and Deep Time Decolonial Reconstellations, Volume 1*, Routledge, pp 175–205.

Doyle, L., wa Gĩthĩnji, M. and Gikandi, S. (eds) (2025) *Decolonial Reconstellations* [three volumes published simultaneously: *Dynamics of Deep Place and Deep Time*, Volume 1; *Dissolving Master Narratives*, Volume Two; and *Rethinking Identities in Political Economy*, Volume Three], Routledge.

Drucker-Brown, S. (1999) The politics of calendars, *Cambridge Anthropology*, 9–17.

Edmondson, B. (1998) *Making Men: Gender, Literary Authority, and Women's Writing in Caribbean Narrative*, Duke University Press.

Emmet, R. (nd) The speech from the dock. www.robertemmet.org/speech.htm

Escobar, A. (2007) Worlds and knowledge otherwise: The Latin American modernity/coloniality research program, *Cultural Studies*, 179–210.

Escobar, A. (2018) *Designs for the Pluriverse: Radical Interdependence, Autonomy, and the Making of World*, Duke University Press.

Escobar, A. (2020) *Pluriversal Politics: The Real and the Possible*, Duke University Press.

Fabian, J. (1983) *Time and the Other: How Anthropology Makes Its Object*, Columbia University Press.

Ferguson, N. (2003) *Empire: How Britain Made the Modern World*, Allen.

Francis, D. (2010) *Fictions of Feminine Citizenship: Sexuality and the Nation in Contemporary Caribbean Literature*, Palgrave Macmillan.

Francis, D. (2025) Sedimentary arrangements: Decorative objects of deep time and place, in L.Doyle, M. wa Gĩthĩnji and S. Gikandi (eds) *Reconceiving Identities in Political Economy: Decolonial Reconstellations, Volume One*, Routledge, pp 67–81.

Freeman, E. (ed) (2007) Special issue of *GLQ: A Journal and Lesbian and Gay Studies*, 13(2–3).

Freeman, E. (2010) *Time Binds: Queer Temporalities, Queer Histories*, Duke University Press.

Fricker, M. (2007) *Epistemic Injustice: Power and the Ethics of Knowing*, Oxford University Press.

Gatsheni-Ndlovu, S. (2020) *Decolonization, Development, and Knowledge in Africa*, Routledge.

Giddings, P.J. (ed) (1984) *When and Where I Enter: The Impact of Black Women on Race and Sex in America*, William Morrow.

Hegel, G.W.F. (1977 [1807]) *Phenomenology of Spirit*, translated by A.V. Miller, Clarendon Press.

Holbrook, J.R., Medupe, T. and Urama, J.O. (eds) (2008) *African Cultural Astronomy: Current Archaeoastronomy and Ethnoastronomy Research in Africa*, Springer Science & Business Media.

James, W. (1977) *A Pluralistic Universe*, Harvard University Press.

Joyce, J. (1986) *Ulysses*, edited by H. Gabler, Vintage.

Kelley, R.D.G. (1999) But a local phase of a world problem: Black history's global.

Lavan, M., Payne, R.W. and Weisweiler, J. (eds) (2016) *Cosmopolitanism and Empire: Universal Rulers, Local Elites, and Cultural integration in the Ancient Near East and Mediterranean*, Oxford University Press.

LeDonne, J. (1997) *The Russian Empire and the World, 1700–1917: The Geopolitics of Expansion and Containment*, Oxford University Press.

Ledoux, E.M. (2013) *Social Reform in Gothic Writing: Fantastic Forms of Change, 1764–1834*, Palgrave.
Lerner, G. (1987) *The Creation of Patriarchy*, Oxford University Press.
Lewis, M.E. (1999) *Writing and Authority in Early China*, SUNY Press.
Liboiron, M. (2021) *Pollution is Colonialism*, Duke University Press.
Lugones, M. (2010) Towards a decolonial feminism, *Hypatia*, 25(4): 742–59.
Lugones, M., Espinosa-Miñoso, Y. and Maldonado-Torres, N. (eds) (2022) *Decolonial Feminism in Abya Yala: Caribbean, Meso, and South American Contributions and Challenges*, Rowman & Littlefield.
MacLean, G. (2007) *Looking East: English Writing and the Ottoman Empire Before 1800*, Palgrave.
Mann, M. (1986) *The Sources of Social Power*, Volume I, Cambridge University Press.
Martin, A.E. (2017) Gothic internationalism: Irish nationalist critiques of empire as a system of violence and trauma, in L. Kasmer (ed) *Traumatic Tales: British Nationhood and National Trauma in Nineteenth Century Literature*, Routledge, pp 97–117.
Massey, D. (1999) Spaces of politics, in D. Massey, J. Allen and P. Sarre (eds) *Human Geography Today*, Polity Press, pp 279–93.
Mazumdar, S. (2003) The politics of religion and national origin: rediscovering Hindu Indian, in V. Kaiwar and S. Mazumdar (eds) *Antinomies of Modernity*, Duke University, pp 223–60.
Mbembe, A. (2019) *Necropolitics*, Duke University Press.
Mercier, T.C. (2019) Uses of 'the pluriverse': Cosmos, interrupted – or the others of humanities, *Ostium*, 15(2): 1–18.
Mignolo, W.D. (2005) *The Idea of Latin America*, Blackwell.
Mignolo, W.D. (2018) Foreword, in B. Reiter (ed) *Constructing the Pluriverse*, Duke University Press, pp ix–xvi.
Moraga, C. and Anzaldúa, G.E. (eds) (1981) *This Bridge Called My Back: Writings by Radical Women of Color*, Persephone Press.
Na'puti, T. and Rohrer, J. (2025) Moves beyond Pacific colonialism, in L. Doyle, M. wa Gĩthĩnji and S. Gikandi (eds) *Dynamisms of Deep Time and Deep Place: Decolonial Reconstellations, Volume One*, Routledge, 270–83.
Nixon, R. (2013) *Slow Violence and the Environmentalism of the Poor*, Harvard University Press.
Nwankwo, I.C.K. (2014) *Black Cosmopolitanism: Racial Consciousness and Transnational Identity in the Nineteenth-Century Americas (Rethinking the Americas)*, University of Pennsylvania Press.
Olaniyi, A.O. (2014) Historical analysis of calendars: Chinese calendars and world calendars, *Asian Journal of Research in Social Sciences and Humanities*, 4(11): 114–30.
Oxby, C. (1998) The manipulation of time: Calendars and power in the Sahara, *Nomadic Peoples*, 2(1–2): 137–49.

Piggott, J.R. (1997) *The Emergence of Japanese Kingship*, Stanford University Press.
Pratt, M.L. (2015) Language and the afterlives of Empire, *PMLA*, 130(2): 348–57.
Ramamurthy, P. and Tambe, A. (eds) (2017) Preface: Decolonial and postcolonial approaches: A Dialogue, *Feminist Studies*, 43(3): 503–9.
Reiter, B. (ed) (2018) *Constructing the Pluriverse*, Duke University Press.
Rowbotham, S. (2015 [1973]) *Women's Consciousness, Men's World*, Verso.
Roy, A. (1998 [1997]) *God of Small Things*, Harper Perennial.
Rubin, G. (1997) The traffic in women: Notes on the 'political economy' of sex, in L. Nicholson (ed) *The Second Wave: A Reader in Feminist Theory*, Routledge, pp 27–62.
Rushdie, S. (1981) *Midnight's Children*, Jonathan Cape Press.
Sabelo, G.-N. (2013) *Empire, Global Coloniality and African Subjectivity*, Berghahn Books.
Sabelo, G.-N. (2020) *Decolonization, Development, and Knowledge in Africa: Turning Over a New Leaf*, Routledge.
Salleh, A., Demaria, F., Escobar, A., Kothari, A. and Acosta, A. (eds) (2019) *Pluriverse: A Post-Development Dictionary*, Columbia University Press.
Sedgwick, E.K. (1985) *Between Men: English Literature and Male Homosocial Desire*, Columbia University Press.
Simpson, A. (2014) *Mohawk Interruptus: Political Life across the Borders of Settler States*, Duke University Press.
Smith, L.T. (2013) *Decolonizing Methodologies: Research and Indigenous Peoples*, Zed Books.
Starblanket, G. and Stark, H.K. (2018) Towards a relational paradigm, in M. Asch, J. Borrows and J. Tully (eds) *Resurgence and Reconciliation*, University of Toronto Press, pp 175–208.
Steele, J.M. (2007) *Calendars and Years II: Astronomy and Time in the Ancient and Medieval World*, Oxbow Press.
Stowasser, B.F. (2014) *The Day Begins at Sunset: Perceptions of Time in the Islamic World*, Bloomsbury Publishing.
Suárez-Krabbe, J. (2012) Rights Confinement and liberation: Rearguard theory and Freedom of movements, in B. de Sousa Santos and B. Martins (eds) *The Pluriverse of Human Rights*, Routledge, pp 218–36.
Suárez-Krabbe, J. (2023) Relinking as healing: on crisis, whiteness and the existential dimensions of decolonization, *Globalizations*, 20(2): 304–15. https://doi.org/10.1080/14747731.2021.2025293.
Suárez-Krabbe, J. (2025) Relinking to the struggles at the heart of the world, in L. Doyle, M. wa Gĩthĩnji and S. Gikandi (eds) *Dynamisms of Deep Time and Deep Place: Decolonial Reconstellations, Volume One*, Routledge, pp 248–69.
Tadiar, N.X.M. (2009) *Things Fall Away: Philippine Historical Experience and the Makings of Globalization*, Duke University Press.
Tadiar, N.X.M. (2022) *Remaindered Life*, Duke University Press.

Thiong'o, N. (1986) *Decolonising the Mind: The Politics of Language in African Literature*, Heinemann Educational.

Tran, B. (2017) *Post-Mandarin: Masculinity and Aesthetic Modernity in Colonial Vietnam*, Fordham University Press.

Trask, H.-K. (1991) Natives and anthropologists: The colonial struggle, *The Contemporary Pacific*, 3(1): 159–67.

Tuck, E. and Yang, K.W. (2012) Decolonization is not a metaphor, *Decolonization: Indigeneity, Education, and Society*, 1(1): 1–40.

Walsh, C.D. (2008) (Post)coloniality in Ecuador: The indigenous movement's practices and politics of (re)signification and decolonization, in M. Moraña, E. Dussel and C. Jauregui (eds) *Coloniality at Large: The Latin America and the Postcolonial Debate*, Duke University Press, pp 506–18.

Walsh, C.D. and Mignolo, W. (2018) *On Decoloniality: Concepts, Analytics, Praxis*, Duke University Press.

Woons, M. and Weier, S. (eds) (2016) *Critical Epistemologies of Global Politics*, E-International Relations Publishing.

Wynter, S. (2003) Unsettling the coloniality of being/power/truth/freedom: Towards the human, after man, its overrepresentation – an argument, *CR: The New Centennial Review*, 3(3): 257–337.

7

Anti-Colonial Planetary Struggle: History, Humans, and Us

Neferti X.M. Tadiar

Introduction

Every book is belated, my friend Saidiya consoled me when I bemoaned how long it takes me to complete one, how slow I am to write. The belatedness is related to something. Some might think it is belated in relation to the debates of the day, or the fashion, perhaps the news, the change in regimes, the change in political demands and public feeling. There would seem to be a current, a temporal movement, taking place, even inside the halls of the academy, but more so in the larger world outside of it, traversing it. What is that current, that movement happening seemingly without pause, the measure for the belatedness of our writing? Is it not what we habitually call history?

History

In the Philippines, battles have been raging over history, as the 2022 presidential election of the son of the former dictator, Ferdinand Marcos, and the vice-presidential election of the daughter of former autocrat, Rodrigo Duterte, to the vice-presidency threaten at once to revise the past and to repeat it. The adage, 'history is written by the victors', has now become a maxim repeated by Marcos supporters to clear the way for a retelling of the period of Martial Law as a golden age, and to put to rest the stories of financial plunder, violence, torture, and murder that otherwise haunt it. 'History' is under attack, trivialized as no more than politically motivated hearsay, and targeted as pernicious liberal propaganda. The dismissal and threat of erasure of the historical experiences and documentary records of a whole era, less than 50 years ago, the besmirching of the memories of this particular living past for many who survived the worst of its experiences, and the imminent dismantling of institutions built to ensure the recovery of the Marcos' stolen wealth and the prevention of similar abuses of power – all of this has been met with reinvigorated campaigns by writers, artists, activists, and other ordinary people to remember, document, and defend historical truth (the truth of dictatorship), as part of an intensifying recommitment to struggles for change. Is not change, after all, what is meant by the phrase 'to make history'? Yet in the face of this recent electoral triumph, it is impossible not to feel the daunting force of history repeating.

The repetition of history and the conflict over history, which the return to power of the Marcoses and Dutertes occasioned, were at the forefront of my mind while I was in the Philippines during the 2022 presidential elections, staying in the same house we lived in when my family and I participated in the People Power revolt that deposed the dictator Marcos in 1986. From that same house I was now witnessing the repudiation of that popular revolt, which inaugurated the world-historical wave of people power movements across the world from the Tianamen Square protests, to the fall of the Berlin Wall, to the revolts of the Arab Spring. The current wilful return to a previous historical moment and order, which these movements had sought to transform, has prompted me to reflect on my own approach to history in my recent book, *Remaindered Life* – to probe that sense of untimeliness that its belatedness might signal.

Certainly, many scholars, including many now engaged in this particular skirmish over history, do not understand it in the narrow political terms and shallow temporal frame within which the debate has been cast by the upholders of the Marcos golden age thesis. Even as many, including myself, consider social, political, and economic transformations wrought by the decisive actions and policies made and acted on by particular presidents, governments, and mega capitalists, we do not see these big men and like personages as making history as they please or under circumstances of their own choosing.[1] We know all too well that experience of ongoing catastrophe that is elided by the modernist temporality of progress, development, and evolution (Benjamin, 1968).

Colonial history is neither past event nor past structure. In 2024, colonialism continues to beat down its self-righteously dispossessive, catastrophic rain of genocidal violence on Palestinians in Gaza and the West Bank, at the hands of the ethnosupremacist state of Israel with the weapons, international diplomatic and media cover, and financial backing of its colonial predecessors, the imperial powers of the United States and most Western European states. Certainly, in the 21st century, we feel the nightmare of dead generations weighing on the living (Marx, 1978). Still we endeavour to grasp marked changes in the orders of things, in the political, economic, social and cultural, psychic and affective, structures and practices wrought by systems, such as colonialism, slavery, and capitalism, changes that spell our own narrative habits of periodization, and the stories we tell about the past, present, and future. Undoubtedly, the currents and countercurrents in this conflict over history is also the turbulence that will determine the stories we will pass on or not, the stories we will want to tell, remit, withhold, or finally let go.[2]

I am not a historian, but I too have a story to tell about this time, which is also the time of my life as well as the lives of many, both living and dead. It is a time which is not one, a time that is not contained within the bounds of a single designable historical age, simply containing multiple tailings of past eras.

My own analytical-political tale is a retelling of the dominant story of our global present that continues to be told as fundamentally the story of capital, even when that story of the restructuring of capital is told as the consequential response to worker's radical struggles in the Global North. If I borrow from the latter autonomist Marxist version of this tale in my own retelling of the story of our global present as the aftermath and afterlife of decolonization – the story of continuing struggle on the part of the colonized to live beyond the bounds of life set by an imperial, racial capitalist order – it is to honour and tend to the subaltern lives of the colonized and their descendants in the long and continuing making of another present.

It is not, after all, only the recent tendentious revisions of Philippine political history that call into question what we mean by and expect of History – what it means to write it or to make it, and the relation between the two. Postcolonial, feminist, and anti-colonial native intellectuals have long interrogated dominant histories that have reduced the role of the colonized to no more than the backdrop or receiving ground of a (colonizing) sovereign European male subject's actions and agency in the world. They have challenged the epistemic framework and categories with which such History subsumes the lifeworlds and experiences of modernity's others into the main story of that very sovereign subject's own worldly evolution and progress, as mere predicates and objects of that subject's narrative of freedom and as mere preparatory acts and developmental stages in the genealogy of a universal modernity (Guha, 1982; Trouillot, 1995; Dayan, 1998; Smith, 1999; Spivak, 1999; Chakrabarty, 2000). The erasures and foreclosures enacted by what we call History have thus marked the sites of a radical subalternization and dispossession of pluriverses of peoples in the course of that history's making. It is a deliberate sidelining and undoing of those peoples' struggles to survive their willed decimation, struggles at the heart of an unfinished movement of decolonization that, today, burns brightly with the renewed fervour of a generation of youth uncowed by the promises of capitalist futures and ignited by the ecocidal consequences of business-as-usual profit-making ventures, with their genocidal wars.

Humans

Under the pressures of climate change-induced environmental disasters, discourses of the Anthropocene have further challenged the adequacy of our social, historical, and cultural disciplinary frameworks for understanding the past, present, and future of human communities in a rapidly transforming 'planetary conjuncture'. The Anthropocene is in the order of geological time, in which species come and go, encompassing tens of millions of years of 'earth history'. This order of time is in stark contrast to even the half millennium that anti-colonial scholars identify as the time of racial Capitolocene, a renaming of the epoch and a revision of the dated origins of humanity's geological agency from the narrow timeline dating from British industrialization to the centuries earlier Western European conquest of the New World (Vergès, 2017). Processes of earth history 'outscale our very sense of human time', spurring a search for new methods adequate to the magnitude of that challenge to the disciplinary assumptions of the humanities (Baucom, 2020: 15; Chakrabarty, 2021: 156). 'The time of such history is the time of Earth System Science, vast and incomprehensible in terms of the concerns of human history though it is available to our cognitive and affective faculties' (Chakrabarty, 2021: 173).

As Françoise Vergès writes, the Anthropocene is a 'narrative centered on the threat to human beings as an undifferentiated whole', even as the prime victims of the consequences of global warming and climate change have in fact been minorities and peoples of the South (Vergès, 2017). Although postcolonial scholars pondering the implications of climate change for the critical humanities acknowledge the power differences among humans and the role of colonialism and capitalism in creating climate change, still some continue to speak of 'human time' and 'human horizons of time', as flat, fully known phenomena, shrunken in scale and significance in relation to the vastness and complexity of planetary processes.

It seems to me to be a mistake to assume that a new imperative 'history' that can address our planetary crisis must now take on and encompass the very scale of geological time in which the aggregate activity of humans has assumed transformative agency. Or to assume that 'humanity' as a species must now take precedence as the subject of that history, 'an emergent, new universal history of humans that flashes up in the moment of the danger that is climate change' (Chakrabarty, 2021: 45).

Do we in fact need a new universal history? Do we need to match the scale of planetary crisis, to approximate the geological agency of anthropogenic climate change? If 'climate change poses for us a question of human collectivity, an us pointing to a figure of the universal that escapes our capacity to experience the world', certainly such premises put into question the salience of the partial figure of humanity, the Global South, as a postcolonial historical subject, an organizing political and theoretical framework, and a decolonial and decolonizing project, for addressing our current planetary crisis.

While reflections on climate change importantly call attention to the vast and infinitely diverse more-than-human living and nonliving worlds composing the planet, which is the very condition of possibility of continued existence of human life, the opposition that these scholars foreground between 'the forces of history' and 'the forcings of climate change' only serves to naturalize both 'humanity' as a uniform biological being and 'history' as the universal horizon of time of humans. They forget that the very differentiation of humans into graded orders – distinctions assumed and implemented between the human, less human, and the nonhuman – has itself acted as a destructive organizing force of colonialism with planetary effects.

The magnitude of ecological disruption caused by European colonization of the New World has been indexed, for example, to the century and a half of planetary cooling from the late 16th to mid-17th century, a period referred to as the 'Little Ice Age'. Recent research has linked the sudden drop in atmospheric carbon and global mean temperatures (in a reverse greenhouse effect) during this time to the massive re-forestation of vast tracts of cultivated land that took place in the wake of the catastrophic decimation of native populations in the Americas – 'the Great Dying' – brought about by European conquest (Koch et al, 2019; Ghosh, 2021: 52–3). Far from being an incidental effect of European invasion, genocide and widespread forms of violence against native peoples and their 'webs of life' have been viewed by feminist, Indigenous, and postcolonial scholars as intrinsic to the ecology of settler-colonial domination, which is predicated on a metaphysic of 'human' life opposed to 'nature', over which 'Man' has been granted full dominion (as the image and representative of God on earth) (Simpson, 2016; Tsing, 2016; Federici, 2004; Merchant, 1980; Mies et al, 1988; Ghosh, 2021; Whyte, 2022). European expansion was a project of 'ecological and topographic transformation' geared towards remaking alien terrains and lifeworlds into a proper environment for European colonial settlement (Ghosh, 2021: 52). This was a project of 'ecological imperialism' insofar as it established the lifeways of colonists over and above and at the expense of Indigenous ecologies through violence, conscripting the agencies of other accompanying species (what Alfred Crosby calls the European 'portmanteau of biota') in a mode of biopolitical warfare against the ecologies (and ontologies) of Indigenous peoples, deemed less than or not human (Crosby, 1986; Ghosh, 2021: 55).

The 'ecology of settler-colonial domination' entails the erasure of and assault on Indigenous ecologies, strategically undermining what Kyle Whyte calls 'collective continuance', the adaptive capacities and relations of interdependence and responsibility with a broader lifeworld of the earth

(Whyte, 2022). Colonization's principal action, Malcolm Ferdinand argues, was this act of inhabiting, 'based upon a set of actions that determined the boundaries between those who inhabit and those who do not inhabit', between lands that are inhabited and others not, between homes and ways of living that are proper forms of habitation and those that are not (Ferdinand, 2018: 27). Structured by principles of territorial domination, exploitation and extraction of land and nature, and othericide, that is the denial of Otherness and its reduction to the Same of the colonizer, this colonial inhabitation establish forms of habitation based on intensive monocultures and mass exploitation of human beings, paradigmatically exemplified by colonial plantations and slavery.

Anna Tsing argues that it is the proliferation and generalization of plantations, 'those ecological simplifications in which living things are transformed into resources – future assets – by removing them from their life worlds', that has produced contemporary environmental disasters. 'Anthropogenic climate change, the extinction crisis and radioactive pollution ... are all produced through the search for assets through simplified ecologies and the industrial processes these ecologies have made possible' (Tsing, 2016: 4). This mode of being and inhabitation and its catastrophic planetary consequences is the bequest and accomplishment of the category of human called Man.

As the agent and consequence of colonial power, the very category of 'human' thus acts at once as a 'force of history' and a 'forcing of climate change', or at least a crucial precipitant. And yet, the universalization and totalization of 'humanity' as a planetary agent, which is held to supersede its now reduced role as subject of history, only further subalternizes the very lives of the colonized and their descendants. No longer considered part of a degraded, violated, and uninhabitable 'nature', the most disenfranchised peoples of the world are folded into a unified human subject held responsible for environmental catastrophes whose worst consequences they are the first and most likely to suffer.

'History was the story of people who were regarded as fully human', the Māori scholar Linda Tuhiwai Smith writes (Smith, 1999: 32). So it continues to be today. In this very late moment of colonialism, a story is being shoved in our faces of the plight of a Zionist humanity surrounded and besieged by terror. That surrounding terror is figured by an entire people, the Palestinian people, whose colonially deemed fate is to be eradicated for their oppressors' paramount humanity to persist.

More than only a story of the past, the history of the already fully human is a contemporary material force, means, and impetus of a revanchist global imperial war, the open declaration of which was signalled with the 2001 launch of the global war on terror, when the United States without shame claimed for itself the name of the aggrieved subject in the phrase 'crimes against humanity', writing out by means of this world-historical act of unending war, all manner of violence that the United States itself, along with its imperial partners and proxies, had carried out with impunity everywhere in the name of a colonial humanity.

When the United States began bombing Afghanistan in October 2001, I called this revanchist global war, 'the war to be human', seeing this spectacular unleashing of violence as an aggressive insistence on and protection of the global mode of life embodied by the 'already human' at the helm of this war. In that moment, more than 20 years ago, it became brutally apparent that the global war on terror was the vindication and practical measure for securing the exclusive rights of freedom and privileges of the already human. This now endless war reprises the neocolonial wars, with which the West had answered the decolonization struggles of 'the wretched of the earth' half a century earlier, in Algeria, Kenya, Guatemala, the Congo, Vietnam, Nicaragua, the Philippines, as well as in the urban streets, rural plains, and island territories of the United States itself. If decolonization had posed the question of what it might mean to become human in the wake of the destruction of a colonial, racist humanism, neocolonial war was nothing less than a war for the West to remain human in the face of the monstrous barbarism that people's struggles revealed to be but the West's own.

The war to be human suggests that the master code of the human as Sylvia Wynter understands it continues to propel the history we see being made all around us, its forces and agents driving the relentless production of stratospheric wealth and violent powers of impunity out of the disposability and liquidity of life that it has secured. This war bears and realizes the specific anthropogenic logic and action that has created the conditions of planetary catastrophe.

War is the force of history waged by many new and old agents seeking those very privileges of the already human and their life of value, as no better epitomized than the case of Israel on behalf of those who were themselves less than a century ago deemed less than human and therefore exterminable. It is a 500-year-old hurt, a global and planetary wounding that has not ceased but rather only accelerated and spread farther and wider across whole swathes of existence, engraving pain onto hitherto unreachable interiors and surfaces of living on earth. The history of the present recedes further back in time. Twenty years, 75 years, 500 years, and more. And still the hour grows late.

Perhaps my own sense of the belatedness of this writing on remaindered life in the context of 21st-century imperialism pertains less to being behind, happening later than due or expected, and more to what is still arriving, what is happening still, beyond the beginnings and endings in historical accounts, an untimeliness that haunts the time of human freedom. It is this haunting, as Saidiya Hartman writes of other belated encounters, that accounts for 'the living presence of slavery', the 'duration of injury' that she understands as 'the time of slavery', which negates the common-sense intuition of time as progression and the easy separation of then and now, which co-exist (Hartman, 2002: 763). 'Plantation time', Katherine McKittrick shows, is this lingering and migration of a logic 'characteristic of (but not identical to) slavery' in geographies through which 'we can trace the past to the present and the present to the past', 'in agriculture, banking, and mining, in trade and tourism, and across other colonial and postcolonial spaces – the prison, the city, the resort' regulating the distinction between inhabitable, human geographies and uninhabitable geographies 'designated as incongruous with humanness' (McKittrick, 2014: 3, 6, 7).

Like the time of slavery and plantation time, the time of primitive accumulation, the violence of dispossession that is the genesis of capital, cannot be contained in the past. As Lenape scholar Joanne Barker and Diné scholar Glen Coulthard, and many other Native scholars argue, settler-colonial dispossession is not only foundational to racial capitalism, but also ongoing and recurrent, consisting of brutal processes that entail the erasure and writing over of Indigenous land and life in the establishment of the legal, territorial, financial, discursive, and epistemological order through which such dispossession is naturalized, guaranteed, and further enabled. These are times that figure in my own account of the present, times seemingly anachronistic or outside the time of history, yet marking and shaping the very environs – *the enabling means, media, and milieu* – for the discernible transformations that constitute the contemporary history of capital as well as the earth's current geological epoch.

In being confined to all the developments that capital itself introduces, disappearing all other capacities and agencies that capital requires and freely disposes of to exercise its own, the history of capital recapitulates the gendered story of the sovereign, self-actualizing human subject set against the backdrop of an impassive, inert, and disposable nature. All other times become, like the times of reproduction in relation to the productive time of the capital–labour relation, diminished and deemed historically and politically inconsequential.

It is these very times of reproduction, seemingly superfluous plural times of life-making and survival, however, that I see as central to our current global and planetary moment – central to the history and continuing active forces of its making, and hence also to the possibility of its unravelling.

The time of imperialism is also a time of reproduction, but the reproduction of capital in its expansion and growth, without which it would not exist. It is a form of reproduction, however, that requires the paradoxical destruction and preservation of other forms of living – the colonization of noncapitalist human and more-than-human formations – to serve as the milieu or environment for the growth and therefore continuing existence of capitalist accumulation. War, Rosa Luxemburg argued, is a constant method of capital accumulation, a violence that is, one could say, *terraforming*. War here is to be understood not only as physical, material violence and destruction but also as productive, developmental projects of reconstruction and rehabilitative engineering of social and subjective capacities of the defeated, which includes the transformation of the very ecologies and terrains of their prior living.

Reinterpreted through Simondon's concept of the 'associated milieu' with respect to the concrete technical object, *milieu* can be viewed as the very enabling environs of colonial human inhabitation as well as the medium or ground that seemingly autonomous capital processes harness and shape as the indispensable condition of their own operation. 'Milieu' suggests the abiding force of the imperial relation in positing constitutively discrepant spheres or strata and subordinating them to and in the service of the most advanced technological modes of contemporary capitalist production – that is, in the project of terraforming as 'in itself a mode of warfare, of a distinctive kind', operating in the global platform economy (Ghosh, 2021: 55). As a discrepant sphere harnessed and shaped but not fabricated by the technical object that it sustains, however, associated milieu also suggests a realm of mixed and fused agencies whose own times of reproduction exceed the time of capital.

Milieus of human life

One of the principal ways that I see these milieus at work today is in the very capitalization of reproduction in industries of global servitude. By global servitude I mean to refer to the myriad ways in which the lives of people from disposable colonial and postcolonial populations are put to work (by themselves and by others) in the social reproduction of a globopolitical humanity (through domestic and care work, service, and agricultural industries, as well as other 'reproductive labour' industries), a humanity which is defined by a life worth living or value-productive life, that is, life with the capacity to yield accumulable value transmissible across generations.

Particularly exemplary of global servitude is the phenomenon of overseas Filipina domestic and care workers, on which topic a large body of literature has grown. Migrant reproductive workers are part of an entire global stratum of formal and informal service workers, itinerant, migrant, and urban excess populations, who act as time-saving and time-producing machines, facilitators of the value-productive activities and movement of an ascendant global class as well as other forms of mobile capital. They serve as *vital infrastructures* for the social reproduction of lives of value, wielded as human capital, as well as the means of reproduction of global capital as a whole.

Philippine domestic workers, nurses and caregivers, sex workers, seafarers, call agents, military base maintenance workers, social media operators, servants, drivers, and couriers are all instruments for the facilitation of the value-productive global circulation and mobility of capital, whether in the form of people, information, goods, or money. Their life-capacities placed at the disposal of the sheer life activity and circulation of (human, commodity, investment) capital, the 'vitality' that is at the core of a financialized global economy increasingly driven by capitalist platforms, and in a context of what I have called uber-urbanization, the processes of building and transforming cities and urban life into total mediatic platforms owned and regulated by a few conglomerates capitalizing on the social productivity and connectivity of entire populations of content providers.

Here I draw my understanding of vital infrastructure from the context of migrant domestic work. In placing their bodily, life-making capacities at the intimate disposition of their employers, migrant domestic workers function as 'all-around' household appliances and domestic implements, whose design is to 'save' their employers' valuable life-times. As machines for other humans' valuable life-production, they are producers of the valorizable life-times (life as labour) of others. Like convenience foods and food services, 'servitude' provides, besides immeasurable social and subjective values of well-being, comfort, intimacy, and self-esteem, 'savings' in that non-material use-value of time. Instead of being 'wasted' on the chores of life-maintenance, the 'surplus' time saved can then be absorbed into the higher value and valorizable life-times of employers. What is one's life to spend depends on the expenditure of the life-times of others.

Today, servitude acts as a generalized social protocol in contemporary modes of value-extraction, exemplified in software-as-a-service (SaaS) business models, which convert people's times of waiting or 'idled' life-times into the work of waiting on others, and On Demand Mobile Services, which through the disaggregation and distribution of traditional whole jobs, convert what would be understood as the waste that is unemployed people's life-times or the unemployed 'free time' of the partially employed (times of waste) into productive 'on demand' or 'on call' work detail. Aiming for friction-less efficiency through the elimination of the inevitable slack in older (personal, bonded as well as industrial, Fordist) models of service labour, leading mobile-app-based service enterprises seek to effectuate a perfect meshing of two orders of media: technological and human. They seek to fuse and incorporate the disaggregated, 'dividuated' human parts of the enterprise as component media within a total, integrated platform – to program the function of humans as media for other humans.

As a form of organized servitude, vital infrastructure consists of capitalist-coordinated aggregates of human instruments, undertaking what built physical environments, technical systems, and technological infrastructure cannot fully undertake (book scanners, copy machine operators, content moderators, troll armies) or facilitating connections and interfaces between capitalist machines as effectively their replaceable components (couriers, runners, and cursors for machines, as transmission agents enabling capital machines to communicate with each other, or as essential ghosts in the machine). If global service workers – 'helper' humans meshed with machines – are placed in the service of the reproduction of valorizable life, they comprise in aggregate form, capitalist means of production of capital life, which often capital does not itself pay for.

In addition to its prominence in the global reproductive labour economy, the Philippines is the second largest single source of seafarers in the global shipping industry, which transports 90 per cent, by weight, of all global trade. The Philippines has also become the world's largest destination for business process outsourcing, with the majority of its clients comprising US companies, and the leading call centre country globally. It is in this capacity – as a major producer and provider of deterritorialized, serviceable, ancillary humans as disposable service labour in industries of global reproduction and as mediatic components of critical global infrastructure – that we see the importance of the Philippines' historical transformation for today's new global political economy, and its parsing of life-times between value and waste.

Undoubtedly, the racialized and gendered deployment of humans as media in these examples is a testament to how the legacies of colonialism and slavery continue to inform the dominant (racial, sex-gender) protocols codified in the most advanced capitalist media technologies. We see the striking continuity between, on the one hand, the function of colonial slaves as the bodily instruments and tools of sovereign masters and, on the other, the contemporary function of non-subject humans as media for the servicing of the 'demands' of full-subject humans. Alden Marte-Wood and Stephanie Santos (2021) rightly observe, for example, the continuity between domestic work and nursing and content moderation, seeing the latter as a remediation of exported Filipino care, which Jan Padios (2018) additionally notes becomes encoded into the architecture of information technologies.

This view of the contemporary deployment of humans as media enables us to track these submerged lineages to continuing pasts of slavery and colonialism, further suggested by the creation through racial violence (of punitive, criminalizing and rights-denying laws as well as of physical acts of injuring) of a permanent or standing population pool of those charged with what Arendt denigrates as 'labours of necessity' – labours of merely reproductive life of native savages and slaves (as opposed to the culture-producing work of a civilized, free humanity). However, the view of humans as media also allows us to glimpse forms of mediatory agency that the colonized and their descendants have developed and depend upon. To see global servants as a means of labour (or media) rather than as human subjects of labour, allows us to see other possibilities in their 'agency' than what a humanist history would consider.

Global servants and their dispersed networks deploy their own distributed selves, capacities, and channels as collective liquid assets for survival, relying on a social calculus that exceeds the neoliberal financialization of everyday life. As creative media, their forms of social calculus consist of dividing and distributing, but also integrating and coordinating, persons and their substances and faculties, in order to ensure *social* as well as individual survival. These forms of coordinated capacities – the partibility, substitutability, and transmutability of persons as auxiliary parts and components of elastic social bodies – are what enable their social kin networks to function not only as vital infrastructural support for human capital or capitalizable life, but also as *vital platforms* of their own life-making ventures.

Vital platforms are dynamic human-mediatic systems composed of kin and affiliative connections, which act as active mediatic conduits of transmission, transaction, augmentation, conversion, and redemption of values in multiple life currencies. Consisting of people lending themselves, their bodily capacities and faculties, and their connections, vital platforms act as collective means of life and the very life itself of shared being, whose members are components, programmers, and users.

The vital platforms of Filipino kin-based social networks are not only 'support systems' that allow them to adapt and survive in the host country. As pragmatic, affective, distributional, allocational social logics, the networks of Filipinos consist of coordinated channels of information, goods, funds, persons, and actions – organized recruitment systems, credit systems. Such is their importance that employment and state agencies themselves rely on and tap them as reliable mechanisms of their capitalist industries and as systems of welfare provision, which thereby subsidizes the costs of 'production' of this stratum of servitude as a permanent, self-replenishing, if continually depleted, resource.

The social reproduction of serviceable life must thus be seen as modes of life-making sociality developed as resources of survival under colonial and postcolonial conditions of dispossession that has undergirded the urbanizing expansion of capital and its new forms of valorization. More, that these social forces of survival have also served as a subaltern driver of the global urbanist economy.

Yet, this global stratum of serviceable life put to work in the social reproduction of a globopolitical humanity issues out of pools of so-called redundant populations of the Global South, produced as expendable life-times through increasingly financialized permanent wars of dispossession and securitization. Indeed, what underlies the Philippines' 'success' as major provider of global reproductive labor is a postcolonial history of international loans and national debt-servicing conditioned by World Bank economic development and restructuring programmes, violent land dispossessions at the hands of agribusiness, real estate development, resource extraction industries, and endless brutal counter-insurgent war continuing into the present.

The global serviceability of Philippine human life-capacities has been produced through these systemic processes of devastation that has impoverished and devalued the majority of the national population, dispossessing them of survival at home and rendering them disposable for the needs of capital everywhere. Such serviceable life has been secured and securitized by the violence of ceaseless domestic Cold War and post-Cold War counter-insurgent campaigns, including the current 'war on drugs' and 'war on terrorism' waged by the Duterte state as 'just wars', examples of financialized enterprises of punishment that create the conditions of absolute expendability of the urban poor, rural farmers, Indigenous and Muslim communities – the pool or fund of life as waste out of which serviceable life can be temporarily (and cheaply) redeemed and transacted.

Serviceable life is completely intertwined with absolutely expendable life in more than one way. Filipino workers replaced expulsed Palestinian labour after the second Intifada, and now compose the largest ethnic group of caregivers in Israel. In 2018, two years into the 'war on drugs' that has now killed almost 30,000 people, mostly the urban poor, Duterte signed memoranda of agreements with Netanyahu, reducing brokerage fees for the 28,000 Filipino caregivers in Israel in exchange for mutual investments, part of a set of agreements that includes the Israeli Defence Force training the Armed Forces of the Philippines in counterterrorism techniques in exchange for the Philippines' direct purchase of missiles, radars, and drones from Israel. The direct exchange of weapons and reproductive care points to the broader circuits within which serviceability and expendability are mutually entangled, the conditions for the provision of one dependent on the provision of the other. These dead exchanges prove that the valued humanity of some, which serviceable life upholds, commands the absolute life expenditures of the great many.

In the global-US war on terror, the Philippines also functioned as logistical and maintenance support for the global-US invasion and occupation of Iraq, supplying the largest number of foreign contract workers to service US military coalition camps and to work for private military contractors charged with postwar reconstruction. Together with other third country nationals maintaining US detention facilities and military bases, Filipino contract workers continue to play important labouring and non-labouring auxiliary parts supporting contemporary US security architecture and logistics at home and abroad, within which Israel too plays its own central role. As part of the vital infrastructure of global security and reproduction of the capital life of its select humanity, Filipino service workers in both global care and military industries contribute to the general expansion of expendable life. All of this too is part of the war to be human.

If the history of the present is the story of this revanchist war, whose time is the time of relentless productive expenditure of the disposable lives and life-times of the descendants of the damned of the earth – the 'becoming-human' intertwined with the non-human *earth*, who continue to be the unspoken objects of this war of punishment – how do we tell their story? How do we tell the stories of those who serve as enabling milieus of the subjects of history, whether the already human or capital, the model and epitome of the sovereign human subject that was once its controlling agent, without simply making them the protagonists of their own proper story? How do we tell a story of the colonized that does not simply fold them into the very category of humanity animating the Anthropocene, the category of a humanity whose definitive condition of freedom and value depends on the destruction of their own prior lifeworlds? Black and postcolonial feminists have grappled with the predicament – the impossibility of restoring the colonized and enslaved, without subsuming them in the categories of understanding – the subject of human will, agency, consciousness, voice, feeling, and binary gender – that were the very codes of negation of their own lifeworlds in the first place.

Heeding their work, I have attempted to foreground the forms of people's living that exceed the premised shape and character of the human subject as the life-form of value, or of the subject of capital, which is its apotheosis. And I have turned my attention to remaindered life – not disposable life but the superfluous effect and performances of life-times made and lived by such disposable life in its social reproduction, the leftover and excess of the social reproductive work of living and life-making that is not absorbed by either the serviceability or absolute expendability of life required by capital.

Though it is a colonial axiom that the past is overcome or superseded by the present, that what continues through time is only the essence or spirit of matter in some value-form, which sovereign agency itself introduces as the fruit of its own, proper seed, *many pasts continue, many presents lie in wait*. Pasts continue not least in the organized and unorganized everyday resistance without which there would be even less survival. These are pasts of unfinished decolonizing struggles, which bequeath to generations the methods and memories of communal aspiration and life-making. It is these immaterial inheritances – ways of living, passed on and adapted, the invention and convention of assaulted life – that are also important to the present: the pasts present in continuing living.

We can glean pasts present in the mediatic, dividual capacities comprising both vital infrastructure and vital platforms, the extensive filiative and affiliative modes of sociality that are 'still unconquered remnants' of prior modes of life. These are the deep social bonds that Luxemburg had surmised formed 'the strongest bulwark' against imperialism, but did not anticipate that those very social bonds, the social organizational means of survival of social formations meant to be destroyed, would themselves become part of the directly appropriable means of production of capital, subsumed as forms of infrastructure and machinery – nonhuman milieus – for contemporary capitalist enterprises through relentless war. Yet, as Joi Barrios' poem, *Ang pagiging babae ay pamumuhay sa panahon ng digma* (*Becoming-woman is living in a time of war*), encapsulates, zones of war are also times of living. As becoming-woman, so too becoming-human is a living, a form of work and survival in a time of war. We are encouraged by Black, postcolonial, queer, and trans scholars to consider that such times (and spaces) of becoming and living are plural and manifold, forms of subaltern making and happening coursing through ontologies of the global present.

We see, for example, complex reckonings with and negotiations of time among overseas Filipinx domestic workers in Hong Kong, navigating what they see as *times of drudgery*, unending life-times of giving and giving up of oneself to the point of nearly having nothing left, and *times of flourishing*, brief life-times of personal self-realization and thriving in beauty pageants, where one's invention and expressivity can be outwardly performed (Villarama, 2016). We see urban slum dwellers in the Global South, deploying their fungible, distributed, bodily rhythmic capacities to absorb the friction, shock, bumps, and drag that delay and detain the value-producing circulation of uber-urban life. Working for a living that is shared, pooled, and apportioned, coordinated within a network of family, friends, and consociates, they wield time not only as the key commodity and medium of exchange, but also as the central category of their experiences, their activities and social identities coordinated and framed in terms of time.

In both contexts of overseas work and the urban excess, people talk of their ventures as *pakikipagasapalaran*, adventure, but better translated as fate-playing, the hazarding of fate, a cosmic gamble, a recasting of the die with one's bodily self as legal tender for the ante of a collective as well as individual wager; a hazarding of one's present fate (*palad*) to create an opening for the immanent possibility of a radical change in fortune and destiny. These are actions and habits I trace to older practices of roaming, flight, and mediumship, and forms of dividual personhood and mutual being that permeate the land-mottled oceanic space of insular Southeast Asia across pre-colonial, colonial, and postcolonial times. Such times of fate-playing and their long and wide travels through space and time point us to a fuller expanse of life-times of struggle under global capital than what our dominant political imaginations might allow. They point us to another timeline of global capitalism's duration and end, what I call the 'time of expectation' when the sum of our decolonizing efforts will bring about the hoped-for change in planetary life.

In their renderings of places of bypass, seemingly dead ends yet also places of spillover, things spreading beyond their bounds, wandering and unravelling, the work of Global South artists – the art work of Lyra Garcellano and Kiri Dalena, and the films of Abderrahmane Sissako, Tsai Ming-Liang, and Apichatpong Weersathakul – convey a sensibility of the surrounds, the mediating atmospheres and landscapes that are also people's matrices of living as also replete with bursts of unexpected, gratuitous vitality, which I describe as some kind of splendour unfolding in the everyday arts of survival. Their lingering attentiveness to and tenderness for these bypassed lives has offered me a form of regard as I cast my eye towards the waysides of the globopolis closer to home.

Us

If History is the intertwined story of the Human and Capital, the two ever more united in the age of the Anthropocene as dual, complementary 'forces of history' and 'forcings of climate change', how might a regard for remaindered life unravel its relentless unfolding? As imperial wars see to the devastation of entire earthly lifeworlds to secure the dominant order and value of colonial inhabitation, how might such a regard propel and shape anti-colonial planetary struggles today?

In the penultimate chapter of my book *Remaindered Life*, I describe the destructive environmental aftermath of the June 1991 eruption of Mt. Pinatubo, in the province of Pampanga, Philippines, the second largest volcanic eruption of the 20th century, which caused a drop in global temperatures by 1°F (0.5 °C) that lasted a couple of years. The massive eruption also precipitated the evacuation and abandonment of Clark Air Base and Subic Bay Naval Base, two of the largest overseas US military bases crucial to US imperial security operations (including outright wars in Korea and Vietnam) in the Asia-Pacific during the Cold War. The volcanic eruption was catastrophic for local Philippine life, but the catastrophe was not confined to the three days in which over 700 people were killed. For years following the eruption, flows of *lahar* – mudflows of volcanic ash and pyroclastic debris mixed with rainwater – buried 28 villages under almost ten feet of volcanic debris, blanketing hundreds of thousands of acres of agricultural land and forest and detrimentally impacting the lives of over two million people, none more so than the aboriginal Aeta communities who were forced to flee the slopes of the mountain where they had lived for centuries. Around 35,000 of them placed in evacuation centres with poor sanitation and shelter conditions, many Aetas lost their children to fatal disease and exposure. With much of the mountain forests of their homes buried or destroyed by the flows of *lahar* over the following years, dispossessing them of their own life ways of hunting, fishing, foraging, and swidden farming, many were forced to adapt to the ways of life of their lowland neighbours by becoming janitors, construction workers, maintenance staff, and mountain tour guides in the Clark Freeport and Special Economic Zone and New Clark City, duty-free industrial, commercial, and urban residential projects built out of the economic reclamation and conversion of the US military base abandoned in the wake of the eruption. These infrastructural projects are part of uber-urbanization, the terraforming development of the physical, technological, communicative, and social structures required by the global platform economy, and secured by the global security apparatus led by the US military (effectively returned to the Philippines through the 1999 Visiting Forces Agreement).

It is impossible not to see in this short episode the contours of an ever-repeated colonial story of dispossession and displacement, whereby a 'natural disaster' in an already conquered land destroys life in the same patterns of destruction that decades and centuries of colonialism had laid down before, and where the waste and loss precipitated and enhanced by the 'forcings of nature' in tandem with the 'forces of history' serve to prepare the ground – the milieu – for a new round of capitalist accumulation. Yet in my regard for the waysides, I cannot also help but gaze at the wide stretches of splendiferous grasses of *talahib* (*Saccharum spontaneum*) that have grown in abundance on the carpet of *lahar* blanketing the surrounding lands. Deemed useless by villagers who cannot make baskets, roof thatching, animal bedding, or stock fodder, as they do with other grasses, *talahib* is periodically burned down and eliminated to make land available for agricultural plantations and other capitalist industries. In the foreshortened timescale of capitalism and its history, *Saccharum spontaneum* is considered a coarse, uncultivated invasive species with no discernible use, remaining no more than a placeholder, literally what holds the shifting terrain together, preventing erosion and the collapse of river banks, and playing a small helping part in the slow environmental restoration of soil productivity and vegetation recovery. It is merely a 'helper' in the enhancement of the fertility and growth of other more useful species – we might say, it is a vital component in the reproduction of enabling milieus for colonial inhabitation of that paradigmatic life-form of value, the human.

In fact, genomic studies show that *Saccharum spontaneum* or 'wild or spontaneous sugar' has evolutionarily contributed to the 'nobilization' of *Saccharum officinarum*, the cultivated sugarcane first domesticated in New Guinea and the Philippines and Indonesia, and the consequential primary sugarcane species for modern capitalist sugar production in plantations forcibly reduplicated across the colonial world. As one such study found, *Saccharum spontaneum* has 'contributed to the development of modern cultivars by conferring resistance to most major diseases, providing vigor and hardiness for increased abiotic stress tolerance (such as cold and drought), increased tillering and improved ratoonability' (Paterson et al, 2013).

Like so many seemingly inconsequential, useless, and disposable, even deleterious beings, *talahib* is a material trace, consequence, and minor elemental agent of a global history of devastation and survival. I do not dwell on it, however, as a symbol of disposability or resilience, or a metaphor for the value of the most diminished, most exterminable, most damned of the earth and their survival. Rather, I see this beautiful, splendiferous, almost fluorescent grass as simply another vital component of cooperative life-making in the scenes of human disaster. Indeed, together with the slash-and-burn or swidden farming practice of the Aeta who have returned to the surrounding hills, its abundant growth alongside the growth of ararong (*Trema orientalis*) have contributed to the restoration of the soil fertility and recovery of these scorched lands of ash. It is therefore not merely a symbolic figure but rather also, and significantly, a material actor taking part in and shaping the stories and forms of know-how – those practices of social resilience of self-determining collectives, which Anishinaabe scholar Kyle Whyte calls 'collective continuance' – that we might want to recuperate as well as craft and pass on (Whyte, 2022).

If over the centuries such natural beings have been rendered mute as part of the brute Nature that colonialism made to be conquered, mastered, comprehended, manipulated, and spoken for by the colonial sciences and arts on which contemporary disciplines have been founded, it is not necessarily the task of anti-colonial scholarship to give them 'voice' or to humanize them in forms that would make them new subjects of history.[3] Yet it is important to heed their presence as co-inhabitants and actors and even addressees in the worlds we ourselves are embedded in and seek to understand.

In my own meditation, I attend to these grasses as they speak to me of broader milieus of our possible thriving than what History and Humans have promised and bequeathed and might allow. The elemental part these grasses play as full agents in the recovery of the land, in interaction with the activity of the Aeta and other beings both close and far and wide, raises the question of who might compose these decolonized milieus of mutual flourishing. Who in actuality might the 'us' be in our efforts to know, understand, and radically change the iniquitous colonial orders that overdetermine our lives? Not simply who this 'us' already is, but who might emerge to become this 'us' as part of the process of decolonizing our relations to the land and to each other.

This, I believe, is what Sylvia Wynter asked us to participate in making: a new poetics of the *propter nos*, which she defines as 'the us for whose sake, and in whose name we act', 'those with whom we are languagingly co-identified; those with whom we are made symbolically conspecific by our orders of discourse, and their systems of symbolic representation' (Wynter, 1995: 30). If scholarship wields important influence over prevailing orders of discourse, anti-colonial scholarship must understand not only its own worldly bearings but also its worldly effects, including its constitution of the 'we' who seek, produce, and exchange knowledge and the 'us' with and for whom we do so.

The knowledge we produce reflects and to no small degree reproduces the world we inhabit, a mode of inhabitation that we see, more clearly than ever, is an abiding structure of colonialism. In contrast to the worldliness of people, objects, images, and texts taught in Northern American and European universities, which are vacated of true social relations and their material realities, Stephen Sheehi reminds us that Said's own concept of worldliness – of *being in the world* and *of the world* – is what millions of people alongside Palestinians are fighting for (Sheehi, 2024). As Sheehi writes, '[w]orldliness is *being of the world*, a world of relationality with one another in a world of disavowals governed by coloniality, whiteness, cisheteronormativity, and capitalism, a worldliness excluded, negated, or denied by the ontologies mediated by the "Western ethnoclass of Man"' (Sheehi, 2024, emphasis original).[4]

Against the abstract worldliness that Western academia permits in its spaces, Said's worldliness is 'in relation to a shared and co-created, albeit asymmetrical, world of exploitation, violence, and genocide, as is happening now in Gaza, and also, creativity, beauty, and defiance'. It is a relation in which 'colonial, marginalized, and racialized subjects know a world that is otherwise imperceptible and illegible to – if negated by – those in power and those of privilege, those who themselves have dragged so many to genocide, to the "abyss"'. As an *engaged* Palestinian intellectual, Said's anti-colonial thought extends and realizes itself in the stone he picks up from the land on the Lebanese border to throw at the Israeli Occupying Forces, a gesture of community in Palestinian resistance and belonging to the land, whose physical remnant in the form of the stone bears the sedimented 'remainders of ongoing native life and living Palestinian practices of a sustainable human ecology' (Sheehi, 2024). Sheehi reads the stone Said picks up as part of his theory in the world, as part of an affiliative grammar of resistance binding Palestinians across time, a poetics of filiative and affiliative relations defying settler-colonial time, which I have also understood and depicted as the time of the war to be human.

Sheehi dwells on Said's stone, as I dwell on the *talahib*, as material parts of a specific landscapes of struggle that at once bear meaning and action in and for the world. They foreground the actual earth and its manifold material beings as part of the project of worldly poeisis (of world-making) that anti-colonial thought must necessarily be engaged in. Such a project deeply questions and transforms the methods of our knowing and the categories of valuation and distinction, which comprise a colonial order of knowledge, including the hard distinction between myth and science. More, it draws on ways of knowing, ways of doing, epistemic, social, and practical traditions of shared thriving, which communities subjugated and negated by colonialism rely on to continue to live, and sometimes flourish, in this time of war.

If stone and grass are therefore meaningful to us, still we must remember that the abundance of their being and living and of what they carry and transmit exceeds any vital instrumental or infrastructural parts they might play in the reproduction of collective life in one moment.[5] In this way, they beckon us not only to consider but also to summon deeper, more diverse timelines and farther-reaching, more discontinuous and variegated yet connected geographies for inquiring into our worldliness than a modern, anthropogenic logic of history or social science can conjure.

As I pen the end of this chapter, a colonial genocide in Palestine continues to be mercilessly carried out by Israel and its imperial enablers, genocide's time of war overruling the plural and manifold times of living and defiant survival subsisting within its present dominion. What is the time of genocide? The time of genocide is the time of imperial reproduction and relentless productive expenditure – the time of producing value and the valued life of a globopolitical humanity through the expenditure of the life-times of its others. It is the time of relentless progress and growth, pursued by means of absolute dispossession of the 'damned of the earth' as the pathway and grounds for seemingly infinite and righteous gain.

What is the time of living for those struggling against dispossession? Looking at an archival photograph of Palestinian children from Lydda and Ramla at a checkpoint in 1948 where they are being stripped of their belongings by Israeli soldiers, Palestinian historian Sherene Seikaly finds something other than the sheer passage of time and inevitable death and catastrophe. What she finds is a thread, a bridge, that links the experiential time in the photograph and the time of her own searching, between the Palestinian girls whose faces she reads and her own self reading them: 'It is the permanent temporary, suspension and abeyance, a prolonged and fragmented state of waiting. Dispossession tries to vanquish the past, besiege the present, foreclose the future. Through and despite conquest, a fragile, tangible thread defies time and space' (Seikaly, 2023, 2).

I too glimpse fragile, tangible threads connecting different colonized communities of the more-than-human and the becoming-human and their stories across imperial unities and segregations of time and space that History and Humans continue to impose on us. They guide the thinking and feeling constituting my own research and writing, the analytical-political tale of my work. Following and weaving these threads into another space-time matrix of inquiry, another poetics of social relation, another lively milieu and vibrant field of orientation for engagement can be one way for anti-colonial scholarship to resist the habitual ways of approaching a world made amenable for colonial inhabitation – disenchanted, objectified, and mute, otherwise already dead (and past) without the animating spirit and agency of the sovereign subject. These habitual forms of knowledge-production and their technological applications in the world are part of the 'organizing technics' for the capitalist world-ecology (Moore, 2015), which codify and quantify an external nature as merely the conditions, instruments, objects, and resources of and for the well-being and understanding of the paramount universal life-form, the human, whose social nature is also overcoded by the measures and categories of colonial epistemes.

A colonial regard persists in the broader humanities and social sciences, 'producing and hiding the abyssal line that creates zones of nonbeing' (De Sousa Santos, 2018: 107). To resist this colonial regard, composed of habitual forms of seeing and understanding the world that unite the forces of history and the forcings of climate change in the destruction and closing of the earth, as Mahmoud Darwish described for Palestinians, is hence a vital way for anti-colonial scholarship to engage in anti-colonial planetary struggle. To decolonize is, after all, to imagine and realize life-making practices, meanings, and agencies that would not only bring a history of ecocidal catastrophe to an end, but also bring about possibilities of ecological flourishing for all.

Coda

I began this chapter with a reflection on the phenomenon of history seemingly repeating itself in the Philippines, with the 2022 presidential election of Ferdinand Marcos, Jr., the son of the dictator who was deposed by popular revolt in 1986. The repetition of political history achieved by the return of the Marcos family to power compelled me to reflect on the broader question of History, which much postcolonial and Indigenous scholarship had already long critiqued as the province of a universal subject that colonialism had deemed Human and from which the descendants of the colonized had always been excluded. Faced with the planetary crisis of climate change, postcolonial scholars have cast doubt on history altogether as the province of humanity, now seemingly no longer viewed in terms of a race marked by white supremacy but rather in terms of a biological species marked by an exceptional geological agency and power beyond all other natural species on earth.

My own reflection on this question of history sees repetition as intrinsic to its very structure both as a practice of global agency and a narrative form. History, as I see it, repeats and bolsters the colonial project, which continues today in what I have called 'the war to be human', a war that is not past but ever-present as the anthropogenic logic propelling planetary catastrophe. History's participation in the project of reproduction of colonial power and colonial inhabitation calls into question our own disciplinary social science and humanities scholarly stories, the forms of knowledge we search for and transmit, the categories and frameworks with which we reproduce the social facts of the life-form of value – the human – and the very world of its colonial inhabitation.

Colonial forms of knowledge importantly include a certain order of time characterized not only by a particular scale and trajectory of progression but also by determinate unities and divisions of space pertaining to the geopolitical order of racial capitalism, which emerged out of Western European colonialism. The time of History is, we might say, the time of reproduction of the modern, global capitalist mode of life that drives and defines this continuing epoch of planetary catastrophe. It is a time in which sovereign subjects on the model of the Human, the species life-form of value, prevail in representation and material structure as paramount agents of History wilfully acting within a global landscape of distinct nations and peoples.

I have tried in my work to explore other forms of agency and action occluded in the time of History that are nevertheless crucial to the global capitalist order. These are agencies which might be viewed in terms of the enabling means, media, and milieus of more properly Human development, movement, and growth, as exemplified by the distributed strata of otherwise disposable Filipinos servicing the global capitalist economy. Observing these agencies in the form of 'helpers' of proper historical subjects – operating as infrastructure, platforms, machines, and engines, or simply the natural environment – constitutes a method of attending to other life-times, times of social reproduction that pass beneath the threshold of understanding and recognition of much disciplinary scholarship in the social sciences and humanities. This method I outline here in the rubric of *remaindered life* is an example of other possible tellings and other times of unfolding we might explore in a struggle against a continuing colonialism and its planetary consequences. Such an anti-colonial planetary struggle requires a revision of the poetics of seeing and making that we necessarily engage in, embedded as we are in the world along with those who we write about and in concert with. A poetics of actively reimagineering the 'us', which tacitly undergirds and orients the knowledges we seek and share, towards the making of other worldly milieus for cooperative, planetary thriving.

Notes

1. 'Men make their own history, but they do not make it just as they please; they do not make it under circumstances chosen by themselves, but under circumstances directly found, given and transmitted from the past. The tradition of all the dead generations weighs like a nightmare on the brain of the living' (Marx, 1978: 595).
2. As Jennifer Morgan writes of the story of reproduction, slavery, and race: 'an origin story that is, in Toni Morrison's words, 'not [one] to pass on' might mean many things: 'a story not to be told, a story not property of one's heirs, and a story one must not fail to tell' (Morgan, 2018: 15).
3. 'As a process, then, the muting of a large part of humanity by European colonizers cannot be separated from the simultaneous muting of "Nature." Colonization was thus not merely a process of establishing dominion over human beings; it was also a process of subjugating, and reducing to muteness, an entire universe of beings that was once thought of as having agency, powers of communication, and the ability to make meaning – animals, trees, volcanoes, nutmegs' Ghosh (2021: 190).

4. The notion of 'Western ethnoclass of Man' is Sylvia Wynter's.
5. The reproduction of life harnessed for capitalism is more than 'unpaid work', as Jason Moore would understand it (Moore, 2015).

References

Baucom, I. (2020) *History 4° Celsius: Search for a Method in the Age of the Anthropocene*, Duke University Press.

Benjamin, W. (1968) Theses on the philosophy of history, in H. Arendt (ed) *Illuminations: Essays and Reflections*, translated by H. Zohn, Schocken Books, pp 253–64.

Chakrabarty, D. (2000) *Provincializing Europe: Postcolonial Thought and Historical Difference*, Princeton University Press.

Chakrabarty, D. (2021) *The Climate of History in a Planetary Age*, University of Chicago Press.

Crosby, A.W. (1986) *Ecological Imperialism: The Biological Expansion of Europe, 900–1900*, Cambridge University Press.

Dayan, J. (1998) *Haiti, History, and the Gods*, University of California Press.

De Sousa Santos, B. (2018) *The End of the Cognitive Empire: The Coming of Age of Epistemologies of the South*, Duke University Press.

Federici, S. (2004) *Caliban and the Witch: Women, the Body, and Primitive*, Autonomedia.

Ferdinand, M. (2018) *Decolonial Ecology: Thinking from the Caribbean World*, Polity.

Ghosh, A. (2021) *The Nutmeg's Curse: Parables for a Planet in Crisis*, University of Chicago Press.

Guha, R. (1982) On some aspects of the historiography of colonial India, in R. Guha (ed) *Subaltern Studies 1: Writings on South Asian History and Society*, Oxford University Press, pp 37–44.

Hartman, S.V. (2002) The time of slavery, *South Atlantic Quarterly*, 101(4): 757–77.

Koch, A., Brierley, C., Maslin, M.M. and Lewis, S.L. (2019) Earth system impacts of the European arrival and great dying in the Americas after 1492, *Quaternary Science Reviews*, 207: 13–36.

Marx, K. (1978) The eighteenth brumaire, in R.C. Tucker (ed) *The Marx-Engels Reader*, W.W. Norton & Company, pp 594–618.

Marte-Wood, A.S. and Santos, S.D. (2021) Circuits of care: Filipino content moderation and American infostructures of feeling, *Verge: Studies in Global Asias*, 7(2): 101–27.

McKittrick, K. (2014) Plantation futures, *Small Axe*, 17(3): 1–15.

Merchant, C. (1980) *The Death of Nature: Women, Ecology and the Scientific Revolution*, Harper & Row.

Mies, M., Bennholdt-Thomsen, V. and von Werlhof, C. (1988) *Women: The Last Colony*, Zed Books.

Moore, J.W. (2015) *Capitalism in the Web of Life: Ecology and the Accumulation of Capital*, Verso.

Morgan, J.L. (2018) *Partus sequitur ventrem:* Law, race, and reproduction in colonial slavery, *Small Axe*, 55: 1–17.

Padios, J.M. (2018) *A Nation on the Line: Call Centers as Postcolonial Predicaments in the Philippines*, Duke University Press.

Paterson, A.H., Moore, P.H. and Tew, T.L. (2013) The gene pool of *Saccharum* species and their improvement, in A.H. Paterson (ed) *Genomics of the Saccharinae*, Spring, pp 43–71.

Seikaly, S. (2023) *Reading in Time*, World Humanities Report, CHCI.

Sheehi, S. (2025) Theory as stone, *Palestine Now, Social Text Online*, 25 January. https://socialtextjournal.org/periscope_article/theory-as-stone/

Simpson, L.B. (2016) *As We Have Always Done: Indigenous Freedom Through Resistance*, University of Minnesota Press.

Smith, L.T. (1999) *Decolonizing Methodologies: Research and Indigenous Peoples*, Zed Books.

Spivak, G.C. (1999) *A Critique of Postcolonial Reason: Toward a History of the Vanishing Present*, Harvard University Press.

Trouillot, M.-R. (1995) *Silencing the Past: Power and the Production of History*, Beacon Press.

Tsing, A. (2016) Earth stalked by man, *The Cambridge Journal of Anthropology*, 34(1): 2–16.

Vergès, F. (2017) Racial capitalocene, in G.T. Johnson and A. Lubin (eds) *Futures of Black Radicalism*, Verso, pp 78–85/289 (ePub).

Villarama, B.R. (dir) (2016) *Sunday Beauty Queen*.

Whyte, K. (2022) Settler colonialism, ecology, and environmental justice, in J. Dhillon (ed) *Indigenous Resurgence: Decolonization and Movements for Environmental Justice*, Berghahn, pp 127–46.

Wynter, S. (1995) 1492: A new view, in V.L. Hyatt and R. Nettleford (eds) *Race, Discourse, and the Origin of the Americas: A New World View*, Smithsonian Institution Press, pp 5–58.

8

Theorizing Hong Kong: From Colonial Collaboration to Inter-Imperial Zone

Hon-Fai Chen

Introduction

In his introduction to an early anthology of postwar Hong Kong studies, Ian Jarvie lamented that 'Hong Kong is well known as a place, but almost unknown as a society' (Jarvie, 1969: xix).[1] For years, Hong Kong did not warrant much social scientific interest as it had been largely seen as an outpost of South China. While in the 1970s sociology and anthropology began to take root on local soils, scholars continued to treat Hong Kong as a variant of traditional Chinese society then undergoing industrialization and urbanization (Topley, 1969; Freedman, 1976; Yang, 1981). Paraphrasing Javie's remark, Hong Kong was then better known as a society but remained almost unknown *as a colony*. British rule was often conceived as secondary, if not residual, in importance compared to traditional Chinese culture and its modern variant of utilitarian familism in shaping Hong Kong society and politics (Lau, 1982). Alternatively, British colonial rule was hailed as non-interventionist and enlightened, which constituted a positive factor behind Hong Kong's 'exceptional' economic prosperity and political stability among developing countries (Endacott, 1964; Miners, 1981).

In the late 1980s, such an understanding was somewhat altered when a younger generation equipped with neo-Marxism and other critical perspectives began to appear on the academic scene. Hong Kong's sovereignty turnover to China in 1997 further provoked scholarly reflections on the legacies of British colonial rule in various arenas, including state–society relations (Ngo, 1999), charity and social organizations (Sinn, 2003) and culture and arts (Abbas, 1997). While furnishing the basis for subsequent studies, some of which I will scrutinize in this chapter, these pioneering works were not followed up by the formulation of new research paradigm. Colonial history and society did not figure prominently in the general surveys of Hong Kong sociology (Tang, 2021) and Hong Kong studies (Lui et al, 2019). While more historical studies of colonial Hong Kong were recently produced (Kong, 2023; Cowell, 2024), it could not match the fast-growing anti-colonial scholarship elsewhere around the world, which amounted to 'decolonial bandwagon' (Moosavi, 2020).

Yet the relative backwardness of Hong Kong in colonial and postcolonial studies should not blind us to its potential relevance and significance. Long regarded as an 'anomaly' among poverty ridden and politically unstable developing countries, Hong Kong arguably possessed distinctive characteristics that could shed light on the manifestations of colonialism and coloniality in diverse sociohistorical contexts. Instead of fitting Hong Kong into preconceived categories, be they Eurocentric or decolonial, I will follow the lead of Yūzō Mizoguchi and Chen Kuan-Hsing in treating Hong Kong as 'method'. In his celebrated essay, Mizoguchi (2016) criticized the tendency to utilize China for illustrating and validating the patterns of modernity, development and civilization as generalized from European experiences. Instead of swinging to the opposite extreme of particularism and exceptionalism, it would be more instructive to place China alongside Europe as mutual references, such that their distinctiveness and interconnectedness could be at once discerned. This line of thought was pursued by Chen (2010), who advocated the paradigm of 'inter-Asia' to move beyond Eurocentrism and towards the reciprocal comparison of Asian societies and cultures. In this chapter I will follow a similar strategy by first pinpointing some defining characteristics of colonialism and coloniality in Hong Kong, thereafter examining them in relation to other comparable sociohistorical contexts. Instead of seeing Hong Kong as either reducible to or incommensurable with other instances of colonial rule, I will seek to articulate its historical trajectory in relation to broader regional and global trends.

To this aim, in the following section I will select and review four major works in Hong Kong studies, which dealt, respectively, with: the central significance of elite collaboration in the colonial formation of Hong Kong society; the *de facto* autonomy negotiated by the local commercial elites in manoeuvring between the British and Qing empires; the bridging role played by a new generation of business cum educational elites in rearticulating Hong Kong and China with the global capitalism/imperialism inaugurated by the United States; and the changing figuration of power, interdependence and contention in Hong Kong amidst China's rise to world power. I will show that these disparate accounts were complementary to each other in addressing the themes of 'colonial collaboration' and 'inter-imperial zone'. In this way, my review will form the basis of further theorizing about Hong Kong in relation to the broader geographical and historical contexts of Asia. Several anti-Eurocentric approaches, including inter-imperiality, world-system theory and ocean studies, will be drawn upon to pinpoint the distinct patterns of collaboration and colonization pertaining to the maritime world of Asia, to which Hong Kong belonged. In what sense should we qualify the Hong Kong experience as 'colonial', and to what extent it was distinctive and/or generalizable? What would be its theoretical and political implications for anti-colonial global scholarship? What kind of critical discourse would be adequate for making sense of 'anomalous' cases such as Hong Kong, while utilizing them as 'method' or global inter-referencing framework to produce alternative, non-Eurocentric social knowledge?

In introducing the concepts of colonial collaboration and the inter-imperial zone, my overall aim will be to extend the scope of anti-colonial global scholarship by addressing the peculiar positions and experiences of places such as Hong Kong and by extension Asia. My premise will be that anti-colonial global scholarship must be duly informed by global political economy and world-system history, for which global capitalism in the course of its expansion had generated different positionalities in the flow of commodities, capital and people. Instead of over-generalizing the decolonial and postcolonial perspectives, which had their respective historical basis in settler-colonialism and non-settler colonialism (Patel, 2024), I will argue that the Asian maritime world was conducive to collaborative colonialism at the interstices of empires. The inter-imperial perspective will not be uncritically adopted either; in the Asian context it should be modified and enriched with additional concepts such as collaboration, network centrality, precarious autonomy, virtuality, conviviality, contingency and connected history (Subrahmanyam, 2022). Altogether, the expanded lexicons will enable us to analyse how far social agents, particularly regional, sub-regional and transregional economic actors, could mediate, navigate and exploit the space in between the multi-vectored forces radiating from competing imperial centres, with all its dialectical ramifications. At a deeper ontological level, the unfolding of dialectics could be conceived in non-Hegelian terms. Alternative models could be found in Daoism and potentially also Buddhism and other civilizations, with their conceptions of power being rooted in the political economy pertaining to specific world-historical regions.

In treating imperial powers, practices and traditions on equal footings regardless of their European (Portuguese, British, American …) or Asian (Indian, Chinese, Japanese …) origins, I will seek to demonstrate that the notion of inter-imperiality could transcend the conventional focus (if not fixation) on European colonialism and coloniality in its original and derivative forms. In this way, the inter-imperial perspective articulated here would follow a more generalized definition of the meaning and scope of anti-colonial global scholarship. The anti-colonial discursive framework critically attended to relations of power and domination as experienced by colonized and marginalized groups (Dei and Asgharzadeh, 2001: 300). This definition could readily cover inter-imperial relations, as its power dynamics were no less multiple and entangled than the intersectionality of class, gender, racial and other inequalities. In directing critical discourses towards the shifting regional centres of the capitalist world-economy, notably from Britain to the United States and China, inter-imperial global social theory could make better sense of 'anomalous' cases such as Hong Kong, in which formal colonial rule had inadvertently contributed to prosperity and autonomy, while the postcolonial condition might yield to new forms of domination. In this context, decolonization and modernity had to be negotiated with multiple and shifting imperial formations, while resistance and counter-hegemony had to be forged against a form of colonial power that was more collaborative than extractive or exploitative.

Theorizing Hong Kong: historical and sociological perspectives

Collaboration and coloniality in the formation of Hong Kong society

My review will start with Law Wing-Sang, a cultural studies scholar who sought to pinpoint how colonial power operated in the Hong Kong context. Central to his *Collaborative Colonial Power: The Making of the Hong Kong Chinese* (Law, 2009) was the idea of 'collaboration', which was adopted from Ronald Robinson's 1972 essay. For Robinson, the collaboration of non-European elites such as 'Ottoman rayahs, Levantine traders, Chinese Mandarins, Indian Brahmins and African chiefs' was indispensable for the rise of European imperialism (Law, 2009: 12). In the case of Hong Kong, colonial collaboration could be traced to those Chinese merchants who had long occupied a dominant role in the regional trade network of Southeast Asia. Since the 18th century, Chinese settlers had become active collaborators of the European colonizers in Southeast Asia by virtue of their business knowledge and networks. The colonization of Hong Kong followed this pattern of European–Chinese collaboration. Migrating from South China or returning from Southeast Asia, most of the early settlers in British Hong Kong were opium smugglers and coolie traders, who were rewarded with land and trade monopoly for collaborating with the colonizers (Law, 2009: 13–17). A more stable collaborative relation was established when Chinese contractors, merchants, compradors and civil servants began to consolidate their status and power. By offering charitable services for the local Chinese community, these elites took over governmental functions in the capacity of 'surrogate gentry'. Repressive measures in early colonial rule were replaced by the self-rule of local community with tacit consent of the British and Chinese empires (Law, 2009: 22–5).

Collaboration and indirect rule did not, however, imply the absence of colonial domination in Hong Kong. The political and cultural life of Hong Kong had been fundamentally shaped by colonial power in accordance with the changing configurations of collaboration. As part of the British civilizing mission, English language education was appropriated by the local elites as a status marker vis-à-vis ordinary Chinese. As an imperial institution, the University of Hong Kong aimed to train up 'native gentlemen' whose vernacular education and nationalism could serve indirect rule. In the 1960s, a modernist discourse was articulated to legitimize the indigenization of colonial rule by a new group of managerial and technocratic local elites. What Law underscored throughout his study was the 'layered colonialities' in the making of Hong Kong society. Instead of a binary power relation between the colonizer and colonized, Hong Kong experienced the formation of a racial and colonial hierarchy stamped with European hegemony while producing the intermediate and contradictory position of the collaborative local elites (Law, 2009: 29).

Between empires: negotiated autonomy of the Hong Kong elites

An alternative interpretation to Law was given by the historian John Carroll in his *Edge of Empires: Chinese Elites and British Colonials in Hong Kong* (2005). Instead of coloniality and its cultural-political repercussions, Carroll aimed to discern how the local business elites could develop a strong sense of identity and build Hong Kong a place of their own out of colonial collaboration. Likewise referring to Ronald Robinson, Carroll interpreted the concept of collaboration more dialectically than Law. Given that colonial power was limited rather than entrenched, collaboration was built upon the convergence of interests between British colonizer and local Chinese elites. Inasmuch as economic and political collaboration co-existed with social and cultural segregation, the relationship between colonizer and colonized in Hong Kong could not be simply characterized as domination or resistance. Conflicts at times occurred, but above all the two parties saw themselves as strategic partners in maintaining order and stability of a global commercial nexus linking the British and Chinese empires (Carroll, 2005: 2–4).

Conceiving collaboration as colonial *and* cooperative, Carroll would readily concur with Law on the existence of racial and colonial hierarchy in Hong Kong, while according a greater room of freedom to the colonial subjects. For instance, the local elites responded to residential segregation and exclusion from the European community by developing their own realm of sociocultural activities, including schools, commercial chambers, sport clubs and associations. Instead of an apology for colonialism, Carroll's purpose was to offer a more balanced appraisal by underscoring the uncertainty of colonial project and its unintended consequences. What was paradoxical about

Hong Kong was that colonialism, by opening up a new space between the Qing and British Empires, empowered the Chinese (and European) settlers by granting them opportunities to ride on the expansion of the capitalist world-economy (Carroll, 2005: 189). Indeed, the title *Edge of Empires* was chosen to highlight Hong Kong's peculiar position between a declining Chinese empire and a rising British empire (Carroll, 2005: 2). By virtue of this location, Hong Kong was more conducive to mutuality of interests than reification of differences.

Straddling late colonial Hong Kong and US-led global capitalism

The strategic pursuit of elite power and autonomy continued to unfold in late colonial Hong Kong, which was the subject matter of Peter Hamilton's *Made in Hong Kong: Transpacific Networks and a New History of Globalization* (2021). As the only crown colony achieving economic growth without formal independence, Hong Kong emerged as a key node in the postwar world economy thanks to a new capitalist class migrating from China in the 1950s. As the successors to earlier Chinese merchants (*huashang*) whose diasporic trade networks were centred in Southeast Asia, these newcomers mostly came from the lower Yangzi region of Shanghai, Zhejiang and Jiangsu. Hamilton called these Chinese entrepreneurs *kuashang* or 'straddling merchants', as they played a pivotal role in forging the commercial linkages of Hong Kong with the United States by virtue of their previous exposure in Republican China. These elites consisted not only of industrialists and bankers but also academics and professionals, as their connections with and knowledge about the US corporate sector were often accumulated in the course of overseas education.

Drawing upon their American-based 'social capital', the *kuashang* could build new careers and enterprises in Hong Kong out of their transpacific networks and bicultural skills. Apart from sending their second generation to the United States to acquire frontier knowledge in business, management and engineering among other fields, the *kuashang* extended their competitive advantage to the broader local community by sponsoring and institutionalizing US-styled higher education in Hong Kong, which culminated in the establishment of the Chinese University of Hong Kong in 1963. These strategies proved to be effective in seizing business opportunities in the US market and later in China's economic reform. Here the key to success lay in adapting the old practices of collaboration (in Robinson's sense) to the new international order resting upon US hegemony. In this vein, Hamilton suggested that Hong Kong had long undergone 'informal decolonization' despite the continuation of British colonial rule until 1997. By virtue of Hong Kong's strategic position in the Cold War, the *kuashang* could wield new forms of power and autonomy by exploiting British imperial decline while brokering Hong Kong's and China's integration with US-led global capitalism (Hamilton, 2021: 12).

Rise of China and the postcolonial condition of Hong Kong

Hung Ho-Fung's *City on the Edge: Hong Kong under Chinese Rule* (2022) served to round up our discussion by charting the postcolonial transformation of Hong Kong with reference to its changing relationship with China. Since the 1990s, China had embarked upon export-oriented industrialization and the global expansion of state-owned enterprises. To these aims, China was dependent on Hong Kong to serve as its offshore trading and financial centre. China's rise to world power would be impossible, Hung argued, without keeping Hong Kong's autonomous status and its international recognition while maintaining a heavily regulated national economy. On the other hand, Hong Kong was increasingly penetrated by Chinese capital backed by state power and neo-imperial ideology. According to Hung, the idea of 'One Country, Two Systems' originated from an attempt at incorporating Tibet in the 1950s, when autonomy and self-rule were promised as the condition of accepting communist rule. This political strategy had its precedent in the Qing imperial policy towards frontier regions, in which local autonomy and self-government were granted but merely as a transition to direct and centralized rule (Hung, 2022: 108). While the Chinese Communist Party at first prepared for Hong Kong's transition to Chinese rule by building a united front with its business elites and other social classes, co-optation and local self-rule eventually gave way to coercive stance and nationalist assimilation.

Like the other authors, Hung highlighted Hong Kong's interstitial location between ascending and declining empires. As 'a city constantly on the edge' (Hung, 2022: 15), Hong Kong had been located at the periphery of the Chinese empire while openly facing a maritime commercial world for millennia. Like other city-states in the history of the capitalist world-economy, Hong Kong had been thriving on a global network of trade, industry and finance, and resisting incorporation by empires and centralized states (Hung, 2022: 12). There was a common urge of the modern nation-states to maintain economic and political control while opening autonomous city-regions at the borders to benefit from integration with the world economy. China's interest to keep colonial Hong Kong's heritage of global connections was manifest in its removal of Hong Kong from the United Nations list of colonies that were entitled to decolonization and self-determination (Hung, 2022: 120). While the situation became complicated with the growing animosity between China and the United States in the trade and tech war, the economic centrality and political marginality of Hong Kong would keep both collaboration and contention alive in the future.

To sum up the review, the four scholars vary to the degree in which they understand and confront colonialism. Law could be regarded as the most strictly adhering to the anti-colonial orientation, as his overarching aim was to expose how the Hong Kong Chinese elites succumbed to colonial rule by contenting themselves with commercial gain and political compromise. Well aware of the brutality of European colonialism, Carroll nevertheless saw in colonial collaboration a feasible way to open and seize opportunities for building one's own identity and place in Hong Kong. Hamilton continued this line of thought by inquiring how a new generation of Hong Kong Chinese elites devised a new strategy of collaboration by tenuously shifting their targets from Britain to the United States and China. Hung completed the story by scrutinizing the relationship between Hong Kong and China in the *longue durée*, which despite socioeconomic changes exhibited notable continuity with imperial ideologies and practices. While differing in their judgements on specific issues, a common feature of these works was to identify elite collaboration as the key to understanding Hong Kong under British colonial, American informal and Chinese direct rule, with relative emphasis being put on the collaborative or subordinative aspect. In addition, the idea of inter-imperial zone was implicit in all these accounts. For example, catchphrases like 'edge of empires' were invoked to capture Hong Kong's in-between position vis-à-vis dominant powers in the world system. But as the idea of inter-imperial space was employed only figuratively, we have to further pinpoint its nature and characteristics by couching the Hong Kong experience in broader theoretical and historical terms.

From colonial Hong Kong to maritime Asia: mapping the inter-imperial zone

Re-orienting inter-imperiality: Asia before Europe in the world system

As formulated by Laura Doyle, *inter-imperiality* referred to the 'multiply vectored relations among empires and among those who endure and maneuver among empires' (Doyle, 2020: 4). The inter-imperial perspective or method aimed to highlight the multilateral interactions and power dynamics through which individuals, communities and states were co-constituted in the contact zones between empires. For Doyle, inter-imperiality was primarily located outside of West Europe before 1500, specifically in the zones of multiple and successive imperial rules in the Middle East, East Europe, the Andes, the Caribbean, the Maghreb and Indonesia (Doyle, 2020: 15–17). Instead of being peripheral and unimportant, the 'inter-imperial zone' should be conceived as a strategic space open to multi-layered contestation, control, cooptation and alliance. Such conception informed Parvulescu and Boatcă's (2022) insightful study of the Transylvania/East Europe, which had been ruled by the Habsburg, Ottoman,

Austro-Hungarian and Tsarist empires before colonization by Europe. Given its imperial and colonial entanglements, this 'creolized' region could not be readily subsumed under the postcolonial or decolonial frame (Parvulescu and Boatcă, 2022: 5–7; see also Radovanović, 2024).

Overall, Doyle's notion of inter-imperiality was intended to conceptualize the world before European hegemony in terms of 'dialectics', that is, the reciprocal interaction and power-ridden interdependence rather than unilateral influence between European and non-European empires. Thus conceived, inter-imperiality left its cultural and political imprints on the formation of the early modern and the modern (colonial) world. While Doyle illustrated the concept with various examples taken from global history, her application of the inter-imperial approach was targeted chiefly at comparative literature. Parvulescu and Boatcă, on the other hand, focused more specifically on Transylvania/East Europe as an instance of inter-imperial zone. I would like to continue the latter's efforts by drawing upon historical-sociological studies of another global region to further substantiate and elaborate the concept of inter-imperiality. While in a previous paper I sought to articulate an inter-imperial perspective on China and East Asia (Chen, 2024), in the following I will seek to extend its scope of applicability to Asia, with particular interest on the nature and characteristics of inter-imperial zone as seen from the vantage point of Hong Kong.

My first step in situating inter-imperiality in the Asian context will be to invoke Andre Gunder Frank's (1998) groundbreaking analysis of the early modern world system (without hyphen), centring upon Asia rather than Europe. Frank's overall aim was to offer a corrective to the hegemonic, Eurocentric explanation of the 'rise of the West' in terms of Europe's putative superiority in 'rationality, institutions, entrepreneurship, technology, geniality, in a word – race' (Frank, 1998: 4). Instead of leading the way to global dominance with its progressive colonization of the Americas, Caribbean and Africa since 1498, Europe had occupied a mere marginal position in the world economy until at least the 18th century. Instead of the expansion of the European capitalist world-economy, what we witnessed in 1400–1800 was an 'Asian century' in which Asia occupied the central position in the then-expanding world economy. The global or 'Afro-Eurasian' trade system and division of labour favoured the growth of productivity, technology and economic institutions in Asia. Compared to Ming-Qing China, Mughal India, Safavid Persia, Tokugawa Japan and the Ottoman Empire, European nation-states, be they 16th-century Portugal, 17th-century Netherlands or 18th-century Britain, were by no means 'hegemonic' in economic, political, technological and military terms (Frank, 1998: 5, 353). Rather, the backwardness *of Europe* was partly compensated through its triangular slave trade and importation of American silver. The relative positions of Asia and Europe were exchanged only with the decline of the East in the 19th century. While Europe was able to climb up on the shoulders of Asia, the rise of the West should be explained in terms of demographic, ecological and economic trends pertaining to the world system as a whole. Yet European hegemony was only temporary; the rise of Asia in the present century represented a return to its long dominant position in the world economy.

While serviceable in problematizing the relationship between European and Asian empires in the context of world economy, Frank's project of 're-orient' was more helpful in rectifying Eurocentrism than specifying the location and dynamics of inter-imperial zone in the Afro-Eurasian world system. In pitting holistic globalism against methodological nationalism, Frank focused on the structure and dynamics of the world economy while attending to its impacts on broad regions in Europe and Asia, including the empires and the oceans connecting them. He was neither interested in lower-level units such as port and hinterland, nor keen on clarifying the relationship between centre and periphery (Frank, 1998: 325, 339). On the other hand, Frank's work contributed to the 'great divergence' debate. Theorists of the California School (Wong, 1997; Pomeranz, 2000) sought to explain the concomitant rise of Europe and decline of Asia with more intricate comparative treatments of macro-historical and sociological factors such as the high-equilibrium trap of agricultural development, coal-mining as an alternative energy source, and the 'industrious revolution' induced by the expansion of commerce (Institute of Historical Research, 2010; Vries, 2010). As the units of comparison were centralized territorial states like China, the *convergence* between port cities such as Hong Kong, Shanghai and Hankow (Rowe, 1984) in their openness to global trade, which allowed them to prosper despite (or rather because of) the imperial decline and national crisis of China, did not receive proper attention. The world system and great divergence perspectives thus failed to live up to their own premises of holism and relationalism, as they sidestepped those regional, sub-regional and transregional economic actors and their mediating role at the interstice or inter-imperial zone of the world economy.

Spatial-temporal extension: commonalities and continuity of the Asian inter-imperial zone

At this juncture, I would like to further introduce the body of scholarship known as 'ocean studies'. My contention would be that *Maritime Asia* constituted an inter-imperial zone *sui generis*. While mediating the interaction between European and Asian powers, port cities or overseas colonies such as Hong Kong occupied a distinctive and partly autonomous position that could not be readily reduced to imperial interests and agendas. Thalassology in Greek, the interdisciplinary field of ocean studies was built upon the 'Mediterranean analogy'. Fernand Braudel's methods and insights in identifying the Mediterranean as the arena whereby civilizations met to constitute the capitalist world-economy were applied to the Indian Ocean, Southeast Asia and beyond. K.N. Chaudhuri, Michael Pearson and Kenneth McPherson, among others, argued that in the early modern period, there was a historical unity in the Indian Ocean revolving around the network of long-distance trade (Vink, 2007: 44–6). While Immanuel Wallerstein conceived the Indian Oceanic 'world' as external or marginal to the European capitalist world-economy, Frank and others regarded it as an alternative world system and characterized its internal dynamism in terms of 'porousness, permeability, connectedness, flexibility, and openness of spatial and temporal boundaries and borders' (Vink, 2007: 52). Similar observations were made about Southeast Asia: thanks to the rich history of transregional trade between the Bay of Bengal and the South China Sea, Southeast Asia was a region defined by 'networks, syncretism, tolerance and openness' (Sutherland, 2003: 3). Ocean studies thus represented a decentered approach questioning the existence of clear boundaries between imperial or national states, which were treated in isolation from each other in the 'regnant paradigm' of area studies (Sutherland, 2003: 2).

As a world of commerce at the interstice of empires, Maritime Asia stood in contrast to Transylvania, which according to Parvulescu and Boatcă (2022) constituted a zone of multiple and successive enslavements between the Habsburg, Ottoman, Austro-Hungarian and Russian empires. Instead of a peasant economy with a peripheral status analogous to that of Latin America and Africa in the Atlantic slave economy, the Afro-Eurasian world system witnessed the (temporary) co-existence of economic prosperity and political marginality, particularly at the trading ports in the Asian waters. What was distinctive about Maritime Asia as an inter-imperial zone was not the absence of domination, but rather the *dialectics* of collaboration and domination that set this region apart from the accretion of imperial subordinations and enslavements in the Transylvania. To understand the unfolding of this dialectics, it was imperative to probe further into the concept of collaboration and its relationship with colonial/imperial power.

Earlier I noted that Ronald Robertson's idea of collaboration was adopted as a common point of reference in the theories of colonial Hong Kong. Yet the idea was used only generally, without considering Robertson's explanation of why and how collaboration arose as a response to imperialism. For Robertson, the necessity of collaboration would depend on the level of resistance to commerce and industry on the part of non-European agrarian empires (Robertson, 1972: 120–4). While giving more weight to local politics outside Europe, Robertson's theory of colonial collaboration inherited Marx's Eurocentrism in positing that European imperialism was a brutal but inevitable force for opening and modernizing an essentially backward and stagnant Orient. A more accurate account of colonial/imperial collaboration was offered by Wills (1993), who explained how European hegemony arose out of interaction with Asian empires in the oceanic world of commerce. Instead of passive victims, Asian 'navigators, merchants, pirates, investors, and merchant-princes' were active collaborators and at times effective competitors of the Europeans in centuries of transatlantic maritime trade (Wills, 1993: 83). While foregrounding the complex interplay of imperial and non-state actors over the oceans, Wills' account would be more convincing if he did not seek to explain the 'interactive emergence' of European hegemony in terms of state mobilization, for which the decline of Asia could be attributed to the lack of organizational cohesion and flexibility (Wills, 1993: 85–7). To overcome the lingering Eurocentrism in Robertson's 'collaboration' and Wills' 'interaction', we shall need a non-teleological explanation in which European hegemony was not treated as a preordained outcome of European superiority, but rather a contingent historical product of inter-imperial relations mediated by Asian waters and ports.

I would suggest that the notions of *network centrality* and *precarious autonomy* could better capture the dynamics and outcomes of collaboration in Maritime Asia. In his classic study, Reid (1993) pointed out that Southeast Asia had undergone an age of commerce and unprecedented prosperity circa 1450–1680. Thanks to their nodal positions in the maritime trade network, coastal cities like Melaka, Aceh and Banten could seize upon the growing demand for spices and pepper to exchange for silver and gold, and in this way wield economic influence and independence vis-à-vis the imperial centres in Europe, India, Japan and China (Reid, 1993: 1–24). Yet economic growth, political power and cultural creativity all came to a standstill in the 'long 17th century' due to a confluence of factors. Of particular importance was colonization and its context-dependent effects. At their inception, Portuguese Melaka, Spanish Manila and Dutch Batavia all contributed to local commercial growth inasmuch as the European settlers were more trade partners than despotic rulers. With the growing tension between Portuguese and Muslim empires and later among European empires, military conflicts, business monopoly and political subjugation eventually sealed an end to the prosperity and autonomy once enjoyed by Southeast Asia (Reid, 1993: 270–81). Here one would recall the analogous historical experience of Hong Kong: while British colonial rule was welcomed because of the unintended trade opportunities it brought to the local elites, in the long run the precarious space for collaboration proved to be unsustainable before contending great powers, most recently being the clash between China and the United States.

Reid's insights were further elaborated by Eric Tagliacozzo's discussion of Maritime Asia, which centered upon Southeast Asia while stretching westward to the Gulf of Hormuz and eastward to Nagasaki in Japan. What deserved attention was the reversal of centre and periphery with the rise of the British empire in the Indian Ocean. The arrival of the Portuguese in India in the 16th century did not much alter the trade system under Mughal rule. Indigenous populations at the coastal region were more benefited than harmed by the expansion of trade network into Spanish Manila, as well as the introduction of capital and technologies from Europe. The situation changed in the 18th century, when entrepot trade was gradually monopolized by British private traders. By infiltrating into the Mughal economic and political system, these private traders could alter its pattern of production by penetrating into the Indian hinterlands and creating relations of dependency. The status of the indigenous traders was reversed, as they served 'first as partners, then as competitors, and finally (often) as subordinates' of the British (Tagliacozzo, 2022: 127). Yet the colonizers were no less vulnerable: they had to adopt expedient means to get into Asian waters and socioeconomic systems before monopolizing or subverting them. This testified to the contingent and improvised character of European colonialism/imperialism, which was a common theme in revisionist historiography of the rise of the West (Erikson, 2014; Sharman, 2019; Flores, 2024).

By better understanding the actual history of events and processes, the Eurocentric narrative of the early modern period became less credible. An interesting consequence of this will be to heighten attention to the role of Asian economic or business elites in this system, especially towards the beginning when the British were more like partners or competitors. As the British and other European empires incorporated Asia as overseas colonies in the 19th century, some port cities such as Singapore continued to exploit their nodal positions in the 'colonial circuit' (Tagliacozzo, 2022: 225). Some common characteristics could be identified among the Asian port cities, including international orientation, the twin administration of commercial and political affairs, sensitivity to changing patterns of global trade, and the segregation of economic activities from external political interferences (Tagliacozzo, 2022: 199–208). In any case, successful adaptation to imperial and colonial rule would be impossible without the *shahbandar* or 'portmaster', who paid deliberate efforts to maintain the prosperity and autonomy of their city-states (Tagliacozzo, 2022: 201). From Carroll and Hamilton, we have seen how the Hong Kong business elites performed a similar strategic role in navigating the inter-imperial space between Britain, China and the United States, preserving the city's precarious survival. From an oceanic perspective, the room for agency and manoeuvring did not come from nowhere. Hong Kong's nodal position in the British colonial network would not be possible without the backing of its 'eight hinterlands' in the nearby regions of China, Japan and Southeast Asia (Hamashita, 1997: 35–9).

Taken together, these insights from ocean studies suggested that the dynamics of power-laden collaboration and inter-imperial interaction were not peculiar to Hong Kong, but rather generalizable to Maritime Asia. By broadening the geographical and historical frame of reference, we can see how imperial powers thrived on commercial networks that were mediated by non-state actors, both European and Asian, at the margin and outside their territorial purview. At first enriching and empowering all parties, the expansion of economic, political and cultural intercourses was increasingly overwhelmed by conflicts and control, thereby paving the road to decline. To draw parallels between early modern Southeast Asia and colonial Hong Kong did not imply that their experiences were the same; rather it was to underscore the spatial commonalities and temporary continuity underlying the Asian maritime/inter-imperial zone. Pursuing anti-colonial scholarship did not only involve an interrogation and rejection of colonial power's incomplete/inaccurate narratives, but also an investigation into variations of colonialism and the active roles played by the colonized.

Dialectical imagination: from contention to virtuality and conviviality

Our discussion of inter-imperiality in the Asian context would be incomplete if we leave out its cultural and political implications. Within the page limits of this chapter, I could only outline some key aspects awaiting more detailed treatments in the future. It could be remembered that according to Hung, contention had always been a prominent feature of Hong Kong given its precarious position between empires. Hung's assertion seemed to contradict Law's observation that class, race and gender inequalities were perpetuated and reinforced by the conservative alliance of local elites with colonial or imperial powers. But the contradiction was more apparent than real, as social injustice and the 'layered colonialities' between elite and ordinary social members could be subordinated under the defence of local autonomy pertaining to the polis as a whole. Behind the facade of social conservatism and rearguard politics, however, was the conception of power deeply ingrained in the Hong Kong people in living with multiple and successive empires.

For Doyle, dialectics was conceived in Hegelian (and feminist) terms, as the process in which individual beings acquired and transformed their identities in combating each other. I would propose that dialectics as *negativity* and power struggle did not exhaust its meanings. Inspired by the works of François Jullien (2004) and Jean François Billeter (2011), an alternative model could be found in the Daoist tradition, for which any opposites, be they good and bad, right and wrong, or *yin* and *yang*, were 'virtual' in the sense that these extremes shaded into each other in the flow of time and life. Inasmuch as any attempts to combat and negate the other would be futile and misplaced, one should rather 'go with the flow' while treating all names as mere labels with no substantial differences. Instead of identity and difference,

Daoist dialectics *as virtuality* valorized spontaneity and indistinction. In this conception, power connoted the efficacy to navigate the world effortlessly by getting around all artificial constraints, as in Zhuangzi's famous fable of 'dismembering a cow'.

The inter-imperial zone in Hong Kong could be conceived as 'virtual' in the Daoist sense, as it opened up potentialities of spontaneous development at those historical moments in which imperial centres refrained from fully asserting their powers over the city. A literary expression of inter-imperial virtuality could be found in the martial art novels of Jin Yong (Louis Cha), which was accorded canonical status in Hong Kong and Sinophone literature. In his early novels, Jin positioned his heroes unambiguously as opponents to alien rule and leaders in the resistance against foreign invasion. Yet this nationalist orientation was progressively weakened in his later works. As an allegory of the Cultural Revolution, *The Smiling, Proud Wanderer* (1967–1969) relativized the distinctions between good and evil, strong and weak, orthodoxy and heterodoxy, and so on, by portraying a hero who cherished spontaneity and flow over vanity and power. The subversion reached its apogee with Jin's last novel, *The Deer and the Cauldron* (1969–1972). That was the story of an anti-hero, a social outcast who happened to climb up the ladder and became the duke by *collaborating* with both the Manchu rulers and Han Chinese rebels. With street-smartness and an unusual combination of hospitality and cunningness, the anti-hero was able to decipher situations and seize opportunities in his best interests. Far from being amoral and cynical, he sought to mitigate conflicts between the opposite camps whenever possible. Seeing no essential difference between alien and indigenous rules, it was his conviction that whoever benefiting the people with benevolent and prudent governance was qualified to be a good ruler.

In fleshing out the Daoist idea of virtuality, Jin's later novels stroke a strong chord with the inter-imperial unconscious of the Hong Kong elites and their ethics of collaboration. One may well argue that Jin's works reflected the hegemonic position of the collaborative elites, and therefore only served to legitimize the capitalist/colonial system they championed. Yet this dominant ideology could be given a dialectical twist as it was being appropriated by the populace. Instead of mere inaction and depoliticization, virtuality could implicate the theme of *conviviality*, that is, the capacity to live in togetherness with differences, and to appropriate whatever tools or institutions serviceable for promoting the common good (Illich, 1973; Nowicka and Vertovec, 2014). Rule of law was widely regarded as a positive legacy of British colonial rule, though the Hong Kong people, especially the older generation, were well aware of the discrepancy between ideal and reality. Legal and other institutions became 'convivial' as they were put to endogenous uses, in the process setting aside cultural-political differences in favour of co-existence and togetherness. In this connection, one might argue that conviviality was nothing but a rhetoric and instrument for policing colonial and other differences (Hernando-Lloréns et al, 2023). But unlike civility, which only served to legitimize the status of the dominant/colonial elites, conviviality presupposed the equal access of social members to efficacious tools and institutions (Costa, 2019). The notion of conviviality thus specified the conditions whence colonial/imperial rule would be considered legitimate or not in Hong Kong. Whether similar conception of power and legitimacy could be found in other inter-imperial settings was worthy of further analysis.

Conclusion

This chapter began with a review of selected works on Hong Kong history and society, all of which highlighting the collaborative relationships that serve to connect the colonizer and colonized while at times blurring the line between them. Nevertheless, such collaboration was neither unconditional nor symmetrical; it was power-laden, hierarchical and in the long run unsustainable, with the room for negotiation dependent on the specific relations and interactions between empires. The co-existence of collaboration and domination in the inter-imperial space was not unique to Hong Kong, but rather signified a common historical experience of port cities and local elites that were positioned along the transregional maritime trade network of Asia. Instead of multiple and superimposing enslavements, the 'dialectics' or power dynamics governing the Asian inter-imperial zone could be captured in terms of network centrality and precarious autonomy, both concepts being adapted from the field of ocean studies. This perspective was also informed by world-system theory, which questioned the conventional assumption that European hegemony was inevitable rather than contingent, persistent rather than transient, and planned rather than improvised. In duly recognizing that Asian empires and cities were not mere passive victims but could be active agents strategically coming to terms with Europe, we can gain additional insights on distinctive cultural-political orientations such as virtuality and conviviality, which arose out of inter-imperial contexts and in turn served to legitimize (and challenge) the political and moral order of imperial/colonial regimes.

While this chapter focused on delineating the spatial commonalities and temporal continuity in inter-imperial Asia, future studies could articulate the 'unity in difference' pertaining to this geographical and historical region. As part of the British overseas empire, Hong Kong was distinguished from other colonies by its proximity and entanglements with China, which constituted a source of both economic opportunities and political turbulences. Likewise a central node in the global trade network, Singapore's political and cultural life was significantly shaped by its strategic and intricate position between the South Asian and Chinese worlds. Another interesting case for comparative analysis would be Taiwan, which had long been experiencing multiple and successive imperial/colonial rules in its history, as well as open clashes of empires such as the war between the Dutch and the Chinese in Zeelandia (Andrade, 2011). The comparative-historical frame could be further expanded to include the oceanic worlds of East Asia (Andrade and Hang, 2016) and the globe at large (Armitage et al, 2017). In specifying these locations, anti-colonial social theory could uncover the varieties of colonial experience in Asia and elsewhere by charting the uneven topography of power as produced in the connected histories of the capitalist/colonial world-system.

What would be the alternative world order as envisioned by global and inter-imperial social theory? Taking the clue again from Frank, we should seek to 're-orient' social theory by shedding off the Eurocentric worldview. But then a question arose: reorient towards what? Instead of decentring Europe by recentring Asia, a more proper task was to identify spatial-temporal locations that had been long deflecting the reach of imperial powers and centralized states. I hope this chapter has convincingly demonstrated that Southeast Asia was one such region. To be sure, under colonial influences modern Southeast Asia occasioned the rise of nationalism, which was often conflict-ridden and exclusionary (Reid, 2010). On the other hand, the noble cause of third worldism had been constrained by poverty and subsided with globalization (Dirlik, 1997). But there were signs of revival in Southeast Asia, as great powers in the West and the East were being fraught with crises and conflicts. Places like Malaysia were important sources of inspiration for intellectual decolonization and autonomous knowledge (Alatas, 2024). Conversely, indigenous and autonomous knowledge traditions could be enriched if they were situated in a broader world-historical region and elaborated along the lines of inter-imperiality, world-system theory, ocean studies and any other perspectives that were underpinned by the comparative-historical analysis of political economy. Whether Southeast Asia could regain its historic prosperity and revitalize its openness and pluralistic traditions, and what would be its implications for small political entities and non-state actors in the inter-imperial zone, would be some questions to ponder for anti-colonial, Southern and global social theorists.

Note

[1] Part of the materials for this chapter comes from the research project 'Yenching, Lingnan, Pittsburgh: C.K. Yang and the Transnational History of Chinese Sociology', funded by the University Grants Committee of Hong Kong (Ref.: LU 13604821).

References

Abbas, A. (1997) *Hong Kong: Culture and the Politics of Disappearance*, University of Minnesota Press.

Alatas, S.F. (2024) Intellectual imperialism, the coloniality of knowledge and the autonomous knowledge tradition, *Sociology Compass*, 18(8): e13256.

Andrade, T. (2011) *Lost Colony: The Untold Story of China's First Great Victory over the West*, Princeton University Press.

Andrade, T. and Hang, X. (2016) *Sea Rovers, Silver, and Samurai: Maritime East Asia in Global History, 1550–1700*, University of Hawai'i Press.

Armitage, D., Bashford, A. and Sivasundaram, S. (eds) (2017) *Oceanic Histories*, Cambridge University Press.

Billeter, J.F. (2011) *Four Lectures on Zhuangzi*, Linking Publishing Company (in Chinese).

Carroll, J. (2005) *Edge of Empires: Chinese Elites and British Colonials in Hong Kong*, Harvard University Press.

Chen, H.-F. (2024) Modernity and inter-imperiality: Rethinking social theory in East Asia, *Sociology Compass*, 18(7): e13251.

Chen, K.-H. (2010) *Asia as Method: Toward Deimperialization*, Duke University Press.

Costa, S. (2019) The neglected nexus between conviviality and inequality, Mecila Working Paper Series, no. 17, The Maria Sibylla Merian International Centre for Advanced Studies in the Humanities and Social Sciences Conviviality-Inequality in Latin America.

Cowell, C. (2024) *Form Follows Fever: Malaria and the Construction of Hong Kong, 1841–1849*, The Chinese University of Hong Kong Press.

Dei, G. and Asgharzadeh, A. (2001) The power of social theory: The anti-colonial discursive framework, *The Journal of Educational Thought*, 35(3): 297–323.

Dirlik, A. (1997) *The Postcolonial Aura: Third World Criticism in the Age of Global Capitalism*, Westview Press.

Doyle, L. (2020) *Inter-Imperiality*, Duke University Press.

Endacott, G. (1964) *Government and People in Hong Kong, 1841–1962: A Constitutional History*, Hong Kong University Press.

Erikson, E. (2014) *Between Monopoly and Free Trade: The English East India Company, 1600–1757*, Princeton University Press.

Flores, J. (2024) *Empire of Contingency: How Portugal Entered the Indo-Persian World*, University of Pennsylvania Press.

Frank, A.G. (1998) *ReOrient: Global Economy in the Asian Age*, University of California Press.

Freedman, M. (1976) A report on social research in the new territories of Hong Kong, 1963, *Journal of the Hong Kong Branch of the Royal Asiatic Society*, 16: 191–261.

Hamashita, T. (1997) *Hong Kong: A Macro History*, Commercial Press (in Chinese).

Hamilton, P. (2021) *Made in Hong Kong: Transpacific Networks and a New History of Globalization*, Columbia University Press.

Hernando-Lloréns, B., López, L.L., Sanya, B.N. and McCarthy, C. (2023) Conviviality and the making of difference: An introduction, *Globalisation, Societies and Education*, 21(4): 431–6.

Hung, H.-F. (2022) *City on the Edge: Hong Kong under Chinese Rule*, Cambridge University Press.

Illich, I. (1973) *Tools for Conviviality*, Harper & Row.

Institute of Historical Research, University of London (2010) Ten years of debate on the origins of the great divergence, *Reviews in History*, review no. 1008.

Jarvie, I.C. (1969) Introduction, in I.C. Jarvie (ed) *Hong Kong: A Society in Transition*, Routledge & Kegan Paul. pp xii–xxviii.

Jullien, F. (2004) *A Treatise on Efficacy: Between Western and Chinese Thinking*, University of Hawai'i Press.

Kong, V. (2023) *Multiracial Britishness: Global Networks in Hong Kong, 1910–45*, Cambridge University Press.

Lau, S.-K. (1982) *Society and Politics in Hong Kong*, Hong Kong University Press.

Law, W.-S. (2009) *Collaborative Colonial Power: The Making of the Hong Kong Chinese*, Hong Kong University Press.

Lui, T.-L., Chui, S.W.K. and Yep, R. (eds) (2019) *Routledge Handbook of Contemporary Hong Kong*, Routledge.

Miners, N. (1981) *The Government and Politics of Hong Kong*, Oxford University Press.

Mizoguchi, Y. (2016) China as method, *Inter-Asia Cultural Studies*, 17(4): 513–18.

Moosavi, L. (2020) The decolonial bandwagon and the dangers of intellectual decolonisation, *International Review of Sociology*, 30(2): 332–54.

Ngo, T.-W. (ed) (1999) *Hong Kong's History: State and Society under Colonial Rule*, Routledge.

Nowicka, M. and Vertovec, S. (2014) Comparing convivialities: Dreams and realities of living-with-difference, *European Journal of Cultural Studies*, 17(4): 341–56.

Parvulescu, A. and Boatcă, M. (2022) *Creolizing the Modern: Transylvania Across Empires*, Cornell University Press.

Patel, S. (2024) What is anti-colonial global social theory?, *Sociology Compass*, 18(8): e13259.

Pomeranz, K. (2000) *The Great Divergence: China, Europe, and the Making of the Modern World Economy*, Princeton University Press.

Radovanović, J. (2024) Legal translation between empires: The case of Çiftlik in Serbia, *Journal of Islamic Law*, 5(1). https://journalofislamiclaw.com/current/article/view/281 (last accessed 30 June 2025).

Reid, A. (1993) *Southeast Asia in the Age of Commerce 1450–1680, Volume 2: Expansion and Crisis*, Yale University Press.

Reid, A. (2010) *Imperial Alchemy: Nationalism and Political Identity in Southeast Asia*, Cambridge University Press.

Robinson, R. (1972) Non-European foundations of European imperialism: Sketch for a theory of collaboration, in R. Owen and B. Sutcliffe (eds) *Studies in the Theory of Imperialism*, Longman, pp 117–42.

Rowe, W. (1984) *Hankow: Commerce and Society in a Chinese City, 1796–1889*, Stanford University Press.

Sharman, J.C. (2019) *Empires of the Weak: The Real Story of European Expansion and the Creation of the New World Order*, Princeton University Press.

Sinn, E. (2003) *Power and Charity: A Chinese Merchant Elite in Colonial Hong Kong*, Hong Kong University Press and Eurospan.

Subrahmanyam, S. (2022) *Connected History: Essays and Arguments*, Verso.

Sutherland, H. (2003) Southeast Asian history and the Mediterranean analogy, *Journal of Southeast Asian Studies*, 34(1): 1–20.

Tagliacozzo, E. (2022) *In Asian Waters: Oceanic Worlds from Yemen to Yokohama*, Princeton University Press.

Tang, T.-S.D. (2021) The production of contemporary sociological knowledge in Hong Kong, *Journal of Historical Sociology*, 34: 120–33.

Topley, M. (ed) (1969) *Anthropology and Sociology in Hong Kong*, Center of Asian Studies, University of Hong Kong.

Vink, M. (2007) Indian Ocean studies and the 'new thalassology', *Journal of Global History*, 2: 41–62.

Vries, P. (2010) The California school and beyond: How to study the great divergence?, *History Compass*, 8(7): 730–51.

Wills, J. (1993) Maritime Asia, 1500–1800: The interactive emergence of European domination, *American Historical Review*, 98(1): 83–105.

Wong, B. (1997) *China Transformed: Historical Change and the Limits of the European Experience*, Cornell University Press.

Yang, C.K. (1981) Introduction, in A.K. Yeo-Chi and R.P.L. Lee (eds) *Social Life and Development in Hong Kong*, Chinese University Press, pp ix–xxv.

9

Humanizing Legacies of Caribbean Slavery and Colonialism in the Contemporary UK

Ann Phoenix

Introduction

Contemporary scholarship on the colonial histories of academic disciplines serves to dispel taken-for-granted assumptions that they are objectively distanced from politics and their objects of study. This chapter engages in anticolonial scholarship by considering some of the ways in which colonial thought is implicated in contemporary everyday life. In doing so, it takes a psychosocial lens to understanding the ways in which colonial histories are part of the present. It interrogates everyday contemporary issues to examine the implicit colonial power relations that fuel them.

Patel (2021) suggests that understanding of the ways in which academia is colonial requires that it is contextualized in time and place. This chapter extends that contextualization by thinking about the ways in which specific groups of people positioned in specific ways in their nation-states experience everyday racism (Essed, 1991) that is implicitly underpinned by colonial constructions. The chapter addresses the question, often ignored in anticolonial scholarship, of how those dehumanized in colonialism and transatlantic slavery are positioned by contemporary events that are redolent of colonial power imbalances. It thus shifts focus away from the colonial gaze as Boatcă and Costa (2016) advocate in order to contribute in small part to unsettling colonial constructions of the human and giving insights into possibilities for anticolonial change.

Methodologically, the chapter does this by paying attention to the narratives of people from minoritized ethnic groups and how they account for, and react to, what is happening to them. It gives them presence as narrators of their own lives rather than rendering them invisible except as members of devalued categories (Lewis, 2017). The examples selected are all located in the UK and show the ubiquity and reach of colonial issues and their situatedness in their particular local histories. The chapter starts by demonstrating this ubiquity in presenting the example of the UK 'anti-immigration riots' in summer 2024, which were fuelled by the same sentiments that sparked the UK vote to leave the European Union (Brexit) in 2016. It then discusses the theoretical and methodological resources on which I draw to conduct the analyses of the third example, the issue that has been called 'the Windrush betrayal' or 'scandal', which shows the relevance of psychosocial analyses to anticolonial scholarship.

Recursive racist violence: contemporary everyday colonialism and anticolonialism

Sometimes, the recursiveness of history is all too evident. This was the case in the UK, following the horrific knife murder, by a 17-year-old, of three girls aged six, seven and nine at their dance class on 29 July 2024. The police announced that they had arrested a 17-year-old young man and that they were not treating the incident as terror-related. However, social media posts began to announce that the murderer was an asylum seeker who arrived in the UK on a small boat in 2023 – a hugely unpopular stereotype for some in the UK. An incorrect name was widely circulated along with unfounded claims that he was Muslim. The following evening, more than a thousand people attended a vigil for the victims in Southport. Later on, some people threw bricks, bottles and other missiles at the local mosque with people inside and at police. A police van was set alight and 27 officers were taken to hospital. The disorder was denounced in the mainstream media and by various politicians and community groups. Police said they believed the violence involved supporters of a disbanded far-right group, the English Defence League.

Throughout the following week the disorder continued, involving white people from all age groups, different social classes and some parents who brought children in England and Northern Ireland. There were attacks on mosques and hotels housing asylum seekers and physical attacks on Asian and Black people. In one case, there was an attempt to burn down a Holiday Inn hotel with asylum seekers and staff barricading themselves inside against those who had smashed their way in. Chants of 'we want our country back' accompanied the riots. BBC analysis of activity on mainstream social media and in smaller public groups found that there was no single organizing force, but that influencers of different social classes and from different social groups promulgated false claims that the attacker was a Muslim migrant and encouraged their followers to gather for protests against migrants in many parts of England and Northern Ireland (BBC, 2024). Over the course of the week, the 'anti-immigration' rioters were opposed by thousands of anti-racists. There was also crowd funding and collective action to, for example, repair mosques that had been attacked in the riots. As Eger and Olzak (2023) suggest for Germany, anti-immigrant violence can have a polarizing effect.

The fear sparked by these events led many Asian and Black people to discuss painful memories of the 1970s and 1980s, when racist violence and National Front demonstrations were frighteningly common in England. Many expressed deep distress that Asian and Black people were again being faced with racist threats (Dhillon, 2024; Kotecha, 2024). This is exemplified by an extract from an interview on the BBC Radio 4 *Today* programme on Saturday 10 August 2024 with Neil Basu, former assistant commissioner at the London Metropolitan Police and former national lead for counterterrorism:

> It won't be immediately apparent to your listeners. But I'm the son of an Indian immigrant, uh, and I am mixed race and I'm also in my 57th year, so I'm a person born in the 60s raised in the 70s who last remembers this being in total fear of people like the National Front skinheads walking down my streets where I was born in the West Midlands. Uh, and this brought all of that back and I've had friends who were too scared to use public transport. I've had people who work in offices where Black and Asian workers were sent home to work from home and it's going to take a very long time for those people to recover their confidence.

Because he is speaking to a radio audience, Basu identifies his characteristics that he considers relevant to understanding the seriousness of the situation. He identifies himself as a British-born 'mixed race' middle-aged man who is the son of an Indian immigrant. This presumably tells us that he is identifiably Asian. He then talks about having been in 'total fear' of the then far-right racist group, the National Front, in the 1970s and how the current situation has brought that memory back. His account is in keeping with those of others who have been subjected to racist attacks earlier in life and are triggered when they see their racialized groups being subjected to the same racist name-calling and attacks they have previously experienced. For some, like Suresh Grover, who co-founded the Asian Youth Movement in the 1970s, the memories are also marked on their bodies in the form of scars, in his case, from stab wounds to his temple and legs (Butt, 2024).

Neil Basu links his past experience with what is currently happening to Black and Asian people who now lack the confidence to go out. He focuses on the fears of visibly racialized people with specific colonial histories in relation to the UK and highlights feelings of fear and loss of confidence.

In the rest of his interview, he points out that violent racism has improved in each generation from his parents' horrific experiences to his children's lack of experience of physical racism. His is, therefore, not a hopeless account. He expresses comfort in the fact that anti-racist demonstrators have outnumbered the anti-immigration demonstrators at some demonstrations, even though the far right is increasing in number. Basu makes clear that the painful emotions generated by the 'anti-immigration' riots are not an end point that strips away agency but that they motivate resistance. The sociostructural background to the generational change he identifies is one in which there was much concerted action, in the 1970s and 1980s, by Black and Asian people, to oppose racism and racist attacks. It took until 1998, however, for the UK Crime and Disorder Act addressing racially and religiously aggravated offences to be passed.

The three-part documentary, *Defiance: Fighting the Far Right*, shown on Channel 4 in April 2024, presented the story of how British Asians in Southall, London and Bradford, Yorkshire achieved the social changes Basu valorizes. They did so by collectively opposing far-right violence and the increasing number of racist murders between 1976 and 1981. Equally, there had long been resistance by Black people to the prevalence of racist attacks against them (Cohen, 1988; Sivanandan, 1990). In a 2024 radio broadcast, Jasvir Singh made this clear in bringing together the 2024 UK riots and the 1958 riots that inspired the British Notting Hill Carnival:

> The August bank holiday weekend is nearly upon us and for many people, one of the highlights is the Notting Hill Carnival. ... The story of how the Notting Hill Carnival came to be celebrated in the first place is a timely one. Late August, in 1958 saw race riots in Notting Hill over the course of a fortnight, with Black residents being the target of white youths and Black youths arming themselves to retaliate. There was also a similar but much shorter riot in Nottingham. In the aftermath a Trinidadian journalist by the name of Claudia Jones, wanted to, in the words of one of her contemporaries, 'wash the taste of Notting Hill and Nottingham out of our mouths'. Her solution was an indoor Caribbean Carnival just six months later, which ended up being televised on the BBC. And some of the money raised went towards paying the court fines of the young people caught up on both sides of the rioting. She had found a unique way to bring people together in celebration and to bridge the divisions highlighted by the riots. That Festival was the first of many others in the local area and they later developed into the Notting Hill Carnival we know today. We're still coming to terms with what the riots this summer mean for us as a nation. And as, for the longer impact, only time will tell. ... This summer has been a

tough one for many people, and there is still a huge amount to do to rebuild communities across the country.

While many politicians and commentators expressed shock about the 2024 riots, successive British governments have paid little attention to the rise of the far right in the UK and the racism that Black and Asian populations identified that they experienced from them. Instead, the UK government has focused on Muslims as potential terrorists, using the 'Prevent' duty enacted in 2015 as a way to 'promote fundamental British values', help to counter terrorism (John, 2024) and create a 'hostile environment' for immigration and potential asylum seekers (SSAHE, 2020). Attempts to understand the riots thus require them to be contextualized in terms of state actions, national histories, struggles over exclusions from citizenship, intersectional positioning, and personal beliefs and experiences at particular times in particular countries. This recognition of the interlinking of time, place, psychological experience and sociostructural context is a central part of understanding how spaces for anticolonial global scholarship are created in the everyday, as well as how implicit colonial ideologies permeate everyday life.

Anti-immigration and anti-minoritized group riots, past and present, are clearly important, but what has this to do with global anticolonial scholarship? To answer this, we need first to ask how it was that anti-immigrant, anti-Muslim, anti-Asian and anti-Black racism were so easily and speedily brought together and mobilized (within hours of the 29 July 2024 murders). Another way of framing this is to think about how it is possible for issues that appear historical to have continuing impact. Second, we need to consider how the burgeoning field of anticolonial global scholarship might aid understanding of the 2024 UK 'anti-immigration' riots and the earlier 'Windrush scandal'. Although these events may be considered microlevel since they focus on effects on individuals, one of the benefits of taking an anticolonial approach is that it may show how the micro, meso and macro level power relations are ontologically linked. However, we still know relatively little about how those subjected to dehumanizing legacies, because of their positioning in colonial histories, experience that dehumanization. It is this gap that gives the impetus to this chapter. The following section presents some theoretical and methodological resources to enable these analyses.

The relevance of anticolonial scholarship to the contemporary everyday: Brexit

If colonial thinking remains relevant, it should be the case that colonial assumptions are evident in analysis of the everyday. It is indisputable that those subjected to colonizing and enslavement are othered as undesirable and inferior to the colonizers and enslavers. This is not, however, only historical since the easy availability of these tropes partly arises from the fact that stereotypes, prejudice and bias are implicitly part of everyday thinking, kept alive and rendered accessible through being mobilized by influential people, including politicians, mainstream media personalities and social media influencers.

It is easy to see that the issues spurring the 2024 British riots are recursive. Since the 1950s, anti-immigration sentiments and protests in the UK have been concentrated on Asian and Black people, who have discursively been constructed as outsiders to the British nation. Martin Barker (1981) coined the term 'new racism' (now referred to as 'cultural racism') to refer to the simultaneous dynamism and recurrence of racism where Black and Asian people are continually constructed as outsiders who do not belong to the British nation, but the grounds on which exclusions are predicated and taken-for-granted shift. For Barker, 'new racism' marked a shift away from racism based solely on biological determinism, or beliefs in white superiority, which were increasingly difficult to sustain, to constructions of the inherent cultural incompatibility of Black and Asian people with white people. Black and Asian people are implicitly viewed as immigrants, regardless of where they were born and it is common to make an elision between Muslims and asylum seekers. All these groups are rendered invisible except as (undesirable) outsiders. 'White amnesiac readings of history' promulgate the notion that the racialized other only comes into contact with Britain through postwar Commonwealth migration (Joseph-Salisbury, 2019). Indeed, the British government's avoidance of mentioning the racism of the 2024 UK riots and focusing instead on 'violent thuggery' (Institute of Race Relations, 2024) also contributes to amnesic readings of history as well as silencing of minoritized ethnic groups' experiences and fears.

It is no surprise then that the result of the 2016 UK referendum, where the majority of voters supported 'Brexit', or the British leaving of the European Union, is inextricably linked with particular readings of British history and racism. As Virdee and McGeever point out, the 'Leave campaign' secured victory by bringing together

> two contradictory but inter-locking visions ... an imperial longing to restore Britain's place in the world as primus inter pares that occludes any coming to terms with the corrosive legacies of colonial conquest and racist subjugation [and] an insular ... narrative of island retreat from a 'globalizing' world, one that is no longer recognizably 'British'. (Virdee and McGeever, 2020: 56)

Brexit thus brings together nostalgia for empire and a sense of British exceptionalism linked to hostility to migrants (Gedalof, 2022), which is promulgated in sections of the mainstream media as well as social media.

The narratives produced by far-right politicians, organizations (such as the UK chapter of the anti-Islamist Pegida organization formed by the remnants of the English Defence League) and social media influencers include notions of swamping and invasion by immigrants and blaming immigrants for economic social ills. This circumlocution avoids charges of direct racism and encourages unity for white British people around anti-immigrant feeling. In addition, the heads of social media companies have enabled the use of social infrastructure to disseminate directly racist rhetoric and spawn racist violence (Bates, 2023; Hylton et al, 2024). While the views of Black and Asian people on Brexit were rarely sought in media, Gina Miller, a British Indian Guyanese businesswoman who was a prominent campaigner against Brexit, explained that the rise in racism sparked by the Brexit campaign silenced them:

> Over the six weeks I've been out [campaigning against Brexit], I've specifically been talking to people in the BAME [Black and Minority Ethnic] community, saying you've got to be part of these panels, you've got to be part of our campaign film.
> We desperately wanted to make a film ... we could not find a single person to agree and that's with me having over 50 conversations. I could not find a single person who was willing to go on camera.
> One of the reasons I think they won't go on camera is because there has been a rise in racism and abuse. I mean, I'm experiencing it every single day and that is palpable and for their children because even if you're mixed race or whatever you can't hide the colour of your skin and so there is a massive concern about what this rise in racism will mean for children and grandchildren and people are really, really upset and angry about it.
> This campaign will increase the hatred towards me, I know that.
> But the fact is I'm a very strong person and I can deal with that. But what I need to do is amplify the concerns of other people. (Francis, 2018)

In order to analyse the ways in which colonialism impacts the everyday, including the normalizing colonial logic in issues such as Brexit and the 2024 'immigration riots', it is important to draw on anticolonial theory and to analyse insider accounts, such as Neil Basu's, and the silences of minoritized ethnic voices and thus lack of representation, as highlighted by Gina Miller.

One of the reasons that colonial histories are attracting current attention is that they have contemporary resonances. Anticolonial scholarship has systematically shown that the social sciences and humanities are intricately interlinked with histories of colonialism and enslavement. Their foundational assumptions were crafted from the epistemological understandings taken for granted in the systems in which they were produced. This serves to invisibilize the experiences and claims of colonial 'others', rendering power relations invisible in the narratives and analytical frameworks of sociology (Wemyss, 2016; Bhambra and Holmwood, 2021). Invisibilization means that 'as modern subjects we breathe coloniality all the time and everyday' (Maldonado-Torres, 2007: 243). The mundanity of coloniality makes it non-conscious, but implicitly taken-for-granted in everyday practices and relations (Maldonado-Torres, 2007). Bhambra (2015) points out that colonial histories have produced amnesia and misunderstandings of the extent to which colonialism and empire are central to modernity. They therefore, naturalize the racialized exclusion and denigration of those whose labour and land were extracted for the benefit of Minority World societies.

Ontologically, constructions of what it is to be human were invented as part of the process of colonization (Bhambra, 2014; Fracchia, 2019; Meghji, 2021). This means that, as Frantz Fanon suggested, the colonizers and colonized are necessarily interlinked in highly unequal power relations inherent in the process of racialization (Fanon, 1967). That process of interlinking of colonizer and colonized dehumanizes the colonized and enslaved (Wynter, 1995, 2003). Achille Mbembe (2017) also shows how the construction of Blackness as non-human allowed for the reproduction of oppressive structures that are often reproduced even by those who critique such ideas. One way to understand this is through Derrida's (1994) notion of 'hauntology', which are 'traumas of previous generations ... [that] disturb the lives of their descendants even and especially if they know nothing about their distant causes' (Davis, 2005: 373).

A psychosocial approach to anticolonial scholarship

The analyses that follow are concerned with the psychosocial, viewing the psychological and social as inextricably linked because psychological issues and subjective experiences can only be understood in societal, cultural and historical contexts and the social world is necessarily also psychological and apprehended subjectively (Redman, 2016).

Anticolonial scholarship thus depends on interdisciplinary thinking. This fits with Laura Doyle's chapter in this volume (Chapter 6) that highlights the multifaceted (and so intersectional) nature of decolonization as both relational and structural. As Frosh et al argue,

> disciplines are themselves socially constructed and tend to become reified as ways to organize and interpret the world that have certain interests embedded in them. Awareness of how this happens is the reason why psychosocial studies is deeply indebted to the challenge to received knowledge mounted by different forms of 'critical' theory,

particularly de- and postcolonial thought, feminism, and queer theory. (Frosh et al, 2024: 5)

There is no one method associated with psychosocial studies. Instead, it is often thought of as a transdisciplinary area that focuses on issues in the social sciences and humanities where the social and the personal are both simultaneously at play, even if different disciplines focus on one, rather than both (Frosh et al, 2024). This means that psychosocial studies take up issues that might be dealt with in many disciplines and probes them from the perspective of an approach that always seeks to think the social and personal together. This sometimes entails critiques of some disciplinary approaches because they neglect identities and subjectivities or avoid social analysis. Methodologically, it is dynamic and often eclectic.

The method used here to take a psychosocial approach to anticolonial scholarship is narrative analysis. Narrative theory recognizes that all narratives are produced from particular viewpoints in the present that build on the past but look to the future. So the stories people tell connect events into a meaningful sequence that gives insights into their processes of making meanings from their experiences as well as the messages they want their readers or listeners to take away (Riessman, 2008). Narratives thus allow engagement with people's own agency and makes their construction of their past, present and constructed futures as well as their identities hearable. It is thus one way to confront and debunk colonial logic by the method of 'presencing' (Lewis, 2017), a method that entails resisting erasure of peoples, lands, relations and histories by making them visible and centring the often marginalized (Nxumalo and Bozalek, 2021).

El Shakry (2024) draws on Frantz Fanon's argument that overturning philosophical assumptions that privilege themselves as universal requires both a critical engagement with whiteness, and a 'turning away from Whiteness as the dominant ontological and epistemological framework for understanding the psychosocial world'. That turning away requires a non-pathologizing turning towards Blackness. This chapter takes a psychosocial approach to examining the contemporary resonances of the dehumanization that attended transatlantic enslavement. The Haitian anthropologist Michel-Rolph Trouillot (2015) argued that unequal power structures work to create and reinforce historical narratives that silence some stories and produce 'bundles of silence' that impact on how societies remember the past and the historical significance they accord to particular events. Trouillot shows how the silencing of certain histories (such as the Haitian revolution) across generations serves to dehumanize people with histories of being enslaved and colonized. Extending Trouillot's theorization to school curricula, Miles (2019) argues that simple multicultural inclusion is insufficient to disrupt current power structures and points to the importance of rethinking and re-storying historical and contemporary narratives in order to interrogate and counter the historical silences in narratives that dominate the present.

Dehumanizing and the 'Windrush scandal' in the UK

This section takes a psychosocial approach to examining the contemporary resonances of the dehumanization that attended transatlantic enslavement. It does so by focusing on an issue (referred to as the 'Windrush scandal') that may be considered microlevel since it focuses on effects on individuals. However, one of the benefits of taking an anticolonial approach is that it shows that micro, meso and macro level power relations are ontologically linked and that what appears individual has to be understood as also sociostructural. Avery Gordon (2008: 53–4) suggests that '[o]nce hauntings, absences and erasures make their ghostly presence felt, repression no longer works, and something must be done'. The discussion that follows addresses some of the ways in which the hauntings associated with the exclusion of the British people subjected to the Windrush betrayal from British citizenship become embodied and provoke resistance.

In the Windrush scandal, thousands of British nationals who had been born in the Caribbean were denied their long-held citizenship status and even deported as part of the UK's 'hostile environment for immigration'. The chapter argues that such episodes result from a dehumanizing history of enslavement and colonialism that has socioemotional consequences that keep those histories in play. The name of the scandal comes from the ship named the *Empire Windrush*, which arrived at Tilbury docks near London on 22 June 1948. It brought 492 people, mainly young men and ex-servicemen, from Caribbean islands colonized by Britain that had been sites of enslavement by the British. The arrival of the ship became iconic as a landmark moment in British history and is retrospectively constructed as marking the start of postwar labour migration from British colonies and the birth of modern multicultural Britain. People from the Caribbean who arrived in Britain between 1948 and 1971 are metaphorically referred to as 'the Windrush generation'. Their contribution to British society in helping to rebuild postwar Britain and in making major contributions to the National Health Service and transport services are widely recognized. Indeed, the opening of the London Olympic Games in 2012 enshrined celebration of Caribbean nurses' contribution to the National Health Service and to making multicultural Britain. They were given recognition as part of the mythology of national identity. However, as Gus John (2023) has repeatedly pointed out, Caribbean migrants had been arriving in Britain long before 1948 by sea and air. They were free to do so since they were British citizens in colonized countries with histories of enslavement by the British. From 1962, however, when the British government enacted the Commonwealth Immigration

Act to restrict open entry to 'coloured immigrants', they were subject to increasing immigration restrictions. John (2023) argues that the continual celebration of the arrival of the *Empire Windrush* is an attempt to embed a colonial mindset in which 'Windrushization' constitutes a homogenizing act of erasure that is colonial, conservative and a distortion of history.

Many people considered scepticism about the Windrush iconography justified when Paulette Wilson began campaigning in 2018 to stop deportations of British Caribbeans. In 2015, Wilson had received notification that she was an illegal immigrant and was required to leave the UK. Her housing and healthcare benefits were stopped; she became homeless and was denied the right to seek work. She was arrested and detained prior to deportation in 2017. Following her successful appeal with the help of the Refugee and Migrant Centre, Paulette Wilson publicized the Windrush scandal and began campaigning against it. The scandal became widely known when in 2018, the journalist Amelia Gentleman, supported by her newspaper, *The Guardian*, took up Paulette Wilson's story and conducted a careful investigation. Paulette Wilson, who was pivotal to highlighting the miscarriage of justice involved in the Windrush scandal, died suddenly and unexpectedly in 2020.

Amelia Gentleman found that many British Caribbeans were being refused the rights accorded to British citizens because they had no passports and could not prove when they had come to the UK. They had always been British citizens because the countries in which they were born were British colonies at the time they arrived in the UK. They had not, therefore, needed documentation to enter Britain since children did not need their own passports at the time and their adult relatives were also British. With increasingly restrictive changes from the 1962 immigration law, those rights were denied. Those who had no passports (or four pieces of evidence for each year they had been in the UK proving that they had continually lived in the UK) were unable to prove their legal right to remain. Although they had lived and worked in the UK for most of their lives, they found themselves being evicted, sacked from jobs, denied free healthcare and refused social security benefits.

In the 2019 book carefully documenting her painstaking work on this issue and the experiences of the people she interviewed, Gentleman referred to this issue as the *Windrush Betrayal*. Those British Caribbeans involved had fallen foul of what the then British prime minister, Theresa May, termed the 'hostile environment' for illegal immigration in 2012, when she had been Home Secretary. The 'Windrush generation' found that the fact that they were not illegal immigrants was irrelevant if they could not prove it to the Home Office's satisfaction. While the then Conservative government suggested that the Windrush scandal was the 'unintended consequence' of the hostile environment policy, this assertion was rejected after it was revealed that as home secretary, Theresa May received repeated warnings from her officials over the potential discrimination and hardship that the policy could cause. Home Office documentation from as far back as 2014 flagged the adverse consequences of the immigration bill. It was highlighted long before the situation escalated into the crisis that '[s]ome non-UK born older people may have difficulties in providing original documentation. Some may have had their immigration records destroyed. Some will have originally come into the country under old legislation but may have difficulty in evidencing this.' According to Guardian editor-at-large Gary Younge, this persecution was 'no accident' but rather 'cruelty by design'. For Younge, a chronicler of the black experience in Britain, the Caribbean and the US, 'this is not a glitch in the system. It is the system. ... A system cannot fail those it was never meant to protect'. (Hewitt, 2020: 110)

As Cummings (2020) and Hewitt (2020) point out, the Windrush scandal cannot be viewed in isolation from the histories of enslavement and colonialism that, as Fanon, Mbembe, Trouillot and Wynter have demonstrated, have excluded Black people from the category human. It is no surprise then that the immigration system was never designed to protect Black people whose histories are inextricably bound up with enslavement and colonialism. The 275-page report of the UK government review into the Windrush scandal found that hundreds, and maybe thousands, of British Caribbeans had been affected – there are no clear figures because records have not been kept. The review suggests that the 'root cause' of the scandal can be traced back to legislation of the 1960s, 1970s and 1980s, some of which had 'racial motivations' (Williams, 2020). The injustice of the Windrush scandal has inspired many people to turn to hauntological theorizations to explain it:

> [W]hile not all migrants and minoritised/racialised citizens are caught up in the wake of enslavement and empire in the same ways, the treatment of the 'Windrush generation' – themselves descendants of slaves brought to the Caribbean by British slave traders – needs to be seen in this context. The ways in which the hostile environment policy was allowed to turn its dehumanising violence on this group of Black people suggests that the 'afterlife of property' and its refusal of the legitimacy of some genealogies of kinship and belonging is still salient to understanding the place of the Afro-Caribbean population in the UK. (Gedalof, 2022: 548)

Accounts such as Gedalof's are themselves anticolonial, pointing out that slavery and its dehumanizing of Black people is at the heart of the

Windrush scandal. The process through which this occurs is one of amnesia about enslavement, the British Empire and the histories of Black British citizenship as a result of empire (Wardle and Obermuller, 2018). If we take seriously Sylvia Wynter's notion that we have to rethink what it means to be human, the question arises of how we do this for the case of the Windrush scandal. One way of resisting the dehumanizing it produces is by considering the agency and accounts of people who have been adversely affected. To that end, an excerpt from the narrative of Judy Griffith, interviewed for a British Library exhibition, is presented here. It provides a contextualized account of what happened to her and shows how she employs agency to attempt to craft a liveable life (Butler, 2004) and how the affective impact of her experiences has long-lasting consequences. The excerpt selected is lengthy in order to present her narrative from her perspective.

Judy: It was 2014 and I had been made redundant. I wasn't really that bothered about it because I've never had a problem becoming employed. I started applying for work, as anyone else would. I was interviewed successfully for three jobs but then found I couldn't take up any of them. Basically, I was told that I was an illegal immigrant, which was horror, shock, horror, shock, more horror, you know. Having lived and worked here all my life, I was like, well, something is obviously wrong. Initially I didn't really take it to heart because to me it seemed like an impossibility. ... Even before that, I had been writing to the Home Office because I had lost my Barbadian passport through the Royal Mail, which had my stamp of indefinite leave in it. From 2005, I'd been writing backwards and forwards to these people and they kept telling me that I could not be found on their system. I kind of gave up for a while. I thought, whatever this is, it's going to pass. But then I realised, no, this is serious now.

Interviewer: Where did you turn to, and what has happened since 2014?

Judy: I went to see my MP. I went to the immigration drop-in place in Hackney. I think I went everywhere. It wasn't so much as going but it was the amount of time that you have to spend in these places. At the immigration centre in Hackney, I was there from ten in the morning till half past four in the afternoon, just for the woman to tell me, 'No, I can't help you. You should go to the law centre in Camden.' By that time that was like the last resort, and thankfully I found some help there.

I think I was fortunate regarding the fact that I was not without documents. I'm what they might call a hoarder of paperwork [laughs] and I kept all my payslips from when I started work, you know, my children's documents, antenatal clinic, all this kind of thing. I had to prove that I had been in the country before 1973. That was the stipulation. I didn't even know then that you had to supply four different pieces of identification for each year. By then my head was so out of it that I was just like, here you are. Sift through that lot [laughs], you know. I brought two sacksful. We sat and went through it together and she was so pleased, the lady that helped me. Annie was her name. I'll never forget her. She was so, so, so helpful. She was pleased to see that I had documentation because by that time she had said to me that there were people coming in with the same problem, but they had like nothing.

I started work as soon as I got the biometric card. I started work and I lost the job. I couldn't cope with what was going on. One of the easiest jobs I've ever had, and I could not pass my probation because I could not get my head around it. I didn't feel like I fit in, felt everybody knew and everybody was looking at me. Do they think it's my fault, you know. All these kinds of thoughts are going around in your head all the time …

Interviewer: Can you describe what effect this has had on you?

Judy: The thing that was so hard for me to get my head around is the sense of loss that came with it, which I'm still feeling today. I've just received a certificate that tells me I'm a British citizen. But it tells me I'm a British citizen from the 12th of July 2018. What's happened to all the other years? Where have they gone? I phoned the hotline and they said, no, it can't be changed, that's it. I felt that at least somebody should have discussed it with me. If, as they claim, they'd have no idea of the dates when people came in because of these landing chapters having been destroyed, then having stipulated that we have to prove we were in the country before 1973, then put the date from 1973. I didn't drop out of the sky into this country, you know [laughs]. I just didn't. I'm not happy about that aspect of it at all.

From Judy Griffith's account, it is difficult to avoid the fact that what she faced were concerted practices that produced a hostile environment for her and hundreds of others. The government destroyed the landing records of Caribbeans of her generation so that they are not available to be used as proof of entry to the UK (Gentleman, 2019). It is also clear that Judy Griffith fights both for citizenship rights so that she can continue to be employed and support herself, and for recognition that it is also an identity issue for her. Having always been a British citizen, she refuses the notion that she became a British citizen in 2018 and that this cannot be changed. Not only has she been denied years of British citizenship, but she has been affectively deskilled, unable to do a job that should be easy for her because of feelings of shame and insecurity.

The fact that the then-Conservative UK government was not committed to redressing the injustice they were forced to acknowledge following the public outcry generated by Amelia Gentleman's publications is illustrated by the fact that it reneged on implementing all the recommendations of the Windrush Inquiry (Williams, 2020).

While Judy Griffiths' story is one of individual action and effect, the Windrush betrayal was a turning point for her and led her to think beyond her own situation once she realized that her experience was something that had happened on a large scale, rather than only to her.

Interviewer: How do you feel about Britain and your identity as a British citizen now?

Judy: I'm a citizen of heaven. Thank God for Jesus. That's the only citizenship I can really acknowledge now, quite frankly. I will go about my daily life and do whatever I have to do but like I said, there's been a great loss, mentally, physically and spiritually.

I'll be quite honest about it, I have considered whether I'll remain living in Britain. We have a saying in the Caribbean: cockroaches don't go to chicken's parties. What that means is, if you're a cockroach, you're not going to go to a party that a chicken is holding 'cause you get eaten, don't you? [Laughs] Basically, I don't feel like I fit here anymore. I don't. I'm uncomfortable in my home, I'm uncomfortable on the street. My thoughts are running, you know, around wondering what next. And not only that, there's a fear. I've seen my children encounter the same racisms that I have. Are they now going to encounter the same thing, even though they were born here? What is next for them?

Interviewer: [What are your] final thoughts?

Judy: My final thoughts are, compensate people properly. You know what they've suffered. They don't need to come and tell you over and over again. All your stories are in the news chapters. The loss, the loss of homes, the loss of employment, the loss of, you know, lives built. Lives stopped in the middle of whatever they were doing, you know. For instance, I'm due to retire next year. How? Where do I start?

Judy Griffiths reports a shift from love of the nation and confidence in her citizenship to fear and discomfort, not only for herself, but for her children. Her metaphor of herself and other Windrush citizens as 'cockroaches' to the government's 'chickens' suggests that she now views the state–Black citizen relationship as that of predator–prey. She also advocates the paying of proper compensation and a sincere apology. While she does not mention histories of enslavement and colonialism, she says that she feels betrayed by the state, particularly because people like her parents contributed so much to Britain. She suggests that she can now only trust heaven as the place in which she can claim citizenship.

Conclusion

This chapter aimed to contribute to the anticolonial global scholarship being developed in this volume by addressing new questions and focusing on the insider narratives of members of racialized groups that are often omitted from social science and humanities scholarship. Its focus has been on the ways in which colonial histories are part of contemporary everyday life in the UK. The chapter took a psychosocial perspective to give attention to the narratives of people from minoritized ethnic groups on the 2024 UK 'immigration riots', Brexit and the Windrush scandal. It explored ways in which the dehumanization of Black people that is an integral part of enslavement and colonial projects has contemporary resonances (Gilroy, 2004; Flax, 2010; Mbembe, 2017). The accounts of the Black and Asian people presented here can be viewed as resisting implicit exclusion from the category human and as anticolonial.

While intersectionality has not been the focus of the chapter, intersections of nation, racialization and generation are evident in the issues discussed. This is more apparent if we consider the ways in which the Windrush scandal has impacted on younger generations of Caribbean people. Stein and Shankley (2023) found that the Caribbean mothers they interviewed, all of whom were younger than the 'Windrush generation', developed or intensified mothering strategies focused on the teaching of historic links between Britain and the Caribbean, with the aim of instilling pride in a diasporic Caribbean identity. They recognized that their belonging to the state is contingent and precarious but resisted racialized exclusion from Britishness for themselves and their children. As mothers, a central site of struggle was clearly the intersection of racialization and gender with concern about the recursiveness of racialized inequalities and exclusions. Their accounts show the contradictions in how histories are an inextricable part of subject formation and how subject formation itself can be riven with contradictions (Lewis, 2009) – in this case recognition of contingent belonging contradicting claims to inclusion. The mothers' narratives and actions give recognition to 'the coloniality of being' (Mignolo, 1995; Wynter, 2003; Maldonado-Torres, 2007) while resisting the dehumanization that is inherent in histories of colonization and refusing to plead for inclusion. They, therefore, contribute to anticolonial everyday practices by humanizing legacies of Caribbean slavery and colonialism in the contemporary UK.

References

Barker, M. (1981) *The New Racism: Conservatives and the Ideology of the Tribe*, Junction Books.

Bates, D. (2023) 'This is Britain, get a grip': Race and racism in Britain today, in T. Sikka, G. Longstaff and S. Walls (eds) *Disrupted Knowledge: Scholarship in a Time of Change*, Haymarket/Brill, pp 97–113.

Basu, N. (2024) Interviewed on Today programme, 10 August, transcribed by author, episode no longer available.

BBC (2024) Why are there riots in the UK? *BBC News*, 8 September. https://www.bbc.co.uk/news/articles/ckg55we5n3xo

Bhambra, G. (2014) *Connected Sociologies*, Bloomsbury Academic.

Bhambra, G. (2015) Citizens and others: The constitution of citizenship through exclusion, *Alternatives*, 40(2): 102–14.

Bhambra, G.K. and Holmwood, J. (2021) *Colonialism and Modern Social Theory*, John Wiley & Sons.

Boatcă, M. and Costa, S. (2016) Postcolonial sociology: A research agenda, in E. Rodríguez, M. Boatca and S. Costa (eds) *Decolonizing European Sociology: Transdisciplinary Approaches*, 2nd edition, Ashgate, pp 13–31.

Butler, J. (2004) *Undoing Gender*, Routledge.

Butt, M. (2024) Riz Ahmed series reveals hidden history of British Asian anti-fascist resistance after UK race riots. *The Independent*, 8 August. https://www.independent.co.uk/arts-entertainment/tv/news/riz-ahmed-documentary-defiance-british-asian-protests-b2593276.html

Cohen, P. (1988) The perversions of inheritance: Studies in the making of multi-racist Britain, in P. Cohen and H.S. Bains (eds) *Multi-Racist Britain. Youth Questions*, Palgrave Macmillan, London, pp 9–118. https://doi.org/10.1007/978-1-349-19399-8

Cummings, R. (2020) Ain't no black in the (Brexit) Union Jack? Race and empire in the era of Brexit and the Windrush scandal, *Journal of Postcolonial Writing*, 56(5): 593–606.

Davis, C. (2005) Hauntology, spectres and phantoms, *French Studies*, 59(3): 373–79.

Derrida, J. (1994) *Specters of Marx: The State of the Debt, the Work of Mourning and the New International*, Routledge.

Dhillon, P. (2024) What the fight against racism in the 1970s can teach us about defeating fascists in 2024, *Byline Times*, 9 August. https://bylinetimes.com/2024/08/09/far-right-riots-southport-lesson-from-1970s/

Eger, M.A. and Olzak, S. (2023) The polarizing effect of anti-immigrant violence on radical right sympathies in Germany, *International Migration Review*, 57(2): 746–77. https://doi.org/10.1177/01979183221126461

El Shakry, O. (2024) Colonialism and postcolonial theory: Race, culture, and religion in psychosocial studies, in S. Frosh, M. Vyrgioti and J. Walsh (eds) *The Palgrave Handbook of Psychosocial Studies*, Springer, pp 307–30.

Essed, P. (1991) *Understanding Everyday Racism: An Interdisciplinary Theory*, SAGE.

Fanon, F. (1967) *The Wretched of the Earth*, Penguin.

Flax, J. (2010) *Resonances of Slavery in Race/gender Relations: Shadow at the Heart of American Politics*, Springer.

Fracchia, C. (2019) *'Black But Human': Slavery and Visual Arts in Hapsburg Spain, 1480–1700*, Oxford University Press. https://doi.org/10.1093/oso/9780198767978.003.0008

Francis, A. (2018) Where are Brexit's black voices? Campaigner Gina Miller says the community needs to be more vocal on the issue to ensure their concerns are heard, *The Voice (Online)*, 23 September. https://www.voice-online.co.uk/news/uk-news/2018/09/23/where-are-brexits-black-voices/

Frosh, S., Vyrgioti, M. and Walsh, J. (2024) *The Palgrave Handbook of Psychosocial Studies*, Springer.

Gedalof, I. (2022) In the wake of the hostile environment: Migration, reproduction and the Windrush scandal, *Feminist Theory*, 23(4): 539–55.

Gentleman, A. (2019) *The Windrush Betrayal: Exposing the Hostile Environment*, Faber & Faber.

Gilroy, P. (2004) *After Empire: Melancholia or Convivial Culture*, Routledge.

Gordon, A.F. (2008) *Ghostly Matters: Haunting and the Sociological Imagination*, University of Minnesota Press.

Hewitt, G. (2020) The Windrush scandal: An insider's reflection, *Caribbean Quarterly*, 66(1): 108–28.

Hylton, K., Kilvington, D., Long, J., Bond, A. and Chaudry, I. (2024) Dear Prime Minister, Mr Musk and Mr Zuckerberg! The challenge of social media and platformed racism in the English premier league and football league, *International Review for the Sociology of Sport*, 59(6): 844–67.

Institute of Race Relations (2024) Editorial: The far right orchestrated riots, 22 August. https://preview.mailerlite.com/d9l7h5i4z1/2552422288897086785/t5j9/?ml_sub=2552422288897086785&ml_sub_hash=t5j9

John, G. (2023) *Don't Salvage the Empire Windrush*, New Beacon Books.

John, G. (2024) You can't sow corn and reap cassava: Prof Gus John reflects upon racial strife in Britain, *The Gleaner*, 7 August.

Joseph-Salisbury, R. (2019) 'Does anybody really care what a racist says?' Anti-racism in 'post-racial' times, *The Sociological Review*, 67(1): 63–78.

Kotecha, S. (2024) 'I thought days of race hatred were over': Riots take British Asians back to 1970s, *BBC News*, 10 August. https://www.bbc.co.uk/news/articles/ckg2r3lxzedo

Lewis, G. (2009) Birthing racial difference: Conversations with my mother and others, *Studies in the Maternal*, 1(1): 1–21. doi: https://doi.org/10.16995/sim.112

Lewis, G. (2017) Questions of presence, *Feminist Review*, 117(1): 1–19.

Maldonado-Torres, N. (2007) On the coloniality of being: Contributions to the development of a concept, *Cultural Studies*, 21: 240–70.

Mbembe, A. (2017) *Critique of Black Reason*, translated L. Dubois, Duke University Press.

Meghji, A. (2021) *Decolonizing Sociology: An Introduction*, John Wiley & Sons.

Mignolo, W.D. (1995) Decires fuera de lugar: Sujetos dicentes, roles sociales y formas de inscripción, *Revista de Crítica Literaria Latinoamericana*, 21(41): 9–31.

Miles, J. (2019) Historical silences and the enduring power of counter storytelling, *Curriculum Inquiry*, 49(3): 253–59.

Nxumalo, F. and Bozalek, V. (2021) Presencing, in Karin Murris (ed) *A Glossary for Doing Postqualitative, New Materialist and Critical Posthumanist Research across Disciplines*, Routledge, pp 102–3.

Patel, S. (2021) Sociology's encounter with the decolonial: The problematique of indigenous vs that of coloniality, extraversion and colonial modernity, *Current Sociology*, 69(3): 372–88.

Redman, P. (2016) Once more with feeling: What is the psychosocial anyway? *The Journal of Psychosocial Studies*, 9(1): 73–93.

Riessman, C. (2008) *Narrative Methods for the Human Sciences*, SAGE.

Singh, J. (2024) Thought for the Day, BBC Radio 4, Today programme, 23 August, transcribed by author. https://www.bbc.co.uk/sounds/play/p0jl5pbv

Sivanandan, A. (1990) *Communities of Resistance: Writings on Black Struggles for Socialism*, Verso Books.

Shankley, W. and Byrne, B. (2020) Citizen rights and immigration, in B. Byrne, C. Alexander, O. Khan, J. Nazroo and W. Shankley (eds) *Ethnicity, Race and Inequality in the UK: State of the Nation*, Policy Press.

SSAHE (Social Scientists Against the Hostile Environment) (2020) *Migration, Racism and the Hostile Environment: Making the Case for the Social Sciences*. London: Academy of Social Sciences special interest group on Migration, Refugees and Settlement. https://ssahe.net/wp-content/uploads/2020/03/ssahe-report-march-2020.pdf

Stein, T. and Shankley, W. (2023) 'Paperwork or no paperwork, we are guests in this country': Mothering and belonging in the wake of the Windrush Scandal, *Identities*, 1–20.

Trouillot, M.-R. (2015) *Silencing the Past: Power and the Production of History*, 2nd edition,, Beacon Press.

Virdee, S. and McGeever, B. (2020) Racism, crisis, Brexit, in S. Gupta and S. Virdee (eds) *Race and Crisis*, Routledge, pp 56–73.

Wardle, H. and Obermuller, L. (2018) The Windrush generation, *Anthropology Today*, 34(4): 3–4.

Wemyss, G. (2016) *The Invisible Empire: White Discourse, Tolerance and Belonging*, Routledge.

Williams, W. (2020) Windrush Lessons Learned Review: Independent review by Wendy Williams Ordered by the House of Commons to be printed on 19 March 2020. https://assets.publishing.service.gov.uk/media/5e74984fd3bf7f4684279faa/6.5577_HO_Windrush_Lessons_Learned_Review_WEB_v2.pdf

Wynter, S. (1995) 'No humans involved': An open letter to my colleagues (revised version), Havens Center Visiting Scholar's Program, Sociology Department, University of Wisconsin-Madison.

Wynter, S. (2003) Unsettling the coloniality of being/power/truth/freedom: Towards the human, after man, its overrepresentation – an argument, *CR: The New Centennial Review*, 3(3): 257–337.

10

The Horrors of Settler-Colonialism: Remote Sites of Refugee Detention in Australia's Carceral Archipelago

Claudia Tazreiter

Introduction

In this chapter, I introduce and analyse a unique contribution to anticolonial thought and the work of decolonizing power structures from marginalized voices that experience directly the harms of continued colonial violence. I focus on the work of refugee writers, creatives and activists through the prism of the lived experience of refugees held in long-term detention in the carceral archipelago – sites of remote immigration detention where the nation-state border is externalized for refugees seeking protection under international law. Australia is among the first nation-states to enact a carceral archipelago, sending asylum seekers to remote islands for detention and assessment of their claims for asylum. From 2001, the Australian government began 'off-shore' detention on remote Pacific Island sites to remove refugees seeking protection from Australia under the 1951 Refugee Convention. This so-called *Pacific Solution* has seen agreements signed with the states of Papua New Guinea (PNG) and the small and impoverished island nation of Nauru, with the Australian government paying its poorer Pacific neighbours to detain refugees that sought protection from Australia. These policies and practices are now also being enacted by the UK and European Union governments, with deals struck with states such as Rwanda to detain asylum seekers and refugees.

In elaborating this empirical field of cases, I begin with a history of these carceral practices, laying out evidence that shows how refugee writing, art and creative practices are not only unique and important examples of resistance and dissent to the dominant discourses and practices of neo- and settler-colonial power and violence, but also constitute unique forms of knowledge production as anticolonial thought. Indeed, the significant creative works that have accumulated over more than a decade from refugees held in the carceral archipelago in the Asia Pacific are much more than a form of resistance or, of speaking back to the colonizers. Rather, these works and the refugees that create them individually and in collaboration, form part of a continuum of resistance, as well as imagining alternative futures through creative voice, performance and various forms of textual production. Many refugees detained by the Australian government in remote sites have also collaborated with Indigenous Australian, Aboriginal and Torres Strait Islander (ATSI) peoples in various visual, performative, literary and other creative works both from detention and once free. These works highlight that in opposing settler-colonial violence and annihilation, people from diverse backgrounds may find commonality and understanding.

The argument I put forward in this chapter relates to the time horizons of settler-colonialism, with continuing cycles of violence and subjugation of targeted populations. This subjugation draws on memories of past practices that have the effect of normalizing contemporary policies and practices. Rather than being a break with the past, as might be expected in a context such as contemporary Australia with a self-understanding as an independent, postcolonial country, the practices of deterrence, detention and harm to refugees link the present to past practices of harm, particularly those of forced removal to camps and settlements, cultural genocide and other forms of subjugation experienced by ATSI peoples. I argue that the majority population in a settler-colonial society such as Australia internalize in subtle, often unconscious ways, the validation of practices of exceptionality towards subjugated and minoritized populations. These practices include the forced removal to camps as remote sites of punishment, deterrence and control of suspect/unwanted populations. At the same time, a settler-colonial society such as Australia perpetuates the self-understanding of principles of fairness and even-handedness through the rule of law and democratic governance, while eschewing this deep, unresolved history and its manifestations in the present. Indeed, I argue that the detention of refugees is a continuation of colonial practices in the Australian case – even in a postcolonial context. There is a difference with the treatment of ATSI peoples, but also continuation. In the colonial period, ATSI peoples were not recognized as fully human. Rather, they were counted among the flora and fauna in the fiction perpetuated by the British colonizers that the land was *terra nullius*, land without people. It was not until the 1967 referendum that ATSI people were recognized and counted as part of the population. In 1992, the *Mabo Case* recognized the land rights of the Meriam people. The decision was also successful in overturning the myth of *terra nullius*.[1] Refugees arriving in contemporary Australia are also effectively dehumanized through the policies, practices and social attitudes that maintain and legitimate remote detention.

For this chapter, an important link with critical migration studies to the experience of refugees can be made at this point with the critique of capitalism that marinates through anticolonial thought, and with other thinkers that critique colonial violence and subjugation. Given the particular history of migration I sketch in relation to Australia, anticolonial thought that relates to settler-colonial societies is most relevant, as outlined by Alatas (Chapter 3, this volume). In this regard, I argue that migration scholars have long assessed colonized countries such as Australia as 'immigration nations'. Only more recently have some scholars instead adopted the term settler-colonial as one type of colonialism. This shift in terminology from some migration scholars is notable, aligning with critical approaches such as those of Anderson (2019) in articulating methodological de-nationalism, theorizing human mobility not as threat, crisis and problem to be solved, but as one aspect of the social transformation of societies in adapting to economic, political and cultural change.

In what follows, I focus on the remote Manus Island, PNG, where a disused Australian naval base was repurposed as an immigration detention facility. My analysis features the period since 2013, drawing on the creative productions, literary and theoretical interventions of refugees held on Manus Island. I argue that refugee voices and the significant contribution they make to understanding colonial violence and power are not limited to the contemporary period, but also challenge the reader/viewer/collaborator to maintain care and attention to continuities with other historical epochs. Specifically, these interventions and creative works from refugees held 'elsewhere' contribute to anticolonial and decolonial ideas and knowledge in at least two ways. First, through their embodied presence in a third state along with their activism, the refugees show the continued colonial violence and power structures used by the Australian state on racialized persons. Second, through the significant accumulated writing, journalism and creative works by refugees, new empirical and epistemic understanding is created, where the contributions of these works to anticolonial thought include the empirical cases detailed here, adding to knowledge production, perhaps in quite unique ways.

Australia as an immigration nation and exceptionalism towards refugee arrivals

In order to provide the context for the contemporary developments in the securitization of refugees and asylum seekers globally, and the particular form it has taken in Australia, I sketch the history of Australia, founded on settler-colonial ideas and values and the key role migration has played in what is often termed 'nation-building'. This history began with the appropriation/theft of land and resources from ATSI peoples, based on the British and European colonial myth that Indigenous peoples were inferior and required civilizing. This myth was used to justify violence, killing and theft of land and resources and arguably remains embedded in contemporary social attitudes. Such ongoing colonial attitudes are exemplified by the majority of the Australian electorate rejecting the proposal to include ATSI peoples in the Australian Constitution and provide an Indigenous voice to parliament in a referendum held in 2023. This history also allows me to situate the overall argument I make on the recurrence of colonial violence even in purportedly postcolonial contexts. Sketching this history is an important reminder of continuities and discontinuities of human mobility (international migration), state planning (migration management) and responses.

Since the first fleet of British colonizers in 1788, Australia has expanded its population through immigration programmes as a settler-colonial state. The first, and subsequent, fleets from England brought convicts, their guards and administrators. Later, voluntary settlers arrived with the promise of large expanses of land often gifted by the Crown to 'squatters'. This theft of land, killing and encampment of ATSI peoples was central to the approach of the British colonizers (Lake and Reynolds, 2008; Moreton-Robinson, 2015). It is notable that the precursor of the modern governance of migration in Australia can be traced to 1901 with the beginning of the federal system, with six states and two territories governed from a federal parliament. The first legislation passed in the new federation was the Immigration Restriction Act of 1901, more commonly known as the 'White Australia Policy', effectively a 'Whites only' policy. From this period, the racialization of immigration was institutionalized in policies and normalized through social practices and attitudes that accompanied policies creating a racial hierarchy of immigrants, hence legitimating and embedding such divisions and exclusions. Australia was late in repealing the White Australia Policy and implementing a non-discriminatory legislative framework to manage the immigration system, accompanied by multicultural, rather than assimilationist, values. A parliamentary review in 1966 began the process of repealing the legislation, however substantial change did not come until 1973 with the Whitlam Labor government introducing legislative change premised on non-discrimination alongside policies and practices of multiculturalism. Notably, ATSI people were also part of the non-white other, though as they were present prior to colonization, could not be physically excluded in the way that Asian migrants were. However, ATSI peoples were, from the beginning of colonization, the target of violent subjugation, cultural genocide, theft of land and resources, and forced removal to encampments.

Today in Australia, as across much of the world, borders and human migration are subject to new, more restrictive and punitive forms of securitization. Since the terrorist events of 9/11 in the United States, the securitization of people categorized as irregular migrants, including refugees and asylum seekers, has accelerated significantly (Pickering et al, 2013; Weber et al, 2014; Tazreiter, 2015a, 2015b, 2015c, 2017a, 2019a; Collins, 2019; Yuval-Davis et al, 2019). People designated as refugees have long been a part of Australia's immigration intake. As a 'classic country of immigration' (similar to Canada and the United States), Australia determines on a yearly basis the number and composition of its immigration intake, including a humanitarian intake. The spontaneous arrival of asylum seekers has in recent years also been tied to the pre-determined humanitarian resettlement numbers. However, the 1951 Refugee Convention that Australia is a signatory to requires states to also receive asylum seekers that arrive spontaneously and provide adequate welfare while their claim for protection is assessed. Many migration scholars indicate the diminution of the international refugee system with actions such as those of the Australian government in externalizing its borders through the carceral archipelago (Juss, 2017; McAdam, 2017; Tazreiter, 2017b; Mountz, 2020).

Some developments in border control over the past two decades are common across Western states and globally. Key among these developments is the physical, digital, temporal and existential securitization of borders. Critical migration scholars show that this securitization extends beyond the obvious barriers of territorial borders, airports, check points, walls and other physical barriers to human movement, but importantly extends beyond the targeting of various categories of unwanted migrants to subjugated and marginalized populations within a state by weaponizing welfare (Puar, 2017; Tazreiter et al, 2023). The synergies between the treatment of refugees and other minorities within the state emerge not only in Australia but globally as citizens are rendered as outsiders while living, working and contributing to society.

Settler-colonial states such as Australia tended to favour permanent migration in the decades after the Second World War, seeking to attract migrants who wished to settle permanently. The state encouraged political membership through access to citizenship. One new development in Australia's migration system is the increasing prevalence over the last two decades of temporary rather than permanent visas (Tazreiter, 2019a, 2019b). Critical migration scholars show how temporary status not only harms individuals and families, but also the social fabric of as society as increasing populations have little to no access to citizenship rights and become exploitable (Hyndman, 2012; Carens, 2013; Juss, 2017; De Genova et al, 2018; Mountz, 2020; Ghosh, 2021; Huynh, 2023). Circumstances of 'permanent temporariness' are now a default approach globally, turning refugees, migrant workers and other categories of foreigners into exploitable and often invisible persons.

An overview of refugee detention by the Australian state

The year 2001 was momentous for the geopolitics of borders and migration. The events of 9/11, with the attacks on the Twin Towers in New York and on the Pentagon in Washington, marked the beginning of the 'War on Terror' and the related global rise in Islamophobia and an intensification of racialization experienced by migrants and refugees. In the Asia-Pacific region, the Australian state carved out a punitive and exclusionary set of policies targeting the arrival of asylum seekers making their journeys by boat. These policies gained widespread public support in the context of political justifications that drew on the 9/11 terror attacks in the United States, with political leaders making explicit links between asylum seekers arriving in Australia and a terrorist threat (Marr and Wilkinson, 2003). While Australia is a specific case and the geography of its relative isolation as an island state are noteworthy, the Australian governance of refugee arrivals after August 2001 is important at regional and global levels for refugee protection. The refugee protection system relies on all signatory states sharing responsibility for maintaining the key norms in international law, including the 1951 Refugee Convention and the 1948 Declaration on Human Rights (McAdam, 2017; Tazreiter, 2017a).

A notable incident in the contemporary perpetuation of crisis narratives in Australia about asylum seekers arriving by boat is the *Tampa* incident of August 2001. This incident became the precursor and justification for the architecture of the carceral archipelago of remote refugee detention sites. The MV *Tampa*, a Norwegian cargo freighter, rescued 433 Afghani asylum seekers from their small sinking boat on 24 August 2001 in international waters close to the coast of Christmas Island, which was at the time part of Australian territory. The Australian government refused the repeated requests of the *Tampa*'s captain to land the asylum-seekers on Australian territory, breaking with international law and protocols on saving lives at sea. Over several tense days international negotiations failed to reach a resolution. Eventually, after several weeks, the Australian navy transferred the asylum seekers from the MV *Tampa* to naval vessels on the high seas. The first iteration of 'off-shore' processing and detention of asylum seekers began with the asylum seekers rescued by the MV *Tampa* moved to the island state of Nauru. From this first incident, the appearance of a war footing in responding to asylum seekers arriving by boat became evident, with heavily armed Special Service soldiers involved in the transfer of asylum seekers. Following the *Tampa* incident, the Australian government passed a number of laws that created the legal framework for what came to be known as the 'Pacific Solution', and the beginning of off-shore detention of asylum seekers in the remote locations of Nauru and Manus Island in Papua New Guinea.

The origins of the more than two decades of Australia's externalization policies, with the territorial border suspended in relation to refugee arrivals, can be traced to the events of 2001 (Gleeson, 2016; Grewcock, 2017; Juss, 2017; Tazreiter et al, 2023). It is beyond the scope of this chapter to review all the legal and policy developments during this period. Instead, I focus on key developments that have built and then entrenched the carceral archipelago as totalizing policies. Moving to mid-2013, one of the first acts of the newly elected conservative government of Prime Minister, Tony Abbott, is a suite of policies announced under the banner of *Operation Sovereign Borders*. The arrival of asylum seekers by boat is defined in these policies as a key threat to Australia (Tazreiter, 2015b, 2017b; Huynh, 2023).

For more than two decades, Australia's carceral archipelago has produced numerous sites of horror, subjugation and death. Australia's relationships with PNG and Nauru demonstrates a neo-colonial dynamic as aid and development are part of the equation, while developing nations remain dependent on richer nations to recover from the continuing legacies of colonialism. A key feature of Australia's border-industrial-complex of incarceration and violence are the multinational companies contracted to build, maintain and manage carceral sites. These companies include, Transfield/Broadspectrum, G4S, Serco, IHMS, Paladin and PIH. These transnational companies have secured lucrative contracts without little oversight or accountability for the care given to traumatized refugees. In Paladin's case, the contract was not made available for public tender. The privatization of immigration detention centres also mirrors similar developments in other Western countries (Mountz, 2020) and is being challenged by new abolitionist demands and movements (Wilson Gilmore, 2022).

People designated as refugees have long been part of Australia's immigration intake. As an immigration country (like Canada and the United States), Australia determines on a yearly basis the number and composition of its immigration intake. This means that various categories of migrant, such as business, student, worker, family reunion and humanitarian are assessed on specific criteria and granted a visa for a specified time and with specified and highly differentiated access to social, political, cultural and economic rights, including access to education, to healthcare and welfare services. In relation to the humanitarian intake, Australia has an 'off-shore' and 'on-shore' approach to refugee arrivals. The 'off-shore', or resettlement programme is the preferred mode in Australia. The 'on-shore' system designates persons arriving spontaneously, often without a visa and documentation and claiming asylum (asylum seekers). The resettlement programme determines a number of refugees to be settled in Australia as part of a yearly quota of immigrants.

Refugees who have been assessed as suitable to settle in Australia by Australian immigration officials are considered for such yearly quotas. In the 2022/2023 financial year Australia's annual humanitarian programme was set at a maximum of 17,875 places, which included an additional 4,125 places for Afghans.[2] For many years prior to 2022/2023, the annual programme was capped at 12,000 to 13,000 places. Importantly, the obligations signatory states have under the 1951 Refugee Convention remain for asylum seekers arriving spontaneously. This obligation remains for those countries that take resettlement refugees. From a global perspective, the United Nations High Commissioner for Refugees estimates that at the end of 2023 117.3 million people were forcibly displaced.[3] This figure includes people designated as refugees and under the United Nations High Commissioner for Refugees' mandate, Palestinian refugees under the United Nations Relief and Works Agency's mandate, asylum seekers, other people in need of international protection and internally displaced persons. Approximately 100,000 places annually are available globally under the resettlement programmes of countries such as Australia. These statistics indicate that the need for solutions for forcibly displaced persons far exceed the planned places through resettlement.

In contrast to the planned humanitarian intake in Australia, the precise numbers of people making, or seeking to make, boat journeys to Australia to claim protection is difficult to establish. Since the implementation of the new approach to border control, successive governments do not divulge any detail to the public of the number of boats intercepted on the way to Australia from Indonesia, the number of boat push-backs, or the number of individuals who may have arrived on Australian territory. The justification is national security. The number of refugees currently held on Nauru as of May 2024, published by the Australian Department of Home Affairs, is 63, labelled as transitory persons as their refugee status has not been determined. From 2015 to 2024, the number of persons detained on Nauru is 1,360.[4] On Manus Island, 4,292 boys and men were sent for off-shore processing from the beginning of the policy in late 2001 to 13 August 2013. Forty-seven refugees remain held in PNG and 96 on Nauru.[5] Compared to the numbers of refugees and asylum seekers arriving spontaneously by boat and other means to Europe, the arrivals to Australia are comparatively small. For example, during the so-called 'refugee crisis' of 2014–2015 in Europe, Germany alone received some one million refugees/migrants.

While it is important to consider similarities and differences between Australia and other Western states in how migration policy is developed and the detail of refugee policy, I argue that it is the collective diminishing of the principles of international law and the spirit of the Refugee Convention that all Western states share blame for in the effects of the externalizing of borders. What is unique about the Australian case, even in relation to other settler-colonial states, is the designed ferocity and mendacity of policies and practices targeting subjugated populations, alongside the application of exceptionality as a political weapon to discipline and silence dissent. In many ways geography has much to do with these circumstances with Australia's relative remoteness as a large island nation. Yet the power of neo-colonial attitudes, practices and policies is overwhelmingly at the root of the particularities of Australia's treatment of refugees.

Contributions of refugee thinkers to anticolonial thought

I now develop the empirical cases in creative works of refugees with collaborators. The empirical material drawn on includes two primary sources. First, I draw on observations and field notes from my visit to Manus Island in 2019. During this visit, I held in-depth conversations with refugees and observed the conditions of everyday life for refugees as well as the life of the local people, the *Manusians*. Second, I draw on works created by refugees held on Manus Island. The individual and collaborative works of Behrouz Boochani are a particular focus in this chapter. Behrouz Boochani describes himself as an Indigenous person from Kurdistan. His deep connections to the land, stories, songs and collective memory of his homeland are evident throughout his creative and political interventions. Boochani is also a journalist, film-maker and writer held in the Manus Island detention facility ('Manus Prison' as Boochani calls it), for over six years. During the years Boochani was incarcerated in Manus Prison, he regularly published in international media, gave speeches, taught virtually in classrooms at universities all over the world, posted and engaged in social media, participated in interviews, shot and co-directed a feature film, and wrote a book. These forms of intellectual and cultural production were prepared and created using a mobile phone and virtual technologies, with all texts typed, saved and sent via WhatsApp. Together with his translator, Omid Tofighian, they worked on the book *No Friend but the Mountains: Writing from Manus Prison* (Boochani, 2018; Tofighian, 2018), written and translated simultaneously through the digital screen. The philosophical vision and intellectual framework captured in this collaboration continues to take shape and also benefits from various working relationships and networks that are scholarly and artistic and include collaborations with ATSI peoples (Boochani and Tazreiter, 2019; Boochani et al, 2021; Boochani, 2023).

A visit to Manus Island and Manus Prison

In mid-2019 I travelled to Manus Island (see Figure 10.1). I had long contemplated this journey to visit and talk with the men and boys detained

Figure 10.1: Map of Manus Island

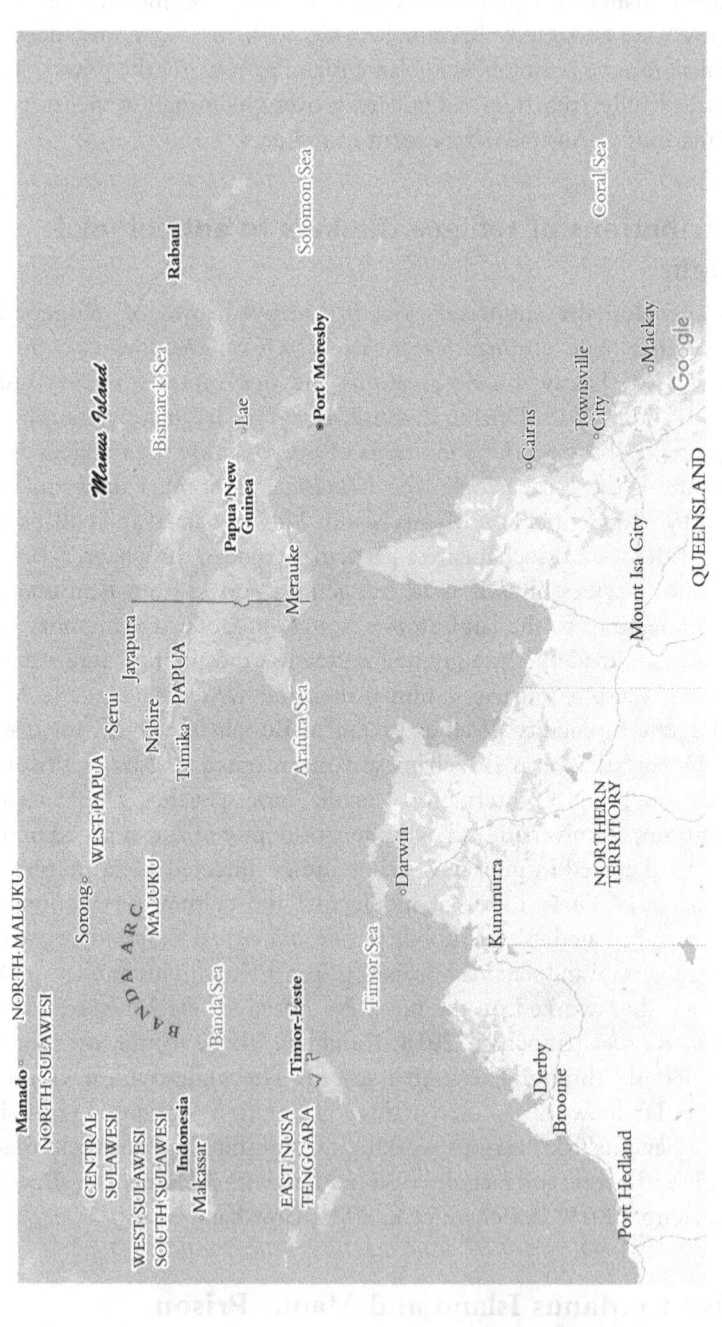

Source: Map data ©2025 Google

there and to bear witness to the lived experience of what politicians and a large part of mainstream media in Australia reported and normalized with the label 'off-shore processing' of refugees. As a sociologist, my research and teaching focuses on the interlinked fields of citizenship, migration, refugeehood and belonging. Engaging in these fields of research brings the everyday realities and stories of marginalized and subjugated peoples to attention. Through this research and teaching practice my biography and positionality have a bearing on my research standpoint, theoretical and methodological orientations. As a first-generation migrant woman, I am part of the settler-colonial landscape in Australia, though having arrived as a child, I am not embedded in colonial practices and attitudes as many of my peers who are multi-generational settler-colonials may be. My speech may be vernacularized to a setter-colonial idiom, but my imagination is not.

The visit to Manus Island was precipitated by discussions with the journalist, writer and refugee, Behrouz Boochani, detained on Manus Island since 2013 and his long-time collaborator and translator, Omid Tofighian. I experienced Manus Island as sensory overload. Manus Island is geographically remote, with great natural beauty, a small population and unrelenting tropical heat. Flying to this remote island, the many stories of harm and abuse of refugees circulated my imagination. There are threads that draw lines between Australia and PNG, between Australians and the refugees imprisoned there, between Australians and the people of Manus. Behrouz Boochani and Shaminda Kanipathi, both imprisoned on Manus Island as refugees, were my companions and guides during my visit, showing me the site of the detention camp, Manus Prison, that had been ruled an illegal site of refugee detention by the PNG Court of Justice, the highest court in PNG, in 2016. Eventually the camp/prison was shut down and refugees were housed in temporary containers on Manus Island from 2017, with a nightly curfew. The Manus Island refugee detention centre was demolished by the Australian government with no material trace left today of what had occurred there. All traces of the cruelty and deaths were erased and the site returned to the jungle. A coalition of researchers, refugees detained on Manus Island and artists collaborated in a digital recreation of the Manus Island detention centre to facilitate ongoing witness to life in the facility through a virtual and interactive recreation. This work mitigates against erasure not only of the physical site but of the memories of what occurred there, and the lives of those who perished there.[6]

One small initiative I was able to begin after my visit to Manus Island was to find a space within university structures and institutional rules to have refugees remotely access education from Manus Island at the Australian university I was working at. The barriers were high and exemplify the university itself as a colonial structure that requires active decolonization.

Over the more than two decades of Australia's policies and practices of the carceral archipelago, many interventions, critiques and alternatives have been formulated, published and shared through various digital and creative means. Of great importance are the voices of those with lived experience of the carceral archipelago and the subjugation administered there, a selection of which are detailed next.

Manus Prison Theory

In drawing on the works that create epistemic knowledge that contributes to anticolonial and decolonial thought, I pay particular attention to the concept of *Manus Prison Theory* (MPT) developed by Boochani and Tofighian in the book *No Friend but the Mountains* (Boochani, 2018),[7] as well as in later writing (Tofighian, 2020). MPT articulates a form of governmentality based on cruelty, domination and submission that is directed onto groups and individuals deemed as marginal, outsiders, disrupters. MPT emerges from Boochani's lived experience of Australia's carceral-border. Rather than being primarily a politics of resistance, MPT offers a contribution to theorizing totalizing systems of domination. In this case, the legacy of settler-colonialism that carried out Indigenous genocide, anti-Blackness and exploitation of bodies as well as excessive resource extraction and destruction of the ecosystem.

MPT, with its critique of the manifold practices of subjugation, is articulated as part of a much wider, indeed global, border-industrial complex (Boochani, 2018: 362). What is detailed throughout the book is the lived experience of Manus Prison, while the conceptualization of MPT seeks to take that experience beyond the confines of the prison to the social imaginary of global publics, especially addressing settler-colonial Australians. What is emphasized is the agency of refugees to describe, understand and critique what is done to them as well as the creativity of imagining an alternate future. What makes MPT an original and unique contribution to anticolonial thought is the way Boochani and Tofighian conceptualize the social and cultural impact of the stories, narratives and realities told and represented by the subjugated – the refugee. They argue that it is the constrained social imaginary of those with citizen privilege, settler-colonial Australians, that can limit and distort meaningful and validating dialogue with the prisoners (refugees) affected by border politics (Boochani, 2018: 363). They posit that injustices are cultivated and maintained through both governmental as well as non-governmental institutions as a result of this embedded (colonial) circumstance.

One important, yet nuanced, elaboration of Boochani and Tofighian is of the duality of pro- and anti-refugee dispositions. They argue that in building awareness and sensitivity to individual and structural forms of discrimination that result in the subjugation of refugees, both an acknowledgement of, and work towards rectification of, a 'pro- and anti-refugee' disposition is required.

> This is a paradoxical posture involving a wide spectrum of roles and practices – a position that forms and evolves when inequitable collaboration, intersectional discrimination and intellectual undermining are not factored into the ethics of organization and action related to refugee support. The same system that spawned Manus Prison created variable manifestations of this paradoxical positioning; therefore, in most instances it becomes possible and acceptable to be both pro-and anti-refugee. (Boochani, 2018: 364)

A central part of MPT is the concept of the kyriarchal system. In explaining how the translation of Boochani's text messages from Manus Island manifest over several years into the book, *No Friend but the Mountains*, Tofighian shows how the idea of a kyriarchal system emerged as relevant to the lived experience in Manus Prison. The concept of kyriarchy was first elaborated by the radical feminist theological Elisabeth Schüssler Fiorenza. She develops the concept to move beyond patriarchy to understand the ways that gender oppression is interlocked with other social systems of domination. In the collaboration between Boochani and Tofighian over a number of years, the intergenerational trauma experienced by generations of the families of both men inform their creative production. Boochani locates himself in Kurdish resistance, with a deep appreciation of Kurdish and Persian literature and a connection to the land, to storytelling and folk ballad traditions of Kurdistan. Tofighian has a family history of persecution and exile from Iranian society, with his family leaving Iran at the time of the Iranian Revolution (Tofighian, 2020: 1140). In translating Boochani's writing on the totalizing system of domination and power in Manus Prison, Tofighian says, 'like Schüssler Fiorenza's notion of kyriarchy, Boochani's kyriarchal system represents a series of intersecting and mutually reinforcing structures bent on domination, repression and submission; and it is also driven by an insatiable desire to reproduce, reinforce and expand its unrelenting oppression' (Tofighian, 2020: 1142).

Other creative works that contribute to anticolonial thought

In 2017, Boochani and his collaborator and co-director Arash Kamali Sarvestani released the film *Chauka, Please Tell us the Time*, documenting life in detention over time, pieced together with hundreds of mobile phone clips and written texts. Along with other forms of visual and material culture and communication, the film has given the Australian public access to counter-narratives to the dominant government narratives of fear, mistrust and hatred of refugees and asylum seekers. In the film, the stories of the men and boys living in Manus Prison are presented in narrative form. The film is a meditation on everyday life in the detention centre on Manus Island. The film gives the viewer a glimpse into the physical and psychological stresses and traumas of the detainees. It is particularly powerful in the context of Australian policies that have made asylum seekers and refugees invisible to the Australian public – they have essentially 'disappeared' through media and information blackouts. With the release of the film, *Chauka*, Boochani received numerous invitations to appear at international film festivals. The Australian government denied him a visa to enter Australia for the premiere of the film. Nevertheless, with the help Omid Tofighian, Boochani appeared virtually for interviews at numerous public events and at the screening of his film on social media. In this way, the Australian public and an international audience have come to know the work, the face and the voice of Boochani and his fellow refugee detainees.

Another notable work created in collaboration is the video work *Remain* created by photographer Hoda Afshar with refugees detained on Manus Island. The work, filmed on Manus Island in 2018, engages with the situation refugees face in being sent to a remote island by the Australian state where they sought protection. It is a layered work that addresses absence and invisibilities. The work depicts the ongoing mistreatment of refugees, including the remembrance invoked of the murdered refugee, Reza Barati, beaten to death by detention centre guards. Yet despite these horrors, the work depicts the beauty of the island setting, of the sand, the ocean and the resilient bodies of the refugees. A haunting presence of their interwoven stories echoes throughout. One man recites poetry, another man sings in the seemingly idyllic tropical setting of the lush tropical rainforest.

In the foreword to a recent publication that gathers Behrouz Boochani's journalism while detained on Manus Island (Boochani, 2023; Tazreiter, 2023), the ATSI author, Tara June Winch, states:

> Refugees and First Nations Australians share an affinity – we've taken control of our narrative and contributed to the retelling of time and space and linguistics, of the past and present and future. Behrouz speaks the language of testifying on our continent. Reading these words in their entirety, written at the edge of the jungle and in the aftermath, and from that uncomfortable position of being free, is not easy. ... Here in these pages is everything we must face if we are to save ourselves from the horror of repetition. (Winch in Boochani, 2023: xiii)

A number of collaborations with subjugated people beyond Manus Island have spawned since the majority of refugees were eventually resettled.[8]

One notable collaboration occurred between Marrugeku, an Australian Indigenous-intercultural dance theatre company, and refugees. The company is based in northwestern Australia on the lands of the Yawuru people who are custodians of the lands and waters of Rubibi. In building the new work, called *Jurrungu Ngan-ga*, two texts were key sources for developing the dance theatre work; the documentary *Australia's Shame* (Meldrum-Hanna and Worthington, 2016) that exposes the abuse of young Indigenous boys in the Don Dale Youth Detention Centre in the Northern Territory and the book *No Friend but the Mountains: Writing from Manus Prison* (Boochani, 2018). Omid Tofighian, involved in the creation of the work as a cultural dramaturg, says:

> Jurrungu Ngan-ga responds to places and peoples that have been targeted by Australia's long-standing neo-colonial appetite for incarceration – particularly addressing events over the past decade. Jurrungu Ngan-ga, meaning 'straight talk' in the language of the Yawuru People, examines the common thread that connects outrageous levels of Indigenous incarceration in Australia to the government's indefinite detention of asylum seekers. The project's creative team interrogate and stage this link as performed in the 'prison of the mind of Australia'. Together they challenge its legitimacy through the lens of what Waanyi writer Alexis Wright explains as 'the sovereignty of the mind'. That is, an Indigenous sovereignty that is outside the reach of the settler state and its mechanisms of policing. This is performed and staged in Jurrungu Ngan-ga through choreopolitical acts of resistance, survivance and straight talking. (Tofighian et al, 2022)

What I have discussed in this chapter as examples of literary, poetic, filmic, artistic and conceptual interventions, reflections and proposals for alternative futures of the settler-colonial violence and subjugation of refugees, is a small sample of the vast archive – digital, analogue and ephemeral – of the experiences, resistance and articulations from children, women and men detained indefinitely in Australia's carceral archipelago.

Conclusion

From the cases developed in this chapter of the impacts of state carceral practices of criminalizing and dehumanizing refugees, I have sought to show how the subjugation of vulnerable populations operates as an inverse logic in a settler-colonial context such as Australia. That is, past colonial practices resurface, morphed into new contexts, yet are motivated through a continuity of exceptionalist logic that justifies violence and harm through the value system of neo-colonial power. What is created through totalizing policies towards asylum seeker and refugee arrivals examined in this chapter is the dismantling of the very framework and mentalities of postcoloniality that imagines renewal and the creation of a new society. In contrast, the horrors of the colonial period are replayed anew, practised on refugees and continued on ATSI peoples. Ann Phoenix (Chapter 9, this volume) shows how everyday racism in contemporary practices of dehumanization have historical links to practices such as the transatlantic slavery. In a similar manner to what I have sought to stress, Phoenix shows the historical connections through the narratives of minoritized ethnic groups. For Phoenix it is the case of the Windrush generation in the UK that is the focus.

I have argued that the histories of racialization entrench the normalization of hierarchies of persons and worldviews, allocating differential value to humans according to scientific racism. From these histories, the relationships between individuals and groups are impacted, naturalizing created divisions over time, making them less visible. Ignorance and indifference to such harms are an important consequence of settler-colonial practices together with the practices of racial capitalism. How we decipher and respond to traumatic pasts experienced by fellow humans guards against ignorance and indifference. The creative works by refugees and other subjugated persons I have presented in this chapter are evidence of the voice and unique positionality of those whose creative energies continue to reverberate beyond the camp, the places of incarceration and separation from members of settler-colonial societies. They also contribute empirical detail and conceptual heft to anticolonial thought. The creative force of testimony, art and story-telling from those with lived experience of the carceral archipelago in the Asia Pacific, and globally, uncovers the systematized and normalized practices of harm – a kind of necropolitics of annihilation (Mbembe, 2017, 2019) of the carceral-border-complex. The activists, artists, writers and thinkers I refer to in this chapter, and many others, collectively offer a powerful critique of settler-colonialism, and in so doing contribute to building unique anticolonial knowledge.

Notes

[1] Despite the legal changes that recognized ATSI peoples in the late 20th century, a number of key violent practices of the colonial era continued. The Aboriginal Protection Act of 1869 of subsequent federal and state legislation authorized the forced removal of ATSI children from their families. The practice continued into the 1970s as form of cultural genocide with the taken children placed in orphanages, institutions and with white families and forbidden to practice their language or cultural practices. In 1997 a long-standing inquiry by the Australian Human Rights and Equal Opportunity Commission published a report titled, *Bringing Them Home*, that detailed the impacts of the practices on individual children and families. Only more recently are the effects of intergenerational trauma resulting from such practices being acknowledged. Deaths in custody of ATSI adults and children in juvenile detention facilities have been the focus of numerous inquiries, yet continue into the present. ATSI peoples make up less than 4 per cent of the Australian population but represent around 25 per cent of the prison population.

2 https://www.homeaffairs.gov.au/research-and-stats/files/australias-ohp-2022-23.pdf
3 https://www.unhcr.org/about-unhcr/who-we-are/figures-glance
4 https://www.homeaffairs.gov.au/about-us-subsite/files/population-number-resettled-31-may-2024.pdf
5 https://asrc.org.au/2024/07/19/11-years-of-costly-cruelty-offshore/
6 https://arts.unimelb.edu.au/school-of-social-and-political-sciences/our-research/research-projects/against-erasure
7 Following the publication of *No Friend but the Mountains* (2018), Boochani was appointed to a number of universities as a honorary and non-residential scholar, including to the University of Sydney, University of New South Wales, Sydney and visiting professor appointments at Birkbeck Law School, University of London. In 2019 Boochani's book won the Victorian Premier's Literary award for the best book of the year.
8 Notably around 100 men are still in PNG, most in Port Moresby, now almost ten years since their applications for protection.

References

Anderson, B. (2019) New directions in migration studies: Towards methodological de-nationalism, *Comparative Migration Studies*, 7(36). https://doi.org/10.1186/s40878-019-0140-8

Boochani, B. (2018) *No Friend but the Mountains: Writing from Manus Prison*, translated by O. Tofighian, Pan Macmillan.

Boochani, B. (2023) *Freedom, Only Freedom: The Prison Writings of Behrouz Boochani*, translated and edited by O. Tofighian and M. Mansoubi, Bloomsbury.

Boochani, B. and Tazreiter, C. (2019) Notes on exile: Behrouz Boochani in conversation with Claudia Tazreiter, *Australian Journal of Human Rights*, 25(3). https://doi.org/10.1080/1323238X.2019.1685768

Boochani, B., Tazreiter, C. and Tofighian, O. (2021) The multiple faces of the people smuggler, in R. Balint and J. Kalman (eds) *Smuggled: An Illegal History of Journeys to Australia*, New South Press, pp 176–90.

Carens, J. (2013) *The Ethics of Immigration*, Oxford University Press.

Collins, J. (2019) Migration to Australia in times of crisis, in C. Menjivar, M. Ruiz and I. Ness (eds) *The Handbook of Migration Crises*, Oxford University Press, pp 817–31.

De Genova, N., Garelli, G. and Tazzioli, M. (2018) Autonomy of asylum? The autonomy of migration: Undoing the refugee crisis script, *The South Atlantic Quarterly*, 117(2): 239–65.

Ghosh, A. (2021) The great uprooting: Migration and displacement in an age of planetary crisis, *The Massachusetts Review*, 62(4): 712–33.

Gleeson, M. (2016) *Offshore: Behind the Wire on Manus and Nauru*, Newsouth.

Grewcock, M. (2017) 'Our lives is (sic) in danger': Manus Island and the end of asylum, *Race & Class*, 1–20.

Huynh, K. (2023) *Australia's Refugee Policy in the 21st Century: Stop the Boats!* Routledge.

Hyndman, J. (2012) The geopolitics of migration and mobility, *Geopolitics*, 17(2): 243–55.

Juss, S. (2017) Detention and delusion in Australia's Kafkaesque refugee law, *Refugee Survey Quarterly*, 36: 146–67.

Lake, M. and Reynolds, H. (2008) *Colour Bar: The International Challenge of Racial Equality*, Cambridge University Press.

Marr, D. and Wilkinson, M. (2003) *Dark Victory*, Allen & Unwin.

Mbembe, A. (2017) *Critique of Black Reason*, translated by L. Dubois, Duke University Press.

Mbembe, A. (2019) *Necropolitics*, translated by S. Corcoran, Duke University Press.

McAdam, J. (2017) The enduring relevance of the 1951 Refugee Convention, *International Journal of Refugee Law*, 29(1): 1–9.

Meldrum-Hanna, C. and Worthington, E. (2016) *Australia's Shame*, Four Corners Australian Broadcast Corporation TV.

Moreton-Robinson, A. (2015) *The White Possessive: Property, Power, and Indigenous Sovereignty*, University of Minnesota Press.

Mountz, A. (2020) *The Death of Asylum: Hidden Geographies of the Enforcement Archipelago*, University of Minnesota Press.

Pickering, S., Segrave, M., Tazreiter, C. and Weber, L. (2013) Migration control and human security, in S. Juss (ed) *The Ashgate Research Companion to Migration Law, Theory and Policy*, Ashgate, pp 535–62.

Puar, J.K. (2017) *The Right to Maim: Debility, Capacity, Disability*, Duke University Press.

Tazreiter, C. (2015a) Insecure communities: Temporary migration status and its impacts in everyday life, in S. Pickering and J. Ham (eds) *Routledge Handbook on Crime and International Migration*, Routledge, pp 193–205.

Tazreiter, C. (2015b) 'Stop the boats'! Externalising the borders of Australia and imaginary pathologies of contagion, *Journal of Immigration, Nationality and Asylum Law*, 29(2): 141–57.

Tazreiter, C. (2015c) Lifeboat politics in the Pacific: Affect and the ripples and shimmers of a migrant saturated future, *Emotion, Space and Society*, 16: 99–107.

Tazreiter, C. (2017a) *Asylum Seekers and the State: The Politics of Protection in a Security-Conscious World*, Routledge.

Tazreiter, C. (2017b) The unlucky in the 'lucky country': Asylum seekers, irregular migrants and refugees and Australia's politics of disappearance, *Australian Journal of Human Rights*, 23(2): 242–60. https://doi.org/10.1080/1323238X.2017.1372039

Tazreiter, C. (2019a) Crisis politics of asylum seekers and migrant arrivals in Australia, in C. Menjivar, M. Ruiz and I. Ness (eds) *The Handbook of Migration Crises*, Oxford University Press, pp 619–34. DOI: 10.1093/oxfordhb/9780190856908.013.71

Tazreiter, C. (2019b) Temporary migrants as an uneasy presence in immigrant societies: Reflections on ambivalence in Australia, *International Journal of Comparative Sociology*, 6(1–2): 91–109.

Tazreiter, C. (2023) Emotion, responsibility and hope for different futures, in O. Tofighinan and M. Mansoubi (eds) *Freedom, Only Freedom: The Prison Writings of Behrouz Boochani*, Bloomsbury Press, pp 208–10.

Tazreiter, C. and Tofighian, O. with Boochani, B. (2023) Spectres of subjugation/inter-subjugation/resubjugation of people seeking asylum: The kyriarchal system in Australia's necropoleis, in P. Billings (ed) *Regulating Refugee Protection through Social Welfare Law, Policy and Praxis*, Routledge, pp 68–90.

Tofighian, O. (2018) No friend but the mountains: Translator's reflections, *In No Friend but the Mountains: Writing from Manus Prison*, translated by O. Tofighian, Picador, pp 359–74.

Tofighian, O. (2020) Introducing Manus Prison theory: Knowing border violence, *Globalizations*, 17(7): 1138–56. DOI: 10.1080/14747731.2020.1713547

Tofighian, O., Swain, R., Pigram, D., Bhenji Ra, Connell, C. and Brown, E.J., et al (2022) Performance as intersectional resistance: Power, polyphony and processes of abolition, *Humanities*, 11(1): 28. https://doi.org/10.3390/h11010028

Weber, L. Pickering, S. and Tazreiter, C. (2014) Border securitization and human security, in S. Takahasi (ed) *Human Rights, Human Security, and National Security* (in 3 volumes), Praeger, Volume 2, pp 21–40.

Wilson Gilmore, R. (2022) *Abolition Geography: Essays Towards Liberation*, Verso.

Yuval-Davis, N., Wemyss, G. and Cassidy, K. (2019) *Bordering*, Polity.

11

Sociology Besides Modernity? *Ontoformative Gestures* and Anti-Colonial Theories

Marcelo C. Rosa

Introduction

Current debates on anti-colonial theory, as proposed in the works of Patel (2023, 2024 and Chapter 2, this volume) and Go (2023 and Chapter 4, this volume), have succeeded in demonstrating the importance of comprehending the effects of colonialism and anti-colonial struggles to challenge the hegemonic understanding of the modern world in the social sciences.[1]

This chapter aims to present a contribution to these debates by affirming the importance of renewing and expanding, beyond modernity, the ontological basis from which the social theory draws to criticize the currently colonial hegemonic formulations. With the aim of complementing anti-colonial writing with the prospect of amplification, I propose the notion of *ontoformative gesture*. It is a theoretical-methodological alternative that requires the development of a specific analytical competence, namely the continuous ontological construction of research objects and subjects that extend beyond the scope of modern colonial effects. If contemporary collective life is not limited to modern elements, why not develop theories and methods to better host *other-than-modern* effects in anti-colonial compositions?

The arguments supporting the proposal and its foundation are divided into four sections. First, I invite a close dialogue with the notions and propositions of anti-colonial social theories from colleagues whose work has inspired this volume. The second part introduces the ontological disciplinary foundation of the colonial problem and its restrictive methodological consequences for a research-based discipline such as sociology. In the third section, it develops the notion of *ontoformative gesture* as a potential way to envision and invigorate an anti-colonial positionality. The final section draws inspiration for an alternative anti-colonial gesture from the works of a group of third-world scholars who, over the last four decades, have made crucial epistemologically relevant contributions to contemporary social sciences. In the writings of three women of Black and indigenous descent, namely Gloria Anzaldúa, Silvia Rivera Cusicanqui and Oyèrónkẹ́ Oyěwùmí, *other-than-modern* agencies and effects are mapped in women's everyday lives and elaborated as analytical tools to escape the constraints of liberal modern ontology.

An invitation to anti-colonial theory debate

In the quest to address the methodological shortfalls translating decolonial and postcolonial onto-epistemological critiques into the practice of research-based sociology, I first coined the term *ontoformative ethics* (Rosa, 2020) to describe a disposition towards an ontological opening within the discipline. Concurrently, a group of colleagues from various parts of the world engaged in a renewed discussion regarding the contemporary necessity for an anti-colonial social theory (Go, 2023; Patel, 2023). After being invited to join the debate raised in this volume, I recognized the profound resonance between colonialism as a theoretical problem and my own intellectual discomfort within the discipline. This encounter prompted me to rework the aforementioned notion presented here as an *ontoformative gesture*, evolving from an epistemologically ethical disposition to define research goals and procedures from a contra-colonial perspective.

Although Patel and Go have slightly distinct empirical sources that inform their anti-colonial theoretical proposals, they share a common ground. For them, the long-term presence of anti-colonial social thought in the colonized world – and beyond – has been reflected in the feelings and actions of political movements and their organic intellectual agendas.

Interactions between movements and intellectuals are not acknowledged in the same manner, yet they lead the authors to reconsider certain conceptual aspects of hegemonic sociology. Despite their differences, these approaches concentrate on anti-colonial practices and thoughts, broadening the theoretical capacity of sociology to address the harmful effects of modernity.

Go (2023 and Chapter 4, this volume) suggests that mapping anti-colonial thought can enable social science theories to better address the issues of self and society, social solidarity, global hierarchies, and the constitutive character of the empire. Alongside his aim to amplify sociology's intellectual grounds, his overarching focus re-enacts an effort to strengthen the hegemonic disciplinary matrices with the inspiration from anti-colonial thinkers. In his own words, his work contributes to connecting struggles and theories from former colonies in a sociological endeavour to 'redeem their humanity and worth' (Go, 2023: 13).

Patel (2023, 2024 and Chapter 2, this volume) proposes that the study of anti-colonial thought, combined with contemporary anti-colonial theory, paves the way for developing a methodology to assess the reasoning behind dominant and hegemonic ways of knowing. She also emphasizes the significance of anti-colonial theory in constructing substantive theories of modernity and addressing global exploitative and exclusionary processes. Beyond a complex understanding of the empire and global hierarchies, Patel expands sociology's goals to the necessary manufacturing of new methodologies and theories, recognizing the necessity for new forms of collective existence beyond those that are hegemonically available.

Inspired by the claims that a 'universal theory, a "one fits all" position, has become dysfunctional' (Patel, 2023: 11) and by the suggestion that 'to consider anti-colonial thought as sociology and social theory, therefore, is to accept an invitation to experiment' (Go, 2023: 6), this chapter follows a particular path. I propose to experiment with assembling anti-colonial thinking with *other-than-modern* components of contemporary existences, transcending the modern political grammar to generate non-hegemonic theories from existences not accounted for in sociological analysis.

To be anti-colonial here requires a deeper exploration of the contradictions and fault lines around which the discipline has evolved into its present form, serving as an instrument of colonial modern political hierarchization of what is deemed significant in transformative thinking. Drawing inspiration from third-world feminist theories, I have opted to experiment with theories that produce *ontoformative gestures* with specific ontological and sociological effects that are not positively accountable to the modern-liberal theoretical repertoire and methodology.

Inspired by Ferreira da Silva (2007), the following pages and sections argue that an anti-colonial social theory must, therefore, tackle the ontological basis of the sociological consensus, which is characterized as a colonial mode of knowledge production due to its stabilized definition of what is considered socially meaningful or not.

Ontology in the theory

As mentioned earlier, in sociology, as it is practised today, theory typically relies on a working ideal type, which serves as an ontological carrier in both teaching and research. To achieve global relevance, research subjects (and researchers) are often first described in relation to a specific hegemonic theory that renders them recognizable and understandable, even in the periphery. Within these contexts, the hegemonic professional challenge has consistently been to translate (and limit) any research element to fit within the canonical frames.

In line with this analysis, among those of us who exist outside hegemonic contexts[2] and could potentially participate in denser theoretical and epistemological debates, the sensation of being '*out of place*' (Tavolaro, 2021) or of encountering theoretical '*discomfort*' (Rosa, 2019, 2020) is prevalent. Extending Fanonian terminology to colonized scholars, at the institutional level, including national and international associations, the discomfort of a few wretched or *damnés* academics is palpable (Fanon, 1961). By reducing their research findings to fit hegemonic theories, these academics, despite feeling discomfort, perpetuate the superiority of a colonial disciplinary form of existence (the modern ontology), which remains geopolitically attractive and coherent for their counterparts who validate the worthiness of peripheral academia.

The common ground for the hegemonic ontology of global social theory is the limitation of social components to particular stabilized general effects of modernity (Karakayali, 2015). Nesting on this onto-epistemological quarrel, we restrict research to a possible and finite set of conditions of existence. This sociological universe of possibilities is defined prior to entering the research, which, in the best-case scenario, merely pays lip-service to regional or temporal details and variations. In doing so, the globally circulating hegemonic theory remains stable, subject to only a handful of empirical variations at the historical (and primarily regional) level in a process described by Costa (2010) as 'theory making by addition' (for example, multiple or connected modernities[3]). In the context of this chapter, I regard this process as central to the geopolitical definition of what is 'general' and 'specific' in our theories (Adésínà, 2006).

By incorporating indigenous and Black contributions to modernity, sociology grants subaltern subjects (and their academic counterparts) the credentials to engage in their limited yet 'general' sociological realm. Non-exemplary existences are invited to share contemporary modes of life in the name of diversity. In doing so, sociologists clearly recognize that *other-than-modern* elements do exist in the collective existences. However, without recognized sociological credentials (concepts and methods) to demonstrate their effects, the *other-than-modern* aspects of their existence remain allegorical and consequently outside the scope of theoretical formulations (not ontological).

I refer to this finite set of inclusion procedures as *onto-reproductive*, as they are incorporated into the theories to reinforce the hierarchical superiority of the 'general' modern ontology, as described by Ferreira da Silva (2007).

Ontoformativity and the problem of dependent ontologies

After outlining these hegemonic tendencies and their geo-onto-political effects, the argument now delineates the hypothesis that a theoretical-epistemic expansion within the discipline can indeed occur. However, it would require an ontological development through a necessary engagement with empirical investigations of non-hegemonic forms of existence.[4]

If the hegemonic is deliberately restrictive, the possible alternatives presented cannot claim a singular anti-hegemonic or anti-colonial theory as a remedy. To diversify theory, we shall work to assemble and incorporate new ontologies into the discipline. In other words, a sociology whose main task is to conduct innovative research in non-hegemonized contexts (with particular advantages for the Global South, as suggested by Moosavi, 2023) should engage in the production of an innovative theoretical-methodological expansion. The inclination towards theoretical transformation becomes a methodological stance in which theory is regarded as an assemblage that remains modestly open to the possibility of being debunked and transformed due to empirical inputs of previously unaccounted elements.

A significant step influencing the recent global debate on geo-ontological boundaries (Rosa, 2016, 2020) of social theory analysed here can be attributed to the publication of Raewyn Connell's *Southern Theory* in 2007 (Connell, 2007). Following the international flourish surrounding the book, Connell aimed to extend the concept of 'Southern' – originally used to refer to social theories developed outside of Europe and the United States – to empirical research contexts, particularly those associated with non-hegemonic notions of gender and body (Connell, 2011, 2012a, 2012b). In these two areas of research, the terms *ontoformative* and *ontoformativity* (both employed by Connell) have been embraced as analytical tools by recent investigations seeking a sociological expression for bodies and genders misplaced in dominant literature (Rudy, 2020; Soldatic, 2020; Nyamnjoh and Morrell, 2021). The question driving Connell and these authors is the new kind of collective existences that social processes continue to create. The most frequently used term, 'ontoformative', appears in *Gender and Power* (Connell, 1987: 211) and is inspired in Karel Kosik's book *Dialectics of the Concrete: A Study on Problems of Man and World*. It denotes that social life, as a process, typically rebuffs and obscures the conditions of its own formation. Revisiting the Marxist-inspired argument also found in Lukács (1979), the ontology of social being is constructed and continuously transformed through the praxis of not only labour and class but also the bodies and genders that evolve within modern colonial processes.

Connell's use of the term and its appropriation points to a virtuous route for social research. It is an empirical path focused on how social interactions in multiple and centralized contexts and circumstances (that is, the Global South) continually take on new forms in the modern world. Her combination of the two terms, 'ontology' and 'formation', illustrates how describing existing matrices and enacting them in specific contexts produces a particular effect on them. Connell's primary contribution was to advocate for the inclusion of colonialism at the core of a global modern social theory.

In colonial contexts, and likely in the metropoles as well, colonialism was a process that generated unexpected, non-uniform effects. According to her, colonialism represents an *ontoformative* context that the global social sciences have yet to address adequately.

According to Kosik (1976: 51), another issue that contemporary debates on social theory must address is that 'methodology is ontologised'. When a theory becomes globally reproduced, it presumes and limits its relevance to specific social ontologies. Under these circumstances, the researchable collective life becomes dependent on and limited to certain key concepts and the conditioning methods necessary to empirically test their effects. In the context of this chapter, those concepts and methods are linked to modernity. Consequently, collective lives within any global disciplinary context remain reliant on the presence of these ontological matrices and effects to be acknowledged at the level of the discipline. One particular outcome of the hegemonic academic training in classrooms is to compel students to pigeonhole any academic topic of interest within constrained and compartmentalized theories and methodologies previously tested to maintain the modern-liberal matrix.

Colonialism is no different. Acknowledging the history of colonization and its modern ontological matrix does not imply that every social action can or should be interpreted through it. When describing collective lives as fundamentally colonized, we tend to emphasize and give prominent *agency* to the colonizer, rendering the subaltern with the sole ontological possibility of a modern reaction to colonization. Even when understood as the result of reciprocal influences, as modernity is currently conceived in the discipline, the colonized must be portrayed as victims, merely reacting to or contributing to the colonizers' dominant narrative. Referring back to the most common outcomes of Connell's notion of *ontoformativity*, non-hegemonic bodies and genders gain sociological relevance only when influenced by colonial/modern processes. Consequently, the discipline has epistemologically worked to obscure any effects other than modern effects on its research subjects, thus preserving its power through an ontologized methodology.

These onto-epistemological processes are explained by Ferreira da Silva (2007), who, in a critical dialogue with certain postmodern and subaltern studies (specifically Chakrabarty, 2000), asserts that the historicized modern rational subject (a sociological and anthropological consequence of Kantian and Hegelian ideas) invariably presupposes the existence of a modern Other. In this conceptualization, the Other (specifically the racialized one) is termed the 'affected'. The one whose historicity and consciousness are externally *determined* in comparison to the exemplary *homo modernus, a self-determined* subject of *transparency*, for whom universal reason serves as an internal guide (in her words, the *transparent I*). The ontology of the colonized, the subaltern, the Blacks, the *damnés*, or the third-world women (Mohanty, 1988) is thus subjected to the consequences of the colonizers' reasoning. The potential for relevant and distinct existences (that is, Connell's *ontoformativity*) is realized by extending modern interiority (for example, reasoning, consciousness) to those historically or culturally excluded from this possibility. Once assimilated (becoming conscious in modern Western terms), they can utilize the colonizer's oppressive tools (Lorde, 2018) to advocate for a better collective existence on the colonizers' own intellectual terrain – the modern human subject according to Ferreira da Silva (2007). After being labelled as enslaved, violated and massacred, they can now harness their bodies, races, genders and other coded exclusions (Tadiar, 2022) to contest and complicate the hegemonic colonial effects.

The *ontoformative gesture*

Ontoforming (assembling an analytical mode of existence) modern existences that are reactive or extended is a palatable, liberal contemporary path to diplomatic influence the hegemonic social sciences globally. However, I would like to pose the following questions: do the people we, as sociologists, describe as the subaltern subjects exist solely under the colonial ontological categorization we have helped build and later demonstrate their ability to react against it? Can the social sciences surpass coding systems that regulate modern normative social identities as transferable disciplinary social and cultural logics (Tadiar, 2022: 47)?

After a long-standing dialogue with the works of Verran (2001, 2014), Law (2004), De la Cadena (2015), and others, I am confident in saying yes. However, through engaging with these authors, I have also learned that going beyond their contributions requires assembling a new form of academic gesture in research processes. To transcend the limitations of the ontological dependency of modern sociology, I offer to the discussion on the promise of anti-colonial scholarship the notion of *ontoformative gesture*. This idea advocates for an open intellectual attitude, positing that all sociologies can and should have a disposition towards empirically produced theoretical scholarship.

In an attempt to avoid the metatheoretical pitfalls of global theories, the proposed *ontoformative* ideas draw significant inspiration from social theories associated with the third-world feminist and gender debates for quite a long time (Mohanty, 1988; Mbilinyi, 2015; Curiel and Pión, 2022 and many others). With the support of these authors, I have come to understand that the everyday lives of contemporary third-world women cannot be represented solely by comparison with or inclusion in the self-determined modes of existence of modern Western women.

To demonstrate that innovative and *ontoformative gestures*, though far from hegemonic, already exist, this section reviews and highlights the contributions of three third-world feminist scholars. Drawing from the works of Chicana

Gloria Anzaldúa, Bolivian Silvia Rivera Cusicanqui and Nigerian Oyèrónkẹ́ Oyěwùmí, the chapter aims to demonstrate their diligent efforts to assemble ontologically distinctive contemporary existences for women, beyond the confines of modern colonialism and the singular political form of liberal rights. In their writings, the exclusive modern ontological representation is rendered impossible because female third-world life is incessantly permeated by *other-than-modern* effects as much as modern ones.

The term 'other-than-modern' is understood here as a broad category describing analytical elements with empirical agencies and effects which are not incorporated into the existing theoretical tools of the dominant social sciences.[5] These elements are currently not yet coded by the prevailing colonial disciplinary matrix, as suggested by Tadiar (2022). One of their primary characteristics is the impossibility of being defined and situated within modern time and space boundaries.

In the context of this chapter, the *other-than-modern* is not necessarily defined in the past; it encompasses pre-colonial times, culture, forests and rural areas (or nature). It is not idyllic. It is part of and affects contemporary collective life, transitioning from past to present, from one space to another, and vice versa, without dwelling in modern predicaments.

As Madhok suggests, when discussing the ontological consequences of feminist intellectual politics, 'there are not enough concepts in place to capture, but also produce theorized accounts of different, historically specific, and located forms of worldmaking in "most of the world"' (Madhok, 2020: 395). The author raises this statement not by chance, but inspired by the ontological challenges posed by the theories and concepts found in the works of Gloria Anzaldúa and Silvia Rivera Cusicanqui, among others.

After the publication of the collective work *This Bridge Called My Back* (Moraga and Anzaldúa, 1981), Gloria Anzaldúa became renowned for ontologically assembling the New Mestiza, women born in the United States but from Mexican descent families in a psychic space called Borderlands. In writing an account of her own collective life, Anzaldúa draws from Mexican indigenous philosophies, esoteric traditions, colonial Catholic religious practices, capitalist agrarian relations, and immigration policies to formulate a set of original concepts that highlight the limitations of Western colonial gendered ontology.

The New Mestiza is a gendered contemporary existence that is distanced from the assimilationist, nation-centred sociological narratives of the 20th century. She is not a second-class female citizen (not yet developed), as the hegemonic Western feminist theories of the 1970s and 1980s asserted (Mohanty, 1988). This notion involves a particular body composed of contemporary indigenous, rural and Black socialites, memories and ideologies that lie at the heart of capitalism, but also encompasses a troubled mind. The mestiza is better described by the indigenous *Nahuatl* notion of the *Nepantla* state, which intentionally transcends the normativity of the nation-state, social sciences and modern self. By exceeding what is politically and epistemologically available, Anzaldúa produces an innovative and unique analytical ontology.

The borderland is not confined to modern spatial and historical positioning. Territorialization occurs in the ambivalent state of mind of someone who does not belong to any fixed culture or social matrix. In Anzaldúa's words, it represents a painful *inner war* leading to despair and a movement towards everyday tolerance amidst ambiguities and contradictions (Anzaldúa, 1987: 78–9)[6] – a tolerance towards a persistent struggle against modern tendencies to singularity and unambiguity.

What brings Anzaldúa's work close to the *ontoformative gesture* proposed here is the fact that, according to her, this turbulent tolerance is borrowed from several indigenous deities and beliefs that actively influence both the objective and subjective existences of queer Chicanas in the United States. Simultaneously, the author does not commit herself to any definite idyllic indigenous existence. Certain aspects of these traditions are also identified as problematic in the lives of non-exemplary gendered bodies and minds. Epistemologically dwelling in the borderlands, the New Mestiza ontology fluctuates from one place to another without the necessity of being settled or discarding the non-modern effects in her actions and thoughts. Rather than a one-way transitional state of crisis from a supposedly limiting indigenous existence to a modern, diverse existence as a subject of multiple rights, which still prevails in hegemonic sociology, Anzaldúa wagers on the construction of ontological instability.

Another in*formative* inspiration is Cusicanqui's (2012) critique of the decolonial and postcolonial projects in Latin America. Analysing the recent incorporation of a multiculturalist discourse in different Latin-American Andean countries, particularly in Bolivia, the author describes it as a strategy to deprive indigenous peoples of their potentially hegemonic status and their ability to affect the state. This strategy echoes the concerns expressed by Ferreira da Silva (2007) and Tadiar (2022) that the cultural coding of indigenous and Black groups reproduces a 'conditional inclusion', a mitigated and 'second-class citizenship that molds subaltern imaginaries and identities' (Cusicanqui, 2003: 100).

In my reading, the author elaborates on a complex category, Ch'ixi, derived from the feminine practices in Bolivia, which accounts for the role of ancestral indigenous existences in constructing the contemporary nation. As she points out, the *Ch'ixi* empirically manifests itself in the modernity of 'the market, the state, the union' (Cusicanqui, 2003: 107), as these serve as the colonial grounds of power. Besides her diplomacy with secular modern categories, her treatment of certain indigenous feminine practices prompts us to consider that a significant research agenda involves examining their effect in the nation-state and understanding how they influence a vast area of feminine existence in that region. *Ch'ixi* is not modern, yet it is pivotal in better confronting the limitations of hegemonic modernity. It arises from ancestral feminine practices but, as seen in Anzaldúa, is not an essentialized indigeneity. It represents an *ontoformative gesture* that has become a consolidated epistemological tool. The central aspect of this analytical ontology is the state of constant indetermination and contradiction.

The writings of Anzaldúa and Cusicanqui can be considered fundamental assemblages where modern and *other-than-modern* elements meet (but not necessarily blend), creating both collective existences and accurate analytical ontologies for the social sciences.

A third ontological possibility arises from the coevalness of unrelated ontologies as described by Oyèrónkẹ́ Oyěwùmí. Oyěwùmí's work is best known for its sustained defence that gender is not a universal ontological condition, but rather a modern colonial imposition established by the Christian-liberal agenda of coding humanity through biological determinism. According to the author, the political and intellectual effect is a *gender-saturated colonial epistemology*, where gender is always regarded as an active power effect, even when it is empirically not (Oyěwùmí, 2016: 2).

In Oyěwùmí (1997), she seeks to demonstrate that gender is not ontological within Yoruba culture and language and, consequently, is not a stable source of power in social relations. Drawing from a particular interpretation of Oyo-Yoruba cosmologies, she introduces innovative concepts such as *anafemale and anamale* to describe male and female bodies without reference to pre-set Western gender power relations.

Her insistence on non-gendered hierarchies in the ancient Oyo-Yoruba collective life sparked a significant feminist reaction from some scholars (Bakare-Yusuf, 2003) who defended the political centrality of gendered categories and patriarchal power structures in interpreting both pre-colonial and colonial societies. Rather than viewing *The Invention of Women* or *What Gender Is Motherhood?* merely as indigenous and non-universalizing ontologies, I interpret Oyěwùmí's proposal as an onto-epistemological construct wherein people dwell in different ontologies through collective interactions. The life of an Oyo-Yoruba mother in contemporary Nigerian society can be gender-saturated in certain Western and colonial-bounded times and spaces demarcated by the modern capitalist nation-state. Nonetheless, her existence cannot simply be empirically and theoretically confined to this, as the Oyo-Yoruba notion of *Ìyá* conveys a procreative role that cannot be easily coded (or translated) as the colonial mother.

According to certain social scientists (Domingues, 2009), the *other-than-modern* ontologies are only feasible in research due to the pluralizing effects of modernity. The very possibility to consider the writings and lives of Yorubas, Chicanas, Latinas, lesbians and indigenous women implies that they are situated and acknowledged within the democratic coding of rights to be human in the modern colonial and imperial order. The specificity I would like to emphasize here is that the provocative epistemological challenge posed by the aforementioned works exceeds and at times contradicts modern coding, yielding unexpected ontological and analytical possibilities (Tadiar, 2022).

The ontologies articulated by Anzaldúa, Cusicanqui and Oyěwùmí, when carried to the field of sociology, clearly operate as *analytical ontologies*, meaning they are assembled out of empirical experiences to assist outsiders in comprehending non-hegemonic existences. They are not merely regional, indigenous or ancestral. The New Mestiza, the *Ch'ixi* and the *Ìyá* ontologies challenge one of the key pillars of modern colonial epistemology: the necessity to be analytically definite either in actions/reactions (effects) or in the dispositions to act (values).

Assembled as undetermined and contradictory but not necessarily problematic, they are virtuous anti-colonial inspirations. Their critical difference to the hegemonic global theories is that they do not claim the analytical universality of social relations but suggest the possibility of generalizing an onto-epistemological attitude.

These anti-colonial methodologies contribute to theoretical constructions in which time and space are not linear and cannot be merged, as demonstrated in Oyěwùmí's work. The women described in each construction navigate through different spatial and historical ontologies, with their intensity and effects in their actions operating under particular regimes of composition and heterogeneity. In my elaboration of these notions, the same entities (which may refer to women, individuals or communities in Western or modern terminology) enact disparate *analytical ontologies*, not only over the *longue durée* of their lives but from one space to another.

It is important to affirm that besides being part of the third-world feminism debates, the analytical constructions presented here are not equal or equivalent. Each of them represents a possible and singular inspiration for *ontoformative gestures*. The *Ch'ixi* can be regarded as a methodological tool developed to enact the ancestral elements of indigeneity in the lives of contemporary women in Bolivia. Anzaldúa's New Mestiza serves as an epistemic intervention, introducing the possibility of considering uncertainties, contradictions and anxieties as positive elements in the coeval existence of modern and *other-than-modern* elements in collective life. The Oyo-Yoruba ontologies in Oyěwùmí's work illustrate the active presence of what is often framed and dismissed as 'metaphysical effects' in the lives of contemporary women in that specific region of the African continent.

Rather than pursuing a universal, all-inclusive ontology (Patel, 2023), we should acknowledge that all ontologies are inherently partial and fragile in their scope. The assembly of analytical (limited) ontologies enacts a stance against the imperial nomothetic gesture in an anti-colonial manner. It positions its scholarship as a privileged foundation for a significant shift in the ontological politics of the social sciences (Mol, 1999). However, engaging in such disputes necessitates the *ontoformative gesture* of perceiving all disciplinary knowledge and conceptual forms as partial and constrained.

Conclusion

The chapter assembled a theoretical-methodological alternative to reinforce and widen the anti-colonial theory project besides modern subjects. It acknowledged the significance of key principles in reinforcing the role of colonialism and the political and intellectual responses to it, thereby strengthening global sociology. Moreover, the chapter sought to emphasize certain aspects of this contemporary initiative that remain constrained by the ontological politics of the modern Western imagination (Mol, 1999; Law, 2004).

The notion of *ontoformative gesture* was conceived to overcome some of the modern ontological limits of the anti-colonial imagination, particularly the ontological definiteness secured by time and space. As with any project confined by disciplinary boundaries, the gesture remains influenced by other modern aspirations, such as inclusion and expansion. Nevertheless, the primary epistemological endeavour is to blur some aspects of these defined modern boundaries with *other-than-modern* ontological effects on collective life that might challenge the exclusivity of modernity.

The need for *other-than-modern* blurring in our theoretical narratives is not merely a product of meta-theoretical-epistemological debates. It stems from a long period of fieldwork with the *abahlali basemapulzani*[7] in South Africa (Rosa, 2012) and from the reading and teaching of some third-world feminist debates (Alzandúa, Cusicanqui and Oyěwùmí, among others). My research experience of theoretical discomfort found solace in the initiatives of scholars who inscribed the *other-than-modern* dimension of contemporary existences in the hegemonic social sciences debates through the production of what I call *analytical ontologies*.

Messy, blurred and not definite sociological descriptions are not necessarily good, but they should not be regarded as bad social science nor as bad politics. If life is typically blurred and messy (Law, 2004), what is the purpose of avoiding this in a virtuous postcolonial moment? The *ontoformative gesture* does not appeal to a definite indigenization or the pursuit of an idyllic and authentic non-modern essence. Rather, it opens up possibilities to consider *other-than-modern* effects in research practices, with theoretical consequences.

Césaire, Fanon, Said, Guha, Chakrabarty, Mignolo or Quijano (to mention the most cited male figures of postcolonial and decolonial thought) helped us to learn and understand the modern ontology of Blackness, indigeneity, the subalternity and the otherness emerging from the colonial and modern encounters. In their work, we learned about despair and desolation, and eventually, we were taught about consistent and conscious reactions to modern colonialism. Nevertheless, we have not yet been able to perform hegemonic sociology beyond the dualistic approach between capitulation and modern conscious revolutionary responses to colonialism. As Ferreira da Silva (2007) and Jones (2004) carefully discuss with the assessment of the modern/liberal racial character of the social sciences, this hegemonic epistemological practice leads to the erasure, disappearance and dismissal of any element escaping the modern grammar.

Part, maybe a small one, of anti-colonial scholarship is resisting the colonial temptation to produce a single dualistic version of life where everyday existence is governed and explained as a product or resistance to modern/imperialist processes. I expect to have demonstrated that the third-world feminists presented here have already done that in an inspiring manner.

The *other-than-modern* should not be deemed relevant to sociology based on its disciplinary value. The *other-than-modern*, however, is relevant to life itself. Therefore, how can an anti-colonial social science theoretically and methodologically address the challenges posed by the empirical complexities of these lives? The proposal of an *ontoformative gesture* drew attention to the need for a public debate on what deserves to exist and how it impacts our work as sociologists.

Notes

[1] The research is supported with funding from CNPq and FAPERJ. I am thankful to Sujata Patel for the careful discussions on the first draft of this chapter, Maureen Eger by careful revisions, and Patricia Lorenzoni and the other participants of the Anti-Colonial Scholarship and Global Social Theory Workshop, who discussed the oral presentation. This version is greatly influenced by the sharp critical appreciation of the Non-Exemplary Sociology Research Laboratory members at the UFRRJ.

[2] Hegemonic here refers to the analytically predominant mode.

[3] Featherstone (1995), Eisenstadt (2017), Therborn (2003), Wagner (2010) and Domingues (2011), among others.

[4] Some of my colleagues who read and listened to preliminary versions of this chapter called my attention to the fact that social anthropology already investigates and assembles theories based in non-hegemonic contemporary existences. I am thankful to this observation and tend to agree with it, but it will be important to note that it is not every anthropological theory that is able to generate analytical effects beyond cultural bounded limits.

[5] It must be considered an ongoing transitional state that is on the verge of being but has not yet been coded by the hegemonic colonial disciplinary matrix, as suggested by Tadiar (2022).

[6] 'Not only does she [the new mestiza] sustain contradictions, she turns the ambivalence into something else' (Anzaldúa, 1987: 79).

[7] The *abahlali basemapulazi* is an isiZulu term to describe the Black rural population forced by the apartheid regime to live in areas converted into modern farms controlled by white farmers only.

References

Adésínà, J. (2006) Sociology, endogeneity and the challenge of transformation, *African Sociological Review/Revue Africaine de Sociologie*, 10(2): 133–50.

Anzaldúa, G. (1987) *The New Mestiza*, Aunt Lute Books.

Bakare-Yusuf, B. (2003) 'Yorubas don't do gender': A critical review of Oyeronke Oyěwùmí's *The Invention of Women: Making an African Sense of Western Gender Discourses*, *African Identities*, 1(1): 122–42.

Chakrabarty, D. (2000) *Provincializing Europe: Postcolonial Thought and Historical Difference – New Edition*, Princeton University Press.

Connell, R. (1987) *Gender and Power: Society, the Person and Sexual Politics*, John Wiley & Sons.

Connell, R.W. (2007) *Southern Theory: Social Science and the Global Dynamics of Knowledge*, Polity.

Connell, R. (2011) Gender and social justice: Southern perspectives, *South African Review of Sociology*, 3: 103–15.

Connell, R. (2012a) Gender, health and theory conceptualising the issue, in local and world perspective, *Social Science & Medicine (1982)*, 74(11): 1675–83.

Connell, R. (2012b) Transsexual women and feminist thought: Toward new understanding and new politics, *Signs: Journal of Women in Culture and Society*, 37(4): 857–81.

Costa, S. (2010) Teoria por adição, in C.B. Martins (ed) *Horizontes das ciências sociais no Brasil: sociologia*, ANPOCS, pp 25–51.

Curiel, O. and Pión, R. (2022) The contributions of Afro-descendant women to feminist theory and practice: Deuniversalizing the subject 'women', *Hypatia*, 37(3): 478–92.

Cusicanqui, S. (2003) El mito de la pertenencia de Bolivia al 'mundo occidental'. Requiem para un Nacionalismo, *Temas sociales*, 24: 64–100.

Cusicanqui, S.R. (2012) Ch'ixinakax *utxiwa*: A reflection on the practices and discourses of decolonization, *The South Atlantic Quarterly*, 111(1): 95–109.

De la Cadena, M. (2015) *Earth Beings: Ecologies of Practice across Andean Worlds*, Duke University Press.

Domingues, J. (2011) Beyond the centre: The third phase of modernity in a globally compared perspective, *European Journal of Social Theory*, 14(4): 517–35.

Domingues, J.M. (2009) Global modernisation, 'coloniality' and a critical sociology for contemporary Latin America, *Theory, Culture & Society*, 26(1): 112–33.

Eisenstadt, S.N. (ed) (2017) *Multiple Modernities*, Routledge.

Fanon, F. (1961) *Les Damnes de la Terre*, La Decouverte Editions.

Featherstone, M. (1995) *Global Modernities*, SAGE.

Ferreira da Silva, D. (2007) *Toward a Global Idea of Race*, University of Minnesota Press.

Go, J. (2023) Thinking against empire: Anti-colonial thought as social theory, *The British Journal of Sociology*, 74(3): 279–93.

Jones, J. (2004) The impairment of empathy in goodwill whites for African Americans, in G. Yancy (ed) *What White Looks Like: African-American Philosophers on the Whiteness Question*, Routledge, pp 65–86.

Karakayali, N. (2015) Two ontological orientations in sociology: Building social ontologies and blurring the boundaries of the 'social', *Sociology*, 49(4): 732–47.

Kosik, K. (1976) *Dialectics of the Concrete: A Study on Problems of Man and World*, Springer Science & Business Media.

Law, J. (2004) *After Method: Mess in Social Science Research*, Routledge.

Lorde, A. (2018) *The Master's Tools Will Never Dismantle the Master's House*, Penguin Classics.

Lukács, G. (1979) *Ontology of Social Being*, Merlin Press.

Madhok, S. (2020) A critical reflexive politics of location, 'feminist debt' and thinking from the Global South, *European Journal of Women's Studies*, 27(4): 394–412.

Mbilinyi, M. (2015) Transformative feminism in Tanzania, in R. Baksh-Soodeen and W. Harcourt (eds) *The Oxford Handbook of Transnational Feminist Movements*, Oxford University Press, pp 507–30.

Mohanty, C. (1988) Under western eyes: Feminist scholarship and colonial discourses, *Feminist Review*, 30(1): 61–88.

Mol, A. (1999) Ontological politics: A word and some questions, *The Sociological Review*, 47(1): 74–89.

Moosavi, L. (2023) Turning the decolonial gaze towards ourselves: Decolonising the curriculum and 'decolonial reflexivity' in sociology and social theory, *Sociology*, 57(1): 137–56.

Moraga, C. and Anzaldúa, G. (1981) *This Bridge Called My Back*, Kitchen Table.

Nyamnjoh, A.-N. and Morrell, R. (2021) Southern theory and how it aids in engaging Southern youth, in S. Swartz, A. Cooper, C.M. Batan and L.K. Causa (eds) *The Oxford Handbook of Global South Youth Studies*, Oxford University Press, pp 77–92.

Oyěwùmí, O. (1997) *Invention of Women: Making an African Sense of Western Gender Discourses*, University of Minnesota Press.

Oyěwùmí, O. (2016) *What Gender is Motherhood? Changing Yorúbá Ideas on Power, Identity, and Procreation in the Age of Modernity*, 1st edition, Palgrave Macmillan.

Patel, S. (2023) Anti-colonial thought and global social theory, *Frontiers in Sociology*, 8(1). doi: 10.3389/fsoc.2023.1143776

Patel, S. (2024) What is anti-colonial global social theory? *Sociology Compass*, 18(8): 1–10.

Rosa, M.C. (2012) A terra e seus vários sentidos: por uma sociologia e etnologia dos moradores de fazenda na África do Sul contemporânea, *Sociedade e Estado*, 27(2): 361–85.

Rosa, M.C. (2016) Sociologies of the South and the actor-network-theory: Possible convergences for an ontoformative sociology, *European Journal of Social Theory*, 19(4): 485–502.

Rosa, M.C. (2019) How to stage a convergence between ANT and Southern sociologies?, in A. Blok, I. Farías and C. Roberts (eds) *The Routledge Companion to Actor-Network Theory*, Routledge, pp 210–19.

Rosa, M.C. (2020) Sociologias Emergentes: uma agenda não-exemplar, *Caderno Eletrônico de Ciências Sociais*, 8(1): 136–48.

Rudy, S. (2020) Gender's ontoformativity, or refusing to be spat out of reality: Reclaiming queer women's solidarity through experimental writing, *Feminist Theory*, 21(3): 351–65.

Soldatic, K. (2020) Disability's circularity: Presence, absence and erasure in Australian settler colonial biopolitical population regimes, *Studies in Social Justice*, 14(2): 306–20.

Tadiar, N.X.M. (2022) *Remaindered Life*, Duke University Press.

Tavolaro, S. (2021) Interpretações do Brasil e a temporalidade moderna: do sentimento de descompasso à crítica epistemológica, *Sociedade e Estado*, 36(3): 1059–82.

Therborn, G. (2003) Entangled modernities, *European Journal of Social Theory*, 6(3): 293–305.

Verran, H. (2001) *Science and an African Logic*, 2nd edition, University of Chicago Press.

Verran, H. (2014) Working with those who think otherwise, *Common Knowledge*, 20(3): 527–39.

Wagner, P. (2010) Multiple trajectories of modernity: Why social theory needs historical sociology, *Thesis Eleven*, 100(1): 53–60.

Index

References to figures appear in *italic* type. References to notes show both the page number and the note number (231n3).

A

Abbott, Tony 223
Aboriginal Protection Act (1869) 232n1
Abu-Lughod, J. 128, 146n4
academic tourism 38, 52n32
Adorno, Theodor 141
Afghanistan 159, 222, 224
Africa 36–8, 87, 96, 133, 145n2–3
Afshar, Hoda 230
Agamben, Giorgio 135
Akiwowo, Akinsola 31, 32, 51n23, 94
Alatas, Syed Farid 12, 92, 219
Alatas, Syed Hussein 60, 71, 72, 73
Alavi, H. 73
Algeria 41, 95, 96, 98
al-Khwarizmi 134
al-Maqdum, Shaykh Zayn al-Din 68
Amin, Samir 8, 9, 38, 131
analytical ontologies 244, 245, 246–7
Anand, Mulk Raj 143
Anderson, B. 219
Anthropocene 14, 156, 166, 168
anthropology 26, 71, 99n6, 106–7, 109, 138, 177, 248n4
Anthropology and the Colonial Encounter (Asad) 106, 119n2
anti-colonial/anticolonial (the term) 59, 124
anti-colonial/anticolonial scholarship 9–10, 11, 103 *see also* anti-colonial/anticolonial social theory; anti-colonial/anticolonial social thought; scholarship
anti-colonial/anticolonial social theory
  author's overview of 11–12, 113
  author's summary of 45–9, 76, 98–9
  beginnings of 22–3, 24, 28–32, 46–7, 50n2
  challenges to 116–18
  critiques of 23, 32
  debates on 236–7
  definitions of 103
  generalizability of 12–13, 15, 85
  metatheories, and 11, 20–1, 49, 62
  methodologies 22, 24, 33, 39, 241, 243–6
  other-than-modern 238, 243, 245, 246, 247, 248
  peripheral gaze 21, 23–4, 25–8, 47, 50n10, 238
  perspectives of 21–2, 84–5
  politics of location 13, 104–10, 111–13, 116–17, 118, 119n1, 119n3
  reframing of 32–3
  social thought, compared to 60–1, 237–8
  the term *theory* 238–9
  see also coloniality of power; endogeneity; exceptionalism; extraversion; ontoformative gestures; subalternity/subaltern studies
anti-colonial/anticolonial social thought
anti-neocolonial thought 74
author's overview of 9–10, 12, 50n12, 58, 83–4
author's summary of 75–6, 99
critiques 6, 7–8, 11
definitions of 60–3
dimensions of 59–60, 68–75
early 3, 4, 58–9
economic nationalism and 29
generalizability of 12–13, 95–8, 100n9
geoepistemic essentialism 12, 62, 85, 91–2, 93–4, 94
history of 88–9
intellectual decolonization 7, 193
Marxism and 6
metatheories, and 62
peripheral gaze 23–4, 26–7
proto-philosophical/sociological approach 20, 27–8
refugees/asylum seekers, by 217–18, 225, 228–9, 229–31
resistance and 16
social theory, compared to 60–1, 237–8

252

INDEX

the term *anti-colonial/anticolonial* 59, 124
  thinkers 89–90
anti-colonialism/anticolonialism
  author's overview of 94–5
  as planetary struggle 14–15
  the term 1, 4, 59
  see also decolonization
anti-immigration riots *see* riots (2024 UK)
anti-neocolonial thought 74
Arendt, H. 163
Armah, Ayi Kwei 143
artists 141–4
Asad, Talal 106, 107, 119n2
Asia 184–6 *see also* inter-imperial approach; Maritime Asia; Southeast Asia; *specific countries (e.g., China)*
Asian Conference on Teaching and Research in Social Sciences 29–30
associated milieu 161
asuwada 32
ATSI peoples *see* Indigenous Australian, Aboriginal, and Torres Strait Islander (ATSI) peoples
Australia
  counter-narratives, refugee 229–30
  externalization policies 16, 223
  Indigenous Australian, Aboriginal, and Torres Strait Islander (ATSI) peoples 218–19, 220, 232n1
  refugee detention by 16, 217, 219, 222–4
  securitization 221
  settler-colonialism 47, 218, 219–20
  Tampa incident 222–3
  terra nullius, as 218–19
Australian Human Rights and Equal Opportunity Commission 232n1
Australia's Shame (Meldrum-Hanna and Worthington) 231

B

Bagú, Sergio 73
Banaji, J. 73
Bandung conference 28–9, 88
Barati, Reza 230
Barker, Joanne 160
Barker, Martin 202
Barlow, Tani 48
Barrera, M. 67
Barrios, Joi 167
Basu, Neil 199–200, 203
becoming-human 159, 166, 167, 172
Before European Hegemony (Abu-Lughod) 146n4
Bell, Kirsten 112–13
Bernal, Martin 8, 51n25
Bhabha, Homi 51n30, 105–6, 107
Bhambra, Gurminder 62, 120n12, 204
biases 2–3, 202

Billeter, Jean François 190
binaries 11–12, 26, 43, 44, 50n8, 62–3, 124, 145n2, 181
biracial model 51n26
Black Athena (Bernal) 8, 51n25
Black feminist theory 87
Blackness 204, 205
Blauner, Robert 66–7
Bloom, Jonathan 133
Boatcă, Manuela 127, 184–5, 187, 197
Boochani, Behrouz 16, 225, 227, 228–9, 229–30, 233n7
books *see* literature; *specific books (e.g. No Friend but the Mountains)*
border epistemology 43, 62
Bourdieu, Pierre 21, 106–7
Braudel, Fernand 187
Breman, Jan 65
Brexit 15–16, 198, 202–3
Bringing Them Home (Australian Human Rights and Equal Opportunity Commission) 232n1
Britain *see* Great Britain
British India 2, 5, 29, 34, 50n15, 64, 65, 189
British Malaya 64, 65, 72
Buck-Morss, Susan 136
Bunker, Stephen 64
Burawoy, M. 94, 120n11
Burke, Edmund 134

C

Calculation of the Hindu Numerals (al-Khwarizmi) 134
capitalism
  Eurocentrism and 8
  impacts of 73
  imperial capitalism 7, 48
  racial capitalism 14, 155, 160, 174, 232
  reproductive labour 14, 136–7, 140, 160, 161, 163–4, 165–6, 175n5
  slavery and 76
  trade colonialism 64
  world-systems approach 25
  see also colonial capitalism
Capitolocene 14, 156
care *see* labours of care
Carroll, John 181–2, 184, 189
Césaire, Aimé 5, 70, 100n9, 247–8
Chabal, E. 1
Chatterjee, Partha 35, 36, 51n21–2
Chauka, Please Tell us the Time (Boochani and Sarvestani) 229–30
Chen, Hon-Fai 15
Chen, Kuan-Hsing 178
China
  Hong Kong 15, 177–8, 180–4, 184–5, 186, 188, 189, 192, 193
  imperialism 6, 99

influence of 32
infrastructures 132–3, 133–4
resistance movements 130
semi-colonization of 66
Ch'ixi 244, 245, 246
City on the Edge (Hung) 183
Cliff, Michelle 144
climate change 14–15, 156–8, 173
coeval (the term) 138–9
coevality 126, 138–9, 140
collaboration 178–9, 180–1, 182, 183–4, 187–8, 191, 192, 230–1
Collaborative Colonial Power (Law) 180
collective continuance 157–8, 170
Collins, Patricia Hill 86, 146n10
colonial capitalism
  critiques of 27–8, 60
  indolence and 71, 72
  scholarship on 38–9, 56, 58, 73
colonial collaboration 178–9, 180–1, 182, 183–4, 187–8, 191, 192
colonial countries
  actions by 158
  biases of 2–3
  challenges faced by 5
  scholarship on, general 69–70
  see also specific countries (e.g. Great Britain, Spain)
colonial difference 43, 84, 99
colonialism
  actions of 158
  author's overview of 4–5, 63
  author's summary of 98–9
  beneficiaries of 2
  climate change, and 14–15, 156–8, 173
  dehumanization, and 197, 201, 204, 205–6, 208–9, 212, 213, 219, 231–2
  discourses of 72
  history of 2, 3
  impacts of 100n9
  invisibilization 204
  marginalization and 15–16
  modular forms of 2, 3
  slow violence 140
  the term *colonialism* 1, 4
  time 159–60, 173–4
  types of 12, 47–8, 59, 63–7
  see also colonial capitalism; exploitation colonialism; internal colonialism; non-settler colonialism; plantation colonialism; semi-colonialism; settler-colonialism; subalternity/subaltern studies; trade colonialism
coloniality of power 38–40, 43
coloniality thesis 39–40
colonial modernity *see* modernity
colonies 2, 3 *see also* post-colonial nation-states

colonies of exploitation *see* exploitation colonialism; non-settler colonialism
colonies of settlement 2
colonization 65, 157, 174n3, 188, 204, 241
  see also colonialism
colonized, the 96–7, 99n4, 155 *see also* other/Other; post-colonial nation-states; subalterns
colonizers *see* colonial countries
color line 95
Columbus, Christopher 74
communism 28, 32, 92, 108, 183
Connell, Raewyn 62, 87, 94, 99n5, 240–1, 242
contention 190
conviviality 191–2
Coolies, Planters and Colonial Politics (Breman) 65
Coronil, F. 48
Costa, S. 197, 239
Cotler, J. 67
Coulthard, Glen 160
counter-narratives 136–7, 229–30
Crosby, Alfred 157
Cuba 129
cultural genocide 218, 220, 232n1
Cummings, R. 208
Cusicanqui, Silva Rivera 244, 245, 246

D

Daoism 179, 190–1
Darwish, Mahmoud 173
da Silva, Ferreira 238, 239, 241, 242, 244, 248
decolonial (the term) 124–5
decoloniality 7, 8–9, 24, 43–5, 48, 114
Decolonial Reconstellations (Doyle) 126
decolonial studies 124, 146n16
decolonial thought 16, 58, 74–5, 123, 125, 138–9, 228
decolonization
  author's overview of 4
  becoming-human 159, 166, 167, 172
  beginnings of 28
  definitions of 124, 173
  economic nationalism 29
  Hong Kong 180, 182, 183
  India 114–16
  intellectual decolonization 7, 59, 60, 63, 193
  as intersectional 204–5
  phases of 4, 5, 6, 7
  scholarship on 47–8
  the term *decolonization* 4, 114
  third worldism/Thirldworldism 8, 23, 29, 32, 33, 193
Decolonizing the Mind (Thiong'o) 130
Deepak, J. Sai 114

Deer and the Cauldron (Jin) 191
Defiance: Fighting for the Far Right 200
dehumanization 197, 201, 204, 205–6, 208–9, 212, 213, 219, 231–2
De l'égalité des races humaines (On the Equality of Human Races) Firmin 71
de-linking 43, 125
delinking 131
Demeter, Márton 112, 119n7–8
dependency
　colonialism, from 3, 28, 38, 189, 223
　economic dependency 67, 183
　knowledge production and 104, 107, 111
　labour frameworks 125–6, 165–6
　theory of 23, 38, 46, 50n14
Derrida, J. 204
Deshpande, Satish 13
de Silva, S.B.D. 73
destabilization 129, 136
detention *see* Australia; Manus Island; refugees
Dhareshwar, Vivek 109
dialectical decolonial thought
　author's overview of 123
　coevality 138–41
　infrastructures/institutions 131–5
　intersectional thinking 125–6
　labour 135–8
　literature 141–4
　see also inter-imperial approach
Dialectics of the Concrete (Kosik) 240
differences 43, 84, 99
dispossession 155, 160, 164–5, 168–9, 172
domestic workers 161–2, 163, 167
Dominican Republic 2
double-consciousness 96, 97
Douwes Dekker, Eduard 69–70
Doyle, Laura 13–14, 184, 185, 190, 204
Du Bois, W.E.B. 44, 75, 89, 91, 95–8, 100n9
Dutch *see* Netherlands
Duterte, Rodrigo 153, 165

E

economic nationalism 29
Edge of Empires (Carroll) 181, 182
Eger, Maureen 199
El Filibusterismo (The Revolution) (Rizal) 61
elites
　collaboration of 178, 180–1, 184, 188, 190, 191–2
　colonial rule through native 70
　geopolitical histories and 129
　hierarchies 99n4, 181
　Hong Kong 182, 183–4, 189, 190, 191–2
　nationalist historiographies and 34–5, 46
　self-serving biases of 2–3
　society 87–8
El Shakry, O. 205
emic perspectives 31, 32, 36

Emmet, Robert 130
empires 94, 97–9, 126–30, 131–5, 181–2, 184–9, 192–3 *see also* imperialism; inter-imperial approach
Empire Windrush 206, 207
endogeneity 36–8, 46
endogenous perspective 37, 58, 63
environmental catastrophes *see* climate change
Essai sur l'inégalité des races (Essay on the Inequality of the Races) Gobineau 71
essentialism 35, 62–3, 88, 93, 99n5, 104
　see also geoepistemic essentialism
Eurocentrism
　anti-Eurocentric approaches 179
　author's overview of 7–8, 50n11
　binaries 62–3
　colonial collaboration and 187–8
　coloniality of power 38–9
　critical scholarship 9, 51n25, 59, 70, 90, 186
　definitions of 8, 38
　embeddedness of 46
　peripheral gaze 26–7
Europe 184–6 *see also specific countries (e.g., France, Spain)*
exceptionalism 40–1, 51n27, 202, 218, 219–22, 231
ex-colonies *see* post-colonial nation-states
exploitation 64
exploitation colonialism 2, 12, 59, 63, 64–5, 67, 76 *see also* non-settler colonialism
extraversion 36–8, 46

F

Fabian, Johannes 126, 138–9
Fanon, Frantz 89, 90, 95, 96–8, 100n9, 204, 205, 239, 247–8
fascism 5
feminism 105, 106, 108
feminist politics 105
feminist standpoint theory 87, 105, 117
Ferdinand, Malcolm 158
Filipinos *see* Philippines
Firmin, Joseph August Anténor 70–1
First Nations 4, 44, 230
first world 28, 29
former colonies *see* post-colonial nation-states
Foucault, Michel 28, 41–2, 119n1
France 2, 26, 87, 95, 96, 97, 98, 129, 134–5
Frank, Andre Gunder 67, 185, 186, 187, 193
Fricker, Miranda 138
Frosh, S. 204–5

G

Gedalof, I. 208
gender 134–5, 136–7, 240, 243, 244, 245
Gender and Power (Connell) 240

generalizability 12–13, 15, 85, 90, 94, 95–8, 100n9, 179, 190
genocide 104, 118, 154, 171, 172, 228
  see also cultural genocide
Gentleman, Amelia 207, 211
geoepistemic essentialism 12, 62, 85, 91–2, 93–4, 94
geopolitics 32–3, 40, 48–9, 128–9, 138, 174, 222, 239
Germany 5, 26, 87, 129, 199, 224
Giddens, A. 76
Giddings, Paula 144
globalization 7
global war on terror see war on terror
Go, Julian 12, 62, 236, 237
Gobineau, Arthur de 71
God of Small Things (Roy) 143
god trick 105
Gordon, Avery 206
grasses 169–70
Great Britain
  British India 2, 5, 29, 34, 50n15, 64, 65, 189
  colonial discourse of 72
  colonialism by 3
  exploitation colonialism 65
  Hong Kong 15, 177, 180–3, 184, 188–9, 191, 192
  immigration policy 40
  imperialism 129
  internal colonialism 67
  racial/ethnic minorities in 15–16
  settler-colonialism 65
  trade colonialism 64
  Windrush scandal 15–16, 198, 201, 206–12
  see also United Kingdom
Griffith, Judy 209–12
Grover, Suresh 199
Gudynas, Eduardo 139
Guha, Ranajit 34, 46, 247–8

H

Hall, Stuart 108
Hamilton, Peter 182–3, 184
Haraway, Donna 105
Hartman, Saidiya 159–60
Harun, Aminurrashid 61
hauntology 204, 208
Hegel, G.W.F. 97, 135–6, 138, 190, 241
Hewitt, G. 208
high theory 24
historiographies 34–5, 42, 44, 46, 51n31, 189
History 153, 155, 158, 168, 170, 172, 173–4
Holton, R.J. 76
Hong Kong
  Chinese rule 183–4
  colonial collaboration in 180–1, 189
  colonialism in 15
  elites 182, 183–4, 189, 190, 191–2
  Filipinx domestic workers 167
  informal decolonization of 182–3
  inter-imperial perspective 179–80
  literature 191–3
  scholarship on 177–8
  as unknown 177
Hountondji, Paulin 36–8, 46, 52n32
Hung, Ho-Fung 183–4, 190

I

Iberia 2, 4, 38, 39–40
immigration
  anti-immigration narratives 202–3
  hostile environment (United Kingdom) 201, 206, 207, 208, 211
  migrant workers 14, 161–5, 167
  policies 40
  riots (2024 UK) 198–201, 202, 203, 212
  settler-colonialism migration systems 221–2
imperial capitalism 7, 48
imperial difference 43
imperialism
  author's overview of 87, 94
  biases of 2–3
  destabilization 129, 136
  impacts of 128–9
  knowledge production, impact of on 47, 48–9
  repeated invasions, areas of 127–8
  reproduction 160–1
  resistance movements 10, 130
  semi-colonialism and 66
  strategies of 4–5, 6
  world-systems approach 25–6, 27–8
  see also inter-imperial approach
imperial standpoint 85, 86, 87, 88, 91–3, 98
India
  British India 2, 5, 29, 34, 50n15, 64, 65, 189
  decolonization 114–16, 124, 130
  economic nationalism 29, 50n16
  emic perspective on 31, 36
  intellectual infrastructures 133, 134
  nationalist historiography of 34
  social sciences in 50n17, 99n6
  subaltern movement 51n22
India that is Bharat (Deepak) 114
indigenization
  of colonial rule 181
  as ideological 63
  as justification 115
  of social sciences 30, 31, 33, 50n17, 90–1
Indigenous Australian, Aboriginal, and Torres Strait Islander (ATSI) peoples 218–19, 220, 232n1
indigenous groups 4, 39–40

INDEX

indigenous/Indigenous (the term) 36
indolence 71–2, 73
inequalities 13, 111–13, 120n13 *see also* racial inequality
infrastructures
  intellectual infrastructures 29, 37–8, 45, 132–3
  inter-imperiality 131–3, 135, 169
  vital infrastructures 14, 161–2, 164, 165, 166–7
intellectual decolonization 7, 59, 60, 193
intellectual infrastructures 29, 37–8, 45, 132–3
intergenerational trauma 229, 232n1
inter-imperial approach
  Asian context 185–6, 186–93
  author's overview of 13–14, 125, 127–9, 179–80, 184–5
  destabilization 129, 136
  Hong Kong 15, 178–80
  infrastructures 131–5
  literature on 141, 142, 144, 146n6
  the term *inter-imperial* 127
  see also imperialism
Inter-imperiality (Doyle) 126, 131, 146n6
inter-imperial positionality 127, 142–3
inter-imperial zones 127–8, 178, 179, 184–6, 186–90, 191, 192
internal colonialism 4, 12, 59, 63, 66–7, 95, 96, 98
intersectionality
  decolonization, of 204–5
  dialectical decolonial thought 123, 125–6
  inter-imperiality and 179–80
  kyriarchal systems 229
  labour formations 135–8
  politics of location 107–8
  Windrush scandal 212–13
invisibilization 204
Ireland 5, 129, 130, 137
Israel 65, 75, 104, 118–19, 154, 159, 165, 171, 172
Ivy Intifada 13, 118–19

J

James, William 146n16
Japan 3, 48, 66, 99, 130, 131, 133–4
Jarvie, Ian 177
Jews 43, 65
jihad 68
Jin, Yong 191
John, Gus 206–7
John, Mary E. 109
Jones, J. 248
Joyce, James 142–3, 143–4
Jullien, François 190
Jurrungu Ngan-ga 231

K

Kellogg, Laura Cornelius 89, 91
Khaldun, Ibn 61, 62, 91, 100n8
knowledge production
  anti-colonial/anticolonial standpoint 100n7
  colonialism on, impact of 3, 47–8
  coloniality of 74–5
  language of 45, 110, 112–13
  politics of location 111–13
  refugees/asylum seekers, by 217–18, 225, 228–9, 229–31
  time 173–4
Korea 3, 168
Kosik, Karel 240, 241
kyriarchy 229

L

labour
  intersectionality of 135–8
  migrant workers 14, 161–5, 167
  reproductive labour 14, 136–7, 140, 160, 161, 163–4, 165–6, 175n5
labours of care 130, 135, 140, 142, 143, 146n5, 146n9, 161
labours of necessity 163
language
  of colonialism 34
  of knowledge production 45, 110, 112–13
  language/literature 8, 41, 42–3
  of social sciences 30–1
  translations 133–4
Law, Wing-Sang 180–1, 184, 190
laziness 60, 71, 72
Lewis, Mark Edward 132
Liboiron, Max 124
libraries 133
Lindner, K. 50n12
literature 141–3
location
  as challenge to theories 116–17
  colonialism and 13–14
  knowledge production and 13, 105
  politics of location 104–10, 111–13, 116–17, 118, 119n1, 119n3
  the term *location* 104
  see also positionality
long-historical perspective 123, 126, 127, 128, 131–5, 137–8, 139, 145
longue durée 23, 27, 125, 126, 139, 184, 246
lord and bondsman 135–6
Ludden, D. 51n20
Lukács, G. 87, 240
Luxemburg, Rosa 5, 160–1, 166–7

M

MacLean, Gerald 133
Made in Hong Kong (Hamilton) 182
Madhok, S. 243

Malaya 61, 64, 65, 72
Malaysia 69, 193
Mann, Michael 132
Mannheim, K. 86
Manus Island 219, 224, 225, *226*, 227, 230
Manus Prison Theory (MPT) 16, 228–9
Mao, Tse-tung 66, 92
Marcos, Ferdinand 154
Marcos Jr., Ferdinand 153–4, 173
Maritime Asia 186, 187, 188–9, 190
Marte-Wood, Alden 163
Marx, Karl
 colonialism 5, 23, 27, 50n12
 conflict, language of 31
 critiques of 32, 33, 42, 83
 decolonization 6, 155
 Eurocentrism 7–8, 46, 187
 labour 136
 nationalist thought and 36
 social being 240
 subaltern project and 51n31
Massey, Doreen 138
material and social inequalities *see* inequalities
Max Havelaar (Multatuli) 69–70
May, Theresa 207, 208
Mbembe, Achille 136, 140, 204
McGeever, B. 202
McKittrick, Katherine 160
Mead, George Herbert 96, 97
media, humans as 162, 163–4
Memmi, Albert 69, 70
metatheories 11, 20–1, 49, 62, 242
methodologies *see* anti-colonial/anticolonial social theory; modernity; psychosocial methodologies; social sciences
Midnight's Children (Rushdie) 142
Mignolo, Walter 43, 44, 50n10, 62, 74, 114, 120n17, 145n2
migrant workers 14, 161–5, 167
Miles, J. 205–6
milieus 160–1, 166, 167, 169, 170, 172, 174
Miller, Gina 203
Mills, David 112–13
Mizoguchi, Yūzō 178
modernity
 binaries and 62
 coevality and 138, 140–1
 colonized, rethinking of 22, 23, 38–9, 178, 241
 decoloniality and 9, 11, 43–4, 145n2
 infrastructures 131, 132
 methodologies for 45–7
 peripheral gaze and 25, 27, 28–9
 social sciences and 31, 83, 88, 99n6, 239
Modi regime 114, 115
Moore, Jason 175n5
Morgan, Jennifer 174n2
Morrison, Toni 174n2

MPT *see* Manus Prison Theory (MPT)
Mukerji, D.P. 31
Multatuli 69–70
Muslims 43, 68, 69, 124, 143, 165, 188, 198–9, 201, 202
MV *Tampa* 222
The Myth of the Lazy Native (Alatas) 71–2

N

Naoroji, Dadabhai 50n15, 64
Na'puti, Tiara 139
narrative analysis 15–16, 205
narratives
 anti-immigration 202–3
 of colonialism 2–3, 16
 counter-narratives 136–7, 229–30
 of Filipinos 71–2
 power imbalances and 205–6
 Windrush scandal, of 209–12
nationalist historiographies 34, 42
nativism 12, 47, 62, 63
Nauru 217, 222, 223, 224
necropolitics 136, 140, 232
neo-colonialism 3, 6, 39, 109, 117–18, 223, 231–2
neocolonial wars 159
neo-liberalism 5, 7, 9, 45, 145, 164
Netherlands 70, 188, 193
Netherlands East Indies 64, 69–70
network centrality 188, 192
New Mestiza 243–4, 246, 248n6
new racism 202
Nigeria 32, 245
9/11 terror attack 221, 222
Nixon, Rob 140
Nkrumah, Kwame 6, 89–90
No Friend but the Mountains (Boochani) 225, 228, 229, 231, 233n7
Noli Me Tangere (Touch Me Not) (Rizal) 61
non-settler colonialism 2, 25, 47–8, 73, 179
 see also exploitation colonialism
Northern Ireland 198–9
Northern-metropolitan social thought 83–4, 85, 86, 90–1, 93
No Telephone to Heaven (Cliff) 144

O

objective dimensions 73
Occidentalism 43–4, 46, 48
ocean studies 15, 186–7, 189–90, 192, 193
Odyssey 142, 144
Olzak, S. 199
One Thousand and One Nights 14, 126, 142
ontoformative (the term) 240–1
ontoformative ethics 237
ontoformative gestures 16–17, 236–7, 238, 242–3, 244, 245, 246, 247
ontoformativity 240, 241, 242

INDEX

Open Social Sciences (Wallerstein) 26
Orientalism 7, 9, 36, 41–2, 51n30, 59, 92
  see also postcolonialism
Orientalism (Said) 41
Osterhammel, J. 2, 3
othericide 158
other/Other
  affected, as the 241–2
  binaries of 62
  decoloniality and 43, 44
  denial of 158
  indigenous/Indigenous perspective 36–7
  invisibilization of 203–4
  national identities and 5
  peripheral gaze 26–7
other-than-modern 238, 243, 245, 246, 247, 248
Outline of a Theory of Practice (Bourdieu) 106–7, 119n2
Oyěwùmí, Oyèrónkẹ́ 245, 246
Oyo-Yoruba 245, 246

P

Padios, Jan 163
Paladin 223
Palestine 65, 75, 104, 118–19, 130, 154, 158, 165, 171–2
Panglima Awang (Harun) 61
paper 132, 134
Papua New Guinea (PNG) 217, 219, 223, 224, *226*, 227, 233n8
Parker, D. 60
Parsons, Talcott 88
Parvulescu, Anca 127, 184–5, 187
Patel, Sujata 11–12, 60, 62–3, 77n3, 84–5, 99n6, 120n13, 197, 236, 237, 238
peripheral gaze 21, 23–4, 25–8, 47, 50n10
Phenomenology of Spirit (Hegel) 135–6
Philippines
  destabilization 129
  Filipinos, narratives of 71–2
  history, phenomenon of 153–4, 173
  Mt. Pinatubo eruption 168–9
  reproductive labour from 161–5, 167
  talahib (Saccharum spontaneum) 169–70, 171
Philosophy of History (Hegel) 136, 138
Phoenix, Ann 15–16, 232
Piggott, Joan 133–4
plantation colonialism 29, 64–5, 76, 158, 160
plantation time 160
A Pluralistic Universe (James) 146n16
pluriversality 43, 139, 145, 145n2
PNG *see* Papua New Guinea (PNG)
Poland 129
politics of location 104–10, 111–13, 116–17, 118, 119n1, 119n3
Portrait du colonisé—Portrait du colonisateur (The Coloniser and the Colonised) (Memmi) 69

Portugal 2, 39–40, 68, 129, 185, 188–9
positionality 30, 105, 110, 119n1, 141, 145, 227, 232, 237 *see also* inter-imperial positionality
postcolonialism
  author's overview of 7, 8, 42–3, 51n30, 58, 74
  beginnings of 41–2
  binaries 62–3
  critiques of 44, 45
  post-colonial nation-states
  citizenship in 47
  impacts of colonialism on 2, 3, 6, 7
  imperial standpoint 83, 88, 92
  knowledge production 51n19, 109
  scholars from 41
  see also decolonization
postcolonial sociology of knowledge 85, 86–7
postcolonial studies 42, 105, 124, 178
Poverty and Un-British Rule in India (Naoroji) 50n15
power
  coloniality of power 38–40, 43
  global balance of 32–3
  imbalances of 4, 106, 204, 205–6
  imperial, impacts of 15
  knowledge production and 21, 22, 27–8, 46
  peripheral gaze 25, 26
  social theory and 92
  types of colonialism and 63, 66
power/knowledge critique (Foucault) 28, 41, 42
Pramoedya, Ananta Toer 61
precarious autonomy 188, 192
presentism 119n3, 140
proto-philosophical/sociological approach 20, 27–8
psychosocial methodologies 15–16, 197, 198, 204–5, 206–12
Puerto Rico 73–4

Q

Quijano, Anibal 8–9, 38–9, 40, 43, 46, 74, 247–8

R

Rabinow, P. 119n1
racial capitalism 14, 155, 160, 174, 232
racial classification 43
racial inequality 67, 70–1
racialization 96–8, 204, 212–13, 220, 222, 232
racism
  coloniality thesis and 40
  colonial racism 71
  hierarchies, and 39

indigenous perspective 37
institutionalization of 5, 43
internal colonialism 66–7
new racism 202
postcolonialism, and 40, 41, 43
violence and 198–201
referendum (UK) *see* Brexit
refugees
  detention of 16, 217, 219, 222–4
  knowledge production by 217–18, 225, 228–9, 229–31
  statistics 224
Reid, A. 188
re-linking 131
Remain (Afshar) 230
Remaindered Life (Tadiar) 154, 168
reproductive labour 14, 136–7, 140, 160, 161, 163–4, 165–6, 175n5
revolutions 10, 90, 96, 129, 130, 144, 205, 248
Ribeiro, Gustavo Lins 110
riots (2024 UK) 198–201, 202, 203, 212
Rizal, José 60, 61, 64, 71–2, 75. 89
Robinson, Ronald 180, 181
Rodinson, M. 65
Rohrer, Judy 139
Rosa, Marcelo C. 16–17
Roy, Arundhati 143
Rushdie, Salman 142
Russia 3, 6, 28, 32, 48, 99, 129, 131
Rwanda 48, 217

S

Saccharum officinarum 169
Saccharum spontaneum (talahib) 169–70, 171
Said, Edward 41–2, 50n2, 51n30, 92, 171
Salgari, Emilio 69
Santos, Stephanie 163
Sarkar, Sumit 35
Sarvestani, Arash Kamali 229
Savarkar, Vinayak Damodar 120n15
scholarship
  on colonial countries (general) 69–70
  on colonialism 3
  on decolonization 47–8
  on Hong Kong 177–8
  intellectual decolonization 7, 193
  on metatheories 21
  from post-colonial nation-states 41
  see also anti-colonial/anticolonial social theory; anti-colonial/anticolonial social thought; Eurocentrism; Orientalism
Schüssler Fiorenza, Elisabeth 229
Scimago Journal and Country Ranks 111, 112, 119n6–7
Scott, David 109
second world 28, 29, 32
securitization 221

Seikaly, Sherene 172
Selvaratnam, V. 65
semi-colonialism 12, 59, 63, 66
Serbia 129, 130
servitude 14, 161, 162, 164
settler-colonialism
  attributes of 39
  author's overview of 2, 16, 65, 219
  decolonization and 4
  dispossession 155, 160, 164–5, 168–9, 172
  indigenous/Indigenous peoples 157–8
  knowledge production, impact on 47–8
  migration systems, and 221–2
  subjugation/violence by 218–19
Shankley, W. 212
Sharma, Ambika Dutt 120n16
Sheehi, Stephen 171
Simondon 161
Simpson, Audra 124, 138
Singapore 189, 192
Singh, Jasvir 200
slavery
  capitalism and 76
  coloniality of power 38–9
  counter-narratives 136–7
  decolonization and 5
  dehumanization, and 197, 201, 204, 205–6, 208–9, 212, 213, 231–2
  exploitation colonialism and 65
  media, humans as 163
  settler-colonialism and 158
  time of slavery 159–60
slow violence 140
The Smiling, Proud Wanderer (Jin) 191
Smith, Linda Tuhiwai 158
social location 86, 92
social sciences
  analytical ontologies 244, 245, 246–7
  anthropology, and 71
  approaches 1
  author's overview of 87
  colonialism and 38, 43–4, 48, 203–4
  coloniality thesis 39–40
  decolonization of 173, 174
  Eurocentrism 8, 70
  imperial standpoint 85, 86, 87, 88, 91–3, 98
  indigenization of 30, 31, 33, 50n17
  limitations of existing frameworks 83
  material inequalities in 120n13
  metatheories 20–1, 62
  methodologies 33, 46, 75, 237, 241
  ontoformative gestures 242–3
  other-than-modern 238, 243, 245, 246, 247, 248
  peripheral gaze 26–7
  politics of location 104, 111–12

INDEX

psychosocial studies 204–5, 206–12
theory, and 238–9
social theories *see* anti-colonial/anticolonial social theory
social thought *see* anti-colonial/anticolonial social thought; Northern-metropolitan social thought
society 64, 75, 95–7, 109
sociology 83, 84–5, 86–8, 89–90, 91–3, 94, 99n6 *see also* social sciences
The Souls of Black Folk (Du Bois) 95
Sousa Santos, Boaventura de 62, 146n12
Southeast Asia 180, 187, 188, 189–90, 193
Southern theory 94, 240
Spain
 colonialism by 39–40, 188, 189
 critics of colonialism from 69
 decoloniality and 43
 imperialism 129
 infrastructures 131, 133, 134
 laziness discourse 71
 rebellions 130
 Spanish colonies 2
Spivak, Gayatri Chakravorty 50n9, 51n30
Srivinas, S.N. 99n6
standpoints
 anti-colonial/anticolonial 89, 92, 93, 99, 100n7
 challenges to 117–18
 definitions of 49
 emergence of 99n4
 imperial standpoint 85, 86, 87, 88, 91–3, 98
 as location 104
 Northern-metropolitan standpoint 83–4, 85, 86, 90–1, 93
 peripheral gaze 23–4, 27, 28
 see also geoepistemic essentialism
standpoint theory 85, 86, 87, 105, 117
Stavenhagen, R. 67
Stein, T. 212
Steinmetz, G. 88
structuralist/poststructuralist critique (Foucault) 41
Suárez-Krabbe, Julia 131, 146n16
subalternity/subaltern studies 23, 34–6, 42–3, 46, 51n31, 51n20–2, 100n7, 241
subalterns 34, 35–6, 42, 46
subjective dimensions 73
subjugation 63, 97–8, 174n3, 188, 218–19, 228–9, 231
sugarcane 169
Sweden 129

T

Tadiar, Neferti X.M. 14–15, 146n9, 243, 244, 248n5
Tagliacozzo, Eric 188–9

Taíno people 74
Taiwan 3, 192–3, 193
Táíwò, O. 37
talahib (Saccharum spontaneum) 169–70, 171
Tampa incident 222
Tazreiter, Claudia 16
territories of strategic significance 2
Thiong'o, Ngũgĩ wa 124–5, 130
third person consciousness 97
third worldism/Thirldworldism 8, 23, 29, 32, 33, 193
third world/Third World
 decolonizing strategies 130–1
 development models for 51n18
 nation-states in 28–9
 politics of location 106
 women/feminists 242–3, 246, 247, 248
This Bridge Called My Back (Moraga and Anzaldúa) 146n9, 243
thought *see* anti-colonial/anticolonial social thought; decolonial thought
Le Tigri di Mompracem (The Tigers of Mompracem) (Salgari) 69
time 159–60, 173–4
Time and the Other (Fabian) 138
time of slavery 159–60
Tofighian, Omid 225, 227, 228–9, 230, 231
trade colonialism 12, 59, 63–4
Tran, Ben 134
translations 133–4
Trouillot, Michel-Rolph 205
Tsing, Anna 158
Tuck, Eve 124, 145n3
Tuhfat al-Mujahidin (al-Maqdum) 68
Two Thousand Seasons (Armah) 143

U

uber-urbanization 162, 167, 169
UK 2024 riots 198–201, 202, 203, 212
Ulysses (Joyce) 142, 143–4
United Kingdom
 Brexit 15–16, 198, 202–3
 detention of refugees by 217
 hostile environment for immigration 201, 206, 207, 208, 211
 racist violence in 198–201
 see also Great Britain; Northern Ireland
United States
 as colonial country 3
 colonialism in 2, 47, 67, 95–6, 99
 exceptionalism 40–1
 geopolitical history 128
 Hong Kong 182, 183, 184, 188, 189
 immigration policy 40
 imperialism 6, 129, 154, 178
 imperial standpoint 87–8
 military bases 168
 New Mestiza 243–4, 246, 248n6

261

9/11 terror attack 221, 222
Philippines 14
politics of location 109, 110
postcolonialism and 42, 43
society 95–6, 97, 98
war on terror 158–9, 165, 222
Untouchable (Anand) 143

V

Van Leur, Jacob Cornelis 70
veils 95, 96–7
Veracini, L. 47
Vergès, Françoise 156
Vietnam 134–5
Virdee, S. 202
virtuality 190–1, 192
vital infrastructures 14, 161–2, 164, 165, 166–7

W

Wallerstein, Immanuel 8, 26, 128, 187
Walsh, Catherine 145n2
war 160–1, 165–6, 167
war on drugs 165
war on terror 158–9, 165, 222
war to be human 159, 165, 171, 173
Weber, Max 62, 88
whiteness 205
Whyte, Kyle 157–8, 170
Wills, J. 188
Wilson, Paulette 207
Winch, Tara June 230
Windrush scandal 15–16, 198, 201, 206–12
women 134–5, 136–7, 140, 143, 146n9, 242–3, 245–6
work *see* labour
worldliness 171–2
world-systems theory
  author's overview of 25
  critiques, anti-colonial/anticolonial 7–8
  decolonial thought 74, 128
  dependency theory and 38, 46
  inter-imperial approach 179, 192
  peripheral gaze 26, 50n10
world-system/world system 26, 45, 50n11, 185–6
Writing and Authority in Early China (Lewis) 132
Wylie, A. 86
Wynter, Sylvia 159, 170, 175n4, 208, 209

Y

Yahya, Zawiah 72
Yang, K. Wayne 124, 145n3
Young, Robert 5, 9
Younge, Gary 208

www.ingramcontent.com/pod-product-compliance
Lightning Source LLC
Chambersburg PA
CBHW051532020426
42333CB00016B/1894